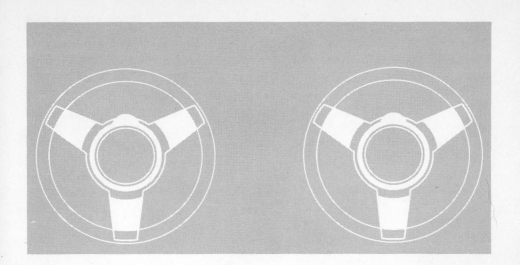

Automatic
Data
Processing

Principles and Procedures

ELIAS M. AWAD
Northwestern University
and
**DATA PROCESSING
MANAGEMENT ASSOCIATION**

PRENTICE-HALL, INC., Englewood Cliffs, New Jersey

Library of Congress Catalog Card No.:
66-22115

Printed in the United States of America,
C-05510

Current printing (last digit):

10 9 8 7 6 5 4 3

PRENTICE-HALL INTERNATIONAL, INC., *London*
PRENTICE-HALL OF AUSTRALIA, PTY., LTD., *Sydney*
PRENTICE-HALL OF CANADA, LTD., *Toronto*
PRENTICE-HALL OF INDIA (PRIVATE) LTD., *New Delhi*
PRENTICE-HALL OF JAPAN, INC., *Tokyo*

Preface

Recognizing the need for a fundamental data-processing text, the Data Processing Management Association set out early in 1963 to sponsor and coordinate a joint writing effort by the major business computer manufacturers. With this goal in mind, Mr. R. Calvin Elliott, DPMA Executive Director, invited national education representatives of all the leading business computer manufacturers to a meeting in Chicago. Six of the companies agreed to participate in the project and sent the following persons as members of the working group:

Harry W. Butts	Burroughs Corporation
William R. Wright	General Electric Company
Richard F. Conn	Honeywell EDP Division
William L. Kelly	International Business Machines
Robert B. Balcomb	National Cash Register Company
Robert J. Brown	National Cash Register Company
W. C. Filbert	Univac Division, Sperry Rand

In addition to Mr. Elliott, the Association was represented by Alfonso G. Pia, Immediate Past President; Elmer F. Judge, International President; John K. Swearingen, Vice President for Education; and James M. Adams, DPMA Education Director.

After formulating the goals and the general outline of the proposed manuscript, representatives from the various companies volunteered to write the preliminary draft of specific sections of the book. As these were completed, they were forwarded to DPMA Headquarters for review and editing.

As might be expected, the assembling of manuscripts written by various people from different parts of the country into a fluent and cohesive textbook was no small task. To give the book proper balance with regard to detail and emphasis, to verify its technical accuracy and completeness, and to make it easily read by the beginning student required more than a cursory edit.

A thorough review of the material was undertaken by Mr. Adams and Philip A. Felber of the DPMA Education Department. Several other people, including Robert H. Gregory, Management Consultant; Mrs. Shannon Fischer, previously of Burroughs Corporation; James A. Campise of Computer Sciences Corporation; and Donald A. Young of General Electric Company made significant technical and editorial contributions.

In the fall of 1964, DPMA contacted Elias M. Awad—then Professor of Business at Rochester Institute of Technology, Rochester, New York, and now a doctoral candidate at Northwestern University—who agreed to perform the necessary final rewriting and editing. In this manner, the book became a shared endeavor of DPMA and Mr. Awad.

Automatic Data Processing: Principles and Procedures, is the result, then, of a combined effort of a number of individuals representing data-processing equipment manufacturers, users, and educators. Its purpose is to provide the beginning student and general reader a basic, yet comprehensive introduction to the field of business data processing, one that requires no previous course work in mathematics or business.

The book is designed for use as the text for a beginning one- or two-term course in automatic data processing. If used in a two-term course, there would probably be time to pursue a more detailed presentation of unit record equipment operation and/or computer programming. If such is the case, operating and programming manuals for specific machines can easily be used as supplementary texts.

Some word about the purposes and activities of the Data Processing Management Association may be in order. The DPMA is an international organization of management and technical staff personnel representing more than 20,000 members in the United States, Canada, and Japan. The Association is dedicated to improving the art and science of data processing through education and service. With its many educational programs DPMA is contributing materially to the advancement of the emerging data-processing profession. Through its publications and broad range of seminars and conferences, its community services, and its professional certification program, DPMA is fast becoming recognized as the spokesman for the business data-processing field.

For their careful review of the manuscript—and for the constructive comments that resulted—special thanks are due to Mr. Nathan Berkowitz of the Graduate School of Business, Fairleigh Dickinson University, and to Mr. Lawrence J. LaFave, Supervisor of Data Processing Education for the Board of Education, Chicago.

ELIAS M. AWAD

and the

DATA PROCESSING MANAGEMENT ASSOCIATION

Contents

v

vii

Complement Method — Decimal System. BINARY SUBTRACTION: One's Complement Method — Binary System; Two's Complement Method — Binary System. DECIMAL MULTIPLICATION. BINARY MULTIPLICATION. BINARY DIVISION. LOGIC. THE CONTROL UNIT: Registers; Branching. INSTRUCTION FORMATS. GLOSSARY OF TERMS. QUESTIONS AND PROBLEMS FOR REVIEW.

the Bond Register; Preparation of the Quarterly Earnings Report; The Withholding Tax Statement. GLOSSARY OF TERMS. QUESTIONS FOR REVIEW.

CAREER POSITIONS IN AUTOMATIC DATA PROCESSING. DATA-PROCESSING MANAGEMENT: The Data-Processing Manager; Manager of Computer Operations. SYSTEMS ANALYSIS AND PROGRAMMING: The Systems Analyst; The Computer Programmer. DATA-PROCESSING OPERATIONS: The Computer Operator: The Tabulator Operator; Keypunch Operator. MANAGEMENT AND AUTOMATIC DATA PROCESSING: The Management Tool.

part 5

Appendices

MACHINE-LANGUAGE CODING: The Processor Program; Languages — Formats and Types; Symbolic Language — Assembler; Macro Languages. GENERALIZED PROGRAMMING AIDS. ASSEMBLERS AND COMPILERS. INPUT/OUTPUT CONTROL SYSTEMS. UTILITIES. GLOSSARY OF TERMS. QUESTIONS FOR REVIEW.

BASIC BOOKS IN AUTOMATIC DATA PROCESSING. PERIODICALS. ASSOCIATIONS AND OTHER SOURCES. MANUFACTURERS.

part 1

Historical Development of Data Processing

chapter 1

The Development
of Aids to Manpower

The rapidity of present-day technological advances makes it difficult to recognize that man's development toward progressively higher standards of living has been relatively slow and sometimes painful. It took him countless years to learn to make use of animals for transportation of materials instead of walking from place to place, carrying his pack on his back. Although the discovery of the wheel revolutionized his thinking, it was many years before he applied his discovery to wagons and bicycles. Decades elapsed between his discovery of the use of steam as a source of power and its eventual use in propelling machinery.

As man discovered new ways to harness the forces of nature to aid him in finding easier methods of doing things, his ingenuity for devising adaptations of these basic discoveries also increased. Thus, the step from the first airplane flight to the development of the jet airplane is shorter than the one from "foot-power" to "animal-power." Once the principles behind jet flight were understood and applied, the transition to manned space flights was relatively easy. In fact, man has become so ingenious and imaginative in his inventive powers that it sometimes seems as if almost any "miracle" could be performed overnight. This is especially evident in what is called the field of automation.

Automation

Automation includes the use of any mechanical device to perform routine work with a minimum of human supervision.

Automation and automatic techniques have been used for mass production at minimal costs. In men's clothing, for instance, tailor-made suits have become less and less common. In preparing ready-made garments, a clothing manufacturer can cut between 25 to 30 pieces of fabric simultaneously for a given size. The various parts go through a standardized process which, when completed, will produce many suits at a time. Although some men (especially those whose proportions are not standard) consider a tailor-made suit a better fit, most find the ready-made garments satisfactory. In the latter case, cost is reduced as much as 60 per cent.

Numeralization has also been applied to areas involving individual identity. The U.S. Internal Revenue Service, for instance, has been using electronic computers to verify and otherwise process the millions of annual tax forms. Each taxpayer is assigned a number which identifies him with the tax return he files each year. The use of numbers, rather than names, greatly speeds up the data processing required to accomplish the desired results, because they are a simpler means for sorting than alphabetic characters.

To find some way to process boring, routine paperwork more efficiently than by human labor has taxed man's mind for many years. The growth of markets and customers has brought with it an increase in business forms, which in turn has created new problems of record keeping. The challenge of paperwork has led to almost daily improvements in our methods of coping with large volumes of routine paper handling and mathematical figuring.

Computers

The amazing and wonderful "world of computers" represents a great step forward in devising better methods to aid man in performing routine and repetitive tasks more efficiently. The principles of uniformity, standardization, and numeralization become the keys to successful performance. Imagination, creativeness, and clever innovation may be used in building the machines, but once they are built, these "human" qualities must be replaced by the "inhuman" qualities surrounding standardization of performance. This is necessary if the machine, especially the computer, is to be useful in accomplishing the work for which it is designed.

Electronic "dehumanization" plays a pleasantly constructive role in wide areas of business and to a limited extent in other fields. It has taken over the drudgery of routine work by processing data more accurately and quickly than man could possibly do it.

The following examples illustrate the range of computer use, and some of the ways they have helped man to do repetitive tasks quickly and with a degree of accuracy not otherwise possible.

A policeman's "watchdog." The use of computers in police headquarters is gaining in popularity. They are used to store and process arrest reports, recovery reports, traffic tickets, gun records, and many other active record files. This gives the police department a file of current information, making it easier to plan and organize its workload. Further, the computer's rapid analysis of crime reports helps the police department to concentrate its manpower in problem areas.

As an example, an officer patrolling a given district may spot a man who he suspects is a wanted criminal. He radios a description of the man to his headquarters. The dispatcher feeds the data into the computer. A positive or a negative response is printed out in less than five seconds, and the result is promptly relayed to the patrolman, who immediately takes the required action.

The post office and mail transportation. Programs have been developed for planning mail transportation by using computers. Factors such as the desired departure time, arrival time, cost, and speed are stored in the computer, which selects the cheapest and fastest route or routes. The use of the computer in mail routing eases time pressures and more efficiently employs different kinds of available transportation.

Book composition. Books are electronically prepared for printing. The computer produces an output tape which is used to operate an automatic typesetting device. A typical four hundred-page book of forty-five lines per page can be processed in about three and one-half hours, a job that usually takes a printer more than a month.

Automated real estate. Realtors are beginning to use automated equipment. Certain data on available houses are stored on punched cards, which are used later to match with customers' specifications such as size, price, location, and other characteristics. When the stack of cards has been processed and a few have been selected for a specific order, the realtor, in effect, has narrowed the range of possible choices from several hundred to about a dozen. Now he is in a position to discuss the selected possibilities with the customer. This automated approach saves times in buying and selling houses, thus helping both the realtor and his customer.

"Computerized" bread. The computer also has entered the bakery business. A nationally known bakery has installed a computer system designed to regulate several factors which previously had to be checked and controlled by people. These include a close check on the various ingredients used, batch blending, mixing operations, and the quality of baked goods. The specific requirements are stored in the computer, and the computer monitors these functions as the baked goods are being prepared.

Banks and "computerized" checks. Since banks deal with volumes of paperwork and require precise control of the smallest detail, they were among the first business organizations to use computers to process their paperwork. To sort the millions of checks which must be processed, many banks have turned to high-speed sorters that can "read" magnetic ink numbers printed at the bottom of each check. These numbers carry information which identifies the bank on which the check is written, and the individual's particular account.

Automated flight reservations. Most airlines have turned to the computer to aid them in the vital job of ticket reservations. One major airline's system makes it possible for any one of 3,000 ticket agents scattered across the country to confirm space on any flight in seconds. The system is capable of handling more than half a million reservations a day.

Hotel reservations. The hotel industry has been trying to reduce the problems of coordinating advance reservations involving many locations and to speed up the task of requesting and confirming these reservations. Through the use of computers, some major hotel chains are now able to confirm reservations in a matter of seconds. Confirmation is made to the requesting branch and a duplicate, complete with the guest's name and address, is mailed to the hotel. If the guest cancels his room reservation, the necessary information is fed to the computer by any branch and the branch can start "selling" the room again. The same approach is used when a certain branch hotel is booked to capacity for a given day or period of time. The computer is instructed to refuse confirmation of any reservations for that branch for the "booked-up" period.

Air traffic control. One of the most complicated computer applications now in operation keeps track of military and commercial air traffic over most of the North American Continent and is constantly on the alert in the defense of our country. Called "SAGE" (Semi-Automatic Ground Environment), it is a vast complex which feeds information from radar stations on the ground, on ships, in aircraft, from Ballistic Missile Early Warning System (BMEWS), and from other sources into a central control. If defensive action ever becomes necessary, the control is set up to send out signals to our aircraft and missiles for action. When commercial air traffic becomes more congested, SAGE or some similar network may take over air traffic control entirely, bringing added safety to air travel.

Computers and the weather. Weather predictions today are far more reliable than they were in the past. While the problem of accurate weather forecasting is a very complex one, methods for solving such problems have been known for some time. Before the advent of computers and rapid data collection, however, the *means* were not available to put this knowledge to use. In 1922, an Englishman named Richardson developed the necessary mathematics for predicting the weather, but it would have taken 60,000 mathematicians working together in a stadium to handle the calculations necessary to predict the weather for one small part of England alone. The advent of computers has made it possible for the U.S. Navy to use this knowledge to plot weather predictions for the entire Northern Hemisphere in 40 minutes.

This text stresses "automatic" rather than "electronic" data-processing principles, because in modern business, mechanical techniques as well as electronic ones are used. Punched-card equipment is widely used and extremely helpful in solving many modern business problems.

The use of the term "automatic data processing," therefore, is much broader than the term "electronic data processing," since all of the data processing methods which will be discussed in later chapters are automatic, although not all are necessarily electronic.

The foregoing examples illustrate the potential of ADP equipment in various fields of endeavor. The gap between what is being done and what can be done does not show clear signs of closing, but it does show the tremendous challenge in developing computer technology.

Automatic data-processing machines seem to accomplish routine jobs so fast that we often overlook the great number of people working behind the scenes to prepare the computers for their data-processing routines. We are often tempted to believe that industry has become completely "dehumanized," but it is an observable fact that the introduction and use of machinery usually results in the employment of more people to handle a wide variety of newly created jobs. Particular jobs may become "dehumanized," but the industry as a whole usually ends up using more, rather than less, humans. Promising rewards as well as new freedom from the frustrations of doing routine, repetitive work await those who are willing to meet the challenge.

GLOSSARY OF TERMS

AUTOMATION: 1. The implementation of processes by automatic means. 2. The theory, art, or technique of making a process more automatic. 3. The investigation, design, development, and application of methods of rendering processes automatic, self-moving, or self-controlling.

NUMERALIZATION: Representation of alphabetic data through the use of digits; a desired step in automatic data processing.

STANDARDIZATION: Establishing specific procedural requirements for the efficient production of a large volume of goods or for automatic processing of data.

QUESTIONS FOR REVIEW

1. What is meant by automation? How is it integrated in electronic data processing? Explain.
2. Describe briefly the role of the computer in:
   (a) Police work
   (b) Mail transportation
   (c) Real estate
   (d) Banking
   (e) Flight reservations
   (f) Air traffic control
   (g) Weather forecasting.

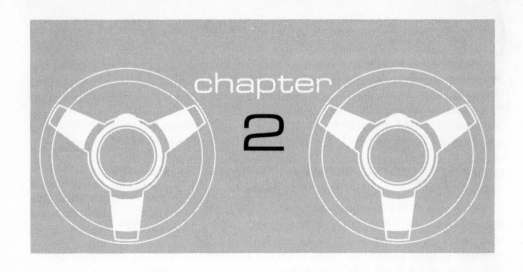

chapter

2

The Development
of the "Thinking Machine"

Data processing, whether manual or automatic, business or scientific, involves collecting, recording, and manipulating the necessary alphabetic and/or numeric symbols to achieve a given result. Data processing is a means to an end, not an end in itself.

Data are everywhere. In writing a term paper, for example, a student goes to the library, reads one or more reference books, records selected ideas or summarizes certain sections, adds more ideas of his own, writes from his notes, and finally, types his findings and presents them to his instructor. Likewise, a housewife first finds out what items she needs for the day, checks the amount of cash available for those items, puts the cash in her purse, goes to the supermarket, selects the needed items, pays the cashier, and drives back home with the groceries.

A businessman processes business data in a similar manner. He determines his needs and checks his budget for the available cash. He orders the needed items and pays for them after an itemized bill has been received. These operations often are done manually with a pencil and paper. Sometimes they are supplemented by an adding machine, a desk calculator, or a slide rule.

The Pre-Automated Data-Processing Era

There always has been a need for man to "calculate." In early times, there was a need to count his family, his flock, and the number of his enemies. As a farmer or a breeder, he found it necessary to keep track of the seasons, and therefore, he developed a calendar. Tying knots in thongs or cutting notches in sticks helped him keep track of such data.

In the early days of banking, notches in a stick were used to keep the borrower and the banker honest. The notches represented the amount of the loan, and the stick was cut in half lengthwise through the notches. The bank kept half the stick and the borrower held the matching half. The half held by the banker was known as the "stock"; hence, the banker became known as the "stockholder."

Other early calculations were recorded by making scratches in the dust. Later, man fitted beads on a series of rods and developed the abacus. Some historians trace the word "abacus" to the semitic *abai*, meaning "dust."

Shopkeepers made use of a similar device. It consisted of beads on a grooved board, and was called a "counter." The name "counter" has been carried down to its present-day use.

Although notches in sticks and straight-line scratches in clay tablets were adequate for man's early needs, it later became necessary for him to create written numbers. Greek and Roman numerals served the purpose of representing numbers, but were cumbersome. It wasn't until Hindu and Arabic numerals were invented that man had a truly workable system of written numbers.

Each number system had its own symbols, beginning with "zero" and progressing through "nine." The use of digits made it possible to use the decimal "place" system, in which the position of a given digit indicated its value (that is, units, tens, hundreds, thousands, and so on).

The foregoing shows us that man was forced to create better calculating devices as his paperwork expanded. In Dickens' *A Christmas Carol*, Bob Cratchit usually is pictured sitting on a high stool working on Mr. Scrooge's books. At that period in history, this was the approved method of calculation and recording. It is quite a contrast to today's bookkeeper, who has adding machines, calculators, and other devices at his disposal. The "green eye-shade" bookkeeper is almost a thing of the past.

An Era of Transition

During the late nineteenth and the early twentieth centuries, man progressed beyond these primitive methods of data recording and processing. He was forced to find better ways of doing things because business was expanding, demand for better products was increasing, and consequently the recording, reporting, and manipulation of data began to present a greater problem. Business went through a transition from the one-man firm, where records were negligible and the need for recording data was slight, to firms owned by many people, employing several hundred or thousand workers. This made it necessary to maintain an endless variety of business records involving the sale of goods, updating the receipt and disbursement of cash, and the periodical preparation of payroll. These and other functions, then, revealed a need for a gradual transition from the use of relatively inadequate tools to a more efficient utilization of an automatic data-processing system.

The Need for and the Cost of Keeping Business Records

If we analyze the needs of a business firm for obtaining accurate and adequate information, we find several areas of business activity that must be controlled. Just as an early shepherd had to keep track of the sheep in his flock, a businessman must keep track of the things he owns. This is known as keeping an inventory. When a businessman's inventory falls below a safe minimum, he must know how many units to reorder and how long it will take to replace his stock so that he may continue to carry on his business activities without interruption.

Large or small, a business firm needs records. An automobile is equipped with an oil pressure gauge to indicate whether or not the engine is receiving proper lubrication. Without this device, it is unlikely that the driver would be aware of a lubrication failure until serious trouble developed. Likewise, a business firm needs "gauges" to determine its operating performance. These "gauges" of business are its accounting records.

Payroll must be prepared regularly. This involves the preparation of a paycheck for each employee, as well as the maintenance of information regarding his earnings and deductions for the year. The firm must have ready cash to pay creditors such as suppliers, the landlord or the mortgage holder, and the advertising agency.

All accounts receivable and accounts payable information must be recorded. City, state, and federal governments require more records and reports from business firms each year. These reports and others of a similar nature must be prepared, and numerous workers often are required to get the job done.

In relation to the total number of workers in a firm, the number of clerical employees is quite high. Clerical requirements have continued to grow each year creating higher costs of doing business. A higher and higher percentage of a firm's working capital and personnel are required for recording, classifying, summarizing, and filing masses of vital business data. If it were possible to total the annual cost of creating and maintaining business records, the sum would be staggering.

At present, it is estimated that one out of every three employees is engaged in clerical work. This ratio seems high, considering the fact that it is the production and sale of goods which sustains the firm and provides the revenue. The salaries of clerical help are direct overhead, eating into business profits. To keep these costs down, business firms are always looking for better and cheaper methods of keeping their records.

Economy is not the only factor that a businessman considers, however.

Speed is equally important. Timing is critical in decision-making, and to aid the executive in arriving at a better decision, business data must be available as soon as possible. Management may speed up the processing of business data by increasing the clerical force, of course, but this would only mean increased clerical costs.

Not only is the volume of data and the need for data increasing, but as businesses become more complex, the distance between a manager and the activity he is to control also is increasing. When the manager becomes farther removed from operations, decisions which previously could be made on the basis of personal knowledge and experience now must be based on "second-hand" information. It is important, then, that this information be accurate and on time to be of use. *Effective* management control requires the "feed-back" of information in time to affect important decisions. If information does not reach the manager when he needs it, it is of little value to him. Since the chief objective of automatic data processing is to *aid* management, the aim of data-processing equipment manufacturers is to build machines that will process information *quickly, accurately,* and *economically.*

Automatic Data Processing—Its Role and Impact

A New Revolution

When the Industrial Revolution began, there were warnings that man would become a "useless slave" of the machines which he had created. Since machines could do the work of many men, it was argued that there soon would be no work for man to do.

The evidence of history has proved these fears groundless. Modern machines and their many uses have freed man from much of his manual labor so that he could devote his energies to more productive work. As a result, it is now possible to communicate instantly with people half a world away. Man can enjoy the music of great orchestras in the comfort of his home. He can travel from continent to continent in a few hours. With the twist of a dial, he can have comfort in his home, whether there is a blizzard or a heat wave outside. Modern man can enjoy things that the most powerful emperors of the past could not.

The developments in automatic data processing are making possible a new kind of industrial revolution. The first revolution relieved man of much of his manual labor and gave him powerful tools to help him accomplish great physical feats. The new revolution gives him powerful new tools that will relieve him of much of his mental drudgery and make it possible for him to use his mind more profitably.

In the scientific field, the computer has made possible many things that could not have been accomplished otherwise. Problems that would require many man-years of human computation are solved by computers in a matter of minutes. No human being would be capable of performing the split-second calculations necessary to orbit a manned spacecraft or direct a missile to the moon.

Many problems were left unsolved for years because there were no computers to handle them. Many areas of research were ignored because it was impossible to complete projects using manual methods of computation. Automatic data processing has opened many doors previously closed to the scientist, as well as to the businessman.

Every business firm has its own data-processing requirements. The manner in which they are handled depends on the volume of work to be done, the elapsed time, the degree of accuracy required, the necessary speed, and the cost. Regardless of its other requirements, however, every business must pay its personnel, make reports to the government, and record the buying and selling of goods or services—all functions involving the processing of data. Information necessary for management decision-making can be obtained from these and other sources of operating data through the use of automatic machines.

In automatic data processing, figures represent facts and are manipulated in various ways to create additional useful information. The original information is referred to as *input*. The result of processing *input* is called *output*. Facts (data) are manipulated (processed) to create information (output) which provides answers to specific problems. Complete, accurate, and timely information aids both the businessman and the scientist to form a sound basis for decisions.

Data can be processed in several ways. In the use of a pencil and paper, the pencil is the *device* and the paper is the *medium*. The development of machines such as the cash register, bookkeeping machine, and accounting machine has been a more advanced answer to data processing. These devices are halfway between the paper-and-pencil method and the relatively complex computer system.

A cash register, for instance, combines the functions of a cash drawer and an adding machine. With its capability to classify data, as in the case of a grocery-store register which identifies items as meat, produce, grocery, etc., it also becomes a sorting machine.

Bookkeeping and accounting machines, on the other hand, combine the functions of a typewriter and a calculator, with controls which permit automating simple operations. When coupled with equipment for producing punched paper tape, these pieces of equipment can be used to prepare *input* data for computers.

Punched-card machines were developed as a step toward the use of fully automatic equipment. Except for the initial preparation of the punched cards and the need to transport them from one machine to another, the entire operation of a punched-card system is automatic. That is, any or all of the necessary calculations are worked out with minimum human intervention.

Next came the electronic computer. Operations became even more automatic. While punched-card data processing requires the handling of cards through various mechanical devices, the components of an electronic system are interconnected in such a way that all processing functions (including input and output) are done automatically.

Electronic data processing transfers data in the form of electrical impulses through electrical circuits, making it possible to attain much greater speeds than can be achieved by a mechanical system. Instructions for processing given data are stored in the *memory* of the computer, and can be changed to suit particular needs, thereby allowing greater flexibility in the system.

To the uninitiated, a computer is a room full of mysterious "boxes" costing millions of dollars. Although there are computer systems that fit this description, computers of smaller size and lower cost are more common. Small to medium-size computers play a vital part in the data-processing field today, and have made it economically possible for many firms to enjoy the benefits of automatic data processing.

Is the Computer a "Thinking Machine"?

Science-fiction books are filled with stories of powerful *thinking machines.* Depending on the whim of the writer, these machines can either become great benefactors or monsters that control or destroy mankind.

The behavior of computers and the tasks they perform are similar to those a human being would perform in the same situations. Because of this similarity, the computer often is referred to as an "electronic brain." While highly flattering to the machine, this comparison is far from accurate.

Computer designers face the challenge of building a computer with the size, function, and storage capacity of the human brain. To do so would mean the creation of a computer the size of a grapefruit, powered by only one-tenth of a watt of electricity, and yet having a memory 10,000 times the size of any computer yet built.

The computer is like a highly efficient, fast, and accurate robot. It must be told when to start, stop, add, and subtract. It must be told precisely what to do, at what time, and in what manner. Although some "sophisticated" computers are capable of catching certain errors in the instructions given to them, data fed into a computer must be accurate and complete. If they are not clear and properly organized, the results of processing will be largely a wasted effort.

Computers can detect but generally cannot correct an inaccurate entry. The initials *GIGO*, meaning "Garbage In, Garbage Out," emphasize the fact that processing is only as accurate as the input received. Since errors in input can be compounded during processing, it is essential to take every precaution to avoid them.

Computers have been used to compose music, write poetry, or play chess, but so far these activities are very limited and involve "thinking" in a very restrictive sense. They are still subject to human direction and control, which presents all kinds of new opportunities for computer scientists and users.

Automatic data-processing equipment puts unique demands on the knowledge of those who use it. Without proper direction, the most sophisticated computer is nothing but a helpless complex of wires. The equipment can be no more accurate than the persons who prepare the instructions and the data for its use.

GLOSSARY OF TERMS

DATA PROCESSING: Any operation or combination of operations on data.

INPUT: 1. The data to be processed. 2. The state or sequence of states occurring on a specified input channel. 3. The device or collective set of devices used for bringing data into another device. 4. A channel for impressing a state on a device or logic element. 5. The processes of transferring data from an external storage to an internal storage. 6. *See* MANUAL INPUT.

INPUT DEVICE: The mechanical unit designed to bring data to be processed into a computer; e.g., a card reader, a tape reader, or a keyboard.

OUTPUT: 1. Data that has been processed. 2. The state or sequence of states occurring on a specified output channel. 3. The device or collective set of devices used for taking data out of a device. 4. A channel for expressing a state of a device or logic element. 5. The process of transferring data from an internal storage to an external storage.

OUTPUT DEVICE: The part of a machine which translates the electrical impulses representing data processed by the machine into permanent results such as printed forms, punched cards, and magnetic writing on tape.

QUESTIONS FOR REVIEW

1. For what reason(s) was man forced to create better calculating devices? Explain.
2. List and explain briefly the factors which led many business firms to resort to automated data processing.
3. What three significant advantages can be achieved from automatic data processing? Discuss.
4. Why is a computer referred to as an "electronic brain"? What are some of its capabilities? Explain.

History
of Data Processing

Chapters 1 and 2 have presented the need for data-processing systems. In order to better understand and appreciate modern data-processing equipment and methods, it would be helpful to review their origin and development.

Early Manual Methods of Calculating

Finger Counting

Man always has been challenged by mathematics and the need to solve mathematical problems. To most people, however, the job of solving a formula is both boring and time-consuming. For this reason, attempts have been made from the very beginning to make calculating less tedious and much faster.

Until the nineteenth century, most business calculations were performed mentally. To reduce this problem, Roman schools taught finger counting and actually devised various methods of doing such advanced operations as multiplication and division on the fingers.

The Roman student was only required to learn the multiplication table up to 5 × 5. To figure out the product of any

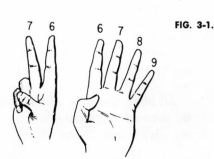

FIG. 3-1.

numbers between 5 and 10, he used his fingers. Suppose, for example, he wished to multiply 7 × 9. To find the product, he would raise two fingers on one hand to represent the numbers over 5 (that is, 6 and 7) plus four fingers on the other hand to represent 6, 7, 8, and 9 (Figure 3-1). He obtained the product as follows:

1. Add the number of fingers raised.

$$2 + 4 = 6 \qquad \text{(the value of ten's position)}$$

2. Multiply the number of fingers not raised in each hand.

$$3 \times 1 = 3 \qquad \text{(the value of the unit's position)}$$

Therefore:

$$7 \times 9 = 63$$

Try this method using other values between 5 and 10. Also consider how impractical such a method would be in computing thousands of customer bills a day.

The Abacus

The abacus is a manual calculating device which uses beads instead of fingers to represent decimal numbers. The beads are strung in rows (Figure 3-2), each row containing 10 beads representing the 10 fingers. The position of the row represents the decimal value of the beads in it. In Figure 3-2, for example, the beads in row A have a value of one each; those in row B have a value of 10 each; those in row C, 100 each; and so on.

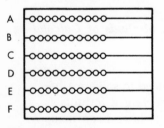

A = Unit's Position

B = Ten's Position

C = Hundred's Position

D = Thousand's Position

E = Ten Thousand's Position

F = Hundred Thousand's Position

FIG. 3-2. An abacus.

Making calculations on the abacus is a manual operation. Beads are moved from left to right to represent values. To represent the number 436, for example, six beads in row A (the unit's position), three beads in row B (the ten's position), and four beads in row C (the hundred's position) are moved (Figure 3-3).

Addition, the most common arithmetic function performed, is accomplished by successively adding values, represented by beads, in the different rows. If we wish to add 255 to 436, for example, we would:

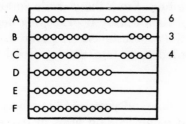

FIG. **3-3.** The number 436 on an abacus.

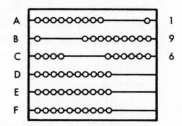

FIG. **3-4.** The number 691 on an abacus.

1. Move two beads in row *C* to the right, showing a total of 6 hundreds.
2. Move five beads in row *B* to the right, giving a total of eight tens.
3. Move five beads in row *A* to the right. Since we only have four beads on the left-hand side of row *A*, however, we move five of the six beads that are on the right *to the left* and move ("carry") one bead to the right in row *B*. (See Figure 3-4).

The abacus was used mostly for addition and subtraction, but many people achieved competence in using it for multiplication and division as well.

In multiplication, successive additions of a value are made. To multiply 5×3, for example, either 3 is added to itself five times $(3 + 3 + 3 + 3 + 3)$ or 5 is added to itself three times $(5 + 5 + 5)$. In either case, the product of 15 is obtained.

Division is executed by successively subtracting the divisor from the dividend until the remainder is equal to zero or is less than the divisor. The number of subtractions determine the quotient. If we wish to divide 15 by 3, for example, we:

$$
\begin{array}{lll}
(1) & 15 - 3 = 12 & 1 \\
(2) & 12 - 3 = 9 & 1 \\
(3) & 9 - 3 = 6 & 1 \\
(4) & 6 - 3 = 3 & 1 \\
(5) & 3 - 3 = 0 & 1 \\
\end{array}
$$

\left.\right\} Number of subtractions

$\overline{5}$ quotient

The origin of the abacus is obscure. Many nations claim to have originated it. It is probable that the idea was developed in several countries and later carried into other parts of the world by travelers and merchants. Its earliest home is believed to have been Babylon or Egypt.

The Primitive Era of Manual Record Keeping

The practice of record keeping existed ages before the recording of formal history. Barbarians kept records by scratching them on rocks. Later, they learned to use their fingers for counting. From these crude forms of picture-writing and counting, the process of rudimentary bookkeeping began, spurred by the growth of civilization and the establishment of government. Later, it became necessary to convert recorded facts into timely, useful information.

Babylon

In Babylonia, clay tablets over four-thousand years old have been discovered, proving to be records of banks and moneylending firms in operation at that time. The code of Hammurabi, ruler of Babylonia (2285–2242 B.C.), includes references to business transactions such as contracts, deeds, bonds, receipts, inventories, sales, and other similar types of accounts. It also reveals that drafts and checks were commonly used and that customs dues and ferry and highway tolls were collected. Similarly, state records of property ownership which were used for taxation purposes have been discovered.

Egypt and Greece

In Egypt, accounts were kept on parchment or papyrus. The state's revenues and disbursements were carefully recorded. Taxes paid in kind caused the building of granaries and warehouses. Taxpayers were given receipts when their grain or livestock was delivered. These receipts were accounted for, along with the inventories of all commodities.

Ancient Greece also required a relatively strict accounting from all public officials. Upon leaving office, an official made a "public accounting" on stone and exposed it to public view. It is also known that the Greeks developed a kind of clearing-house system for financial transactions.

Rome

In ancient Rome, the father of the family kept records of receipts and payments in a memorandum record. Each month, these entries were transferred to a "register," accepted as evidence in lawsuits. Roman bankers also used registers and a kind of account book for clients to show individual deposits, loans, payments, and balances. Checks were used, but evidently only by the wealthy.

Later, the state developed a new system of accounting control. The official in charge of funds (treasurer) had no authority to disburse them without a "voucher" issued by another body of officials to substantiate the payment. Further, the Romans drew up budgets for the needs of the imperial household and the army which served as a basis for levying taxes, which later were collected on a decentralized basis but with central offices handling all of the accounting and control aspects.

England

The Exchequer, established during the reign of Henry I (1100–1135), is the earliest known accounting system in England. This was based on the Domesday

Book, in which was recorded all taxable estates in the country. From it, the treasurer's Great Roll was made up. Each sheriff was held responsible for collecting his portion of taxes and was required to render an account twice a year. On the first accounting, he received half of a tally stick, notched to show the amount; the other half was retained by the treasurer. On the next accounting, the sheriff's tally stick was turned in as evidence of the first payment and matched against the treasurer's half.

Italy's Double-Entry Bookkeeping

Double-entry bookkeeping began in Italy in the fourteenth century. In 1340, a double-entry ledger was used in Genoa which shows a merchandise account for pepper, debited with expenses, credited with receipts, and the balance transferred to "profit and loss." A similar system was also used in Venice.

In Venice, in 1494, Luca Paciolo, a monk, published a book entitled "Everything about Arithmetic, Geometry, and Proportion." At the end of the treatise on arithmetic, Paciolo made a summary of the existing practice in bookkeeping. He stated that the purpose of bookkeeping was the furnishing of timely information in regard to assets and liabilities. The system described the use of three books: a memorial (daybook or blotter), a journal (formal debits and credits in standard currency), and a Quaderno (ledger). Merchandise accounts in the ledger were kept on a single-venture basis, with balances between debits and credits closed out to the Profit and Loss account.

Further Development of Record-keeping Methods

Between the early 1400's and the 1800's, record-keeping methods were developed and expanded, but little was done to *speed up* the process of recording business transactions, calculating various amounts, or producing business reports.

Early Mechanical Calculating Devices

Napier's "Bones"

Arab, Hindi, and European mathematicians were the first to develop techniques of written calculations. However, most of those techniques were in the form of *tables* to aid multiplication and other arithmetic functions. The "table" approach was used in 1614 by John Napier of Merchiston, Scotland, and culminated in the development of Napier's "bones."

Napier divided rods into nine squares. The top square holds a decimal digit (that is, 1–9) and represents the product of its multiplication by 1. Each

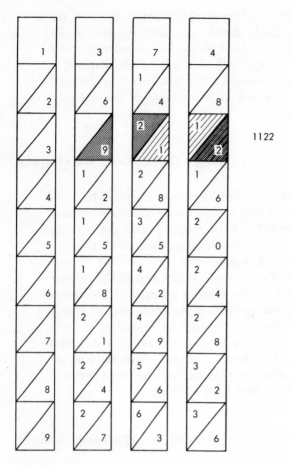

1122

FIG. 3-5. Napier's bones.

of the remaining eight squares is divided diagonally and holds (top to bottom) the product of the digit in the top square by 2, 3, 4, 5, 6, 7, and 8, respectively. Once the set is completed, the product of any two numbers can be obtained by adding the values pertaining to them diagonally.

Figure 3-5 shows the rods for multiplying 1, 3, 7, and 4.

Suppose we wish to multiply 3×374. Using Napier's "bones," we first identify the multiplier (3) in the third square of the left rod. The multiplicand (374) is the remaining three rods. The product is obtained by adding diagonally the values in the third square of each of the rods of the multiplicand (from right):

Unit's position . . . 2 (the contents of the right diagonal column).
Ten's position . . . the sum of the second diagonal column, or $1 + 1 = 2$.
Hundred's position . . . the sum of the third diagonal column, or $2 + 9 = 1$ and a carry 1. The carry is in the thousand's position, therefore the product is 1,122.

Early Calculators

The first mechanical digital calculator was invented by Blaise Pascal in Paris in 1642 (Figure 3-6). It also is referred to as the numerical wheel calculator, because it was the world's first mechanical adding machine.

At age eighteen, Pascal wanted to help his father, who at that time was the

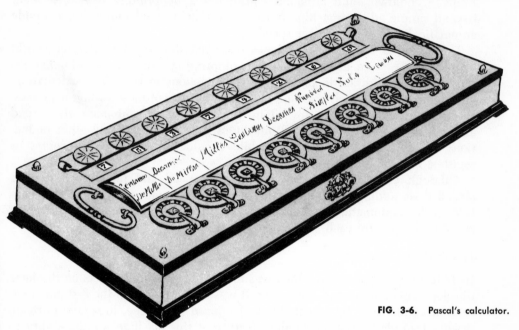

FIG. 3-6. Pascal's calculator.

Superintendent of Taxes. The calculator he designed registered decimal values by rotating a wheel by one to nine steps, with a carry lever to operate the next higher digit wheel whenever the first wheel reached 10 units.

At the age of 25, Gottfried Wilhelm von Leibnitz built his "stepped-wheel" calculator which was manufactured in 1694. It was capable of performing all four arithmetic functions; however, it was not considered dependable in its operation.

Another attempt was made in 1829 by Charles Xavier Thomas of Colmar, France. His calculator was the first to perform all four functions accurately. An idea similar to Thomas' was used in 1872 by Frank Stephen Baldwin, marking the beginning of the calculating-machine industry in the United States.

Key-Driven Calculating Machines

The invention and development of devices and machines such as the type-writer, the letterpress, and the cash register played a big part in the advancement of data processing, particularly in the recording and reporting functions. In 1887, Dorr Eugene Felt patented his comptometer, improved versions of which are still widely used. The first practical adding and listing (printing) machines were produced by Felt in 1889 and, three years later, by W. S. Burroughs. Burroughs developed a 90-key machine with a capacity of up to nine decimal digits.

In 1914, Oscar and David Sundstrand produced a 10-key adding machine. About that time, the Monroe calculator was invented by Jay R. Monroe and Frank S. Baldwin, and although considered a nonprinting device, it went beyond simple adding-machine functions in that it could multiply and divide automatically at much greater speeds.

The so-called accounting machines were not developed until after World War I. These were machines capable of printing values in a columnar arrangement, in addition to performing the functions of recording, calculating, and summarizing, which are common characteristics of most adding machines. Included in this category are billing machines which automatically extend amounts on invoices, and payroll machines that handle tax and other deductions in arriving at the net pay, while simultaneously providing copies or registers for accounting purposes.

Although electric motors provide greater speed and facility, all devices classified as adding machines, calculators, or accounting machines are considered "nonautomatic" equipment. All of them require a human worker to control and operate each step of processing.

Joseph Marie Jacquard

In 1801, an event occurred which was to have far-reaching effects on the later development of automatic equipment. It was the perfection of the first punched-card machine, built by Joseph Marie Jacquard of France, to weave intricate designs into cloth. The outstanding feature of this machine was its ability to follow a set of instructions punched into cards. Due to the "fear of machines," Jacquard had difficulty gaining public acceptance for his machine. In the City of Lyons, he was physically attacked and his machine was destroyed. Through Napoleon's support, he rebuilt his machine and proved its usefulness in weaving. Lyon's prosperity in the mid-1800's was attributed largely to the success of Jacquard's loom.

Herman Hollerith and the Punched-Card Era

The year 1880 marks the beginning of the modern punched-card era. During this year, Dr. Herman Hollerith, a statistician, was engaged by the U.S. Census Bureau as a special agent to speed up the processing of census data.

The 1880 census took seven and a half years to complete. Manual tabulating methods were used in the survey of a population of 50 million people and proved hopelessly inadequate. It was obvious that the 1890 census could not be processed by the same means if the information was to have any real value. Furthermore, many facts of interest could not be compiled at all, or could not be handled in a manner which satisfied the Census Bureau's objectives.

Dr. Hollerith set out to mechanize the census operations. By 1887, he had completed a system using the punched-card principle, although the first machine used paper strips with holes punched into them according to a code, similar to a player-piano roll. The paper strip was found to be impractical, so a standard-size card was developed and the system eventually included 3 in. × 5 in. corner-cut cards, a punch, a "pin-press," electromagnetic counters, and a sorting box.

In operation, a punched card was placed into the pin-press, and a hinged box was lowered to activate a counter and open the lid of a sorting slot. Cards were deposited at a speed of 50 to 80 cards a minute. A test tabulation of 10,000 returns showed that enumeration time was three-fourths and tabulating time was one-eighth of that required for earlier systems. Despite an increase in the population to 63 million, the 1890 census was tabulated in two and a half years, a job which would have taken several more years to do manually.

In 1896, Dr. Hollerith organized the Tabulating Machine Company to develop his machines for commercial sale. In 1901, he introduced the basic form of a numerical punch keyboard, and other system improvements were completed before his retirement in 1914.

James Powers

In the meantime, S. N. D. North, Director of the United States Census Bureau, was making plans for the 1910 census. Realizing the necessity of greater processing speed and accuracy, and in the absence of Hollerith, he engaged James Powers (a comparatively unknown statistician from New Jersey) to develop more equipment in a new mechanical laboratory subsidized by Congress.

Powers designed completely mechanical machines with many desirable features. In 1908, he produced a die-set punch capable of punching 20-column cards on a "simultaneous-punching" principle. The principle involves the accumulation of information to be punched in a card; then, by depressing a key, all the information is punched simultaneously. With this technique, there is an advantage in checking to see that all data to be punched are keyed in correctly. The simultaneous-punching principle presently is used in the Univac keypunch. Later, Powers developed a two-deck horizontal sorter.

Powers' machines performed so well that 300 punches, related sorters, and tabulators were installed for the 1910 census. Powers became convinced that there was a commercial market for his machines. In 1911, he formed the Powers Accounting Machine Company (which was later acquired by Remington Rand Corporation).

Industry Developments

About 1911, punched-card machine developments began to accelerate. During that year, the Tabulating Machine Company, originally organized by Dr. Hollerith, merged with the International Time Recording Company and the Dayton Scale Company to form the Computing-Tabulating Recording Company. Three years later, in 1914, Thomas J. Watson, Sr., became its president. In 1924, the name of the company was changed to the International Business Machines Corporation.

Meanwhile, the Accounting and Tabulating Machine Corporation was organized to distribute internationally the products of Powers Accounting Machine Company. Powers' machines were successfully demonstrated in Europe, and sales agencies were established in several countries. Among these was the Accounting and Tabulating Corporation of Great Britain, Ltd., which separated from Powers in 1919. In 1922, *Samas* (Société Anonyme des Machines à Statistiques), another sales agency, was established in France. In 1929, the French and British companies consolidated, forming Powers-Samas Accounting Machines, Ltd. In 1958, the merger of Power-Samas Accounting Machines, Ltd. and the British Tabulating Machine Company led to the organization of International Computers and Tabulators, Ltd.

In the United States, the Powers line merged in 1927 with other office supply companies to form Remington Rand Corporation, which in 1955 merged with the Sperry Corporation to form Sperry Rand Corporation. Presently, data processing equipment is marketed through the Univac Division of Sperry Rand Corporation.

Developments in Automatic Data Processing

The word *computer* had long been used to describe anything that has a "computing" ability: adding, subtracting, multiplying, or dividing. Only recently has the term come to have its present-day meaning.

Charles P. Babbage

It is generally agreed that the first major step in the development of computers can be attributed to Charles P. Babbage, a professor of mathematics at Trinity College, Cambridge, England.

Babbage became interested in computing extensive mathematical tables which would make the metric system easier to use. In 1812, he selected three groups of people, assigning the first group of five men to the task of defining the formulas and of describing the mathematical methods to be used. The second group was assigned to take these formulas and to compute some numerical values for them. The third group of about 100 men was to complete all necessary computations. Babbage's idea was to replace this third group ultimately with a piece of equipment he called the *Difference Engine*. Unfortunately, it never was perfected.

The Difference Engine

In 1812, Babbage thought of building the Difference Engine, a machine capable of computing mathematical tables automatically. Ten years later, a

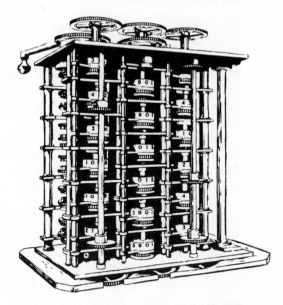

FIG. 3-7. Babbage's Difference Engine.

model of the Difference Engine was completed and received wide attention. This led to a substantial subsidy from the Royal Society and the British Government for the construction of the machine. Soon thereafter, however, Babbage became interested instead in developing a new idea involving a general-purpose machine. This shift in plans left him unsupported by the Government and the original plan for the difference engine was abandoned.

Babbage's Analytical Engine

Babbage's next project was the "analytical engine," designed and partially built in 1830. This was to be the first completely automatic general-purpose digital computer. According to the plan, the machine was to have an arithmetic unit designed to perform calculations based on numbers from a storage unit. Both the arithmetic and the storage units were to be governed by a control unit which would coordinate and supervise the sequence of operations.

Babbage worked on the analytical engine for the remaining years of his life, but died in 1871 with the job uncompleted. Even though the analytical engine was never put into actual use, he must be given credit for having the original idea, and for recognizing the kind of problems which later occupied the efforts and talents of two generations of engineers. He is considered one of the great pioneers in the field of computation. In addition to having been a mathematician and a professor, he wrote over 80 books and papers. His son, Major General H. P. Babbage, took up his father's project and succeeded in completing part of the arithmetic unit after his father's death.

The Mark I Computer

After Babbage died in 1871, no major advance in automatic computation was made until 1937, when Professor Howard Aiken of Harvard University became interested in combining some established principles with the punched cards pioneered by Hollerith and Powers to build an automatic calculating device. In May, 1944, with the cooperation of I.B.M., an automatic-sequence-controlled calculator named the Harvard Mark I was built and formally presented to Harvard University.

Aiken's machine was built on the concept of using information from punched cards as input, making decimal calculations through electromechanical devices, and producing the results on punched cards again. The sequence of calculations was controlled through a wide-punched paper tape.

The machine was adapted to solve various kinds of problems for engineers, physicists, and mathematicians, and was the first machine to do long series of arithmetic and logical problems. After the Mark I, Professor Aiken also constructed three more models, the Mark II, Mark III, and Mark IV.

The Mark I computer is considered to be the first successful general-purpose digital computer. It is now on display at Harvard. Compared to today's computers, it is slow, but is still in working condition.

The Eniac

In the early 1940's, Dr. John W. Mauchly of the University of Pennsylvania became aware of the need for a high-speed electronic device able to do great quantities of statistical calculations for weather data. During World War II, a contract for the project was made between the University of Pennsylvania and the U.S. government.

In 1945, Dr. Mauchly and J. Presper Eckert used the facilities at the Moore School of Electrical Engineering to design and build the Electronic Numerical Integrator and Calculator (ENIAC). Eniac was completely electronic in that it had no moving parts other than input/output gear. It was installed at the Aberdeen Proving Grounds in Maryland and was used until 1956, when it was removed to be placed in the Smithsonian Institution.

Mauchly and Eckert formed a company, subsequently acquired by the Sperry Rand Corporation, that played a major role in the development of the first commercial computer, the Univac.

Eniac was a large machine, containing 18,000 vacuum tubes. It had a small memory of 20 accumulators for storing data. Each accumulator was capable of carrying 10 digits. The accumulators consisted of vacuum tubes, tied together in packages of two, so that two tubes would represent one binary digit (bit) in computer storage. The machine was externally programmed, but had internal capacities of a multiplier, divider (which also functioned as a unit to take a square root), and three function tables. Input and output were made through punched cards.

In the mid-1940's, the best available electromechanical equipment could perform a maximum of one multiplication per second. By contrast, Eniac could process 300 multiplications per second. A job that took 300 days to complete by hand could be accomplished in a day with Eniac. The main point was not so much that the Eniac worked faster than other equipment, but that—by combining operations—jobs that had been considered impossible before could now be performed.

Also in the mid-1940's, Dr. J. von Neumann, another pioneer, issued a report to a group connected with the Moore School of Electrical Engineering at the University of Pennsylvania, in which he described the basic philosophy of computer design. This philosophy has been incorporated in today's computers. Von Neumann himself did not believe that all his theories were practical, but with today's advanced technology, almost everything he described in his theoretical paper has become reality. It is not uncommon to hear that computers were designed based on the "von Neumann concept."

The Edvac

As a result of Dr. von Neumann's paper, the Electronic Discrete Variable Automatic Computer (EDVAC) was built. It was smaller in size, but greater in power, than its predecessors. Numbers were represented internally in powers of 2, or in what is referred to as the *binary* numbering system.

Before Edvac, all computer programs had been wired externally by hand. Coincident with its design, the notion of internal programming was born. In May, 1945, Dr. von Neumann wrote the first program, an internal sorting routine consisting of the rearrangement of numbers in ascending sequences, in an attempt to prove that computers could be used in projects *other than those of a scientific* nature. The sorting routine ran a job three times faster than a card sorter.

The Univac

The Univac (Universal Automatic Calculator), manufactured and designed by the Sperry Rand Corporation, is considered the first step toward completely automatic data processing. Previously, computers had been built only for scientific and engineering data processing purposes. The Univac was popularized through television quiz shows and various other demonstrations, and is well-known for having predicted the victory of President Dwight D. Eisenhower in the presidential election of 1952. It was the Univac that led the public to believe that the computer was an "electronic brain" and might become a replacement for "brains."

Although many tube-type computers are still operating satisfactorily, the advent of the transistor (commonly referred to as "solid state") has greatly improved the efficiency of computer operations. A transistor is much smaller than a vacuum tube. Solid state computers are much more compact than tube-type computers; they require less rigid air-conditioning, have a greater life expectancy, and are less susceptible to failure. Solid state computers are much more reliable than tube-type computers.

Computer manufacturers are constantly trying to develop computers with a longer life and of a smaller size capable of storing more data and operating at greater speeds.

In 1943, there were no electronic computers available. Ten years later (1953), many electronic calculators were commercially available, but the general-purpose, stored-program electronic digital computer was not yet widely used. Between that time and 1958, hundreds of vacuum-tube computers were put into operations. Most of the small-size to medium-size models had magnetic drum storage, while only the largest computers contained magnetic core storage. In 1959, the use of vacuum-tube computers almost ceased when transistorized computers began to appear on the market. Since their appearance, thousands of transistorized computers have been delivered and installed.

Computers are generally classified as small-, medium-, or large-scale. This classification is not necessarily an indication of their physical size (although large-scale computers do require more floor space), but rather is used as a general price-scale categorization. Small-scale computers range up to $100,000 each; medium-scale computers between $100,000 and $750,000; and large-scale computers, from $750,000 upward.

Based on a late 1965 survey of computer installations in the United States,* 7,288 small-scale, 14,128 medium-scale, and 1,678 large-scale computers had been installed: a total of 23,094 computers. Examples of the small-scale computer are the Friden 6010, IBM 1620, and NCR 390. Medium-scale computers include the Burroughs B 200, GE 215, Honeywell 200, IBM 360 (small configuration), IBM 1401, NCR 315, RCA 3301, and Univac 418. Some of the large-scale computers are the Burroughs 5500, Control Data 6400, GE 635, IBM 360 (large configuration), RCA Spectra 70, and Univac 490.

In recent years, the trend has been toward producing medium-scale computer systems. The larger, more powerful computer systems have been used primarily for scientific and engineering purposes. Current and future trends may very likely move toward the production of small-scale computers, especially since electronic data processing has made a powerful appeal to the small businessman.

GLOSSARY OF TERMS

ABACUS: A manual calculating device that uses beads to represent decimal values.

EDVAC: An electronic automatic computer which represents data in a binary form.

ENIAC: A high-speed electronic computer designed and built by Mauchly and Eckert at the University of Pennsylvania.

NAPIER's "BONES": A technique introduced by John Napier to aid multiplication through the use of data tables or rods.

---

* *Business Automation,* OA Business Publication Inc., 288 Park Avenue West, Elmhurst, Illinois, February 1966, pp. 54-56.

SIMULTANEOUS-PUNCHING PRINCIPLE: Introduced by James Powers, whereby all the required information to be punched is initially accumulated and then punched simultaneously in a card.

UNIVAC: An early automatic computer designed and manufactured by the Sperry Rand Corporation.

QUESTIONS FOR REVIEW

1. What is finger counting? Show how the product of multiplying 7×8 is obtained.
2. What is an abacus? Explain its basic operation.
3. Discuss the origin of the abacus.
4. Explain the primitive era of manual record keeping.
5. List and describe briefly three early mechanical calculating devices.
6. How do Napier's "bones" perform multiplication?
7. Who invented the first mechanical digital calculator? Why?
8. In what way did Jacquard contribute toward the development of automatic equipment? Explain.
9. Describe the main contributions of Hollerith to the development of punched-card data processing.
10. Explain the main contributions of Powers to punched-card data processing. What company currently practices and develops machines based on his ideas?
11. Present a brief historical review of I.B.M. How is Hollerith related to this firm?
12. What is the idea behind Babbage's difference engine? Illustrate.
13. What are some of the unique characteristics of the Mark I?
14. Describe the Eniac. Who built it? When?

chapter

4

Business and Scientific Data Processing

It has been estimated that at least one-sixth of our total gross national product (GNP) is devoted to handling paper. Computers make a tremendous contribution by doing this work more quickly, efficiently, and economically.

A businessman's judgment can be no better than his source of information. Through the use of automatic data processing, today's decisions can be based on today's conditions, not last month's. Masses of confusing details can quickly be analyzed to produce the information needed to operate the business. Changes in business requirements, in turn, encourage a sustaining development of new data processing systems.

There are three main ways in which computers are used in business. First, they are used to print the necessary information for instructing the organization to act in accordance with certain predetermined decisions. Second, routine management decisions may be made by programming the computers to signal certain conditions and perform the necessary action, such as recording stock when the inventory reaches a predetermined "low limit." Finally, the most important way in which computers are being used in business is in the preparation of feedback information and progress reports for management's use in controlling the whole operation.

With these factors in mind, it becomes increasingly evident that a knowledge of the principles of automatic data processing is essential to anyone who plans to enter the business world. In this chapter, the term "business" is used in a broad sense, and "business applications" are any nonscientific data-processing requirements of government as well as industry.

Business Data Processing

Business data processing is an area including the storage and maintenance of records required in the everyday conduct of a business organization. The business may be as small as the corner soda fountain or as large and complex as General Motors. The more complex a business organization, the greater is the amount of data.

Regardless of size, the general requirements of data processing are about the same. Records must be maintained and periodically updated. Reports must be prepared and presented to the proper administrators. Materials must be ordered at the proper time. Employees must be paid the correct amount and on time.

For illustrative purposes, let us take a look at a corner soda fountain and see just what requirements the proprietor has for a data-processing system. He sells ice cream and a few other refreshments. When the need arises, he employs part-time student help after school hours and on weekends. His business is considered a one-man operation and is referred to as a "proprietorship."

A small business like this would not require the use of a computer, perhaps not even an adding machine, to keep going. Despite the simplicity of a small business, however, certain records must be kept, and other details related to those records must be filed for future reference. They may be filed either in one's head, as might be the case here, or in the case of documents such as receipts and tax reports, filed in an old roll-top desk or a filing cabinet.

Suppose that the proprietor has introduced a special sale on strawberry sundaes. For what reason is a reduction in price made? Does he need to increase his sales because of his immediate need for cash, or is it done out of the goodness of his heart? Assuming that he is an experienced businessman, the introduction of a "special" on any item presumably is done to minimize costs (or losses) and to maximize profits. The store's proprietor might have looked in his back room the day before the sale and found an excess of six gallons of strawberry syrup. He knew then that if he did not sell it quickly, it might spoil and he would have to throw it out. Besides, since his stock room is limited in size, he probably felt the need to conserve space. Expected delivery of other items may have put pressure on him to find room for the new merchandise. Regardless of the exact reason for the sale, it is obvious that the proprietor must keep regular control over his salable stock. This practice is one of the main functions performed by data processing.

For his part-time helper, the owner determines the amount of time he should work, his hourly rate and his total weekly pay. This process is as simple, in some instances, as multiplying 22 hours of work by $1.50 per hour, arriving at $33.00 in weekly wages. The problem becomes more involved when we consider the fact that the proprietor is required by law to withhold federal income tax, state tax (if any), social security (FICA), and other related taxes from his helper's earnings each week. At the end of the year, he also must be prepared to report both to his helper and to the Internal Revenue

Service the exact earnings of his employee and the amount(s) withheld. The procedure of determining employee earnings, and the preparation of their checks for a given period, is referred to as preparing "payroll."

This payroll problem, even when it involves only one employee, is not simple. There is the need to prepare some sort of Profit and Loss Statement, compute various taxes, pay a variety of insurance premiums, and other similar items. One may wonder how the owner ever has enough time to do anything but keep records.

The proprietor must have a system which he follows regularly. As soon as data originate, he files them away—in his head or in his desk—for future reference. After the data are processed in some way (such as filling out a tax form), the results, or reports, are filed for future reference.

Not all business firms operate in this relatively simple manner. Larger firms have established more advanced and more highly efficient systems of processing data due to the fact they have more paperwork problems to be handled, the magnitude of each problem is greater, and the problems are infinitely more complex.

The Business Organization—Its Makeup and Information Flow

To get a better understanding of the factors involved in processing business data, it is necessary to understand the makeup of a business organization and the way in which information flows between its various departments or divisions.

FIG. 4-1.

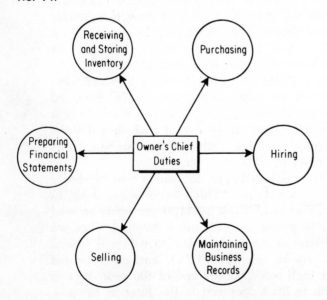

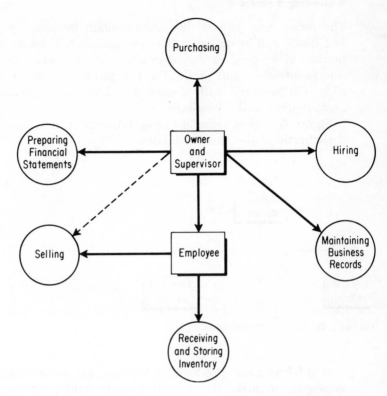

FIG. 4-2. The expanding business.

A business organization is defined as a human relationship in group activity, similar to that of a social structure. It usually consists of a group of people whose activities are varied and who are related to one another by a superior–subordinate relationship, referred to as the "chain of command." Its function is to accomplish a major goal or combination of goals, such as the manufacture of a product or the rendering of a service.

In Figure 4-1, we diagram the functions of the proprietor of a soda fountain. These functions include buying, selling, receiving, maintaining records, hiring, and preparing financial statements.

As a small business concern expands, additional help is needed. This point usually is reached when the owner and a helper no longer can handle all the various activities effectively. The helper probably was hired originally because of sporadic increases in sales during some store hours, especially on weekends. In this case, the subordinate may be assigned to do certain chores, thus relieving his superior to do other things or to help keep up with the extra work generated as a result of the increase in business.

Figure 4-2 shows how this subordinate–superior relationship affects a reorganization of the workload.

A Growing Business

The owner may expand his soda-fountain business by adding more tables and stools, and by ordering more merchandise. If he desires to have a unique product of his own, he may decide to make his own ice cream. When a decision to introduce and produce a new product is made, the owner quite possibly will be faced with a need for more men, materials, money, methods (techniques), and "know-how."

Figure 4-3 shows the growing business, which now includes two main departments, Sales and Production.

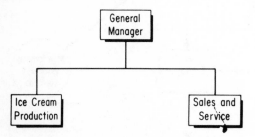

FIG. 4-3. The new organization chart.

In order to begin producing ice cream, the owner will need to hire enough employees to make the desired quantity within the required specifications. Having more employees will increase the payroll problem. A bookkeeper may be hired to maintain records, file reports, prepare financial statements, and produce the payroll. Two girls may be needed as sales clerks.

Figure 4-4 is an organization chart showing these new employees, the work they do, and their relationship to the boss and to each other. Rectangles denote the position held. Circles stand for the duties performed.

Basic Requirements of a Business

In order to set up and operate this growing business, the owner (or perhaps, by now, he has taken in a partner) must (1) buy from other companies, called vendors, such items as machinery, equipment, paper supplies, and other goods needed to make and package the product he wishes to sell; and (2) sell, or market, his product either to the consumer or to other companies or both.

Production Planning

Figure 4-4 shows the areas in which data are originated, collected, manipulated, and later summarized in the form of financial reports for the manager. A description of how the information flows and the data it creates is helpful in understanding the stages of data processing to be described later.

In a large manufacturing firm, a decision is made involving the quantity and

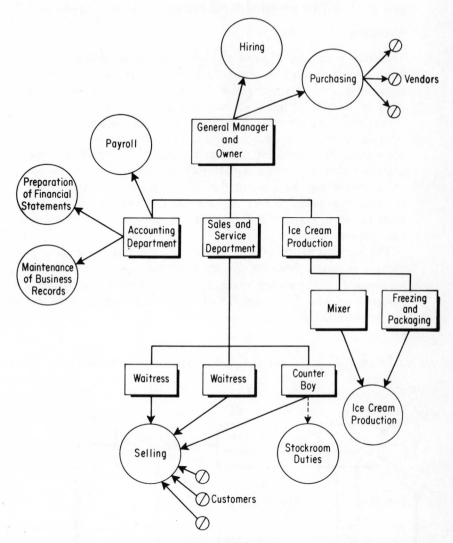

FIG. 4-4. The business structure—selling and producing.

type of products to be made. A quota is determined, based on the actual amount sold, the quantity on hand, and the estimated sales volume for a specified period of time in the future. The sales department provides information concerning the actual quantity sold to date and also helps to forecast future sales. A production order is prepared, authorizing the manufacture of the needed quantity.

Suppose, for example, the owner estimates sales of 1,000 gallons of ice cream during the month of December. A check on the warehouse shows a stock of 800 gallons on hand. This means that a production order for 200 gallons should be executed to fill the projected sales quota of 1,000 gallons.

Purchasing

The stock room should hold all raw materials needed for the production of a finished unit. It must be prepared to give the production department the right quantity of each raw material at the time it is needed. Any depleted ingredient must be reordered and restocked promptly.

Suppose there are enough ingredients in the stock room to manufacture only 80 gallons of ice cream. A purchase order must be issued to authorize the acquisition of ingredients for an additional 120 gallons, plus enough extra ingredients to provide a satisfactory inventory backup to cover unforeseen emergencies and the start of the following month's production. If the vendor requires two weeks to receive, process, and deliver the order, the stock room must maintain enough "safety stock" to prevent a complete shutdown during that period.

The purchasing process is a common application of data processing. Purchasing involves obtaining the materials that go into the finished product and making sure that they are available on time. Before purchasing an item, several competitive brands of similar quality are sampled. After consideration of factors such as price, quality, and value is made, a purchase order for the

FIG. 4-5. The flow of materials and related information—a schematic diagram.

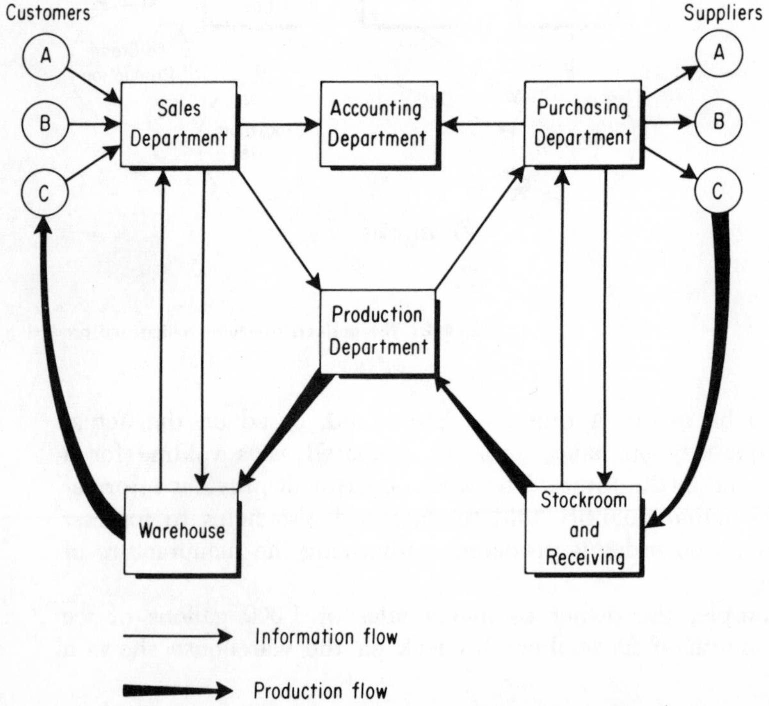

Customers   Suppliers

A → Sales Department → Accounting Department ← Purchasing Department → A
B → → B
C → → C

Production Department

Warehouse   Stockroom and Receiving

———→ Information flow

━━━▶ Production flow

needed quantity is mailed to the chosen vendor. A carbon copy of the order is sent also to the stock room as advance notice of the forthcoming shipment.

Figure 4-5 shows the relationship of this function to the operation of a manufacturing business.

Receiving

When a shipment arrives from a vendor, the stock-room clerk verifies the items in the shipment, their quantity, and their specifications against a copy of the original purchase order. Next he notifies the purchasing department of its arrival and the satisfactory condition of the contents. Upon receiving an invoice from the supplier, the purchasing department approves payment and sends the invoice to the accounting department for payment.

An invoice is a detailed account of the merchandise shipped by the vendor, including the quantity, the unit price, and the total dollar value of the order, including any allowable discounts to which the purchaser is entitled.

Disbursements

Once the accounting department receives the invoice, the bookkeeper goes through the routine of writing and mailing a check for the amount owed, less any applicable discounts.

Discounts frequently are offered to those who order merchandise in relatively large quantities (for example, units of 100 or 1,000 case lots, etc., depending upon the product involved). The idea is that such a discount will encourage volume buying and that the person or company that does so is entitled to a reduced unit price.

Cash discounts, on the other hand, are designed to encourage prompt payment. It is common for a vendor to allow a discount of, say, 2 per cent if the bill is paid within a specified period of time (for example, 10 days from the date of the invoice).

Stockkeeping

The incoming shipment of materials is sent to the stock room, where a record is marked to indicate that such items now are "on hand." Every time the production department requisitions part of the stock, this record is used to indicate the amount withdrawn and the amount remaining on hand. This procedure, referred to as inventory keeping, lets management know its materials situation at all times, and is helpful in assuring that production will never have to stop for lack of materials.

Periodically, a physical count of the inventory in stock is taken to verify the actual materials on hand with those shown on the records. This operation not only verifies the accuracy of the inventory records, but it also performs two other vital functions: (1) it helps to pinpoint waste, loss, or pilferage; and (2) it provides management with important information to be used for cost analyses, financial reports (inventory, after all, is an "asset"), government reports, and the like.

Production

No sale can be made unless a product is available, both for sale and delivery. Products are made either by special order or in advance of sale. In the former case, orders first must be received from a customer and then the production department begins to manufacture the merchandise to meet the customer's requirements.

The more common type of production is the manufacture of merchandise in advance of its sale or the receipt of an order. This requires a reasonable forecast of future sales volume, and the risk is commensurate with the reliability of the data from which such a forecast is made. If the forecast was low, the company will run out of merchandise and have to pass up sales. If it was high, the company will overproduce and an excess of merchandise will have to be held in costly warehouses or be sold at reduced prices in order to prevent it from spoiling, going out of style, etc.

All finished merchandise is transferred from the production department to a warehouse, where it is stored until receipt of authorization to ship it to a specific customer.

Sales

Basically, the ice-cream company used in our example—like any other business organization—operates with *profit* as its ultimate goal. Profit comes from sales, either of a product or a service. Thus, in most organizations, a sales department is set up. The number of salesmen depends largely on the volume of sales, the type of product, the number of customers, the demand for the product, and the geographic area to be covered.

When a customer orders a given product, the transaction may be in cash or in credit. If the order is on credit, approval of the customer's credit rating becomes necessary. A copy of the sales invoices is sent to the credit or accounting department, along with the customer's history card (if any). The history card contains a complete record of the customer's past purchases and history of payment.

Usually, customers have a credit limit, based on their ability to pay and on their reliability. If the present order exceeds the credit limit, the credit manager may either disapprove the sale or may ask the customer for an advance payment equal to the amount beyond this limit.

Assuming that an agreement is reached regarding credit terms, the credit department approves the sale, setting a number of activities into action. A copy of the invoice is sent to the warehouse, authorizing shipment of the merchandise. When the merchandise is shipped, the sales and credit departments are notified. The sale is recorded in the accounts-receivable journal, where an entry is made to debit the customer's account by the amount of the purchase. Next, a statement is prepared and mailed to the customer for payment. When the bill is paid, an entry is made in the journal to reduce the customer's obligation by that amount, and a suitable entry is recorded on the customer's credit history card.

Preparation of the Profit and Loss (P & L) Statement

The foregoing illustration described a manufacturing and distributing cycle which begins with planning for production and ends in the sale of a finished product. This cycle continues as long as the firm remains in *profitable* operation.

The company's earning capability usually is shown through a Profit and Loss Statement. This financial statement is constructed from data collected in the general ledger and contains all financial details pertaining to sales, cost of goods sold, operating expenses, and other related information. The basic outline of a typical P & L Statement follows:

BENNETT MUSICAL SUPPLIES

Income Statement
For Year Ended December 31, 1966

Revenue from Sales	$16,000
Cost of goods sold	11,000
Gross profit on sales	$ 5,000
Total operating expenses	2,000
Net income from operations	$ 3,000
Income tax	1,300
Net income	$ 1,700

Note that the statement is developed by subtracting expenses from revenues. If revenues exceed expenses, the remainder is profit. If expenses exceed revenues, the difference is loss.

It can be seen from the foregoing example that a volume of information flows through the various departments of a typical business organization. Much of the information is of a routine, repetitive nature, especially in the areas of production, order writing, billing, accounts receivable, and purchasing. Integrating these areas into a data-processing system is not always easy to do, but accomplishing such a goal usually reduces data-processing costs and produces more meaningful reports for more effective control of the organization. This is the aim and objective of an automatic data-processing system.

Automatic Data Processing in the Scientific World

In the past, many scientific problems were left unsolved because of the seemingly impossible task of processing a variety of complex formulas by manual methods. The present use of automatic data processing has given the scientist and engineer tools with which to handle such involved computations. Problems that would have taken a lifetime of calculations in the past now are being processed by computers in a matter of minutes. Some problems with a large number of variables and restrictions could never have been handled by ordinary means; today, computers process them with comparative ease. With the new tools of automatic data processing, scientists in both basic and applied research have widened their horizons and have given new freedom to creative thought.

What Is Scientific Data Processing?

Scientific data processing consists mainly of solving mathematical problems such as engineering formulas, research and development problems, or any type of calculation that normally requires a "one-time" solution. Unlike most business problems, scientific problems are generally not repetitive.

The scientist and engineer must solve problems with many variables, dealing with probabilities, statistical equations, and so on. This presents a different kind of problem for the computer than the typical business application, which usually involves a high volume of input and output, but limited arithmetic requirements. Consequently, scientific and business computers have generally been different in design, despite the fact that many so-called business computers are being used for certain scientific and engineering applications. The reverse is also true in a few cases.

Although scientific data may differ from business data, the pattern of processing is quite similar. First, a *system* must be devised. Second, a *problem* must exist that can be represented in a form acceptable to the data-processing system.

As tools for the engineer, computers are one of the vital elements in the field of automation. They have been linked to metal-working tools, production mills, and processing plants. Some computers are even being used to design other computers—planning the wiring circuitry and issuing instructions to the automatic equipment which physically wires the circuits.

Through the use of a device called a *plotter,* which may be connected to a computer, charts and graphs may be produced. By the introduction of engineering specifications into such a machine, mechanical drawings can be created. Multiple drawings, representing views from changing angles, also have been used to "animate" movies of such complex things as the approach of an attacking aircraft on a "pursuit curve."

Researchers at the University of Pennsylvania in Philadelphia, working with the American Cancer Society, are using computers to simulate the growth of cancer cells, saving many years of study. Computer analyses of millions of medical records are giving the medical profession new insights into causes and possible cures of many diseases. Other uses include certain specialized applications. A patient's symptoms can be entered into the computer as source data, for example, and then the system can manipulate these data and correctly diagnose the patient's illness.

The Armed Forces require many types of problem solutions produced by a workable data-processing system. After missiles are launched into orbit, for example, they are constantly checked to make sure they are following a pre-planned course.

Enemy aircraft are detected and positioned by radar. Courses and speed are worked out by data-processing systems to enable our own fighter planes or rockets to intercept and destroy them.

These and other problems can be solved in fractions of seconds, provided the proper data-processing techniques are employed. But again, regardless of the system used, the steps in solving the problem are much the same as those described earlier.

GLOSSARY OF TERMS

BUSINESS DATA PROCESSING: Data processing for business purposes, e.g., recording and summarizing the financial transactions of a business.

BUSINESS ORGANIZATION: A framework which ties together the activities of a business to induce integrated performance. Also, a human relationship in group activity.

CASH DISCOUNT: A fixed amount or a percentage deducted by the seller from the price of an item for inducing cash payment by the buyer.

PLOTTER: A visual display or board in which a dependent variable is graphed by an automatically controlled pen or pencil as a function of one or more variables.

PRODUCTION: Conversion of basic raw materials into a product sold by a business firm.

PROFIT AND LOSS STATEMENT: A financial statement showing the company's earning capability during a specific period of time.

PURCHASE ORDER: A requisition made by the purchasing department to a supplier for meeting the needs of a division or a department (for example, production department) of the firm.

QUESTIONS FOR REVIEW

1. In what ways are computers used in business? Explain.
2. What is business data processing? What are some of its requirements?
3. Prepare a 300–400 word report about the data-processing requirements of a small business in your neighborhood.
4. Discuss the primary functions of a business organization.
5. Explain briefly the information flow that takes place in a manufacturing enterprise.
6. What is purchasing? How does a purchasing department contribute to the smooth operation of the production division of a business firm?
7. Why are discounts of various types introduced? Explain.
8. What are the chief reasons for taking a physical count of inventory in stock?

9. "Persia, Incorporated," is an independent rug dealer in Chicago, Ill. His ledger accounts for the month of January, 1966 show the following data:

Sales for the month	$27,000
Cost of goods sold	11,000
Rent expense	1,200
Salaries	3,400
Office supplies	200

Based on the above account balances, prepare a profit and loss statement.

10. How is scientific data processing similar to business data processing? For what reason(s) is it used?

chapter

5

The Data-Processing Cycle

Chapter 4 presented the makeup of a business organization, the major departments it contains, and the flow of information between those departments. To facilitate this flow of information, many steps are necessary. They might be as easy as typing a purchase order or transferring an invoice from one department to another, or as complex as determining a detailed payroll of several hundred employees each week.

Data processing may be divided into five separate but related steps. They are: (1) origination, (2) input, (3) manipulation, (4) output, and (5) storage.

Origination

It should be kept in mind that "to process" means to do something with or to "manipulate" existing information so that the result is a meaningful contribution to the goals set by the company. The existing information is generally original in nature and is either handwritten or typewritten. Original papers are commonly referred to as *source documents*. Examples of source documents are checks, time cards, and sales orders.

What type of source documents did the soda-fountain proprietor have, for example, and where did they originate? The proprietor received an invoice from the vendor every time merchandise was delivered. The invoice is a source document. The number of hours the clerks and those who produced ice cream worked constituted the source information to be used by the bookkeeper. Presumably, those hours were recorded on some sort of time card or sheet—a source document. The "checks" that were written by the waitresses, presented to the customers, and paid to the cashier contained source information regarding the day's sales. They are source documents.

In Figure 5-1, two transactions have been completed: (1) the sale of two radios, and (2) the sale of one television set. The invoice containing these two transactions is a source document. Producing source documents, then, is the first step in a series of steps included in the data-processing cycle.

Input

After certain source documents are originated, or have been made available, the next step is to introduce the information they contain into the data processing system. This system may be manual, mechanical, electromechanical, or electronic. Let us assume, for this illustration, that the system is manual, where people are used to process data with the aid of paper and pencil.

Input data consist of original (raw) transactions in need of processing. The device used to record the two transactions in Figure 5-1 is called an input device. In manual data processing, a pencil is an input device, since it records the transaction and other related information. The pencil also is used as an output device, since once a computation has been completed, it records the answer.

Recording is the means by which an input device facilitates the presentation of source data for processing. Proper recording of source data involves: (1) determining what transaction needs processing. This is necessary especially in cases where the result of processing a given transaction is required for the successful processing of subsequent transactions. (2) The transaction should be checked to make sure it accurately represents the event or condition involved. Manual recording of transactions is not as accurate as machine recording. The human eye can deceive. Catalog number 56041 in Figure 5-1 may be incorrectly recorded as 56401 or 50641. This type of error is referred to as "transposition." Extra care must be taken to assure the accuracy of recorded data.

A given transaction can be coded, or condensed, to help make further processing more efficient and convenient. For ex-

FIG. 5-1. Source document—a sales invoice showing two transactions.

ABC Company Alton, Illiniois				
Cat. No.	Quantity	Description	Unit Cost	Total
56041	2	Radio	1500	3000
42461	1	Television	9500	9500

ample, an employee's name may be coded by assigning him a number (for example, your Social Security number or telephone number). Reading a number is more convenient and more accurate than reading a name since several people may have the same name.

The result of data processing can be no more accurate than the source information, so input accuracy is paramount.

Manipulation

When input data are recorded and verified, they are ready to be processed. The human eye is the device used to feed input data to the brain, where mental calculations are made. The "eye" of a punched-card data-processing system is the reading brush, which is installed in an input device to "read" input data and transfer them into the system for manipulation or processing.

"Manipulation" involves the actual work performed on the source data before any meaningful results can be realized. To *manipulate* data means to perform any or all of the subfunctions of (1) classifying, (2) sorting, (3) calculating, (4) recording, and (5) summarizing.

Classifying

Classifying facilitates the arrangement of data in a proper form so that they can be used effectively in the preparation of reports. Assume, for example, that a stack of invoices needs to be filed.

Following the manual process, a filing clerk can do one of two things. He can take the first invoice in the stack and file it in the proper folder by locating the identifying code name, number, etc., as in Figure 5-2, where the clerk would take the invoice bearing the name "Jones" and file it in the "Jones" folder in the file cabinet.

Locating Jones's folder involves searching the file alphabetically until Jones's file is found. This becomes time-consuming when a great number of names are involved, ranging from "Adams" to "Zona," and the entire file must be searched for each name as it appears.

A more convenient and faster approach to the filing procedure is to *classify* all invoices by pre-grouping or pre-sorting them into alphabetical order. Following this approach the 10 invoices in Figure 5-2 would be grouped as shown in Figure 5-3. It is easier to file each invoice by dropping it into its proper location during a single alphabetical search through the cabinet.

In a mechanized procedure, a machine called the keypunch punches holes in standard-size cards to record coded data representing each invoice. The data cards then can be fed through a *sorter* which places them in the same order as the existing file, and then into a *collator* which is wired to "merge" the new cards with the existing file automatically, producing the same result as that shown in Figure 5-3.

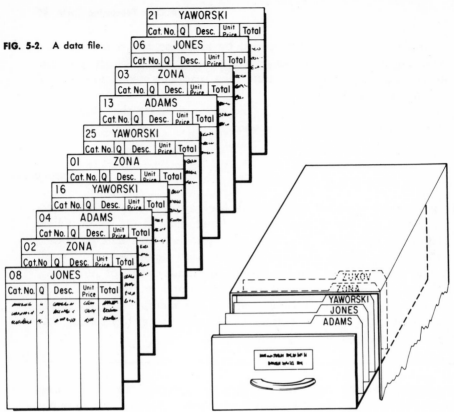

FIG. 5-2. A data file.

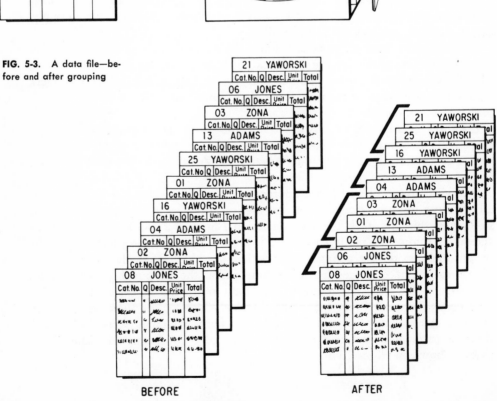

FIG. 5-3. A data file—before and after grouping

BEFORE

AFTER

46

Sorting

Sorting is the process of arranging data into a pre-determined alphabetic or numeric order, or of selecting particular data from a file according to some predetermined code classification.

Once the invoices in Figure 5-3 are classified, further sorting of each group by invoice number before filing would help the filing clerk to complete his job much more quickly and efficiently (see Figure 5-4).

After having sorted the invoices within each group by number, the clerk may simply pull out a group at a time and file the appropriate invoices accordingly.

These procedures could well be applied to many types of business. In the case of inventory work, for example, classification takes place when a stack of receipts is sorted by type, such as frozen foods, canned goods, school supplies, and so on. Once classified, each "sub-stack" of receipts is used to verify the quantity of merchandise available in the store. Failure to classify and/or sort the receipts will cause the clerk to make a great many unnecessary visits to various parts of the store—to the freezer, where frozen foods are stored; to the back room, where canned goods are kept; and to the front of the store, where school supplies are displayed.

Even a small business can entail a great deal of time and trouble recording, classifying, and sorting data, as the previous examples illustrate. By contrast, a large business finds it an unacceptably time-consuming—and expensive—task to do the same thing, using manual methods. Most businesses, therefore, have resorted to a more efficient and sophisticated classifying and sorting technique.

FIG. 5-4. A grouped data file sorted by invoice number.

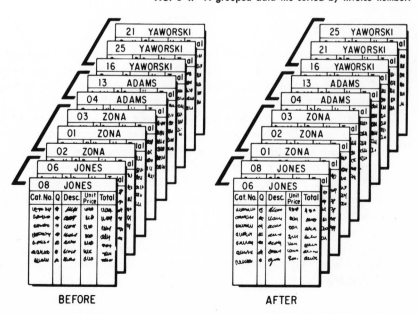

BEFORE   AFTER

The more up-to-date firm already has resorted to mechanical, electromechanical, or electronic data-processing equipment, motivated by the factors of accuracy, speed, and economy.

Calculating

Calculating aids in the reconstruction of data by condensing and/or "rephrasing" certain facts leading to a desired solution. For example, to multiply five cans of soup by 10 cents per can produces a total value of 50 cents for the lot. Calculating is the most crucial phase of data manipulation, since it is in this stage that most of the work is performed toward the solution of a given problem. Calculating involves one or more of the four arithmetic functions of addition, subtraction, multiplication, and division.

Referring to the inventory problem, items received (say, 10 units of frozen goods) are added to the balance on hand, at last inventory 85 units, for a new total of 95 units—the *amount of goods available for sale.* In order to calculate the number of units sold, one would reduce the total quantity available for sale (95) by the number of units available in the freezer (say, 60); and the difference (35 units) would constitute the desired information.

Recording

Often, the answer to a given *part* of a problem is only a partial solution to the *over-all* problem. In such cases, the recording of the intermediate answer is required until further processing can take place. This process is similar to that of a calculator that prints one or more subtotals, while retaining them in storage until a grand total can be reached. The subtotal is a partial answer which is recorded as a part of the report, but must be used later to produce the final result (the grand total).

Summarizing

Summarizing involves the compression of a mass of data into a concise and meaningful form. For decision-making or control purposes, it is not necessary to present all the facts (for example, the entire list of items in inventory) to management if the total (say, the combined dollar value of the inventory) is all that management requires. As a manager, the storekeeper doesn't necessarily care to know that there are six gallons of strawberry syrup at the soda counter and 12 more in the back room; all he cares to know is that the total on hand equals 18 gallons, or that the value of those 18 gallons is so many dollars.

Summary reports are used for various purposes, some of which include income-tax reporting, preparation of inventory status, profit and loss statements, and many others pertaining to the internal, as well as the external activities of the business. It is important to remember at this point that the purpose of data processing is to provide useful management information, not to see how many calculations can be performed or how many reports can be generated.

Output

After input data have been fed into a data-processing system and properly manipulated, the result is called "output." Output can be in either summary or detail form. The type of output desired must be planned in advance so that no waste of time occurs in processing the source data.

Included in "output" is *communication*. Output is of little value unless it is communicated promptly and effectively. A report which indicates that a certain variety of frozen foods is out of stock is of no value until it reaches the attention of the manager who is responsible for ordering a new supply. Failure to communicate this information promptly—and to the proper person—is as wasteful as figuring out one's income tax and then failing to file the return.

The output, then, is the ultimate goal in data processing. The system must be capable of communicating quickly, completely, and accurately with the outside world (that is, with people who are related to the data processed by the system), in order to make available the results of its calculations. Only by communicating properly can corrective action be initiated.

The data processing cycle is incomplete without the concept (loop) of control. In a business organization, control depends basically upon a comparison between the attained results and the predetermined goals. When the results are compared with the goals, they either agree or they are different. If they agree, no action is taken and the operation is repeated as before. However, if a disagreement is detected, a decision is made to make the necessary changes before the operation is repeated again. This *feedback concept of control* is an essential part of data processing. That is, output is compared with a predetermined standard and a decision is made (if necessary) on a course of action and is communicated to the stage where it is to be taken.

Storage

Data related to or resulting from the previous four data-processing steps can be *stored,* either temporarily or permanently, for future reference. It is necessary to store data, especially that pertaining to periodic reports, since they often are used over and over again in other related applications. A monthly profit and loss statement, for example, is used in compiling an annual report. A bank statement is carried over from one month to another in determining the balance-to-date. Employees' weekly wages are accumulated from payday to payday for use in annual and social security (FICA) reports.

Stored information can be either raw, semiprocessed, or output data. Quite often, the output of one problem becomes the input to another. When this occurs, a cycle is created that can be repeated continuously until the major application is completely processed. In the case of inventory, any unsold canned goods at the end of the year (*ending* inventory) constitute the *beginning* inventory for the ensuing year.

There are several ways of storing information, ranging from a simple record in a ledger book (manual data storage) to the "memory" of a large-scale electronic computer (automatic data storage).

Summary

The five basic functions of data processing are:

1. *Origination.* Determination of the nature, type, and origin of source documents.
2. *Input.* The introduction and feeding of source documents into a data-processing system.
3. *Manipulation.* The performance of certain necessary operations on source data or input.
   (a) *Classifying.* Identification of like data according to common characteristics or types.
   (b) *Sorting.* Re-sequencing source data into some logical order or form.
   (c) *Calculating.* Reconstructing source data to create meaningful results through addition, subtraction, multiplication, or division.
   (d) *Recording.* Registering the result of calculations in a written or other suitable form.
   (e) *Summarizing.* Reducing a mass of data into a meaningful and concise form.
4. *Output.* Producing and communicating the results of data manipulation in an intelligible form to the appropriate user.
5. *Storage.* Retaining a record of the output for future use or reference.

FIG. 5-5. The data-processing cycle.

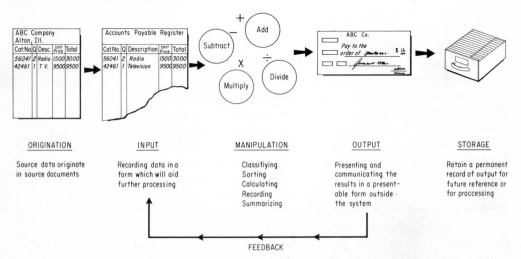

ORIGINATION	INPUT	MANIPULATION	OUTPUT	STORAGE
Source data originate in source documents	Recording data in a form which will aid further processing	Classifiying Sorting Calculating Recording Summarizing	Presenting and communicating the results in a presentable form outside the system	Retain a permanent record of output for future reference or for proccessing

FEEDBACK

GLOSSARY OF TERMS

FEEDBACK: The part of a closed loop system which automatically brings back information about the condition under control.

MERGE: To combine two or more sets of data into one, usually in a specified sequence.

SOURCE DOCUMENT: A document from which basic data is extracted.

QUESTIONS FOR REVIEW

1. What is a source document? Give examples.
2. List the five steps of data processing. Define each step briefly.
3. What is the difference between an input device and input medium? Explain by defining each and giving an example.
4. What factors are involved in the recording of source data? Explain.
5. Define the following terms:
   (a) Originating
   (b) Classifying
   (c) Calculating
   (d) Summarizing
   (e) Merging.
6. What is meant by feedback? Explain and give an example.

chapter

6

Case Illustration—
Payroll

To further illustrate the fundamentals of data processing, a payroll application has been chosen to emphasize the five functions performed in the data-processing cycle.

One of the most common routines in a business organization is the preparation of its employees' paychecks. To an employee, his paycheck represents the time and effort he exerts on a given job for his employer. Financial remuneration is considered the most effective incentive an employer can offer an employee to retain him and to induce him to do his job well.

All of us make plans to spend or to save our earnings during a given period of time. There are long-term debts to pay, current bills to be cleared, and shopping to do. It is important for the employer, then, to keep in mind that every one of his employees looks forward to being paid on time. In the event the regular payroll is expected to be delayed due to unavoidable circumstances, employees should be notified as early as possible so that they may make their plans accordingly.

Payrolls are usually prepared once a week, once every other week, twice a month, or once a month. In preparing the payroll on time, an organization must accurately compute each employee's earnings and any other data related to them. The job becomes more involved in firms employing several thousand workers.

Problems Involved in the Preparation of a Payroll

Various Types of Earnings Within the Organization

The common types of wages paid today include those computed on a (1) salaried, (2) hourly, or (3) piecework basis.

A salaried employee is someone who regularly is paid a fixed amount. This sum frequently is determined as a portion of a predetermined annual salary. For example, if a man is hired at an annual salary of $8,400 and is paid monthly, his gross monthly salary (before deductions) would be $700. Depending upon the policy of the company, he may or may not be eligible for overtime, special incentives (commissions, bonuses, etc.), and an expense account.

Skilled workers usually are paid a fixed hourly rate, plus additional payment for any extra time (overtime) beyond the normal workday. For example, a man may be hired by a retail firm at $2.00 an hour, plus time and a half for overtime. For an eight-hour day, the employee's pay would be 8 × $2.00 or $16.00; and for a five-day week at eight hours per day:

$$8 \text{ hours} \times 5 \text{ days} = 40 \text{ hours}$$
$$40 \times \$2.00 = \$80.00 \text{ gross pay}$$

If six hours' overtime was worked during the same week, the additional pay is determined by multiplying 6 hours × $3.00 (one and one-half times the hourly pay) = $18.00. Therefore, the employee's total gross earnings for the week would be $80.00 + $18.00 = $98.00.

In some cases, workers are paid on a piecework basis; that is, pay rate based on the number of units he can complete during the normal pay period. If, for example, an employee is paid 50 cents for every unit he can complete during an eight-hour shift, and he completes 20 units each day during a six-day work week, his gross pay would be:

$$20 \text{ units} \times 6 \text{ days} = 120 \text{ units}$$
$$120 \times 50\cent = \$60.00 \text{ gross pay}$$

The Time Factor

Due to the various frequencies of payment—and these widely divergent methods of determining an employee's earnings—the processing of payroll data can become exceedingly complex. Further, employees' earnings (especially those who are paid on an hourly or piece-rate basis) cannot be determined accurately in advance. For that reason, a time lag usually occurs between the end of a specified pay period and the time a paycheck finally can be drawn.

The speed at which checks can be processed depends on the number of employees on the payroll, the complexity of their earnings data, and the type of data-processing system in use.

Various Types of Deductions to Be Determined

Unlike "the good old days," when an employee's earnings were his "take-home" pay, today's payroll requires the withholding of various types of deductions. The most important of these are the federal income tax, social security (FICA), state and local income tax, union dues, savings bonds, and insurance. These deductions must be recorded both for present payroll calculations and for future use in various reports.

Despite the fact that they are paid the same hourly rate, two employees can receive widely divergent amounts on their paychecks. Their marital status may differ, the number of their dependents may differ (or he may declare them differently), one may not belong to the union, etc. For example, a married worker with three dependents has less federal income tax deducted than a single employee or a married employee with no children. Therefore, in processing a payroll, each employee's pay record must be manipulated individually to take these and other factors into account.

The Data-Processing Cycle in Action

Origination

Before any payroll can be processed, some type of source data is required. In the case of some employees, a time card is used to record the number of hours the employee has worked each day. Figure 6-1 shows an employee time card on which the employee number, employee name, and the appropriate pay week are reflected. Such a card serves as a complete record of the employee's work week. More complete time cards even include the employee's payroll deduction data.

In Figure 6-1, the time card shows that on Monday, December 7, John Hartfield reported to work by punching in at 8:00 A.M., punched again at noon for lunch, returned at 1:02 P.M. (two minutes late), punched out again at 5:00 P.M. His overtime later in the evening amounted to an hour and a half (7:00 to 8:30 P.M.).

Some firms require their white-collar workers to record by hand the amount of time they work during the week, while they require their production maintenance and certain other workers to punch in and out by means of a time clock. Other firms require every employee, regardless of his rank or status, to use the time clock.

FIG. 6-1. A time card.

	AM		PM		EVE	
	IN	OUT	IN	OUT	IN	OUT
M O N	8:00	12:00	1:02	5:00	7:00	8:30
T U E S						
W E D						
T H U R						
F R I						
S A T						
S U N						

Employee No. _40125_

Employee Name _John Hartfield_

Dept. _Production_ Week Beginning _Dec. 6, 1965_

The reason for the use of a time clock is to discourage (if not prevent) tampering with or "rounding off" the amount of time worked. For example, with manual recording, it is common for an employee who arrives at work at 8:04 A.M. to enter 8:00 on his time card.

A time clock records the exact time (to the nearest minute) of the arrival or departure of any employee, simply by inserting and depressing the time card into a slot (Figure 6-2). However, considering the origination function, either a manual or an automatic method is considered fairly adequate to provide the necessary data for further processing.

Input

The source document (time card) constitutes the input to the data-processing system. Under the manual data-processing system, input usually is gathered by dispatching a messenger from the payroll department to collect all employee time cards

FIG. 6-2. A time clock with card inserted.

at the end of the last working day of the week. These are delivered to the person in charge of using these data in the final preparation of the payroll.

Manipulation

Before any processing steps are taken, employee time cards are *classified* according to categories of compensation: hourly, salaried, or piecework. For purposes of illustration, the remaining part of this chapter centers around the hourly type of employees.

After time cards are classified, the hourly time cards are *sorted* into a given order, either alphabetically (by employee name) or numerically (by employee number). If sorting by employee name is desired, the cards will end up in alphabetical order, such as: Al *Bliss*, Sid *Boyd*, Philip *Hays*, Joe *Hunt*, and Fred *Karmie*.

Arranging time cards by employee name is desirable in manual data processing systems. After an employee's pay has been computed, certain data (results) must be transferred to a permanent record, which is filed in the payroll department. Assuming that the permanent record is kept in alphabetical order, results can be recorded more efficiently if the time cards are arranged in the same order.

After time cards have been classified and sorted, the *calculation* of the employee's pay follows. This involves determining the gross pay, the amount of the deductions, and the net pay. As previously explained, gross pay is determined by multiplying the number of work-hours by the hourly rate. In Figure

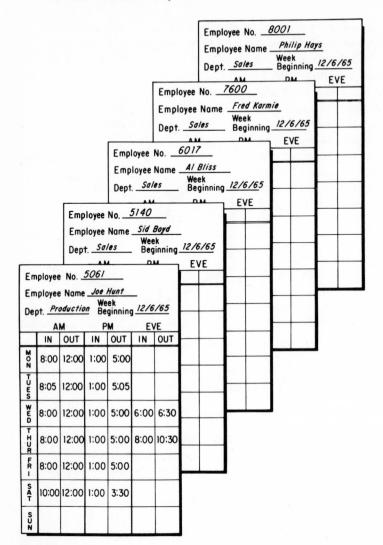

FIG. 6-3. A deck of five time cards sorted sequentially by employee number.

6-3, Joe Hunt worked 40 regular hours, plus 7½ hours of overtime. Assuming that Joe is paid $2.00 an hour and time and a half ($3.00) for overtime, his gross pay would be computed as follows:

$$40 \text{ hours} \times \$2.00 = \$80.00 \text{ regular pay}$$
$$7\frac{1}{2} \text{ hours} \times \$3.00 = \$22.50 \text{ overtime pay}$$
$$\overline{\$102.50} \text{ total gross pay}$$

Net pay is determined by subtracting from the gross pay the federal income tax, social security tax (FICA), hospitalization insurance premium, union dues (if any), and other voluntary deductions. The amount of net pay,

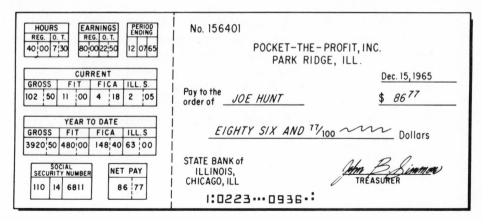

HOURS		EARNINGS		PERIOD ENDING
REG.	O.T.	REG.	O.T.	
40 00	7 30	80 00	22 50	12 07 65

CURRENT			
GROSS	FIT	FICA	ILL. S.
102 50	11 00	4 18	2 05

YEAR TO DATE			
GROSS	FIT	FICA	ILL.S
3920 50	480 00	148 40	63 00

SOCIAL SECURITY NUMBER			NET PAY
110	14	6811	86 77

No. 156401

POCKET–THE–PROFIT, INC.
PARK RIDGE, ILL.

Dec. 15, 1965

Pay to the order of *JOE HUNT* $ 86 77

EIGHTY SIX AND 77/100 ~~~~~ Dollars

STATE BANK of
ILLINOIS,
CHICAGO, ILL

John B Simmon
TREASURER

I:0223 ··· 0936 ·:

FIG. 6-4. A paycheck—an example.

along with the related details, usually is printed on a two-part form, the left section of which is the check stub and the right section, the paycheck (Figure 6-4). The employee cashes or deposits the right-hand section of the check after removing and retaining the stub for future reference.

When employee paychecks are prepared (drawn), the current pay of each employee and his deductions are *recorded* on a permanent record in the payroll department. This recording step is necessary because the recorded data are used at the end of the calendar year to summarize income-tax information, determine the company's cost of doing business, etc.

Output

Paychecks constitute the *output* of the system. Each employee receives his check, and here the data-processing function in regard to payroll ends; but it starts all over again when blank time cards are distributed to begin compiling data for the next payroll period.

Storage

Employees' permanent records are stored for future reference. Incidental to a payroll application, however, is the need for the preparation of various financial reports. Top managers, for example, often ask the payroll department for a summary statement showing the amounts (salaries and wages) paid by departments and/or divisions. When data related to such statements are available in storage, their preparation becomes relatively simple.

These reports provide "feedback" on labor and other costs which may cause adjustments in the future. Also there is check-cashing and reconciliation which must be balanced, closing the control loop for the cycle.

The foregoing has attempted to explain the basic elements involved in the preparation of a payroll and their relationships to the functions of data processing. In Chapter 10, a more detailed payroll application will be illustrated.

It would be helpful to remember that, regardless of the type of data processing system in use (manual, mechanical, electromechanical, or electronic), the routine of processing source data includes the same basic steps of origination, input, manipulation, output, and storage. Mechanized systems condense these five steps into three (input, processing, and output). This does not mean, however, that data origination is no longer necessary, nor does it suggest that the storage function should be ignored. In the chapters describing punched-card and electronic data-processing equipment, emphasis will be placed upon input, processing, and output, with due consideration of data origination, data recording, and data storage.

QUESTIONS FOR REVIEW

1. What problems are involved in the preparation of a payroll? Explain.
2. Explain the main types of deductions that are withheld from an employee's earnings.

part 2

Punched-Card Data Processing

chapter

7

The Punched Card

Part 2 of this text describes the basic steps of punched-card data processing and the equipment involved.

The data-processing cycle presented in Chapters 4 and 5 is the same as the data-processing cycle employed in punched-card processing. The chief differences are that punched-card machines are mechanical (or electromechanical) rather than electronic and that each performs its function independent of the other machines in the system. The input medium is the punched card, and most card handling must be performed manually.

Punched-Card Cycle

The following outline introduces the punched-card data-processing cycle (see Figure 7-1):

(1) *Data Origination.* This involves the preparation of source documents, such as time cards, checks, and invoices. These are prepared manually, either by manipulating a keyboard machine (for example, a typewriter or adding machine) or by using a pencil and paper (filling out a purchase order). A source document itself may be used as input under some circumstances.

(2) *Data Input.* Information from the source document is copied (recorded) on punched cards or punched paper tape. Represented by a coded system of holes, round or rectangular, it can be read by various machines. It is now ready to be used for machine input.

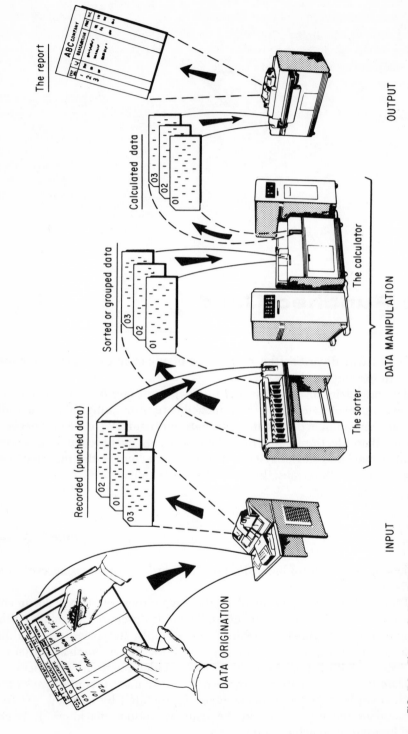

The report

ABC COMPANY

Calculated data

OUTPUT

Sorted or grouped data

The calculator

DATA MANIPULATION

Recorded (punched data)

The sorter

INPUT

DATA ORIGINATION

FIG. 7-1. The punched-card data-processing cycle.

62

(3) *Data Manipulation.* Once input cards are prepared, they are sorted, classified, and/or calculated, depending on the type of results required. Sorting is accomplished on a machine referred to as the *sorter.* Classifying is performed on a *collator,* and calculating is worked out on a *calculator.*

The subsequent chapters discuss these and other related machines, the functions of which are recording, reproducing, verifying, sorting, merging, calculating, and reporting facts, using the punched card as an input medium.

Types of Punched Card

There are two common types of punched card in use today: the Hollerith card (referred to as the IBM card) and the Powers card (referred to as the Remington Rand card). The size of both cards is the same: 7⅜ in. × 4¼ in. × .007 in. The Hollerith card contains 80 vertical columns; the Powers card, divided into upper and lower halves of 45 columns each, contains 90 columns. The holes punched in a Hollerith card are rectangular; those in a Powers card are round.

What Is a Punched Card?

The punched card is a common sight to almost everyone. Gas and electric companies bill their customers on punched cards. High schools, colleges, and universities use them as a class admission card at the beginning of each term. Paychecks often are printed on them. They frequently are used, not only as an input medium, but as a source document and as an output medium.

Figure 7-2 is a blank Hollerith card with a right corner cut. This cut aids the operator in visually checking to see that all cards in a given deck are facing in the same direction. Made of sturdy, high-quality paper, punched cards are capable of withstanding changes in temperature and humidity which would affect the physical shape of ordinary paper, causing it to jam in the machines.

FIG. 7-2. A Hollerith card.

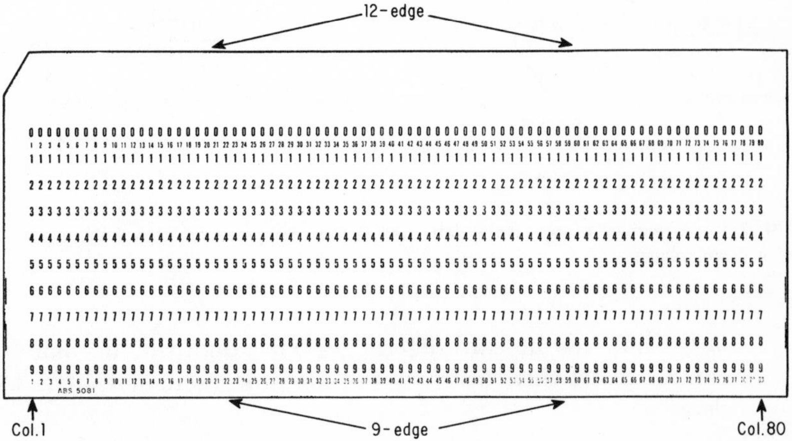

Columns and rows. The Hollerith card is divided into 80 columns, numbered 1 through 80, left to right. Since each column can store one character of information, up to 80 characters of information can be stored on each card.

Horizontally, the punched card is divided into 12 punching positions, called *rows.* Row numbers 0 through 9 are shown on the card in Figure 7-2, and are used to represent numeric data. The remaining two rows are 11 and 12 at the top of the card. Alphabetic information is represented by combining a punch in one of the top three rows with a punch in one of the numeric rows below.

"Edges" and "Faces." Cards are fed into a machine either "12-edge first" or "9-edge first." The top of a punched card is called the 12-edge; the bottom is called the 9-edge (Figure 7-2).

Because of the positions of their reading brushes, certain machines require that punched cards be fed 12-edge first; other machines read from the 9-edge first.

Certain machines further require that the deck be either "face up" or "face down" in the hopper. The term "12-edge first, face down" means that the top edge of each card is fed through the slot first, with the printed side of the card down.

Methods of Recording Data on Punched Cards

Data, whether they are numeric (for example, employee number 14060), alphabetic (John Hill), or special (such as characters $, *, &, etc.), are recorded permanently on a card by punching holes in it with a keypunch. These holes code the data in a language understandable to the machines. As the cards pass through the machine, the data are "read" by a reading brush which makes contact with a roller beneath the card whenever one of the punched holes appears. When a hole is detected, the brush makes contact with the roller to complete an electrical circuit (Figure 7-3). The specific position

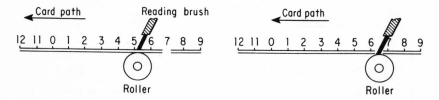

FIG. 7-3. A reading brush before (left) and during the detection of a hole in row 7 of a given column.

of the hole on the card determines what digit the machine will read. A wired control panel then instructs the machine as to how it is to manipulate this data.

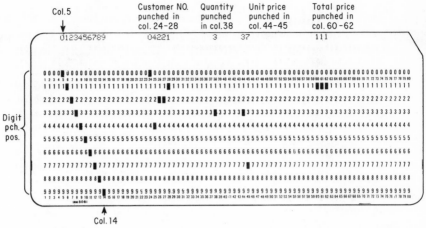

FIG. 7-4. An IBM card showing the digit-punching position—digits 0, 1 through 9, and an example.

The Card-Punching Positions

In order to determine the location of numeric and alphabetic characters on a card, the 12 horizontal card rows are divided into two categories: the digit-punching positions and the zone-punching positions. The digit-punching positions include ten rows in which digits 0 through 9 are stored, respectively. Figure 7-4 shows the locations of these rows.

The zone-punching positions consist of rows 0, 11, and 12. They are used in conjunction with the digit-punching positions to store alphabetic data. Note that row zero is used for storing either numeric or alphabetic characters in a given column.

Numeric Data Recording

Numbers are recorded in a card by punching *one* hole in any given column for each digit. In Figure 7-4, a quantity of 3 is recorded in column 38 by punching a hole in row 3 of that column. A unit price of 37 is recorded in columns 44 and 45 by punching a 3 in column 44 and a 7 in column 45.

There are two important points to be noted. First, a value consisting of two or more digits must be punched in two or more *consecutive* columns. Second, one and only one hole should be punched in a given column for each digit. If more than one hole is punched in a column, the machine will not be able to interpret them.

Alphabetic Data Recording

To record alphabetic information in cards, *two* holes must be punched in each column. If the word "student" is to be punched in a card, for example, it will require seven consecutive columns, each of which is punched with two holes, one in the digit-punching position and the other in the zone-punching position.

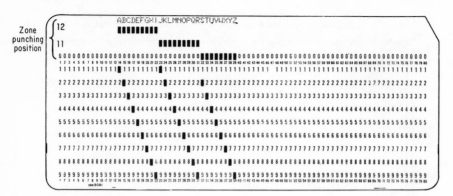

FIG. 7-5. An IBM card showing the zone-punching positions and the alphabet.

Figure 7-5 shows the zone-punching positions (that is, rows 0, 11, and 12). Row 11 is often referred to as the X-row; row 12 is sometimes called the Y-row. The alphabet is punched in columns 15–45.

It should be noted that the zero position can be used either as a zone or as a digit punch. If it stands alone in a given column, it represents a digit and is called a *digit punch*. On the other hand, if a zero punch is used along with another hole in the same column, it signifies an alphabetic code and is called a *zone punch*.

To represent alphabetic information in cards, the 26 letters of the alphabet are divided into three parts. They are: A through I (9 letters), J through R (9 letters), and S through Z (8 letters). Each part is coded by one of the three zone rows (that is, 0, 11, or 12) and contains one of the remaining 9 rows for nine letters, respectively. This means that a given letter must be represented by two holes in a specific column; one hole in row 12, 11, or 0, and another hole in row 1, 2, 3, 4, 5, 6, 7, 8, or 9.

A through I Coding. The first part of the alphabet consists of the first nine letters: A, B, C, D, E, F, G, H, and I. Each is coded by a hole punched in row 12 and another hole in rows 1 through 9, respectively. For example, letter A is coded by two holes: one hole in row 12 and another hole in row 1 of the same column. Letter A is punched in column 15 in Figure 7-5. Letter B is coded by a punch in row 12 and one in row 2, and so on. Figure 7-6 shows the codes of the first nine letters. Note that each of letters A through I takes a zone punch (row 12) plus a digit punch in that column in one of rows 1 through 9, respectively. Letter A, being the first letter, is coded by punches in rows 12 and 1; letter B, the second letter, in sequence, is coded by punches in rows 12 and 2; letter I, being the last letter in the part containing A through I, is coded by punches in 12 and 9. Refer to Figure 7-5 as you check the coding for each of the letters A through I in Figure 7-6.

J through R Coding. The second part of the alphabet contains letters J, K, L, M, N, O, P, Q, and R. The last letter of part 1 (letter I) is coded by a hole in row 9 (the last usable row). It is now necessary to start from the

Letter	Zone Punching Position	Digit Punching Position	Word "DEAF" Punched columns 26–29
A	12	1	
B	12	2	
C	12	3	
D	12	4	
E	12	5	
F	12	6	
G	12	7	
H	12	8	
I	12	9	

FIG. 7-6. Alphabetic coding table—letters A through I.

Letter	Zone Punching Position	Digit Punching Position	The Word "PORK" Coded in col. 51–55
J	11	1	
K	11	2	
L	11	3	
M	11	4	
N	11	5	
O	11	6	
P	11	7	
Q	11	8	
R	11	9	

FIG. 7-7. Alphabetic coding table—letters J through R.

beginning (rows 1 through 9) to code the next 9 letters (that is *J* through *R*) by assigning a *different zone punch* to distinguish them from the first nine letters. To do this, a punch in *row 11* for a zone punch is assigned to each of the letters *J* through *R* and a punch in rows 1 through 9, respectively, for the digit punch. For example, letter *J*, the first letter in the *J–R* group, is coded by a hole in row 11 in a given column (zone-punching position) and another hole in row 1 of that column (digit-punching position). Figure 7-7.

S through Z Coding. The third and last part of the alphabet consists of eight letters only: *S, T, U, V, W, X, Y,* and *Z.* Each of these letters is coded by a punch in row zero (zone punching position) and another punch in rows 2 through 9 (digit-punching position), respectively. Since there are only eight letters in this part, row 1 is left blank and remaining rows (2 through 9) are used for representing letters S through Z. For example, letter S takes a zone punch in row zero and a digit punch in row 2. Both punches must be in the same column. Letter Z, the last letter in part S through Z, is represented by a zone punch (row zero) and a digit punch (row 9). Refer to Figure 7-8 for the coding of letters S through Z.

It should be noted that any number of consecutive columns in a card can be used to record a given word. In Figure 7-6, the word *DEAF* is stored in columns 26–29, *STY* (Figure 7-8) in columns 64–66. The alphabetic and numeric codes are built into the keypunch machine, which is designed somewhat like a typewriter. In order to punch holes in a card representing a digit, a letter, or a group of letters, the operator needs only to depress certain keys on the keyboard.

Letter	Zone Punching Position	Digit Punching Position	Word "sty" punched in columns 64–66
S	0	2	
T	0	3	
U	0	4	
V	0	5	
W	0	6	
X	0	7	
Y	0	8	
Z	0	9	

FIG. 7-8. Alphabetic coding table—letters S through Z.

The Unit-Record Principle

A punched card is called a *unit record* because it is used to record information about one transaction only in its 80 columns. Recording only one transaction in a card makes the punched card mobile, in that it can be used later with other cards bearing different, related information, to obtain special reports.

What happens if a transaction contains more characters than can be recorded in a card? Each vertical card column corresponds to a space on a typewriter. If the data to be recorded from an original source document exceed the capacity of the card, it becomes necessary to use more than one card. Every effort is made, however, to avoid this so as to keep all relevant facts on one card. This is done by various methods of coding and condensing

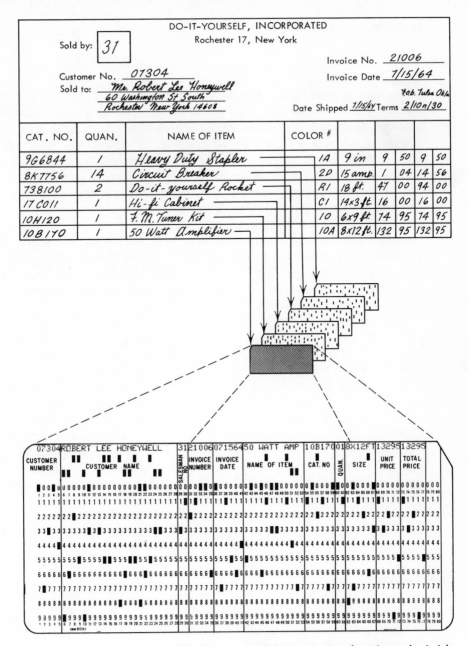

FIG. 7-9.   A partial invoice stressing the unit-record principle.

data, such as using numeric dates (for example, 071564 instead of July 15, 1964), common abbreviations (for example, amp. to stand for amplifier), and eliminating dollar signs, commas, and decimal points.

Figure 7-9 is an invoice containing six transactions, each of which must be punched in a separate card. The last transaction involving the 50-watt amplifier is punched in a card to illustrate the unit-record principle.

Card Fields

A transaction consists of a number of related details, called units of information. In Figure 7-9, each transaction contains a catalog number, quantity sold, name of the item sold, column number, size of the item, unit price, and total price: a total of seven units of information. Looking at the punched card in which transaction 6 is recorded, we find that each unit of information is recorded in a number of adjacent, consecutive columns. For example, customer number is recorded in columns 1, 2, 3, 4, and 5. Customer name is punched in columns 6 through 28, and so on. The consecutive columns reserved for storing a specific unit of information are referred to as a *field*.

From the foregoing, then, we can conclude that the punched card in which transaction 6 is punched contains 11 fields in addition to columns 78, 79, and 80, which are left blank. Vertical lines are drawn between the fields for clarity. Card fields for recording identification data such as date, employee number, invoice number are often called *designating* fields. Fields used to record quantities or amounts are called *adding*, or accumulating, fields. The length of a given field varies with the size of the unit of information it contains. It can be as small as one character, in which case it is punched in one card column, or as large as 80 characters, which would occupy the whole card.

Determining the size of a given field(s) is an arbitrary matter. In Figure 7-9, the customer number field, for example, is punched in columns 1–5. The decision to allow five columns is based on the assumption that the number of customers of Do-It-Yourself, Inc., in the future is likely to exceed 9999 customers and thus will require a 5-digit field for recording the 10,000th customer and above. A 5-digit number is judged to be adequate since it is not anticipated that the firm will have more than 99,999 customers within the next decade. Meanwhile, the unused column is filled with a zero as shown in column 1. Therefore, in designing a field, enough columns must be reserved so that the longest anticipated group of digits or alphabetic characters pertaining to that field can be accommodated.

Card Design

The planning of the arrangement of fields on a card for an application is called *card design*. In designing a card, it is necessary to study the requirements of the application in order to determine the sequence and size of each field. The proper field sequence is important especially for keypunching. When fields are punched in a card in the same sequence as they appear in the source document, this makes the keypunching operation more convenient as well as faster. This is especially true when the reading function is performed manually through the keypunch. In order to standardize and speed up the recording process, it is helpful to keep certain fields common to all cards by placing them in the same position in each card of the deck. For example, if the name-and-address fields are punched in columns 17–56 in one card, all other names and addresses must be punched in the same location in those cards.

As mentioned before, the size of each field must accommodate the longest entry that will be encountered. In the case of a name field consisting of 20 columns, for example, unused columns resulting from shorter names may be left blank. An amount field, on the other hand, may be set up for six digits, total capacity of which is 999,999. Any unused columns *to the left* of a smaller amount (for example, 85968) are often filled with zeros to indicate that no digit was ignored (result 085968).

When the card design is completed, it is customary to have a supply of cards printed with appropriate identification and headings of the various fields for ease of handling. Each card thus becomes a document, supporting details for the processing of a particular application. The various machines used in processing recognize the holes but not the printing on the cards. The printing is for the benefit of the human worker so that recognition of what the code represents will be speeded up.

Card Classifications and Types

Cards are classified by use into three major classes: Unit Record (detail), Summary Unit Record (summary), and Master Unit Record (master).

A detail card usually represents one transaction, with pertinent statistical designations. Suppliers, for example, keep a card representing each item sold or shipped to their customers. The card contains information such as customer's name, quantity sold, item's code or catalog number, and cost of sale of the item. The card pertaining to transaction 6 in Figure 7-9 is a detail card.

A summary card contains totals of a group of similar detail cards. This is usually the sum of all sales made to a given customer during a specific period of time. In Figure 7-9, a summary card may be prepared to include the name of the customer (Robert Lee Honeywell), the total number of items shipped (6), date of the shipment (7/15/65), and the total price ($341.96).

This summary is generally obtained automatically by means of a summary card punch during a tabulating or accumulating operation. For report preparation, a summary card is substituted for a whole host of detail cards. A monthly report of sales by customer, for example, can be prepared from 20 daily summary cards instead of from 2,000 detail cards for each product. This is time-saving and becomes especially important when time and cost of operating the equipment are at a premium.

A master card contains information that is somewhat fixed or permanent in nature. A customer master card, for example, would contain all information associated with one particular customer; that is, name, address, account number, class, codes, etc. The card is punched with an account number, item description, size, cost, selling prices, and other related data. This fixed information may be reproduced into a detail card for a given transaction, thus eliminating manual punching of the fixed data.

There are many types of cards within the three major classifications. Among them are:

(1) *Dual Use Cards.* A written record from which subsequent punching on a card is made. For example, a time card is manually filled out daily by an employee. At the end of the week, data are copied from the time card and punched in punched cards for payroll processing purposes.

(2) *Composite Cards.* Cards which are used for several different applications or for different uses in the same application. For example, a customer's balance card can be used either to prepare a sales report or to determine the number of items left in stock, or to prepare a statement for billing purposes.

(3) *Prepunched Cards.* Detail cards partially or completely punched from a master card. For example, a detail payroll card may be prepunched with employee number, department number, name, and card code prior to giving it to the employee for daily use.

(4) *Stub Card.* A card containing a detachable stub which serves as a receipt. For example, most electric bills come with a tear-off portion or a perforation across the width of the bill. One section is kept for customer's future reference and the other section is sent back with the payment.

(5) *Mark-sense or Optical Scanning Card.* A card designed for marking amounts with a special pencil. The marks are later converted automatically to punches (holes) in the same card by a special machine (Figure 7-10).

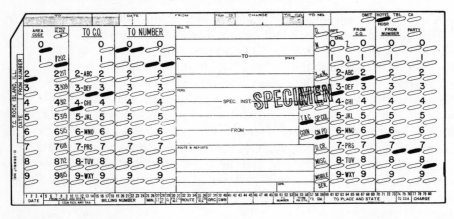

FIG. 7-10. A mark-sensed card.

FIG. 7-11. A tumble card.

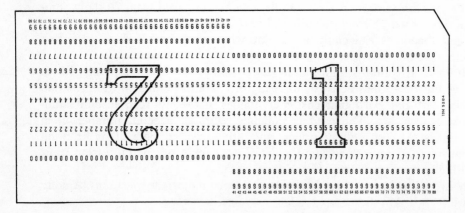

(6) *Multiple-use or Tumble Card.* A card designed for re-use for data requiring less than the capacity of a standard-size card. For example, in an 80-column card, the first 40 columns are handled as one unit at one time, while the second 40 columns are handled as a second unit at a later time (Figure 7-11).

(7) *Document Cards.* Standard or special punch-card forms to prepare checks, bills, toll tickets, airline tickets, purchase orders, etc.

Control Punches

It has been pointed out that holes in cards serve to code numeric, alphabetic, or special characters. There are also other purposes for which code punches are used. A punch or group of punches can be used to instruct a certain machine to do a specific operation. For example, assuming that the control panel is wired properly, a hole in row 11 (X-punch) over the units column of a numeric field (a group of consecutive columns reserved for an amount) can be made to cause the entire amount to be treated as a credit (minus). The absence of that hole indicates that the amount is a debit (plus). Control holes are also used to do things such as printing three lines from one card (instead of the usual one line per card) on an accounting machine which is used for accumulating totals and printing reports.

Another common use of an X-punch or control punch is in separating or extracting a specific card or a group of cards from a deck for a predetermined operation. For example, in an employee file, female employees may have an X-punched in a specific column so as to make it possible to extract all their cards from the major file of all employees for a specific event. When the X-punch is made in column 27, for example, of each female employee's card, the machine can be wired to eject in a designated pocket every card it senses having the X-punch in that column. When this operation is completed, the main employee file would be divided into two smaller files or decks: male and female decks.

To conclude, a control punch aids in locating or rearranging a deck of cards into two or more decks based on the specific objective in mind.

The Remington Rand Card

Like the IBM card, the Remington Rand card measures 7⅜ in. × 4¼ in. and is similar in thickness and quality. See Figure 7-12. Unlike the IBM card, the Remington card holes are circular, arranged in 90 vertical columns organized into two sections; i.e., an upper section containing columns 1–45 and a lower section containing columns 46–90. Each of these sections contains six rows in each column which are utilized to code numeric, alphabetic, or special characters by single, double, or triple punches in a given column for each character. Digits *0, 1, 3, 5, 7,* and *9* are single-punched (1 hole) in their respective rows. Each of the even digits *2, 4, 6,* and *8* is double-punched (2 holes); one hole in row 9 and the other hole in rows 2, 4, 6, or 8, respectively. In Figure 7-12, you will note that digits are punched in the lower half of the card, whereas alphabetic data are punched in the upper half.

Coding alphabetic characters does not follow an easily identified pattern. Letters are coded by a combination of double or triple hole punches. A single key depression on the keypunch machine creates the required pattern of holes automatically.

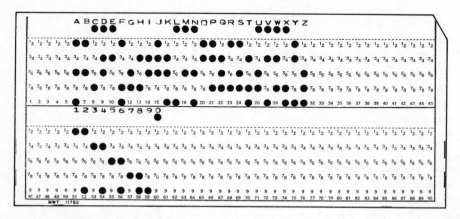

FIG. 7-12. A Remington Rand card with alphabet.

GLOSSARY OF TERMS

COMPOSITE CARD: A multipurpose data card, or a card that contains data which are needed in the processing of various applications.

CONTROL PUNCH: A specific code punched in a card to cause the machine to perform a specific operation.

DATA-PROCESSING CYCLE: The sequence of steps involved in manipulating business information.

DIGIT-PUNCHING POSITION: The area on a punched card reserved to represent a decimal digit.

DOCUMENT CARD: A special card form used in preparing a document such as a check, a purchase order, etc.

FIELD: A specified area of a record used for a particular category of data, e.g., a group of card columns used to represent a wage rate or a set of bit locations in a computer word used to express the address of the operand.

HOLLERITH: A widely used system of encoding alphanumeric information onto cards, hence Hollerith cards is synonymous with punch cards.

9-EDGE: Denotes the bottom edge of a punched card.

PUNCHED CARD: 1. A card punched with a pattern of holes to represent data. 2. A card as in (1) before being punched.

Stub Card: A card containing a detachable stub to serve as a receipt for future reference.

12-edge: A term used to designate the top edge of a punched card.

Unit Record: 1. A separate record that is similar in form and content to other records; e.g., a summary of a particular employee's earnings to date. 2. Sometimes refers to a piece of nontape auxiliary equipment; e.g., card reader, printer, or console typewriter.

X-punch: A punch in the second row, one row above the zero row, on a Hollerith punched card.

Zone Punch: A punch in the O, X, or Y row on a Hollerith punched card.

QUESTIONS FOR REVIEW

1. Explain the steps involved in the punched-card data-processing cycle. Give an example to illustrate these steps.
2. What are the two main types of punched cards? What is the size of each type?
3. What is the primary difference between the Hollerith and the Powers code?
4. What is a punched card? Give an example of its use.
5. What is meant by "9-edge first, face down"? What is meant by "12-edge first, face up"?
6. How is alphabetic recording of data different from numeric recording in a card? Explain briefly.
7. What is the zone-punching position of each of the following letters? C, S, U, K, F, X, Q, Y.
8. What is the digit-punching position of each of the following characters? 4, S, 7, P, I, 8.
9. What is the unit-record principle? Explain.
10. What is a card field? Give an example.
11. What is the difference between a designating field and an accumulating field? Give an example to illustrate.
12. What factors must be considered in designing a card? Explain.
13. What is the difference between a detail card and a summary card? Give an example.
14. Describe briefly the three main classifications of a punched card.
15. Define the following:
    (a) Composite card
    (b) Stub card
    (c) Mark-sense card
    (d) Tumble card
    (e) Document card.
16. For what reason(s) is a control punch used? Explain.
17. Describe briefly the Remington Rand card. How is it different from the IBM card?

chapter

8

Input Preparation
and Entry

Original documents form the basis for future data processing. They are important because they represent the ultimate proof of a transaction. Each of these documents must go through a process which includes the use of one or more punched-card machines before meaningful results can be obtained. The number and type of machines used depend on the kind of work to be performed. A sales invoice, for example, contains source information which is usually handwritten: processing, therefore, must begin with the conversion of the handwritten data into a punched card. This is referred to as the recording function, and is one of the most frequently used steps in the processing cycle. The other steps are classifying, calculating, summarizing, and reporting. All these steps will be covered separately in later chapters.

Recording by Keypunching

As mentioned in earlier chapters, a machine capable of reading and processing handwritten information accurately and completely has yet to become available on a commercial basis. The most common practice today is to record source data by punching them in cards. Once recorded, they can be handled easily by various data processing machines.

The Keypunch

The recording of data is done by a machine called a keypunch (Figure 8-1). Keypunching is the most widely used method of recording data. It is as easy to keypunch as it is to typewrite on an electric typewriter. Both machines have a keyboard containing numeric, alphabetic, and special characters. The mere depression of a certain key causes the character it represents to be recorded. Another similarity is that both machines perform the recording function one character at a time. The typewriter *prints* one character at a time on a sheet of paper as the carriage moves from right to left. The keypunch, on the other hand, *punches* one character at a time in a standard-size card as the card moves from right to left.

Some keypunches (Figure 8-1) have the optional feature of printing the character on the top of the column at the same time the character is punched. This means that a maximum of 80 characters can be printed on the top edge of the card, corresponding to the total number of columns on the card.

The IBM method of keypunching is referred to as the *serial* method. That is, keys representing certain characters are depressed a key at a time, causing consecutive punching until the job is done.

FIG. 8-1. Keypunch—IBM 26.

The other method of keypunching is called the *parallel* method, which is used on the Remington Rand card-punch machine (Figure 8-2). The desired number of characters to be punched in a blank card are "keyed-in" first; then, by means of a release key, are punched in the card *simultaneously.*

FIG. 8-2. Parallel punch—Remington Rand.

FIG. 8-3. Keyboard of the IBM keypunch.

The Card-Punch Keyboard

The keyboard of the IBM keypunch (Figure 8-3) is like a regular typewriter keyboard. If the letters A-B-E-L are to be punched, the keypunch operator depresses these four keys consecutively. Every time a given key is depressed, it immediately punches the character in the card.

Unlike a typewriter, however, the arrangement of the numeric keys is such that the operator only need use her right hand to punch them. In Figure 8-3, keys representing digits 0 through 9 are located close to one another in the right-hand section of the keyboard. In a typewriter keyboard, the numeric keys are located horizontally across the top of the keyboard.

The Card Path

A blank card becomes a data card after it has been punched with the necessary data. The *card path* begins in the card hopper, where all blank cards are placed, and ends in the card stacker, which holds the recently punched cards (Figure 8-4).

The card hopper. The card hopper located on the right side of the machine, holds approximately 500 cards, which are to be fed through the punching unit one at a time.

The punching station. All recording is performed when a card moves to and passes under the punching station (Figure 8-4). In order to move a card to the punching station, the "Feed" key is depressed, causing the first card in the hopper to drop onto the card bed. The feed key is depressed a second time, causing another card to drop while column 1 of the first card is aligned under the punches. This step sets the stage for the recording (punching) function.

FIG. 8-4. Components of the keypunch showing the path of the card through the punch.

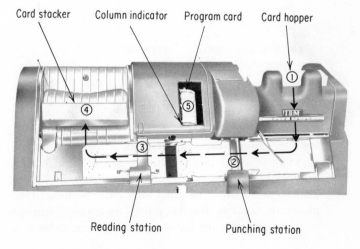

Card stacker   Column indicator   Program card   Card hopper

Reading station   Punching station

Single cards also may be fed manually under the punching station by depressing the "Reg" key. Once the key is depressed, the first column of the card is aligned under the punches, ready for punching. This method often is preferred when only a few cards are involved.

The punching station contains 12 punches, aligned vertically to punch a hole or a combination of holes (representing a numeric, alphabetic, or special character) in a given column. Figure 8-5 shows the location of the 12 punches and the location of the letter *C* in a card column. The punches are vertically aligned to conform to the locations of the 12 punching positions in each of the 80 columns of a card.

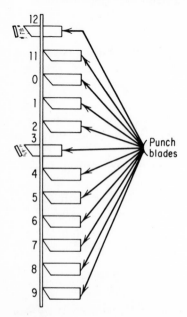

FIG. 8-5. Letter "C" punched in a card column.

The reading station. After column 80 of a given card passes through the punching station, the card moves under the reading station and the next card moves under the punching station. From this moment on, both cards will move in synchronization; that is, as the first card passes under the reading station, the next one passes under the punching station.

Synchronization between the reading station and the punching station allows for duplication of punching in cards. Duplicating is done simply by depressing a "dup" key for the length of time it takes to duplicate the desired number of columns of data. For example, if it is desired to duplicate columns 1 through 15 from the card under the reading station onto the card under the punching station, the keypunch operator depresses the "dup" key until the column indicator on the keypunch passes column 15.

▮ Skip	Duplicate	Shift	Duplicate by the operator

```
0 0 0 0 0 0 0 0 0 0 0 0 0 0 0 0 0 0 0 0 0 0 0 0 0 0 0 0 0 0 0 0 0 0 0 0 0 0 0 0 0 0 0 0 0 0 0 0 0 0 0 0 0 0 0 0 0 0 0 0 0 0 0 0 0 0 0 0 0 0 0 0 0 0 0 0 0 0 0 0
 1  2  3  4  5  6  7  8  9 10 11 12 13 14 15 16 17 18 19 20 21 22 23 24 25 26 27 28 29 30 31 32 33 34 35 36 37 38 39 40 41 42 43 44 45 46 47 48 49 50 51 52 53 54 55 56 57 58 59 60 61 62 63 64 65 66 67 68 69 70 71 72 73 74 75 76 77 78 79 80
1 1 1 1 1 1 1 1 1 1 1 1 1 1 1 1 1 1 1 1 1 1 1 1 1 1 1 1 1 1 1 1 ▮ 1 1 1 1 1 1 1 1 1 1 1 1 1 1 1 1 1 1 1 1 1 1 1 1 1 1 1 1 1 1 1 1 1 1 1 1 1 1 1 1 1 1 1 1 1
2 2 2 2 2 2 2 2 2 2 2 2 2 2 2 2 2 2 2 2 2 2 2 2 2 2 2 2 2 2 2 2 2 2 2 2 2 2 2 2 2 2 2 2 2 2 2 2 2 2 2 2 2 2 2 2 2 2 2 2 2 2 2 2 2 2 2 2 2 2 2 2 2 2 2 2 2 2 2 2
3 3 3 3 3 3 3 3 3 3 3 3 3 3 3 3 3 3 3 3 3 3 3 3 3 3 3 3 3 3 3 3 3 3 3 3 3 3 3 3 3 3 3 3 3 3 3 3 3 3 3 3 3 3 3 3 3 3 3 3 3 3 3 3 3 3 3 3 3 3 3 3 3 3 3 3 3 3 3 3
4 4 4 4 4 4 4 4 4 4 4 4 4 4 4 4 4 4 4 4 4 4 4 4 4 4 4 4 4 4 4 4 4 4 4 4 4 4 4 4 4 4 4 4 4 4 4 4 4 4 4 4 4 4 4 4 4 4 4 4 4 4 4 4 4 4 4 4 4 4 4 4 4 4 4 4 4 4 4 4
5 5 5 5 5 5 5 5 5 5 5 5 5 5 5 5 5 5 5 5 5 5 5 5 5 5 5 5 5 5 5 5 5 5 5 5 5 5 5 5 5 5 5 5 5 5 5 5 5 5 5 5 5 5 5 5 5 5 5 5 5 5 5 5 5 5 5 5 5 5 5 5 5 5 5 5 5 5 5 5
6 6 6 6 6 6 6 6 6 6 6 6 6 6 6 6 6 6 6 6 6 6 6 6 6 6 6 6 6 6 6 6 6 6 6 6 6 6 6 6 6 6 6 6 6 6 6 6 6 6 6 6 6 6 6 6 6 6 6 6 6 6 6 6 6 6 6 6 6 6 6 6 6 6 6 6 6 6 6 6
7 7 7 7 7 7 7 7 7 7 7 7 7 7 7 7 7 7 7 7 7 7 7 7 7 7 7 7 7 7 7 7 7 7 7 7 7 7 7 7 7 7 7 7 7 7 7 7 7 7 7 7 7 7 7 7 7 7 7 7 7 7 7 7 7 7 7 7 7 7 7 7 7 7 7 7 7 7 7 7
8 8 8 8 8 8 8 8 8 8 8 8 8 8 8 8 8 8 8 8 8 8 8 8 8 8 8 8 8 8 8 8 8 8 8 8 8 8 8 8 8 8 8 8 8 8 8 8 8 8 8 8 8 8 8 8 8 8 8 8 8 8 8 8 8 8 8 8 8 8 8 8 8 8 8 8 8 8 8 8
9 9 9 9 9 9 9 9 9 9 9 9 9 9 9 9 9 9 9 9 9 9 9 9 9 9 9 9 9 9 9 9 9 9 9 9 9 9 9 9 9 9 9 9 9 9 9 9 9 9 9 9 9 9 9 9 9 9 9 9 9 9 9 9 9 9 9 9 9 9 9 9 9 9 9 9 9 9 9 9
 1  2  3  4  5  6  7  8  9 10 11 12 13 14 15 16 17 18 19 20 21 22 23 24 25 26 27 28 29 30 31 32 33 34 35 36 37 38 39 40 41 42 43 44 45 46 47 48 49 50 51 52 53 54 55 56 57 58 59 60 61 62 63 64 65 66 67 68 69 70 71 72 73 74 75 76 77 78 79 80
ISC 5081
```

FIG. 8-6. A program card.

Duplicating data from one card to another by means of a keypunch is useful and convenient when the number of columns to be duplicated is limited and only a few cards are involved. Mass duplication, or reproducing, from one card into several other cards is done on a machine called the reproducer.

The card stacker. When column 80 of the card under the reading station is released, it moves horizontally until it is aligned opposite the card stacker and then turned 9-edge up, in the stacker. The card stacker is located on the left side of the keypunch and holds approximately 500 cards (Figure 8-4).

Automatic Recording on the Keypunch

The keypunch can be "programmed" to do certain routine jobs automatically, thus minimizing the drudgery of manual work that otherwise would be done by the keypunch operator. The device that controls this automatic feature is called the "program control unit" (Figure 8-4). Through this unit, duplicating, skipping, and shifting can be done automatically.

In order for the program control unit to perform these functions, a blank card must first be punched with the pertinent codes to tell the machine what to do, and when and where to start performing the desired function (Figure 8-6). Next, the coded program card is wrapped around a drum and placed in the program control unit. Duplicating, skipping, and shifting to alphabetic mode may be performed automatically by appropriate punches in the

FIG. 8-7. An IBM program control drum.

program card, thus speeding up keypunching operations and reducing the possibility of error. Figure 8-7 shows the program card wrapped around a drum.

Verification of Recorded Data

Regardless of the experience of the keypunch operator, it is always possible for him to make errors during the keypunching routine. In order to increase the accuracy of recorded data, another machine is used: the *verifier* (Figure 8-8).

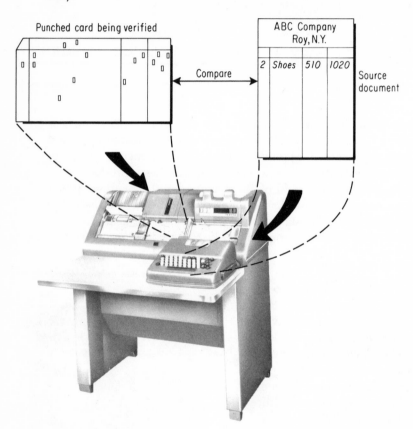

FIG. 8-8. The IBM verifier.

The IBM verifier is similar to the keypunch, except that its main function is to check, rather than to punch, data in a card. The verifier operator feeds the data cards into the hopper and keys in the information from the source document (that is, the one from which the cards originally were punched). As the operator keys in the data, a metal plunger passes through (senses) the punched holes. If the holes are not where they should be, meaning that they do not represent the proper character, then an error is indicated by a notch on the top of each incorrectly punched column. If the sensed holes match the

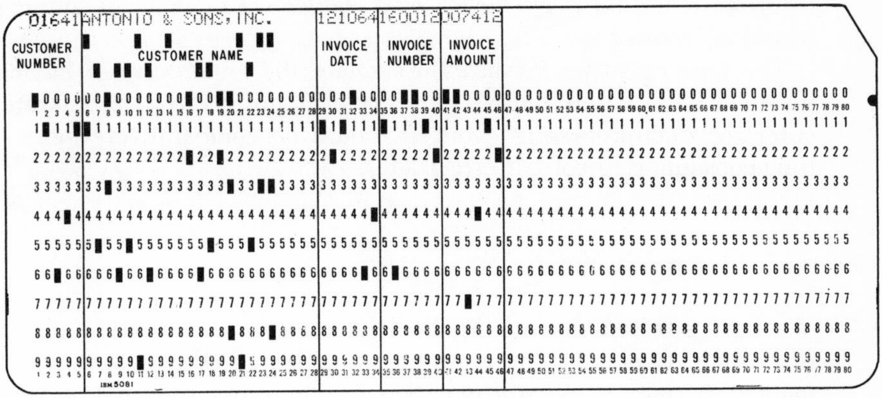

FIG. 8-9. A verified card.

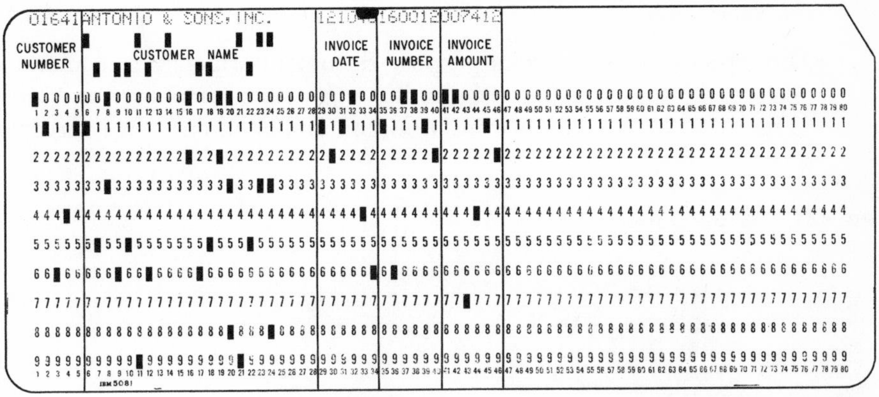

FIG. 8-10. An error-notched card.

correct characters, as keyed-in by the operator, a notch indicating the correctness of the punched data is made on the right edge of the card, opposite row 1.

Figure 8-9 shows a correctly punched card compared to the source document. Note the notch on the right edge, indicating its verification. Figure 8-10 shows two error notches on the top of columns 33 and 34, where the year (19)*64* has been incorrectly punched *46*.

Remington Rand also has a verifier to check the accuracy of punched data. Briefly, the Remington Rand (Powers) card is raised about $\frac{1}{16}$ in. in the keypunch and repunched with the same data. This gives the once-round holes an oval shape, indicating the correctness of the data they represent. Remaining round holes indicate errors. The deck is placed in the verifier, which considers round holes as errors, and each card containing a round hole is separated from the other cards by means of a "finder card" which is automatically **in-**serted in front of it.

The time taken for verification signifies the importance of having accurate punched data. Errors must be corrected at this stage or inaccurate data will enter the data-processing cycle. It would be comparatively more costly and time-consuming to correct errors later.

Recording by Reproducing

We have stressed the use of the keypunch to record input data for future processing. Generally, the recording function of the keypunch is considered manual, in that an operator must key-in the desired information from a source document. Although the keypunch can be used to duplicate certain data from one card into another card automatically, it is not the best machine for the job. Large scale reproduction of recorded data is done by a special-purpose machine called the *reproducer*.

The Reproducer

The reproducer is a special-purpose document-originating machine capable of performing the functions of duplicating, gang punching, and mark sensing (Figure 8-11). For duplicating a large number of cards it is favored over **the**

FIG. 8-11. IBM 519 reproducer.

keypunch because of its greater speed and flexibility in the reproduction of input and other data cards.

Before presenting any details regarding its main functions, it would be helpful to discuss the reproducer's features and main component parts.

The IBM reproducer contains two major units: the reading unit and the punching unit. The primary function of the reading unit is to read data cards and, through a control panel, which is specially wired by the operator or analyst, to cause certain dies to punch the information they contain into blank cards.

Control panels are wired boards which are used by the reproducer and certain other punched-card processors to allow flexibility in the manner with which specific cards are handled. The panel is inserted into the machine by the operator, is easily removed, and may be rewired for different applications. Panels will be discussed at greater length in the section on accounting machines (Chapter 10).

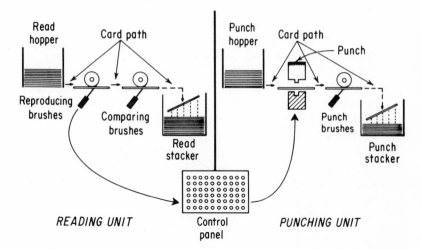

FIG. 8-12. Component parts of the IBM reproducer.

In order to reproduce cards, data cards are placed in the "Read" hopper 12-edge first, face down, and pass over two sets of reading brushes, each of which contains 80 brushes, corresponding to the 80 columns on a card (Figure 8-12). The first set, called the *reproducing brushes*, are connected to the control panel, which is wired to perform a specific operation. When a card is read, its data are transferred by the reproducing brushes to the punches through the control panel where an exact duplicate of the data is punched into a blank card. The other reading brushes are called the *comparing brushes*, whose main function is to read the data card and compare it with the data punched into the new card to insure accuracy.

The punch unit contains a card hopper in which a deck of blank cards is

placed 12-edge first, face down. When a data card is fed through the reproducing brushes in the reading unit, a blank card also is moved under the punch
unit where it will be punched with whatever information is received. It is important to remember that both the data card and the blank card move in
synchronization; that is, when row 1 on the data card is over the reproducing
brushes, row 1 on the blank card is under the punches. This synchronization
makes it possible to duplicate data from one card into another.

Suppose we have employee number *3456* punched in columns 1 through 4
and that a duplicate card is desired. To do this, the card bearing the employee's number is placed in the "Read" hopper and a blank card is placed
in the "Punch" hopper. Assuming that the control panel is wired to reproduce
these columns, the depression of the "START" button causes both cards to
move through the machine simultaneously, one card from each hopper at a
time. The cards keep moving until the reproducing brush for column 1 detects
a hole in row 3 of that column. At that moment, the punch for column 1 is
aligned on top of row 3 and produces a punch. Reproducing brush 2 then
reads a hole in row 4, causing punch 2 to punch a hole in row 4 of the blank
card. And so on until the whole employee-number field is punched.

It should be noted that the reproducer provides the flexibility of being able
to copy only selected data from one card into another. Figure 8-13 shows a
sales card (left), punched with the customer's account number, name, and
the amount sold. The amount sold, punched in columns 35–38, is reproduced
into the master card for subsequent calculation of the total balance due. In
this case, the control panel is wired to read columns 35–38 and punch their
contents in the same location in the master card. The data in the remaining
columns are not read for this specific application.

Another point which should be noted is that selected information from the
data card (for example, "amount sold" in columns 35–38) may be duplicated
in any four consecutive columns in the master card. In this case, the control
panel can be wired to read columns 35–38 of the data card and activate dies

FIG. 8-13. Selected reproduction of data from one card into another—
an example.

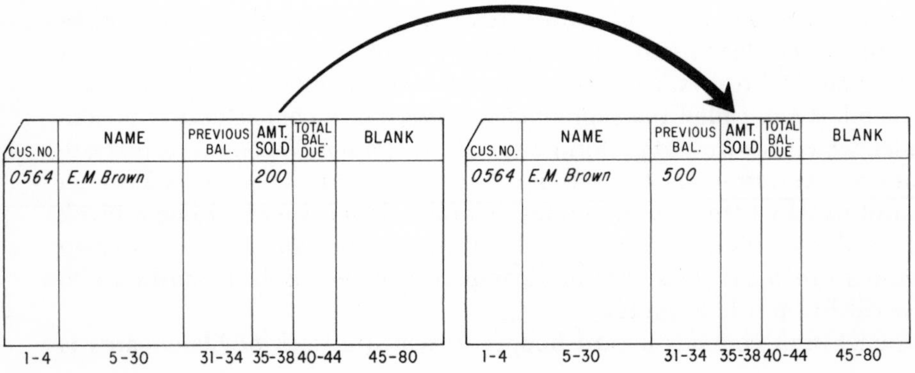

CUS. NO.	NAME	PREVIOUS BAL.	AMT. SOLD	TOTAL BAL. DUE	BLANK		CUS. NO.	NAME	PREVIOUS BAL.	AMT. SOLD	TOTAL BAL. DUE	BLANK
0564	E.M. Brown		200				0564	E.M. Brown	500			
1-4	5-30	31-34	35-38	40-44	45-80		1-4	5-30	31-34	35-38	40-44	45-80

to punch their contents elsewhere in the master card (for example, columns 50–53). This flexibility is useful in cases where the card being punched does not have the same design or layout as that from which the data are read.

In reproducing, Remington Rand equipment follows a similar technique. Naturally, the design and specifications of each machine are different. Figure 8-14 shows a Remington Rand multicontrol reproducer with two hoppers: the "Read" hopper and the "Punch" hopper.

Gang Punching

Gang punching is defined as the automatic copying of punched data from a master card into one or more detail cards following it. This process is accomplished by using the punching unit only, since it is assumed that the blank cards are merged behind their master card(s) in advance of the gang-punching operation, thus providing one complete deck to be placed in the "Punch" hopper of the reproducer (Figure 8-15).

In gang punching, the master card moves past the punches and to the punch brushes, followed by the first blank card, which moves under the punches. Through a control panel, wired for a gang-punching operation, the desired data read from the master card are punched into the blank card. The master card drops into the stacker, the gang-punched card moves to the punch brushes, and a second blank card moves from the punch hopper to the punches to be punched. This operation goes on until the last blank card in the hopper is gang-punched and finally dropped into the stacker.

Four cycles are involved in gang punching four blank cards. They are:

FIG. 8-14. Multicontrol reproducer—Remington Rand.

Cycle 1	blank card *1* to be punched with data from the master card
Cycle 2	blank card *2* to be punched with data from gang-punched *1* card
Cycle 3	blank card *3* to be punched with data from gang-punched *2* card
Cycle 4	blank card *4* to be punched with data from gang-punched *3* card

When only one master card is involved, followed by one or more blank cards constituting the deck, the operation is referred to as *single master-card gang punching* (Figure 8-15).

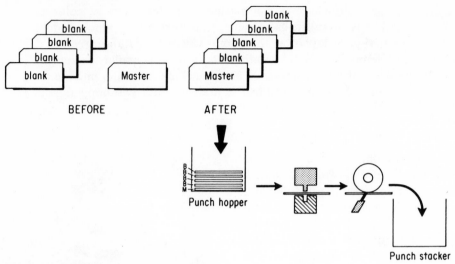

FIG. 8-15. Single master-card gang punching.

Interspersed gang punching. Interspersed gang punching is different from single master-card gang punching in that the card deck contains two or more master cards, each of which is followed by a number of blank cards to be gang-punched. In Figure 8-16, the first master card and the following two blank cards are gang-punched as they would be with the single master-card gang punching method. The fourth card (master card 2) is detected by the machine as a master card and is not gang-punched as is the blank card, but, rather, moves past the punches and to the punch brushes to activate the gang punching of the blank cards which follow it. The ability of the machine to detect a master card from any other card in the deck by use of a punch in a specific location makes interspersed gang punching possible. Special wiring of the control panel is the key to this operation.

FIG. 8-16. Interspersed gang punching.

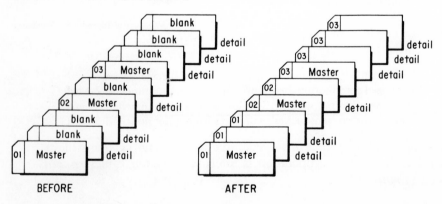

End Printing and Mark Sensing

Besides duplicating and gang punching, the reproducer can also perform the functions of end printing and mark sensing.

The end-printing function of the IBM reproducer is simply that of convert-ing punched information into printing across the end of a card. It is similar to that of *interpreting* punched data which prints across the top of the card. End printing makes it possible to have a quick reference to the data on a given card (Figure 8-17). This capability is a unique feature of the reproducer and may be performed at the same time that other functions, such as gang punching, summary punching, or mark sensing are performed.

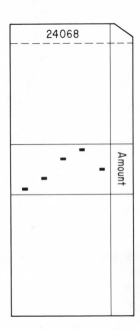

24068

Amount

FIG. 8-17.   End printing—an example.

Mark sensing is a copying process in which the user marks special areas of a punched card with an electrographic pencil to represent (record) data. When these cards are fed into the reproducer, the machine senses the marks and punches their values into the card (Figure 8-18). Mark-sense cards are placed in the "Punch" hopper and, assuming that the control panel is wired to do this job, the cards are ejected into the punch stacker after they have been punched. This conversion step is necessary before the mark-sensed cards can be processed further.

The Remington Rand machine has an optical scanning punch which reads and automatically punches a 90-column card marked with penciled strokes, circles, or the digit itself on the proper position (Figure 8-19).

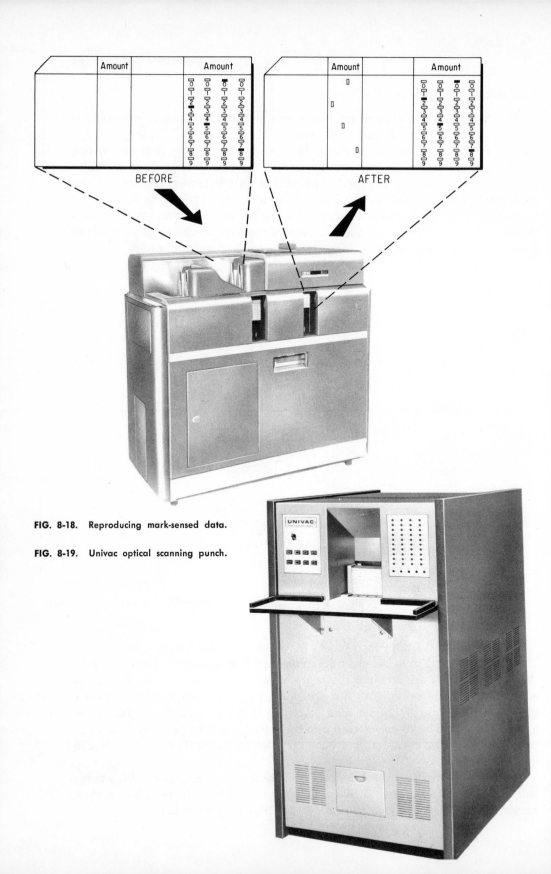

FIG. 8-18. Reproducing mark-sensed data.

FIG. 8-19. Univac optical scanning punch.

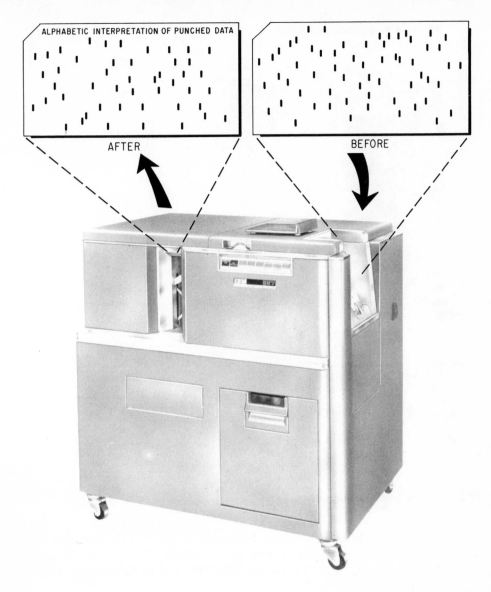

ALPHABETIC INTERPRETATION OF PUNCHED DATA

AFTER

BEFORE

FIG. 8-20. Interpreter—IBM.

Interpreting

Interpreting is the process of converting punched-card holes into human language. It is done mainly by sensing alphabetic or numeric data punched in a card and printing it on the same card. Often duplicated, gang-punched, or otherwise reproduced cards do not give a visual interpretation of the holes punched into them. In order to make it convenient for the user to interpret these holes, the cards are placed in the hopper of the interpreter, and with the insertion of the proper control panel, each card is read. The desired interpretation is printed at the top of the card (Figures 8-20 and 8-21).

FIG. 8-21. Interpreter—Remington Rand.

Unlike the keypunch, which is capable of printing the meaning of the character it contains on the top of each column, the interpreter prints across the face of the card, in specific locations and in larger type than the keypunch.

Interpreting is a helpful supplementary aid in the reproducing function. Because many cards are reproduced or gang-punched, a person can read them more easily if the cards are first interpreted than if he has to read the punched holes, a job which is both time-consuming and extremely boring.

GLOSSARY OF TERMS

CARD STACKER: An output device that accumulates punched cards in a deck. Contrast with card hopper.

CONTROL PANEL: 1. A part of a computer console that contains manual controls. 2. Same as plugboard.

GANG PUNCH: To punch identical or constant information into a group of punched cards.

INTERPRETER: 1. A program that translates and executes each source language expression before translating and executing the next one. 2. A device that prints on a punched card the data already punched in the card.

KEYBOARD: A group of marked levers operated manually for recording characters.

KEYPUNCH: A keyboard-operated device that punches holes in a card to represent data.

MARK-SENSE CARD: A card designed to allow entering data on it with an electrographic pencil.

PROGRAM CARD: A coded card inserted in the program control unit of the keypunch to control operations such as skipping, duplicating, and shifting, automatically.

PUNCHING STATION: The area on the keypunch where a card is aligned for the punching process.

READING STATION: The area on the keypunch where a data card is aligned for reading by a sensing mechanism to duplicate it automatically into another card located in the punching station.

REPRODUCER: A machine that duplicates a punched card by punching another one.

VERIFIER: A device on which a record can be compared or tested for identity character-by-character with a retranscription or copy as it is being prepared.

QUESTIONS FOR REVIEW

1. Give a general description of the keypunch.
2. Compare a keypunch to a typewriter. How are they similar? How are they dissimilar?
3. What is meant by the serial method of keypunching? How is it different from the parallel method?
4. What is the function of the punching station? The reading station?
5. What procedure is usually followed in punching data in a deck of cards?
6. How are data duplicated manually from one card into another card through the use of the keypunch?
7. How are data duplicated automatically on a keypunch?
8. What is the function of a verifier? What happens when an error is detected in a certain column (for example, column 16)? Explain.
9. Describe the reproducer, its functions, and main units.
10. What is gang punching? Explain how data are gang-punched.
11. What is mark sensing? What is end printing?
12. What is the difference between interpreting and mark sensing? What machine is used by each process?

chapter

9

Classifying
Recorded Data

Chapter 8 described the recording process and the methods by which input data are prepared. This chapter brings us a step further into the data-processing cycle by introducing the classifying function, the various ways of sorting input data, and the machines used in the preparation of the data for further processing.

Generally, most recorded data are compiled and filed as they are received. In a banking application, for instance, loan instalment tickets accepted by the teller are recorded in punched cards in the order in which they are received. Once these "input" data are recorded, they must be *classified* (for example, by loan number or by customer account number), and later merged with the main file to determine the balance outstanding on accounts for which payments have been received.

What is classifying? What machines are involved? What operations are performed on these machines? Answers to these and other questions comprise the subject matter of this chapter.

What Is Classifying?

Classifying is defined as a process in which like transactions are prepared, in either numeric or alphabetic order, based on the data they contain. Classifying includes sorting, grouping, and selecting.

Sorting is the arrangement of numeric or alphabetic data in a given sequence. Although descending sequence is possible, ascending sequence is the more popular method (Figures 9-1 and 9-2).

Grouping is the arrangement of a mass of data into related groups, all of which have common characteristics. For example, in a deck of student admission cards arranged by student number, the cards may be rearranged by class, so that each student is identified as freshman, sophomore, junior, or senior. Figure 9-3 shows a deck of student admission cards filed by student number (left), and later grouped by class.

Selecting is defined as the process of extracting a number of cards from a deck for a specific purpose, without disturbing the sequence in which they originally were filed. The selecting process is widely used in various business applications. Usually, selected cards contain a code (for example, an X-punch) in a specific location. The sorter is set (or wired, in the case of the collator) to detect and extract such cards from the main file and eject them into a separate pocket. If a code is not already punched in the cards to be selected, the sorter can be set to read a specific digit (for example, 2) in a given column and suppress the reading of any other digit or characters punched in that column. In either case, a selection is made and the net results are the same. When the process is completed, the original deck has been separated into two smaller decks: (1) the selected cards and (2) the remaining file (Figure 9-4).

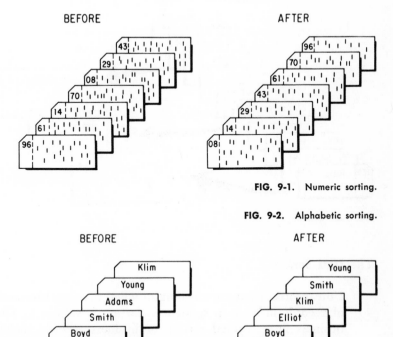

BEFORE

AFTER

FIG. 9-1. Numeric sorting.

FIG. 9-2. Alphabetic sorting.

BEFORE

AFTER

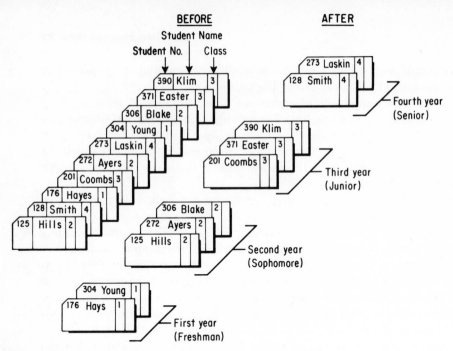

FIG. 9-3. Grouping—by class.

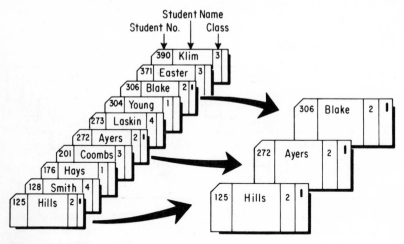

FIG. 9-4. Selecting.

The IBM Sorters

Unit records are more meaningful when they are arranged as parts of a group of records in a given sequence. Sorting is similar to filing. In a progressive business firm, manual sorting of business records is considered both costly and time-consuming. When a punched-card data-processing system is in use, it is necessary to integrate a sorter into the system to speed up the process of re-sequencing business records.

All sorters on the market today operate in a similar manner. They each perform the basic job of rearranging records in a given sequence. The main differences between them are the rate of speed, method of editing, and convenience of operation. Rated sort speeds are commonly 650, 1,000, and 2,000 cards per minute.

A Typical Sorter

The IBM 82 sorter is an example of a widely used, relatively fast model. It has 13 pockets, into which processed cards are ejected (Figure 9-5). From the right, they are: *Reject, 12, 11, 0, 1, 2, 3, 4, 5, 6, 7, 8,* and *9.*

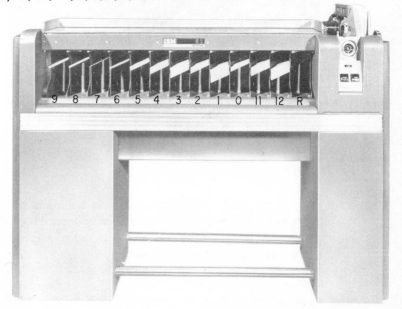

FIG. 9-5.   IBM 82 sorter.

The "reject" pocket usually receives cards that contain an invalid character in the card column being sorted, or cards which do not belong in any of the other 12 pockets, such as a blank column. The remaining pockets conform to the card format and are used for both numeric and alphabetic sorting; that is, pockets 0 through 9 are used in numeric sorting, and pockets 12, 11, and 0 are used in combination with pockets 1 through 9 for alphabetic sorting (Figure 9-5).

As in other sorters, the IBM 82 follows the reverse-digit method of sorting; that is, sorting begins with the unit's position of a given field and proceeds one column at a time (from right to left) until the field is completely sorted. In numeric sorting, the number of passes required to sort a field is equal to the number of columns it contains, because the sorter sorts only one column at a time.

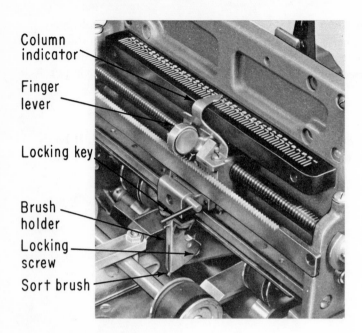

Column indicator

Finger lever

Locking key

Brush holder

Locking screw

Sort brush

FIG. 9-6. Sort brush—IBM 82 sorter.

In a one-column field, card-column 37, containing a punch in row 4, will drop into pocket 4. Before any sorting is done, the card is placed in the hopper. The single sorter brush is moved to align with column 37 and then the "START" button is depressed. This causes the card sorting on column 37 to move under the brush and be ejected into pocket 4. Figure 9-6 shows the single sort brush of the 82 sorter, positioned to sort on column 37.

The reverse-digit method of sorting is applicable on a field of two or more columns. Assume, for instance, that we desire to sort a deck of cards in columns 17–19. First, the deck is placed in the hopper and the sort brush is set at the unit's position of the sort field (or column 19). When the sorter starts, cards move under the sort brush and eject into any one of the 10 pockets (0–9), based on the digit punched in that column; that is, a card punched with digit 8 in column 19 will drop into pocket 8, digit 6 into pocket 6, etc. (Figure 9-7).

When the machine stops, the cards are taken out of their pockets and re-assembled. This marks the end of Pass One. The sort brush is reset to column 18 (the ten's position), and the reassembled deck is placed in the hopper again as Pass Two begins. The reassembled deck at the end of Pass Two and the setting of the sort brush on column 17 marks the beginning of Pass Three. After Pass Three is completed, the entire 19-card deck has been sorted into the proper sequence (Figure 9-7).

Alphabetic sorting requires twice as many passes as numeric sorting. Since each letter is represented by two holes, it takes two passes to sort each alpha-

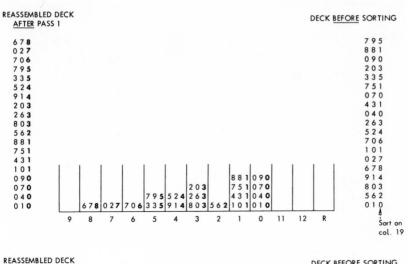

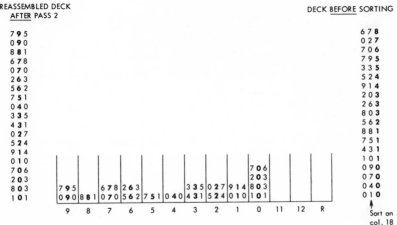

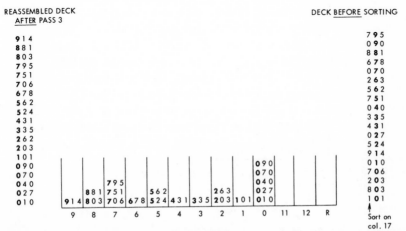

FIG. 9-7. Numeric sorting—reverse digit method.

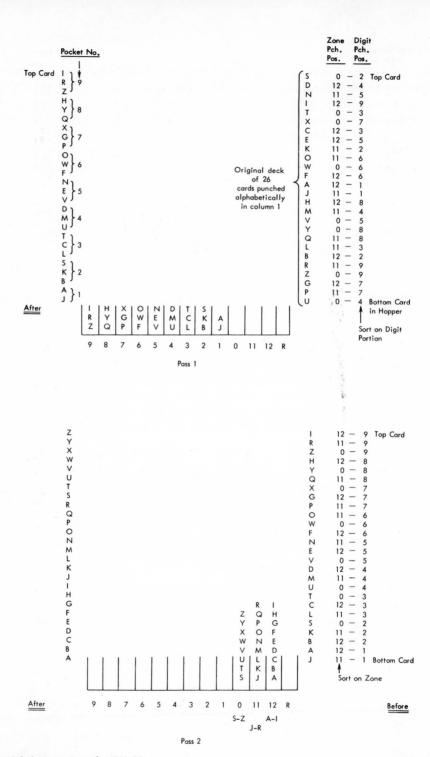

FIG. 9-8. Alphabetic sorting—the IBM 82 sorter.

betic column: the first pass by digit, and the second pass by zone. To illustrate, suppose we have 26 cards, each of which contains a different letter punched in a given column. To sort these cards into the proper alphabetic sequence, Pass One must sort the 26 cards on the digit portion; that is, the sort brush is directed to read only the holes in the digit-punching positions (0–9). This sort ejects the cards into one of the 0 through 9 pockets. In Figure 9-8, Pass One causes letter A to drop into pocket 1, B into pocket 2, C into pocket 3, etc.

When the cards are reassembled, they are placed in the hopper and the sort brush is directed to the zone portion (that is, 12, 11, or 0), ignoring any punches in the digit-punching positions. On the second sort, cards punched with letters A through I will drop into pocket 12; letters J through R, into pocket 11; and letters S through Z, into pocket 0. When the cards are taken out of the three pockets and assembled, they will be sorted into the proper alphabetic sequence, A through Z (Figure 9-8).

In summary, it takes two passes to sort each alphabetic column, compared to one pass to sort a numeric column. Thus, if we wish to sort a four-column field containing alphabetic information, it will take eight passes (4 × 2) to sort the whole field.

Computation of sorting time. Sorting time is computed by multiplying the number of cards to be sorted by the number of passes that must be made, then dividing the product by the speed of the sorter. For example, the time it would take to sort 1,300 cards, each of which is punched with a five-digit numeric field, on a machine capable of sorting 650 cards per minute is computed as follows:

$$\frac{1,300 \times 5}{650} = 10 \text{ minutes}$$

Assuming that we have a five-column alphabetic field in each of 1,300 cards, the sorting time is doubled:

$$\frac{1,300 \times 10}{650} = 20 \text{ minutes}$$

In addition to machine sorting time, it is a common practice to allow some percentage of sorting time for the handling of cards between passes. Approximately 25 per cent of the sorting time is considered average. In the case of our last example, *total* sorting time would be 10 + 2.5 = 12.5 minutes for the numeric sort, and 20 + 5 = 25 minutes for the alphabetic sort.

Other Types of Sorters

Newer and faster sorters are available which sort electronically or with "electric-eye" contact rather than with brushes. These generally have more efficiently designed machine controls as well. Some feature special devices which provide certain types of computation and statistical functions as well as the primary sorting functions (Figures 9-9 and 9-10).

FIG. 9-9. IBM statistical sorter.

FIG. 9-10. Electronic sorter—
Remington Rand.

The Collator

Collation of sorted data is accomplished by bringing together (interfiling) two decks of cards in a given order. The sorter is capable of performing this routine on a limited scale providing that the merging field is in the same location in each card. This requirement is often difficult to meet, however, because two decks may have the same data punched in different locations to suit the needs of two specific applications. To repunch one deck in order to make it conform to the format of the other deck is both costly and time-consuming. To avoid this, another filing machine has been developed called the collator.

A Typical Collator

The IBM 88 collator is an auxiliary, special-purpose, filing machine designed to do various routines at high speed (Figure 9-11). These routines include merging, matching, selecting, and sequence checking. Other IBM collators and the Remington Rand numerical collator also are available and perform essentially the same functions, differing mainly in rates of speed.

FIG. 9-11. IBM 88 collator.

Figure 9-11 shows two feed hoppers: on the right is the primary hopper, and on the left, the secondary hopper. The primary hopper has an extension for holding more cards than the secondary hopper, because the primary deck of cards normally is larger than the secondary deck. Other components include two sets of 80 reading brushes each (secondary and primary), and five stackers.

Initially, two decks of cards are placed in the primary and secondary hoppers. Cards moving from either of two directions drop into one of the five stackers and pass under their respective reading brushes based on the type of operation in action. The collator carries out a given operation (for example, merging) by comparing a card from the primary with one from the secondary hopper. Based on the way the control panel is wired, it "decides" on the location and the sequence in which the cards must drop.

The Merging Function

Merging is defined as combining two decks of cards into one deck of a given sequence. To perform a merging operation manually involves the use of the eyes and the mind—the eyes to see and read the data, and the mind to de-

FIG. 9-12. Merging—an example.

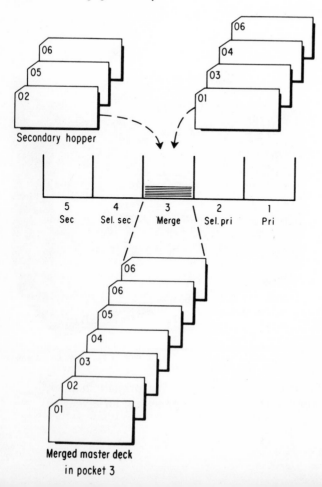

Secondary hopper

5	4	3	2	1
Sec	Sel. sec	Merge	Sel. pri	Pri

Merged master deck
in pocket 3

termine the sequence into which these data must be placed. Likewise, a collator merges similar data punched in cards through the use of brushes and a control panel. The brushes are the "eyes" of the machine and the control panel is its "mind."

The control panel is wired to merge two decks of cards into one deck of a given sequence, usually an ascending sequence. The two decks, each of which must already be in sequence, are placed in the primary and secondary feed hoppers. When the collator starts, a card from the primary hopper (primary card) moves under the primary reading brushes. At the same time, a card from the secondary feed hopper (secondary card) moves under the secondary reading brushes. A comparison is made between the values in the primary and secondary cards. The card with the smaller value drops into pocket 3 (the middle pocket), followed by another card either equal to or smaller than the value of the card to which it is compared. When the two cards are of equal value, the machine drops the primary card first, followed by the secondary card.

To illustrate, Figure 9-12 presents a merging operation involving two decks of cards. The deck of three cards (numbers 02, 05, and 06) in the secondary hopper is merged with the deck of four cards (numbers 01, 03, 04, and 06) in the primary hopper. In merging the two decks, six comparisons are made. They are:

	Secondary Card No.		Primary Card No.	
1	02	–	01	Primary card 01 drops in pocket 3 and card 03 moves under the primary reading brushes.
2	02	–	03	Secondary card 02 drops in pocket 3 and card 05 moves under the secondary reading brushes.
3	05	–	03	Primary card 03 drops in pocket 3 and card 04 moves under the primary reading brushes.
4	05	–	04	Primary card 04 drops in pocket 3 and card 06 moves under the primary reading brushes.
5	05	–	06	Secondary card 05 drops in pocket 3 and secondary card 06 moves under the secondary reading brushes.
6	06	–	06	Primary card 06 drops in pocket 3 first, followed by secondary card 06.

The Matching Function

Matching is checking on the equality of a specific field in two decks of cards. To perform this operation, the control panel is rewired from the arrangement used in merging, and the two decks of cards are fed through the primary and secondary hoppers. Next, a card from each deck is compared. If the values are equal, both cards drop into the matched pockets, the primary card into pocket 2 (the matched primary pocket), and the secondary card into pocket 4 (the matched secondary pocket). In an unequal comparison (that is, if the two cards do *not* match), they drop into the pockets 1 and 5 (Figure 9-13).

FIG. 9-13. Matching—an example.

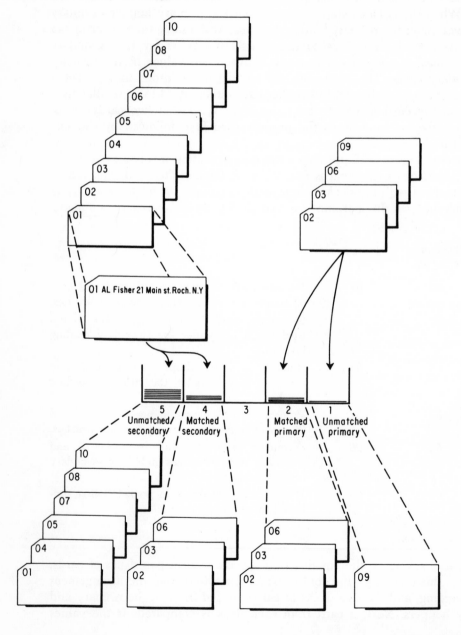

Often, a combination of "merge" and "match" operations is performed, whereby two decks of cards are compared. The cards that match are directed to merge into the middle pocket, rather than pockets 2 and 4. Unmatched secondary cards drop into pocket 5, and unmatched primary cards drop into pocket 1. This routine is referred to as the "match-merge" operation.

The Selecting Function

Selecting is defined as extracting certain cards from a deck for a specific purpose. In the match-merging operation, for example, unmatched cards dropping into pocket 1 are said to be *selected* (through control-panel wiring) to drop into that pocket. There are situations in which cards are selected because they require special attention; for example, in checking on the proper sequence of a deck of cards, any or all that are out of sequence can be selected to drop into a separate pocket without disturbing remaining cards of the deck.

Other examples of selecting include extracting from a given deck (1) any cards having no specific code, (2) cards that have a zero balance in a given location, (3) cards that have a code, such as an X-punch in a given column, and (4) cards that have a value punched in a specific field which falls between specified limits. For example, in a business application, delinquent accounts between five and ten days from the due date may be extracted from the file for future action. A card is punched with the maximum and minimum date and is fed into the machine as the first card of the deck. With proper control-panel wiring, all cards that contain dates within the limits punched in the "lead" card are separated (or selected) into a given pocket.

The Sequence-Checking Function

Sequence checking is the act of determining the order in which the cards of a given deck are filed. In sequence checking, only the primary hopper is used, since the operation involves just one deck of cards. The control panel can be wired to divert cards that are out of sequence into a separate pocket without disturbing the processing routine. Under normal circumstances, however, the machine is wired to stop automatically upon the detection of an "out-of-sequence" card.

Sequence checking is performed by comparing a value in two consecutive cards for one of three possibilities: high sequence, low sequence, or equal sequence. In Figure 9-14, card *01* is compared with card *04*, reflecting a "high sequence." Card *01* drops into the designated pocket, leaving card *04* under the reading brushes to be compared with card *03*.

In a second comparison, the result is "low sequence," meaning that in an ascending-sequence checking operation, card *04* would be considered out of sequence. If the machine is wired to stop automatically as a result of a low-sequence comparison, the machine would be "run out," thus ejecting the two cards (*04* and *03*) into the pocket. The operator at that time re-sequences the two cards manually and then restarts the machine to continue the operation.

A third comparison can be made between card *05* and the following card

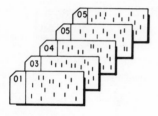

FIG. 9-14. Sequence checking.

05. The result is "equal sequence." **Both** cards drop into the pocket in the order in which they are fed. Technically, the last two cards are processed after a "Run-out" button is depressed.

Although sequence checking is used as a separate operation, it can be, and usually is, used in conjunction with other operations, such as merging, matching, match-merging, and selecting. While any one of these operations is being performed, the control panel can be wired to sequence-check the cards in each of the two decks simultaneously to make sure they are in the right order. The application of sequence checking with other operations saves time and insures accuracy.

GLOSSARY OF TERMS

CLASSIFYING: Arranging data in a specific form, usually by sorting, grouping, or extracting.

COLLATOR: A device to collate or merge sets of cards or other documents into a sequence.

GROUPING: Arranging a mass of data into related groups, having common characteristics.

MATCHING: A data-processing operation similar to a merge, except that instead of producing a sequence of items made up from the input, sequences are matched against each other on the basis of some key.

MERGE: To combine items into one, sequenced file from two or more similarly sequenced files without changing the order of the items.

SELECTING: Extracting certain cards from a deck for a specific purpose without disturbing the sequence in which they were originally filed.

SEQUENCE CHECK: A data-processing operation designed to check the sequence of the items in a file assumed to be already in sequence.

SORTER: A machine capable of sorting punched cards either alphabetically or numerically.

SORTING: Arranging numeric or alphabetic data in a given sequence.

QUESTIONS AND PROBLEMS FOR REVIEW

1. What is meant by classifying? What are its three main types? Explain each type briefly.

2. What is the primary difference between grouping and sorting? Between grouping and selecting?

3. The following is a deck of 8 cards, each of which contains a customer account number in columns 1 and 2. Sort these cards in ascending sequence.

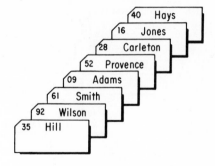

4. Assume the following deck of 20 numbers, each of which represents a card:

(top card) 20	67	10	80	18
08	75	72	95	26
20	11	52	33	51
33	46	07	64	93 (bottom card)

(a) How many passes are required to sort the deck?
(b) Using the reverse-digit method of sorting, present in ascending order a reassembled deck after each pass.

5. Sort the following letters, each representing a card, using the IBM 82 sorter, by showing their location in the proper sorter pockets:

(top card) Q	T	L	E	F
S	K	G	V	P
N	L	C	U	R
B	J	W	M	Y (bottom card)

6. Suppose we wish to sort 9,000 cards on a four-digit numeric field,
(a) How many passes would be required to sort the deck?
(b) Assuming a speed of 650 cards per minute, what is the running time of this sort?
(c) What is the total sorting time if 10 per cent of the running time is allowed for handling?

7. What advantage does a collator have over a sorter?

8. Describe the IBM 88 collator. What are its chief functions?

9. Define the following terms:
(a) Matching
(b) Merging
(c) Selecting
(d) Sequence checking
(e) Match-merging
(f) High sequence
(g) Equal sequence
(h) Low sequence.

10. Suppose we wish to merge the following two decks of cards:

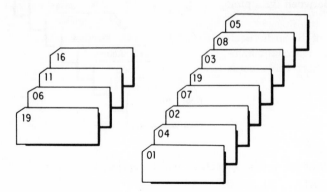

(a) What step(s) must be taken before any merging can take place?
(b) How many comparisons are made by the collator during the merging operation?

11. Assume two decks of data cards: the primary deck consisting of employees' withholding-tax information, and the secondary deck including the employee's name-and-address cards. In a matching operation:
(a) Which cards (or card) in both decks match?
(b) Which cards (or card) in both decks do not match? In which pocket(s) do they drop?

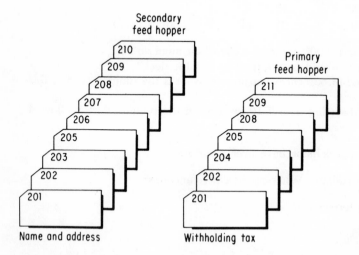

12. Suppose we wish to match-merge the two decks of cards in Problem 5 above with each employee's withholding-tax card behind his name-and-address card. Assuming that the control panel of the collator is wired to perform a match-merge operation,

   (a) In which hopper (that is, primary or secondary) is the name-and-address deck placed? Why?
   (b) In which pocket do the merged cards drop?
   (c) In which pocket do the rest of the cards from both decks drop? Specify.
13. What types of cards can be selected out of a deck of punched cards? Explain each type briefly.

chapter

10

The Calculating Function
and Preparation of Reports

Generally every business application involves some calculation on the data it contains. Previous chapters pointed out the stages through which source data must go before they are ready to be calculated and later produced in the form of reports. These stages, in effect, are steps in a process whereby certain information is recorded, sorted, interfiled, and otherwise manipulated toward the ultimate goal of realizing meaningful reports. The results are not considered until after the function of calculating has been carried out and the reconstructed data, along with other pertinent information, have been summarized and printed.

The Calculating Function

Most calculations performed in solving business problems involve one or a combination of the four arithmetic functions: addition, subtraction, multiplication, and division. Considering the thousands of records to be updated periodically, a business firm of average size finds it difficult and costly to calculate them by hand or even with the help of basic mechanical devices. In a punched-card data-processing installation, a calculator is used: the electronic calculating punch (Figure 10-1).

The IBM punched-card calculator determines a result, based on the instructions wired in the machine's control panel. It takes one instruction at a time and carries it out until the answer is obtained. Normally, calculating begins by feeding data cards from the hopper of the punch unit. Next, a field—or several fields—of a card are read and transferred to the calculating unit. If the operation is to multiply one field by another, for example, this arithmetic function is performed in the calculating unit, and the product promptly transferred to the punches, which punch the answer into a designated location in the same card or into another card following it.

A typical application involving the use of the calculating punch is payroll. In processing the payroll, several steps are involved, which are divided into substeps for the purpose of simplifying the calculating routine. Gross pay is reduced by federal and other applicable taxes and deductions before arriving at the net pay.

To illustrate the basic steps taken in computing the net pay, we shall introduce the elements required in (1) computing an employee's gross pay and (2) computing his federal withholding tax. Federal tax is mandatory, and therefore, calculation of the exact amount is necessary before arriving at the net pay.

Calculations for Gross Pay

Gross pay at the average employee's level is determined by multiplying the number of hours worked by the pay rate per hour. When overtime is involved, an employee is generally paid time and a half, or one-and-a-half times the regular hourly rate. These amounts are new, reconstructed data resulting from calculations involving the employee's rate of pay and the amount of time he worked. These factors are punched into a card(s) and fed into the punch

FIG. 10-1. The IBM electronic calculating punch.

unit before they are calculated; and the result is punched into that card following the calculation.

Calculations for Federal Income Tax

An employee's net pay is equal to his gross earnings less certain deductions, the type and number of which depend on such factors as his marital status, number of dependents, and size of income. The federal income-tax schedule is constructed in such a way that a taxpayer pays proportionately less tax as the number of his dependents (exemptions) increases. For instance, a single taxpayer earning $8,000 per year pays more federal income tax than a married taxpayer earning the same amount.

To compute the federal income tax, three main elements are required: (1) the total hours worked, (2) the rate per hour, and (3) the number of exemptions. The first step is to compute the gross pay (hours worked × rate per hour), and then subtract from it the sum allowed for the employee's total declared exemptions. The remainder, the balance referred to as the taxable income, is the amount to be used in figuring out the federal income tax withholding.

To illustrate, assume that an employee works 40 hours per week at $2.00 per hour and claims three exemptions (his wife, his son, and himself). To calculate the federal income tax, assume further that (1) $13.00 is deducted from gross pay for each exemption, and (2) 18 per cent of the taxable amount is withheld for federal income tax.* The federal income tax withholding is calculated according to the following formulas:

> Gross pay = number of hours worked × rate per hour
> Taxable income = gross pay − nontaxable amount
> Federal income tax withholding = taxable income × 18 per cent

To substitute:

> Gross pay = 40 × $2.00 = $80.00
> Taxable income = $80.00 − $39.00 (3 × $13.00) = $41.00
> Federal income tax withholding = $41.00 × $\dfrac{18}{100}$ = $7.38

Other deductions, such as social security (FICA), insurance premiums of various types, and the like, further reduce an employee's gross earnings. Each of these deductions is a problem by itself, consisting of performing a series of arithmetic calculations in a definite sequence. Use of the calculating punch involves prepunching the data to be worked up into cards, then wiring the control panels to do the required work.

All "input" data must be as accurate and complete as possible, since the accuracy of the results obtained by the calculating unit depends upon the accuracy and validity of the input information.

* The tax rate used is for illustrative purposes only.

The Preparation of Reports

One of the most important steps in the punched-card data processing cycle is the printing and preparation of needed reports. Managers cannot function effectively without these reports, since they represent condensed data which often are vital to the over-all operation of the business. Furthermore, the functions of recording, classifying, and calculating data (discussed in previous chapters) would be meaningless unless they contribute to the finished product —printed reports.

Reports are prepared on continuous paper forms on an accounting machine, more commonly referred to as a tabulator. (Figures 10-2 and 10-3.)

FIG. 10-2. IBM 407 accounting machine.

FIG. 10-3. Alphabetic tabulator—Remington Rand.

Originally machines did not print; they merely accumulated amounts in counters. The amounts were transcribed manually at the end of the operation. Later, when printing tabulators were developed, two options were provided: (1) to print (list) each card passing through the machine, plus the necessary totals accumulated (added or subtracted) during the run, and (2) to print the totals only (referred to as tabulating or group printing). Alphabetical information, naturally, is only printed, not accumulated as would be the case involving amounts.

A tabulator is capable of reading data by means of its reading brushes and of processing the data it reads. Based upon instructions it receives via a control panel (in the case of IBM equipment) or wired unit (in the case of the Sperry Rand Tabulator), the control panel or wired unit "tells" the tabulator what field(s) to read, what to do with the data read, and where to print them on the paper form.

Figure 10-4 is a control panel inserted in the IBM 407 accounting machine. Printing is "activated" by means of a connection (through the control panel)

FIG. 10-4. A control panel (courtesy *International Business Machines Corp.*).

between the reading brushes and the print wheel (older models print by means of type bars instead of print wheels). A wire causes the connection of a specific reading brush to activate a selected print wheel to print the contents of a given column. For example, if column 40 of a given card is to be printed in the middle of a form, the operator uses a connecting wire, and (1) inserts one end in a hole (or hub) in the control panel, which corresponds to reading brush 40, and (2) inserts the other end into another hub, which completes a circuit that will allow the proper print wheel to print at the middle of the paper form (Figure 10-5).

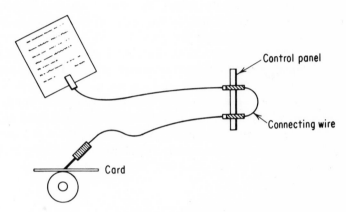

FIG. 10-5.   Control panel wiring.

When the deck of cards is fed into the card hopper and the control panel is properly wired and inserted in the machine, the reading brushes read each card, and through the control panel, cause data to be printed on a paper form, one line at a time. This "one-line-at-a-time" printing is referred to as "parallel" printing, which is compared to "serial" printing, an example of which is "typewriting." The operator should take time to look over the printed data to make sure that no obvious errors have been made.

The Summarizing Function

Tabulators perform the functions of summarizing, printing, and summary punching. *Summarizing* is the compression of certain data into a more meaningful and concise form. An income statement *summarizes* the primary revenues and expenses of a given firm for a specific period of time; the balance sheet *summarizes* the chief assets, liabilities, and owners' equities of that firm at a given point in time.

Generally, tabulators contain a number of counters, which are used to accumulate totals as a result of the addition or subtraction of two or more values.

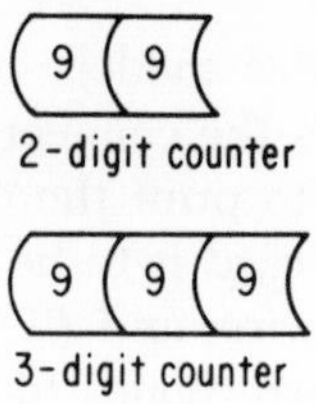

2-digit counter

3-digit counter

FIG. 10-6.

In the preparation of a sales report, for instance, a counter is used to accumulate each of three main types of total: minor, intermediate, and major totals. A counter can accumulate any maximum amount desired. For example, a two-digit counter can accumulate up to 99; a three-digit counter, up to 999; etc. (Figure 10-6). In planning the use of the machine and the preparation of a given report, counters must be identified and set so that the maximum anticipated amount can be accommodated by that counter. Next, the control panel should be wired to print, that is, "dump," the contents of certain counters into a specific location and at a given time on the form.

A minor total is the smallest unit or total in a report. Total sales made by a given salesman in the hardware department of a specific store, for instance, could be referred to as a "minor" total, whereas intermediate totals involve the sum of many smaller units, such as those within a given branch or office. In the above example, the "intermediate" total would be the total amount sold by all the salesmen in the hardware department of the store, and the "major" total would sum up the total of the entire store, including all the departments. The "grand" total would be achieved by adding up the sales volumes of all the branches of the company throughout the state or across the nation (Figure 10-7).

The Printing Function

The most important function and a required role of the tabulator is its ability to print summarized and other data on a continuous paper form. The form is mounted on sprocket wheels which help to advance it every time a line is printed (Figure 10-8).

Depending on the model and make, tabulators print either by means of type bars or print wheels. The IBM 402 alphabetic tabulator employs 88 type bars aligned across the width of the form. A maximum of 43 type bars, grouped on the right half of the printing mechanism, print numeric characters. The remaining 45 type bars are alphanumeric, each capable of printing any of the 26 letters, 10 digits, or special characters. When a combination of alphabetic and numeric printing is desired, the designated type bars are raised, or positioned, for printing one complete line at a time; that is, all the required type characters are pressed against the paper simultaneously.

Type wheels (referred to as print wheels) perform the same function as type bars and can print alphabetic, numeric, or special characters (Figure 10-9).

The IBM 407 tabulator uses 120 print wheels, arranged in one group to

ABC Company

Sales Report for the month ended Dec. 31, 1965

Division	Branch	Salesman	Sales Total by Salesman	Total by Branch	Total by Division
Eastern	A	1	100		
		2	200		
		3	150	450	
	B	4	200		
		5	300		
		6	250	750	1200*
Western	C	7	400		
		8	600	1000	
	D	9	180		
		10	120		
		11	300	600	1600*
					2800**

* Major Total
**Grand Total

FIG. 10-7.

FIG. 10-8. IBM 402 accounting machine.

print up to 120 characters within a maximum width of 12 inches. It prints a number of required characters in a specific location on the form. Activated by electrical impulses generated by holes in the punched card, certain print wheels are rotated so that the proper character is aligned to print in the proper position on the line. In actual operation, you will notice that a *print wheel* rotates to position the desired character to the line, compared to the type bar, which moves vertically to position the same character.

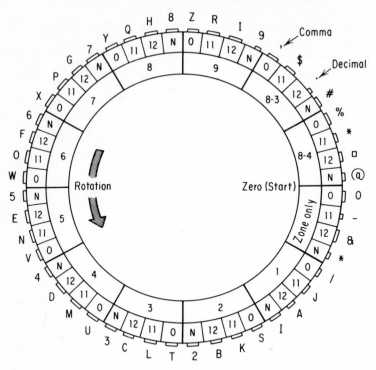

FIG. 10-9. IBM 407 print wheel.

Detail and Group Printing

Detail printing, or listing, involves printing one line for each card fed from the hopper. Providing the tabulator's control panel is wired to detail-print, each card is read and the printing mechanism is activated to print any or all of its data on a line. If we have a deck of 10 cards, 10 lines will be printed.

Group printing, on the other hand, means printing one line for each *group* of cards having similar characteristics. For example, suppose we have 10 punched cards: the first five contain a product number (for example, 714), the number of units sold, and the unit price. The remaining five cards contain a different product number (for example, 800), the quantity sold, and the unit price. The group-printing routine includes that of adding the quantity sold under each of the products (714 and 800), determining the total amount, and printing two lines including the necessary details (Figure 10-10).

The tabulator group-prints by comparing specified columns of each card with the one following it. When two cards are equal they are considered part of a group, and their selected values are accumulated. This process continues until an unequal comparison occurs, denoting the end of one group and the beginning of another. At that time, the tabulator prints the accumulated amount in its counters and begins again, following the same routine on the succeeding group.

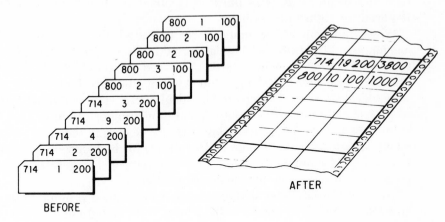

BEFORE

AFTER

FIG. 10-10. Group printing.

Summary Punching

Summary punching is defined as the act of automatically converting data accumulated from detail cards into punched holes. In Figure 10-11, the summarized data group-printed on the form also may be punched into a card or

FIG. 10-11. Tabulator with summary punch hooked up.

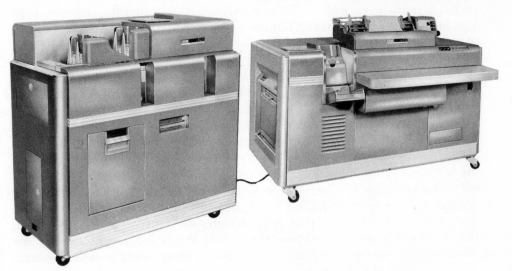

cards through the coordinated use (by a direct connection) of both the accounting machine and the reproducer. While the accounting machine is group printing on a paper form, the reproducer is copying (punching) the same data into blank cards. This function is valuable when group-printed data are required for future processing.

When punched-card equipment was first used, the tabulator or accounting machine could perform accumulation, addition, or subtraction while printing information from punched cards. This led to simultaneous summary-card punching by means of linking a punch to the tabulator. Later, when calculators were developed, cards were read, calculations were performed, and results were punched into cards for subsequent tabulating or printing. This, of course, is the punched-card approach closest to the electronic data-processing system, which also uses magnetic tape and/or drums for high-speed input and output. Punched-card equipment includes calculating punches, electronic calculating punches, and electronic punched-card computers.

The trend in tabulator design is toward high-speed printing only as part of an integrated system. Machines have been built, and are in use, which produce printed and punched cards; one is called the card-punching printer, which prints on both sides of a standard punched-card and punches data during the same run. Another development provides for printing in magnetic ink or for printing with special type fonts, acceptable to optical scanners when re-entered into the processing system. We may look forward to future developments in this area optimistically.

An Application of the Punched-Card System

Typically, a punched-card system consists of a keypunch, a sorter, an interpreter, a reproducer, and a tabulator (with summary punch). Assume "Pep-Up, Inc." has such a system. Prepunched item cards (one card for each case of soft drinks) are filed in a tub file, by brand. For each order received, the required number of cards is extracted from the file. The reproducer is used to punch new cards which will be inserted into the file when the company replenishes its stock. In this case, the file represents the actual inventory of cases in the warehouse.

Next, customer cards are taken out of a master customer file and reproduced and merged with the "item" cards to form a customer billing deck. The various billing decks are sorted according to the customers' geographical locations and are fed through the tabulator, which prints out the day's orders in quadruplicate. One copy goes to the sales department; another to a routing clerk, who combines the various orders by truck and route; and two are given to the drivers. One of these is the customer's copy; the other is turned in by the driver with the empty bottles he returns. As the orders are printed by the tabulator, the summary punch creates a gross-charge card for each customer. These are held in a "suspense" file.

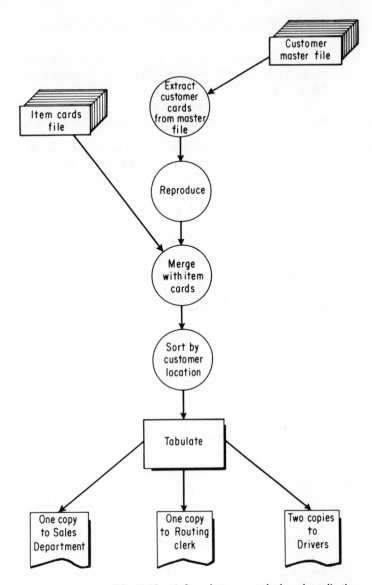

FIG. 10-12. A flow chart—a punched card application.

Another tub file contains prepunched item cards for empty bottles. A clerk pulls the proper number of cards indicated by the driver on the returned order-copy, and matches them with the gross-charge cards in the suspense file. The combined deck of cards is run through the tabulator to obtain a listing (detail printing). In the same operation, a summary punch creates net-charge cards, which are run through the tabulator to print invoices for each customer. About 5,000 separate orders may be included in these invoices.

Next, the cards are sorted and run through the tabulator to produce an "aged" trial balance of accounts receivable (total dollars owed Pep-Up, Inc.).

The result shows the age of any unpaid bill and, as payments are received during the month, the corresponding accounts-receivable cards are removed from the file.

A number of management reports are prepared from the cards created during the foregoing procedure. Among them are the following:

Daily: Sales analysis by item, updated for the month.
Weekly: (a) Customer sales analysis by item, updated for the month.
(b) Salesman's sales analysis by item, updated for the month.
(c) Wholesaler's sales analysis by item, updated for the month.
Monthly: Sales report by item, sales report by brand, sales report by state—all updated for the year. Sales report by customer and item for this year and last year. Sales report by state and item, for this year and last year. Sales report by salesman, updated for the year.

In this instance, we may conclude that the punched-card system is primarily responsible for speeding up service to customers, a factor considered vital in today's competitive market.

GLOSSARY OF TERMS

ACCOUNTING MACHINE: 1. A keyboard actuated machine that prepares accounting records. 2. A machine that reads data from external storage media, such as cards or tapes, and automatically produces accounting records or tabulations, usually on continuous forms.

CALCULATOR: 1. A device capable of performing arithmetic. 2. A calculator as in (1) that requires frequent manual intervention. 3. Generally and historically, a device for carrying out logic and arithmetic digital operations of any kind.

COUNTER: A device such as a register or storage location used to represent the number of occurrences of an event.

DETAIL PRINTING (listing): The printing of one line for each card read by the tabulator.

GROUP PRINTING: A procedure whereby one line is printed for each group of cards having similar characteristics.

SUMMARIZING: Condensing a mass of data into a concise and meaningful form.

SUMMARY PUNCH: A card punch operating in conjunction with another machine, commonly a tabulator, to punch into cards data which have been summarized or calculated by the other machine.

QUESTIONS AND PROBLEMS FOR REVIEW

1. What is meant by the term *calculate*? Give an example.
2. What are the main arithmetic functions of the IBM punched-card calculator? Explain.

3. Explain how the punch and the calculating units are used to calculate a given problem.

4. Show (by giving an example) how new data are created in a "gross-pay" calculation.

5. What factors are needed in calculating federal income-tax withholding? Explain by giving an example.

6. Bob Sanderson, a college student, accepted a summer job with a local contractor to pave driveways. He worked 32 hours a week and was paid at the rate of $4.35 per hour. His year-to-date gross earnings are $4,680. He is single and has no dependents. Assuming that Bob's employer deducted federal income-tax withholding and $1.50 for health insurance premium, calculate:
   (a) Gross pay
   (b) Federal income tax withheld
   (c) Net pay.

7. List and explain briefly the main functions of the control panel of an accounting machine.

8. List the four primary functions of an accounting machine. Explain each function briefly.

9. How is summarizing performed in an accounting machine? Illustrate.

10. What is the function of a counter? What is the maximum value which can be stored in a four-position counter?

11. What types of total can be represented or stored in a counter? Define each type and present an illustration of your own, showing their significance and their location on a paper form.

12. How is a final or grand total derived?

13. What are the two methods of printing? Explain and give an example of each method.

14. What is detail printing? What is group printing?

15. A deck containing eight cards (account numbers 201, 202, 203, 203, 204, 205, 205, and 206) are placed in the card hopper of an accounting machine. Assuming that detail printing is desired, how many lines would the machine print? How many lines would be group-printed? Why?

16. What is summary punching? On what machine(s) is it used? Why?

part 3

Electronic Data Processing

chapter

11

The Electronic Computer—
Its Elements and Capabilities

We have been dealing with equipment and methods of data processing using punched-card machines. As business firms expand, their needs for faster means of data-processing increase. Although punched-card data-processing is a major improvement over manual systems for handling data, it has some limitations. Intercommunication between the machines in the system is somewhat limited. They are not capable of handling exceptions within a normal routine, which necessitates manual processing. Further, the punched-card system is limited because of its inability to "make decisions" in the course of processing. This means that complex problems must be solved in pieces, or fractions, rather than in one continuous process. It is only logical to expect, then, that as a punched-card installation's cost increases and rated efficiency declines, a computer system is next to be considered for a replacement.

Why is a computer system often more desirable than a punched-card installation in a growing firm? The latter requires the use of the punched card as the primary unit record, and this unit record aids as a communication link among the various machines, which perform their tasks through the wiring of their control panels. Unlike a punched-card installation, the computer is capable of processing data received through a number of other types of devices beside punched cards. Further, an electronic computer performs the same functions faster and often more economically. Wiring panels are not required by most computers; instructions are received by means of a program, which is loaded into the machine and performs the same function as the wired control panel in a punched-card machine, plus a good many others.

To elaborate further on the unique characteristics of the two systems, a brief mention regarding their physical makeup would be helpful. A punched-card system includes a series of individual pieces of equipment, each of which processes the same unit record (or a summarized form of that record) in different ways. Certain equipment sorts; other equipment calculates, prints, and so on. A computer system, on the other hand, includes equipment which processes the unit record *under control of a central unit* (called a *processor*). All individual units are tied to the processor, and either accept or produce records as a result of the logic it imposes upon them. Whereas both systems are made up of many individual pieces of equipment, the punched-card system is not under a central automatic control as is the computer system.

As we examine both systems, we also find a difference in flexibility. It is true that both systems produce reports based on the information contained in the punched card. Nevertheless, there is a difference in the manner in which data are processed. The punched-card system reads the cards, sequences them, accumulates them, and finally prints out summary reports. The computer system, on the other hand, performs the same routine, but with greatly extended capabilities. That is, it can add, subtract, multiply, or divide; verify the accuracy of incoming information; reject certain cards if they contain invalid coding; and use a preplanned set of logic to deal with output data before a final printout is made.

Elements of an Electronic Data-Processing System

An electronic computer is only one part of an entire data-processing system. The following shows the relationship of computers to the basic functions of data handling:

Communicate—Input Mechanisms and Media

In any data-processing system, there is the need to communicate the originating transaction (input) to the system. Examples of such transactions may be purchase orders, deposit slips, payment of bills, etc. Input transactions must be translated to a language understandable to the computer system. This may require rewriting or typing certain information from the raw data, punching cards from it, checking it for errors, or handling it in some other manner that makes it machine-processable.

In electronic data processing, input can be defined as information of any sort delivered to the computer. Computer input may take the form of punched cards, punched paper tape, magnetic tape, a typewriter keyboard, or documents read by an optical scanner.

Hold Information—Memory

A data-processing system must have the ability to hold information while actions are being performed. In manual systems, this function may be handled by a clerk with a worksheet. The register on a desk calculator holds the result of the latest calculation until the next one is executed. In a unit-record system, information may be held in a punched card until the next step in the procedure.

In the broader sense, storage may be broken down into three types:

(a) *Internal (or primary) storage* is a device which forms an integral part of the central-processing unit of the computer system, and is directly controlled by it. This device, also called the "memory" unit, has the ability to accept, hold, and release information on demand from the control unit.

(b) *Auxiliary storage* devices are outside the central-processing unit, but are controlled by it. Such devices include magnetic disks, drums, and tapes.

(c) *External storage* facilities are apart from the central-processing unit, and include such devices as punched paper tape and punched cards. Magnetic tapes also can be considered a form of external storage.

Manipulate Data-Logic, Arithmetic, and Control

Once information has been received into the system, it is processed in various ways, depending upon the action required. Decisions must be made, arithmetic must be performed, manipulations must occur before action can be taken. In a computer, such activity is performed by the logic and arithmetic elements of the central processing unit (CPU).

Produce Reports—Output Mechanisms and Media

In electronic data processing, output can be defined as information of any sort delivered by the computer. It may be in a form which requires further translation (as in cases involving punched cards, punched paper tape, or magnetic-tape output), but final output generally is delivered to line printers. The results of such data-processing activity (reports) are written, typed, or printed documents.

Basic Types of Computers

Analog and Digital Computers

Electronic computation can be achieved by using digital or analog methods. A digital computer counts, using strings of digits to represent numbers. An analog computer measures, representing numbers by physical magnitudes, such as pressure, temperature, voltage, current, etc. Analog computers are physical systems which behave in a way analogous to some other physical or abstract system. A desk calculator is a digital machine, with cogged wheels serving as digits; a slide rule is an analog device, with length serving as the analog of the logarithm of the numbers.

In an electronic analog computer, the analog of a number generally is a voltage, a resistance, or some similar electrical quantity, and computations are performed by combining these quantities. Simple circuits can be built to add, subtract, multiply, divide, and otherwise combine electrical quantities. Networks of these circuits can compute very complicated mathematical expressions.

A continuous-variable function in an analog computer can be represented in a digital computer by a sequence of discrete numbers in the same way that a distribution function is represented by a bar graph; and with enough digits, the agreement of the analog and digital forms can be as close as required. The digital process sometimes may be slower than its analog counterpart, but the net result will otherwise be the same. A digital computer can even be made to behave as if it were an analog computer by equipping it with devices to convert the input from analog to digital form and to convert the output from digital to analog form.

A further advantage of digital computation is its greater accuracy. The precision with which a voltage can be measured limits the accuracy of an analog computer; an accuracy of better than one part in 1,000 is very difficult to achieve. Digital computation, on the other hand, is accomplished electronically by digits. A digital computer can get any required accuracy by using as many digits as it needs (or to phrase it differently, by carrying the solution to as many decimal places as necessary).

Analog computers are well suited to some types of problems, notably those in which the inputs and outputs are complex functions of time and in which the system being studied is producing inputs to the computer by reacting to its own outputs (that is, acting as part of a *feedback loop*). Thus, analog computers have been used effectively in studying human tracking performance, in building flight simulators, and in network simulation. For business applications, however, analog computers are generally not used.

Special- and General-purpose Computers

The computers already discussed are general-purpose machines. They differ in detail, but are basically similar in arrangement and logical design. They are built to do a variety of jobs through the use of the stored program. In this, they have sacrificed certain aspects of speed or efficiency, which may be extremely desirable for one customer but have little benefit for another. General-purpose computers have the advantage of lower cost, better service, and longer and more extensive testing during production to eliminate "bugs."

In contrast, the special-purpose machine is built for a specific operation, and usually for a single customer. It may incorporate many of the features of a general-purpose machine, but its applicability to a particular problem is a function of design rather than of program. Naturally, it lacks the flexibility of the general-purpose machine.

Examples of successful special-purpose systems are devices for the collection of highway tolls, for air traffic control (which receives such flight information as departure time, destination, route, payload, etc., via teletype), and for airline-reservations systems. Another important special-purpose computer is the ERMA system, originally built for the Bank of America by General Electric Co. and Stanford Research Institute, in which checks and deposit slips are read, using magnetic-ink character recognition (MICR) to identify account numbers.

Classification of general-purpose digital computers is made on the basis of power and speed, measured in terms of data handling and storage capacities and a variety of input-output possibilities. Internal computer speeds are measured by the time required to perform specific operations (for example, add or multiply) and are stated in terms of milliseconds (thousandths), microseconds (millionths), or nanoseconds (billionths).

The Basic Components of a Digital Computer

The five basic components of a computer system are (1) primary storage, (2) the arithmetic unit, (3) the control unit, (4) input devices, and (5) output devices. The first three make up the central processor, which sometimes is referred to as the "computer." They, along with the two remaining components, are referred to as the "computer system."

Primary Storage

Primary storage retains the data which will be used during processing. It is called "internal memory" owing to its similarity in function to human memory. Primary storage, or "memory," is used during the processing of a problem to act upon the data being manipulated, just as the human memory is used to "think out" the logical solution to a given problem. Like the human brain, the computer's memory is not used to retain all answers, nor to retain all the elements of a problem. Answers usually are written down, rather than committed to memory permanently; in other words, computer memory is based on the temporary retention of information, or data. This does not imply that the physical aspects of the memory allow the information to fade away or be lost after a while. To the contrary, once data are written into memory, they are retained permanently unless purposely or accidentally destroyed. Data are retained as long as they are being processed. When another problem is fed into the processor, the data it contains replace the data of the previous problem.

Information in computer memory can be numeric, alphabetic, or alphanumeric. A single piece of information in digital or alphabetic form is called a *character*. For the logic of the computer to locate any information it desires, the "character-oriented" computer is designed so that each character position in its memory can be located by an *address* or a location number. A computer having 5,000 character positions of primary storage, for instance, is capable of storing 5,000 alphabetic or numeric characters in all. The address of the first character of a 5,000-character memory, is 0000; the last address is 4999.

In Figure 11-1, 7,912 is stored in position numbers 2401–2404. Number

2401 is the address of digit 7; 2402, the address of digit 9; 2403, of digit 1; and 2404, of digit 2.

Picture a large bank of post-office boxes. Each of the boxes has a number on it and is assigned to a particular individual. A person receives his mail by going to the box which bears his assigned number, or address. It should be noted that the address is not the mail it contains, but merely a location number to aid the owner in finding his mail. Computer memories are similar in structure. Each character in storage is assigned an address. This address has nothing to do with the information it represents.

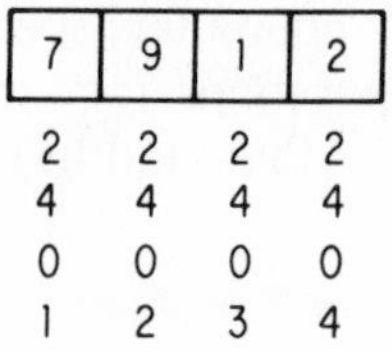

7	9	1	2
2	2	2	2
4	4	4	4
0	0	0	0
1	2	3	4

FIG. 11-1.

Computer memories are divided into two basic categories: character-oriented and word-oriented memories. Most of the early computers had memories which were divided into sections called "words." Each word had a location number, and contained enough bits of binary digits to hold 10 or perhaps 11 numeric positions (the word-size was determined by the manufacturer). These machines lent themselves easily to mathematical or scientific problems, since a word containing a large number could be manipulated as rapidly as one containing a small number. As most scientific and engineering problems deal with a wide range of numbers and usually do not deal with alphabetic information, word machines fit the need of these problems most conveniently.

The inconvenience of programming word-oriented machines for business data processing led to the development of the "character-oriented" computer. In a character-oriented computer, addresses do not refer to a group of positions, but only to one position, so that field sizes may vary from one character to many. Memory can accommodate fields just as they appear on a punched card, as a string of characters divided into fields of various sizes.

Generally speaking, word-oriented machines are best suited for scientific or mathematical applications; character-oriented memories appear to be more efficient for business data-processing applications, although either type of application can be performed on both types of computers. Ideally, a combination of word and character memories would be best. The newer computers are utilizing such memories in an attempt to consolidate both types of problems on the same general-purpose machine. There appear to be definite economical advantages to such an arrangement.

Types of Internal Memory Devices

Early computers. Early in computer development, there were two basic primary-storage devices: Acoustic Delay Line (for example, Univac I) and Electrostatic Storage (for example, the IBM 701 and 702). The methods of these machines were considered adequate for their time, but have been replaced by less expensive, faster, and more reliable types of machines.

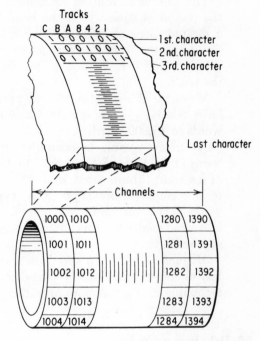

FIG. 11-2. Schematic of magnetic drum.

With the earlier computers, the magnetic drum was a basic storage device. The drum is a cylinder coated with iron oxide, a substance which can maintain a magnetic field. The drum is divided into strips around the circumference called bands; each band is divided into words (Figure 11-2). Think of a large ashcan which has been divided into bands by taking lengths of magnetic tape, such as that used in a tape recorder, and taping the ends together around the can. The words then could be chalked off for proper size. The brownish covering of magnetic tape is similar to the iron oxide used in coating a computer memory drum. Recording information on the bands is done by devices which turn "bits" (binary digits) on or off in BCD or alpha fashion. These codes are explained under "Data Representation" in Chapter 12.

Along the vertical length of the drum, there are a series of devices called read-write heads, one for each band on the drum. Whereas the heads remain stationary, the drums commonly revolve at speeds in excess of 1,500 revolutions per minute. If the computer desires to obtain some information from the drum, it specifies a particular address (band and word on the drum). Since the drum rotates, the desired information may not be immediately available. In fact, it might have just passed the read-write head, in which case the computer must wait one complete revolution before it can obtain the data. On the other hand, the information may be just coming up to the head, and therefore be immediately available.

This period of waiting for information is called "access time"; that is, it is the period of time which the head is required to wait before it can obtain a desired piece of information. Since access time varies with the position of the drum, the term "average access time" is often heard, and usually will be equal to half a revolution unless there is more than one read-write head on the band.

Magnetic drums have the advantage of high capacity and low cost, but have relatively slow speeds. Capacities in common machines go from 220 words to 64,000 words. Costs vary according to size and access time. Timing plays an active role in computer discussions. Modern computers process in terms of fractions of a second. The first level is called a *millisecond*, or 1/1000 of a second (abbreviated, ms). The next level is a *microsecond*, or 1/1,000,000 of a second (abbreviated, μs). Typically, the logic of modern computers works in microseconds. Manufacturers of the most expensive computers have also produced computers that process data in *nanoseconds* (1/1,000,000,000 of a second).

Magnetic cores. To speed up access time and to make it the same regardless of the location of any particular information in storage, another storage technique is in common use: the magnetic core (Figure 11-4). Magnetic

FIG. 11-3. Drum storage unit.

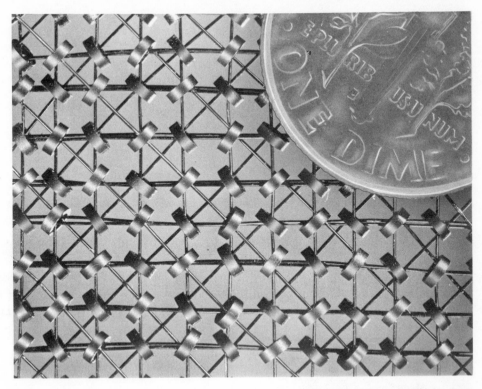

FIG. 11-4. Plane of magnetic cores.

cores are similar to tiny doughnuts. They are ferrite rings capable of being magnetized in one of two states. Each core is equivalent to a bit. Combinations of these cores, strung together, represent numbers or other characters in the same manner as those on a magnetic drum.

Magnetization, or polarity, in the core is made either clockwise or counterclockwise. By convention, when magnetized clockwise, the core is said to be tuned "on" or to represent a binary "one." When magnetized counterclockwise, the core is said to be "off," representing a binary "zero." In order to induce magnetization, or change direction of polarity, the cores are strung on ultra-thin wires, forming grids or "planes." An additional wire runs through the core for the purpose of "reading" its direction of polarity (Figure 11-5).

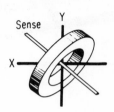

FIG. 11-5.

Electric current passing through each core is able to set and "read" the status of its polarity. The direction of polarity will depend on the direction of the current in the two wires that cross in the center of the core. This bistable nature of the core network

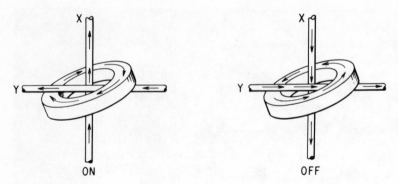

ON   OFF

FIG. 11-6.

enables it to flip from one direction of polarity to the other quite easily by changing the direction of the electricity in the wires (Figure 11-6).

Cores are set up in the form of planes connected to the central processor. The number of planes varies with the size and cost of the computer, but they are stacked in a series to form a basic module of memory (Figure 11-7).

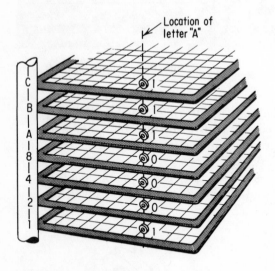

Location of letter "A"

FIG. 11-7. Schematic of character in storage—even parity.

Computer capacity often may be increased simply by adding new memory modules to the same computer.

Core memory is referred to as "non-volatile," meaning that once information is placed in core memory, it remains there until new information replaces it. Further, there is no physical wear on a core since there are no moving or rotating parts to cause friction, as is the case with a drum.

In addition to the foregoing advantages of permanent storage of data and durability of cores, other major advantages of core memories include their compact size, low power consumption, low heat dissipation, and adaptability to word- or character-oriented computers.

Parity checking. In fast core memories, one method of checking takes the form of an extra bit, called a "parity bit." The parity bit serves to check whether bits changed accidentally (Figure 11-7).

A manufacturer using a fixed number of binary bits to code data may decide arbitrarily to set an even number of bits to represent any given character. Codes using an even number of "one-bits" are called *even parity*. Codes using an odd number of "one-bits" are called *odd parity*. For instance, decimal-digit one (1) is coded 0000001. This representation satisfies the requirements of odd parity, since the number of one-bits that stand for digit "one" is odd. However, in even-parity coding, another "one" must be added in the parity bit (left bit) to make the total number of one bits even (therefore, 1000001).

Consequently, in this particular system, any time information is received, the parity bit is turned on or left off, as the case may be, based on what character is represented. Assuming that the information in memory is all "even parity," the wiring logic immediately discovers the error whenever a single bit in any character is dropped or an extra bit is picked up.

One must consider the importance of accuracy in computers. In listening to the radio or listening to music played from a reel of tape, the absence of a few sound "bits" is barely noticeable. Fidelity is important, but not crucial. In computers, however, accuracy is both important and utterly crucial. The loss of one bit of information can cause distortion in processing. The use of parity bits aids in detecting errors in data representation.

Thin film. The most recently marketed computer memory is thin film. Cores are being made smaller and smaller, and are being strung closer and closer together, but as this happens, there are some difficulties with respect to practicability and cost of wiring these tiny cores. The latest thin-film memories are now in operation with access times of 0.4 microseconds (Figure 11-8).

One of the newest thin-film memories consists of a 2.7 in. × 1.7 in. glass plane, .008 in. thick. On this small glass are rectangles of a nickel ferrite substance which are 1,200 angstroms thick (one angstrom is one one-hundred millionth of a centimeter). On this small plane, there is room for 768 rectangles, each representing one bit of storage, or a total capacity of 128 character positions of memory.

When thin-film planes were first being made, they were done by hand. If one bit was not up to standard, the entire plane had to be discarded. Consequently, the initial price of a plane was about a dollar per bit. With new techniques of vacuum depositing, the present cost has brought the thin-film memory into a practical price range. Undoubtedly, there will be further improvements and miniaturization of the films in the future.

Future devices hold a great deal in store. Since the size of a particular

FIG. 11-8. A thin film memory—with its developer, Dr. Sidney Reubens
(courtesy Univac Division, Sperry Rand Corp.).

computer memory often is based on the practical cost for the system, and since it is desirable to have more memory than is made available, a cheaper method of primary storage is constantly being sought. Users of data processing equipment are unwilling to sacrifice speed for a reduction in cost, in that it would be useless to take a step back to the comparatively slow speed of the magnetic drum.

Cryogenic Memories. The latest development involves *cryogenics,* a term derived from a word dealing with the study of cold temperatures. A cryogenic memory is a superconducting memory set at a very low temperature. It is both extremely fast and small. It is now considered too expensive to be marketed competitively.

GLOSSARY OF TERMS

ACCESS TIME: 1. The time interval between the instant at which data are called for from a storage device and the instant delivery is completed, i.e., the read time. 2. The time interval between the instant at which data are requested to be stored and the instant at which storage is completed, i.e., the write time.

ADDRESS: 1. An identification, as represented by a name, label, or number, for a register, location in storage, or any other data source or destination such as the location of a station in a communication network. 2. Loosely, any part of an instruction that specifies the location of an operand for the instruction.

ANALOG COMPUTER: A computer which represents variables by physical analogies. Thus any computer which solves problems by translating physical conditions such as flow, temperature, pressure, angular position, or voltage into related mechanical or electrical quantities and uses mechanical or electrical equivalent circuits as an analog for the physical phenomenon being investigated. In general, it is a computer which uses an analog for each variable and produces analogs as output. Thus an analog computer measures continuously whereas a digital computer counts discretely.

AUXILIARY STORAGE: Storage which is outside the central-processing unit but is controlled by it.

BINARY: 1. Pertaining to a characteristic or property involving a selection, choice, or condition in which there are two possibilities. 2. Pertaining to the number representation system with a radix of two.

BIT: 1. An abbreviation of *bi*nary dig*it*. 2. A single character in a binary number. 3. A single pulse in a group of pulses. 4. A unit of information capacity of a storage device.

CHARACTER: An elementary mark or event that is used to represent data. A character is often in the form of a graphic spatial arrangement of connected or adjacent strokes.

COMPUTER WORD: A sequence of bits or characters treated as a unit. Synonymous with machine word.

CRYOGENICS: The study and use of devices utilizing properties of materials near absolute zero in temperature.

DIGITAL COMPUTER: A computer that operates on discrete data by performing arithmetic and logic processes on these data. Contrast with analog computer.

GENERAL-PURPOSE COMPUTER: A computer that is designed to solve a wide class of problems.

MAGNETIC CORE: A configuration of magnetic material that is, or is intended to be, placed in a spatial relationship to current-carrying conductors and whose magnetic properties are essential to its use. It may be used to concentrate an induced magnetic field as in a transformer induction coil, or armature, to retain a magnetic polarization for the purpose of storing data, or for its nonlinear properties as in a logic element. It may be made of such material as iron, iron oxide, or ferrite, and in such shapes as wires and tapes.

MAGNETIC DRUM: A right circular cylinder with a magnetic surface on which data can be stored by selective magnetization of portions of the curved surface.

MEMORY: 1. Pertaining to a device into which data can be entered, in which it can be held, and from which it can be retrieved at a later time. 2. Loosely, any device that can store data.

MICROSECOND: One millionth of a second.

MILLISECOND: One thousandth of a second.

NANOSECOND: One billionth of a second.

PARITY CHECK: A check that tests whether the number of ones (or zeros) in an array of binary digits is odd or even. Synonymous with odd-even check.

PROCESS: A general term covering such terms as assemble, compile, generate, interpret, and compute.

SPECIAL-PURPOSE COMPUTER: A computer that is designed to solve a restricted class of problems.

QUESTIONS FOR REVIEW

1. What are some of the chief limitations of a punched-card data-processing system?
2. What are some of the unique characteristics of the punched-card and the computer systems?
3. List and explain briefly the primary elements of an electronic data-processing system.
4. What are the three basic types of storage? Explain.
5. List and explain the basic components of a digital computer.
6. What is an address? A character? Give an example to illustrate each.
7. If the amount 946742 is stored in primary storage in location numbers 801 to 806, what is the address of digit 7? 2? 9?
8. What are the two basic primary storage devices? Explain.
9. Describe in detail the magnetic drum.
10. Describe a magnetic core. How does it store information?
11. What is meant by parity check? What is the difference between even- and odd-parity check?
12. What is thin-film memory? Explain.
13. List and describe briefly the basic types of computers.
14. What is the difference between an analog and a digital computer?
15. What is the difference between a special- and a general-purpose computer?

chapter

12

Coded-Data
Representation

To simplify the handling of data electronically, it was important to develop methods of coding decimal and alphabetic information into a form that could be used by computers. Just as punched cards are a form of coded information employing one of two states (either a hole or no hole in a particular position), so electronic computers employ the state of a particular location to represent information. This may be indicated by the direction of a magnetic field, by an open or closed relay, or by a ferrite core magnetized clockwise or counter-clockwise. Such schemes of "yes or no," "on or off," and "zero or one" introduce the important concepts of the binary numbering system. Combinations of the zero- and 1-symbols (bits) are basic to the representation of digits, letters, and/or special characters in primary storage.

Numerical Data Representation

For the user, especially in business data processing, input to the computer is written or printed in standard decimal or alphabetic form. It should be remembered, however, that these characters are first converted into codes by the computer, based on the binary numbering system used within the computer. Next, the coded data is reconverted to decimal and alphabetic characters when printing the output results. Although few people except the micro-programmer need to work in terms of these binary codes, it is desirable to understand something about them and their ability to represent data in computer storage.

To understand the binary system, a review of the basic characteristics of the decimal system would be helpful. Our decimal system probably is used because man's fingers are the most convenient tools nature has provided for counting. The decimal system involves the use of ten different digits: 0 through 9. To represent any amount greater than 9, the proper decimal numbers are positioned side by side. Each position has a value which is a multiple of 10, as these digits are placed from right to left. In Figure 12-1, each box represents one decimal digit and its appropriate power. The decimal value 1 5 6 2 3,

10^4	10^3	10^2	10^1	10^0
10,000	1000	100	10	1
1	5	6	2	3

FIG. 12-1.

then, is the sum of each of the individual numbers after each has been multiplied by the value of its position:

$$
\begin{array}{rrr}
3 \times & 1 = & 3 \\
2 \times & 10 = & 20 \\
6 \times & 100 = & 600 \\
5 \times & 1000 = & 5000 \\
1 \times & 10000 = & 10000 \\
\hline
& & 15623
\end{array}
$$

The answer might seem obvious, since we are accustomed to dealing with decimal numbers. This technique will be helpful in understanding binary figures, however.

In binary, the only acceptable numbers are 0 and 1. Since "bi" means *two*, such a system is called *bi*nary. With these two symbols we can represent the equivalent of any decimal digit by placing them in certain mathematical combinations. The binary numbering system lends itself most easily and economically to the design and function of digital computers.

Decimal	Binary	Decimal	Binary
1	1	11	1011
2	10	12	1100
3	11	13	1101
4	100	14	1110
5	101	15	1111
6	110	16	10000
7	111	17	10001
8	1000	18	10010
9	1001	19	10011
10	1010	20	10100

FIG. 12-2.

To represent decimal data greater than 1 in binary, the next higher binary number is formed by adding 1 to its predecessor (Figure 12-2). In other words, from right to left, the value of each binary digit is a greater power of two (2^0, 2^1, 2^2, etc.) just as the decimal system increases by multiples of ten. In Figure 12-3, the binary powers of two are placed from right to left. To represent decimal amount 10 in binary, for instance, digit 1 is placed in the box of the approximate binary power, as shown in Figure 12-3; that is, it is determined as follows:

binary power		binary bit		decimal equivalent
8	X	1	=	8
plus				
4	X	0	=	0
plus				
2	X	1	=	2
plus				
1	X	0	=	0
				10

32	16	8	4	2	1

(before)

32	16	8	4	2	1
		1	0	1	0

(after)

FIG. 12-3.

As mentioned earlier, most electronic data-processing equipment operates in a binary mode. The devices used in computers are essentially in either of two states: conducting or nonconducting. This stage is analogous to an electric light bulb which is turned either "ON" or "OFF." It is easy to realize, then, that when the device in computer storage is conducting, it has the effect of representing one binary bit; and when it is nonconducting, it represents a zero bit. For example, in Figure 12-4, decimal value 5 is represented by two light bulbs turned on in binary place values 4 and 1. That is, 5 in decimal is determined by the sum of:

FIG. 12-4.

$$4 \times 1 = 4$$

and

$$1 \times 1 = 1$$
$$\overline{5} \text{ (or 0 1 0 1 in binary)}$$

A popular method of converting decimal to binary is to divide the decimal amount successively by two (Figure 12-5). The remainder of each of the suc-

2		85		Remainder
2		42	+	1
2		21	+	0
2		10	+	1
2		5	+	0
2		2	+	1
2		1	+	0
2		0	+	1

FIG. 12-5. Decimal to binary conversion.

Read up

85 in decimal, then, is equivalent to: 1010101 in binary

cessive divisions, reading up, constitutes the binary equivalent. For example:

Binary-to-decimal conversion follows exactly the opposite routine. That is, to convert a binary value to a decimal equivalent, each binary digit (beginning at the left) is multiplied by two, and its product is added to the number until the entire binary amount is converted. For example, in converting binary amount 1 1 1 0 1 0, we proceed as follows:

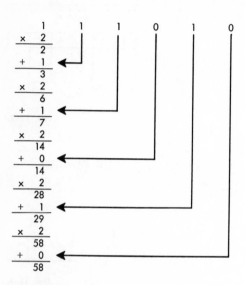

Therefore, 111010 in binary is equivalent to 58 in decimal

FIG. 12-6. Binary to decimal conversion.

Some computers, particularly those which are constructed chiefly for scientific and engineering purposes, represent numbers in a pure binary fashion. In such cases, decimal input is converted to binary, manipulated, and usually converted back into decimal for output. A disadvantage of binary over decimal numbering is that bits (binary digits) require more positions; however, without binary, decimal numbers would have to be represented by ten different quantities of electricity, rather than a simple "on-off" state. This would present many problems of control and reliability to the engineers.

Binary is a way to represent decimal digits without being concerned about the quantity of electricity. On a punched card, for example, the numbers 0 through 9 are represented by a hole in a particular position in the column. A similar approach would involve the use of 10 light bulbs, each one representing a decimal number. When one of the lights is turned on, it represents the particular digit for which it is reserved (Figure 12-7). By installing these "columns" side by side, one could represent a large decimal number.

Figure 12-8 shows that decimal-digit 17 would be represented by two columns of bulbs in straight decimal representation, as compared to a binary representation of the same amount. Whereas the binary code requires five places (five

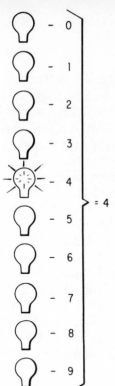

= 4

FIG. 12-7.

Binary	Decimal	
●0000●	00	0
	●0	1
	00	2
	00	3
	00	4
	00	5
	00	6
	0●	7
	00	8
	00	9

FIG. 12-8.

light bulbs) to represent decimal value 17, the decimal system (although it uses only two places) requires 20. From the human point of view, it might be better to use the extra "light bulbs" and eliminate the binary-to-decimal conversion, but it should be remembered that this conversion is done automatically by a computer at a great rate of speed. For simplicity, the filled-in zero's in Figure 12-8 represent "on" light bulbs.

Binary-Coded Decimal: 8-4-2-1

The most common method of reconciling the decimal-versus-binary conflict has been to represent each decimal digit with a binary code and to avoid the task of having to convert the number as a whole into binary. Early computers were based on coded combinations of the binary and decimal numbering systems, called Binary Coded Decimal (BCD). These codes represent each decimal digit by a fixed number of binary bits. The representation is detected by the presence of a 1-bit in the appropriate box, or level. Figure 12-9 shows the most popular type of BCD code, based on four binary bits. These are more than adequate to represent any decimal digit (0 through 9); that is, with each of the four positions containing a 1-bit (turned on), the maximum value would be $(8 \times 1) + (4 \times 1) + (2 \times 1) +$

8	
4	
2	
1	

FIG. 12-9. The BCD code.

8	1
4	1
2	1
1	1

FIG. 12-10.

$(1 \times 1) = 15$ (Figure 12-10). See Figure 12-14 for the BCD table.

The 4-bit BCD code is used to represent one decimal digit at a time. If two or more decimal digits are represented, two or more 4-bit combinations are required: one to represent the unit's position, another to represent the ten's position, and so on. For instance, decimal amount 271 is shown in figure 12-11. Therefore, the decimal value can be determined in terms of powers of ten by the position of the bit in the BCD code. A bit in the top position is worth eight; the next, four; then, two; and the bottom position, one.

BCD   Decimal

	2	7	1
8	0	0	0
4	0	1	0
2	1	1	0
1	0	1	1

FIG. 12-11.

It should be remembered that the programmer does not have to convert from the BCD to decimal or vice versa. The wired logic built into the computer circuitry does the translation. When a report is to be printed out, the Binary Coded Decimal numbers are automatically retranslated into printed information.

Excess-Three

The excess-three system is another type of BCD code which is formed by adding 3 to the decimal digit and then forming its BCD equivalent. That is, the coded decimal is three greater than the actual decimal number. For instance, the excess-three code of decimal-digit 6 is formed by adding 3 to 6, totaling 9; and then the BCD equivalent $(1\,0\,0\,1)$ is used. Figure 12-12 shows a complete list of the excess-three codes for 10 decimal digits (also see Figure 12-14 for a related listing of the same code).

Decimal digit	Excess 3
0	0 0 1 1
1	0 1 0 0
2	0 1 0 1
3	0 1 1 0
4	0 1 1 1
5	1 0 0 0
6	1 0 0 1
7	1 0 1 0
8	1 0 1 1
9	1 1 0 0

FIG. 12-12. The excess-three code.

Biquinary Code

The biquinary code makes use of seven possible bits of information. Two of these bits are known as the "binary" portion of the code and have the assigned values of 0 and 5. The remaining five bits are known as the "quinary" portion of the code and have the assigned values of 4, 3, 2, 1, and 0. Any decimal digit is represented by the presence of two 1-bits: one in the binary portion and one in the quinary portion of the code (Figure 12-14).

The advantage of this system is that arithmetic operations are relatively easy and checking the internal circuit for validity is simplified by the constant presence of exactly two bits.

Two-Out-of-Five Code

The two-out-of-five system uses a total of five bits to represent a decimal digit. Bit positions have the values 0, 1, 2, 3, 6 (as opposed to the 1, 2, 4, 8, type BCD). Figure 12-13 shows the numbers in this system and their decimal equivalents. Note that decimal-digit zero is represented by an arbitrary code of two bits (one of one) and (one of two). Again, an internal checking device is simplified. In each character, there must be exactly two 1-bits for representing any decimal number.

Decimal Equivalent	Two-out-of-five binary code
	6 3 2 1 0
0	0 0 1 1 0
1	0 0 0 1 1
2	0 0 1 0 1
3	0 1 0 0 1
4	0 1 0 1 0
5	0 1 1 0 0
6	1 0 0 0 1
7	1 0 0 1 0
8	1 0 1 0 0
9	1 1 0 0 0

FIG. 12-13. The two-out-of-five code.

Octal

Used particularly in scientific-type computers, the octal (or base-eight) system is another popular coding system. It is quite similar to the 8-4-2-1 BCD, except that it does not carry the fourth bit (value 8) of the BCD code. Instead, it uses only the 1-, 2-, and 4-bits for number representation. The three bits (when each bit consists of one) represent a total of 7. In the octal system, therefore, there are only the digits 0 through 7, and 8 and 9 are never used.

To represent decimal-digit 8 or more, another position is added to the left of its predecessor, thus increasing by a multiple of eight, compared to the decimal system, which increases by a multiple of 10, or the binary system, which increases by a multiple of two (see Figure 12-14).

Decimal Digit	Binary	Octal	8421 BCD	Excess 3	Biquinary 50 43210
0	0	0	0000	0011	01 00001
1	1	1	0001	0100	01 00010
2	10	2	0010	0101	01 00100
3	11	3	0011	0110	01 01000
4	100	4	0100	0111	01 10000
5	101	5	0101	1000	10 00001
6	110	6	0110	1001	10 00010
7	111	7	0111	1010	10 00100
8	1000	10	1000	1011	10 01000
9	1001	11	1001	1100	10 10000

FIG. 12-14. Numerical coding systems.

In manual conversion, an octal coded number may be converted into decimal by multiplying each octal digit by 8 (beginning with the left-most digit) and adding its product to the digit to the right until the whole number is included. For instance, 721 in octal is converted to decimal as follows:

$$
\begin{array}{r}
7 \quad 2 \quad 1 \\
\times\ 8 \\
\hline
56 \\
+\ 2 \\
\hline
58 \\
\times\ 8 \\
\hline
464 \\
+\ 1 \\
\hline
465
\end{array}
$$

Therefore, 721 in octal is equal to 465 in decimal.

Another way of expressing 721_8 is as follows: $(7 \times 8^2) + (2 \times 8^1) + (1 \times 8^0)$.

Octal coded numbers may be easily converted into binary by assigning a fixed number of three binary digits to each octal digit. For instance:

Octal number   7   2   1   is converted to binary as follows: 111   010   001

A binary-coded number, on the other hand, is converted into octal simply by dividing the binary value (beginning from the right digit) into an equal portion of three bits each. If the last (left) digit (or digits) do not total 3 in number, add zero(s). For example, binary number 1 1 0 0 1 is converted into octal as follows:

Binary   011   001

Octal   3   1

It is easy to see, then, that the octal system provides a simple "shorthand" for representing long pure binary numbers. Another advantage is that numbers may be represented by fewer bits than BCD. The decimal number 357895674 will take 36 bits in BCD representation (9 decimal digits × 4 bits each), while the octal equivalent of this number is 2525206626, which is ten digits and can be represented by only 30 bits (10 digits × 3 bits each).

Alphanumeric Data Representation

In modern electronic data processing, the need for the central processor to represent alphabetic as well as numeric information has become very important. To be able to do this, manufacturers have settled on an internal representation, a 6-bit alphanumeric code system, which is similar in most computers. This code utilizes a six-bit grouping called a *frame*, in which the lower four bits are the BCD 8, 4, 2, and 1. These four bits alone are sufficient to represent numeric data, but to represent alphabetic data, two more bits are added (bits A and B). Their combination with 8, 4, 2, and 1 in forming alphabetic characters is similar in approach to alphabetic coding in the punched card (through the use of the zone-punching positions). Each computer has its own coding scheme for combining the A- and B- (zone) bits with the numeric bits to form alphanumeric characters.

In one popular code (Figure 12-15), letters *A* through *Z* are represented as follows: letters *A* through *I* are represented by the A- and B-zone bits, in addition to numeric bits 1 through 9. Letters *J* through *R* are represented by the B-zone bit only, in addition to numeric bits 1 through 9. Letters *S* through *Z* are represented by the A-zone bit, along with numeric bits 2 through 9. The

FIG. 12-15. Alphanumeric data representation.

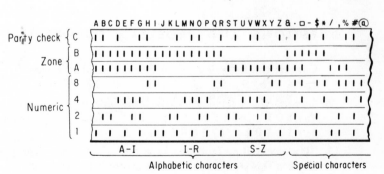

A- and B-bits together perform the same function as the 12-punch in a card; the B-bit is the same as the 11-punch; and the A-bit is similar to the 0-punch.

Special characters representing blank, asterisk, comma, slash, etc., are arbitrarily established by the computer manufacturer and are coded in such a way as to distinguish them from one another. The seventh bit (C-bit) is added in this scheme for parity checking.

To summarize, the foregoing presentation shows that although the user is interested only in decimal numbers as output, the internal operation of electronic computers is based on digits in various binary forms. Having a comprehensive understanding of these forms would give a more meaningful conception of the output realized.

GLOSSARY OF TERMS

BINARY-CODED DECIMAL: Pertaining to a decimal notation in which the individual decimal digits are each represented by a group of binary digits, e.g., in the 8-4-2-1 binary-coded decimal notation, the number twenty-three is represented as 0010 0011 whereas in binary notation, twenty-three is represented as 10111.

BIQUINARY CODE: A two part code in which each decimal digit is represented by the sum of the two parts, one of which has the value of decimal zero or five and the other the values zero through four. The abacus and soroban both use biquinary codes.

OCTAL: 1. Pertaining to a characteristic or property involving a selection, choice, or condition in which there are eight possibilities. 2. Pertaining to the number representation system with a radix of eight.

TWO-OUT-OF-FIVE CODE: A code in which each decimal digit is represented by five binary digits of which two are one kind (e.g., ones) and three are the other kind (e.g., zero).

QUESTIONS AND PROBLEMS FOR REVIEW

1. Convert the following values from decimal to binary:
   (a) 4   (b) 9   (c) 11   (d) 17   (e) 25   (f) 64   (g) 126.
2. Convert the following values from binary to decimal:
   (a) 1 0 1   (b) 1 0 0 0 1   (c) 1 0 0 1   (d) 1 1 1   (e) 1 1 1 0 1   (f) 1 0 1 1 1
   (g) 1 1 1 0 1   (h) 1 0 0 1 1 0 0.
3. "The decimal system uses base ten whereas the binary system uses base two." Explain this statement. Give an example to illustrate.
4. What is a "coding system"?
5. What is the difference between straight binary and binary-coded decimal representation?

6. Explain the two-out-of-five code. How is it different from the biquinary code? Give an example.

7. What is the excess-3 code? In what respect is it similar to the BCD code?

8. Show how the following values are represented in (1) straight binary, (2) BCD, (3) two-out-of-five, (4) the excess-3, and (5) the biquinary code: (a) 3 (b) 4 (c) 8 (d) 13 (e) 89 (f) 98 (g) 106 (h) 890.

9. What is the octal code? Represent decimal values 62 and 74 in octal.

chapter

13

The Arithmetic
and Control Units

Much has been said regarding the role and function of primary storage in electronic data processing. For it to perform an active and effective role in a computer system, supporting devices such as the arithmetic and control units are integrated to achieve the correct result. Harmonious coordination between these devices is imperative since neither device is capable of working alone. Primary storage has been shown to store the data being processed and retain the results until needed; however, in order to get these results, the arithmetic unit must be both present and active for the execution of the various required arithmetic operations.

Parallel Adder

The arithmetic unit is defined as that part of the computer which performs the basic arithmetic functions of addition, subtraction, multiplication, and division under the direction of the control unit. It is composed of adder circuits, electronic devices which perform all arithmetic and logical operations. The adder is like the mechanical wheels of an adding machine, except that computer adders are electronic, rather than mechanical.

Adders are of two kinds: serial and parallel. Since a fixed word-length computer deals with information in groups of several digits at a time, it is necessary to have an adder which is capable of (1) adding a full word of

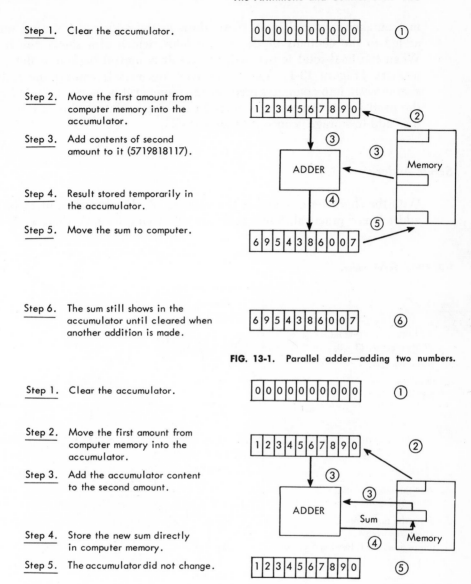

Step 1.   Clear the accumulator.

Step 2.   Move the first amount from
computer memory into the
accumulator.

Step 3.   Add contents of second
amount to it (5719818117).

Step 4.   Result stored temporarily in
the accumulator.

Step 5.   Move the sum to computer.

Step 6.   The sum still shows in the
accumulator until cleared when
another addition is made.

FIG. 13-1.   Parallel adder—adding two numbers.

Step 1.   Clear the accumulator.

Step 2.   Move the first amount from
computer memory into the
accumulator.

Step 3.   Add the accumulator content
to the second amount.

Step 4.   Store the new sum directly
in computer memory.

Step 5.   The accumulator did not change.

FIG. 13-2.   Add to storage concept.

digits to another full word of digits; (2) allowing the result to be accumulated at the same time; and (3) taking care of the carry-over from one decimal position to another. Adders which add several bits simultaneously are called parallel adders.

In addition to a parallel adder, a computer also includes an electronic device called an *accumulator*. Its function is to store values (sums) temporarily. For example, when two numbers are added, an accumulator first is cleared and the first number is stored in it. Next, through the adder, the second number is added to the contents of the accumulator, which also shows the final sum. When the final total is reached, the result is moved back into the computer memory (Figure 13-1). Later improvements in this concept move the final sum directly into computer memory the moment it is realized, thus eliminating the need for its temporary storage in the accumulator. This is referred to as the "add-to-storage" concept (Figure 13-2).

Serial Adder

With the character-oriented or the variable word-length computer, the parallel adder is not practical. Since fields are of varying lengths, there is no require-

FIG. 13-3. Serial adder.

Step 1.

1. Add the two low-order digits together (3 + 8)
2. Store the sum.
3. Note the carry following step 1.

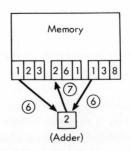

Step 2.

4. Add the next two digits (2 + 3) and the carry of 1.
5. Store the sum with carry from step 1. (Note carry off following Step 2)

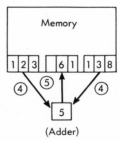

Step 3.

6. Add the last two digits (1 + 1).
7. Store the sum

ment for a specific number of digits involving the adder or the accumulator.

Essentially, a serial adder is a one-digit adder. When two fields are to be added together, the low-order (right-hand) position of the first field is put into the adder. The low-order position of the second field is added to it. The sum is put back directly into computer memory in the low-order position of the area reserved for storing the sum. The arithmetic unit continues this process until all the digits of the two fields (amounts) have been added (Figure 13-3). The serial adder utilizes the "add-to-storage" concept, and makes the need for an accumulator unnecessary.

Binary Addition

The foregoing discussion illustrates the arithmetic unit's capability of adding decimal values through the use of adders and accumulators. Binary addition also is feasible since the electronic state of the computer would provide for the one-versus-zero state.

Addition is performed on binary digits following the same basic rules as those used in the decimal system. It should be noted that a "carry" occurs in binary when a total exceeds one; a carry occurs in decimal after 9 is reached. The rules for binary addition are as follows:

$$0 + 0 = 0$$
$$1 + 0 = 1$$
$$0 + 1 = 1$$
$$1 + 1 = 0 \text{ with a carry-over of 1}$$

For example, the binary addition of 1 0 1 0 and 1 0 1 1 would be performed as follows:

Binary	Decimal
1 0 1 0	10
1 0 1 1	11
1 0 1 0 1	21

The sum of 1 0 1 0 (ten) and 1 0 1 1 (eleven) in binary, then, is equal to 1 0 1 0 1, or 21 in decimal.

Decimal Subtraction

Most digital computers perform binary subtraction first by complementing the subtrahend (lower number) and then adding the complement to the minuend (upper number). This may be best understood by comparing it to decimal subtraction using complements.

There are two complements of interest associated with a decimal digit: one complement is identified by the base of the decimal system, less one. It is called the nine's complement. The other is related to the base of the decimal system, and is called the ten's complement.

Nine's Complement Method—Decimal System

In the nine's system, each decimal digit in the subtrahend is first subtracted from 9. The nine's complement of digit 5 is 4; of digit 6, 3; of digit 7, 2. Subtraction proceeds by adding the complemented subtrahend to the minuend, as shown in Figure 13-4.

However, if no carry is realized in the high-order position, it means that the remainder is in complement form and is also negative. A recomplement is necessary to obtain the true remainder. For example, in subtracting 6 − 8, we proceed as follows:

Step 1. Complement the subtrahend and add.

Before	*After*	
6	6	Minuend
− 8	+ 1	Complemented subtrahend
	7	Remainder in complement form

Step 2. Since there is no carry, 7 must be recomplemented and a minus (−) sign added.

FIG. 13-4.

	Minuend	+ 3 8 9 5	The manual
		−	subtraction
			method.
	Subtrahend	+ 6 4 2	
		+ 3 2 5 3	Remainder

Step 1. Determine the nine's complement of the subtrahend and add.

		BEFORE	*AFTER*
Minuend		+ 3 8 9 5	+ 3 8 9 5
		−	+
Subtrahend		+ 0 6 4 2	+ 9 3 5 7
			1 3 2 5 2

(9999 − 0642 = 9357)

Note: For complementing purposes, both fields used in subtraction must be of equal length. If one field is shorter than another, zero(s) are added in the high-order positions to equalize the length.

Step 2. The end-around carry (encircled) is added to the lower-order position:

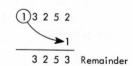

3 2 5 3   Remainder

$$9$$
$$- 7$$
$$\overline{-2}\text{ The true remainder}$$

Therefore, $6 - 8 = -2$.

Ten's Complement Method—Decimal System

In the 10's complement method, a similar procedure is followed: that is, the 10's complement of the subtrahend is determined and added to the minuend, replacing any end-around carry with a plus (+) sign. The 10's complement of digit 6 is 4; of 7 is 3; of 8 is 2; etc. For example, suppose we wish to subtract 17 from 25, using the 10's complement method. We proceed as follows:

Manual Method

Minuend	25
Subtrahend	− 17
	08 Remainder

Step 1. Determine the ten's complement of the subtrahend.

$$(100 - 17 = 83)$$

Step 2. Add the complemented subtrahend to the minuend.

Minuend	25
	+ 83
	①08

Step 3. The encircled digit is a carry, and is changed to a plus (+) sign.

Minuend	25
Subtrahend	+ 83
	+ 08 True remainder

If no carry is realized, a recomplement of the remainder must be made and a negative sign added denoting a negative remainder. For example:

17 Minuend
− 25 Subtrahend   } The manual method of subtraction.
− 08

Step 1. Determine the ten's complement of the subtrahend.

$$(100 - 25 = 75)$$

Step 2. Add the complemented subtrahend to the minuend.

17 Minuend
+ 75 Complemented subtrahend
+ 92 Remainder in complement form

Step 3. Since there is no carry, the remainder should be complemented and a negative sign added, denoting that it is a negative remainder.

$(100 - 92 = 08)$ Adding the negative sign, 08 becomes −08.

Binary Subtraction

One's Complement Method—Binary System

Binary subtraction is performed by reversing the binary state of the subtrahend which gives us the one's complement, adding it to the minuend, and adding any resulting carry to the sum. For example, to subtract 1 0 0 1 (9) from 1 1 0 0 (12), we proceed as follows:

Step 1. Reverse the subtrahend to its opposite state. That is, all 1's are changed to 0's and all 0's changed to 1's. *This is the one's complement.*

	Binary	*Binary*
Decimal	*(before)*	*(after)*
12	1 1 0 0	1 1 0 0
09	1 0 0 1	0 1 1 0
$\overline{03}$		

Step 2. Add

$$
\begin{array}{r}
1\,1\,0\,0 \\
0\,1\,1\,0 \\
\hline
①0\,0\,1\,0
\end{array}
$$

Step 3. If a carry results in the high-order position, it is added to the unit's position, thus:
1 0 0 1 0 becomes

$$
\begin{array}{r}
①0\,0\,1\,0 \\
\longrightarrow 1 \\
\hline
+\,0\,0\,1\,1
\end{array}
$$

Two's Complement Method—Binary System

Binary subtraction may be performed by using the two's complement. As with the 10's complement method an end-around carry is replaced with a (+) sign. If no carry occurs the result must be recomplemented and given a minus sign. For example, suppose we wish to subtract 0101(5) from 1001(9) using the two's complement method. We proceed as follows:

Step 1. Determine the two's complement of the subtrahend.

$$(10000 - 0101) = 1011$$

	Binary	*Binary*
Decimal	*(before)*	*(after)*
9	1 0 0 1	1 0 0 1
− 5	0 1 0 1	1 0 1 1
$\overline{4}$		

Step 2. Add.

$$
\begin{array}{r}
1\,0\,0\,1 \\
1\,0\,1\,1 \\
\hline
①0\,1\,0\,0
\end{array}
$$

Step 3. The encircled digit is a carry, and is charged to a plus (+) sign.

$$
\begin{array}{r}
1\,0\,0\,1 \\
1\,0\,1\,1 \\
\hline
+\,0\,1\,0\,0
\end{array}
$$

If no carry is realized, the complement of the remainder must be taken with a negative sign added denoting a negative remainder. For example, to subtract 9 from 5:

Step 1. Determine the two's complement of the subtrahend.

$$(10000 - 1001) = 0111$$

Decimal	Binary (before)	Binary (after)
5	0 1 0 1	0 1 0 1
− 9	1 0 0 1	0 1 1 1
− 4		

Step 2. Add.

$$
\begin{array}{r}
0\,1\,0\,1 \\
0\,1\,1\,1 \\
\hline
1\,1\,0\,0
\end{array}
$$

Step 3. Since there is no carry the remainder should be recomplemented and given a negative sign.

$$(10000 - 1100) = 0100$$

Adding the negative sign, 0100 becomes −0100.

Decimal Multiplication

Multiplication simply is a series of additions, plus some shifting. Look at the following example:

Multiplicand	1 2 3
Multiplier	3 2

$$
\begin{array}{r}
2\,4\,6 \\
3\,6\,9 \\
\hline
3\,9\,3\,6 \quad \text{The product}
\end{array}
$$

Upon receiving the instruction to perform a multiplication, the arithmetic unit first takes the low-order digit of the multiplier (2) and adds the multiplicand to itself twice, arriving at 246. This sum is put aside temporarily. Second, the next high-order position of the multiplier (3) is used to determine the number of times the multiplicand will be added to itself. Each time the next high-order position of the multiplier is used (as in the case of the multiplier-digit 3), the multiplicand is shifted one position to the left, with a zero filling in on the right. Thus, the second operation in this example adds the multiplicand (which is now 1230) to itself three times, as indicated by the next position in the multiplier (3). This sum will be 3690. The first sum (246) plus the second sum (3690) gives the proper answer (3936).

Any two numbers, regardless of their size, may be multiplied. Each time a digit in the multiplier is used, the multiplicand has one more zero added to its right. Each time a new sum is developed, it is added to the previous one until all multiplier digits have been used.

Binary Multiplication

Binary multiplication follows the method used in decimal multiplication. The binary multiplication table is short and consists of four entries:

$$0 \times 0 = 0$$
$$1 \times 0 = 0$$
$$0 \times 1 = 0$$
$$1 \times 1 = 1$$

For example, 1 1 1 (seven) multiplied by 1 0 1 (five) equals 1 0 0 0 1 1, as follows:

	Decimal
1 1 1	7
1 0 1	× 5
‾‾‾‾‾	‾‾‾‾
1 1 1	35 Product
0 0 0	
1 1 1	
‾‾‾‾‾‾‾	
1 0 0 0 1 1 (35 in decimal)	

Decimal Division—The Decimal Method

Division is a combination of successive subtractions just as multiplication is a series of successive additions. In subtraction, however, there also is the use of the complementing process. Complementing must be done first, and then additions take place. However, assuming that complementing is done every time subtraction is made, division is shown as follows:

		No. of Subtractions
The manual division method.		
4 Quotient	20	
Divisor 5 ⟌ 20 Dividend	−5	1
20	‾‾‾	
‾‾	15	
00	−5	1
	‾‾‾	
	10	
	−5	1
	‾‾	
	5	
	−5	1
	‾‾	‾‾
	0	4

Binary Division

Like the decimal division method, binary division is performed on the basis of the following table:

$$0 \div 1 = 0$$
$$1 \div 1 = 1$$

For example:

```
        1001            9
  11 ⟌ 11011      3 ⟌ 27
       11               27
      ‾‾‾‾‾            ‾‾‾‾
      00011            00
         11
       ‾‾‾‾
       00
```

Logic

Another function of the arithmetic unit is to perform the logic of the computer system. It generally is accepted that one of the primary differences between a typical calculating device and a computer is the computer's logical ability. A computer's logic is relatively simple compared to the complex logical thinking of the human brain. However, the speed of the computer logic, plus its capacity for "remembering" its former steps in reaching a goal or problem solution, compensate for the basic simplicity of its logical operations and make it efficient in the processing of data.

Generally, logical decisions made by computers include the ability to tell (1) if two numbers or characters are equal or unequal, (2) if one number is greater or less than another, and (3) if a quantity is positive, negative, or zero. Decisions made by most computers are based on simple comparisons. For instance, if we have a deck of punched cards, each punched with digit 3 in column 1, we can direct the computer to check the presence of the punched digit in each card. Despite the fact that a computer does not "know" a 3 in the same manner we do, it still is able to "tell" us whether column 1 of each card has a 3 punched in it. To do this involves storing in the computer memory the proper instructions as a part of the program it receives.

A computer determines the equality of two values by comparison. Using the deck of cards in the previous example and assuming the storage of digit 3 in memory location 0006, the computer can be instructed to compare the content of column 1 of each card with that of address 0006 in memory. Further, based on the subtraction of one number from another, the computer can determine whether the remainder is negative or positive. If the result is negative, it can be concluded that the column containing the number is less than 3. If the remainder is zero, it indicates that both numbers (fields) are the same.

If the result is positive, the contents of the card column are greater than digit 3 in memory.

How does the computer compare values? The computer contains indicators (on-off bits used only by the arithmetic unit and not part of primary storage) which have special purposes. Generally, there is a "high-low" toggle (or indicator), "equal/unequal" indicator, "minus" indicator, and "zero/nonzero" indicator. When a computer is asked to test any of these functions (one function at a time), the appropriate indicator is set. The result determined by this setting may be used to provide the desired information.

The Control Unit

The third major part of the central processor is called the control unit. The control unit causes the arithmetic unit and primary storage to be used in a logical fashion. With every computer system, there is a prewired set of instructions, or commands. Electronic circuitry is provided for each of the functions desired in that particular system. For instance, there is an individual circuit to add, to subtract, to divide, to multiply, to compare, to test for plus or minus, etc. Each of these circuits is given an individual number, and the programmer is told what these numbers are. In computer terminology, they are called operation codes (or op-codes). This list of operation codes is furnished to the user by the manufacturer and differs from computer to computer. An operation code of 7 may mean for one computer to add, but it may mean for another computer to compare.

In dealing with the problem within the internal mechanism of a computer, two elements are stressed: the operation to be performed and the data upon which the operation will take place. The operation to be performed is called the *op-code;* the data are referred to as the *operand*. The sequence of instructions determines the manner in which the problem is to be solved. A complete list of instructions is called a *program*. People trained to write the computer instructions are called *programmers*. Since operation codes and primary storage vary from one computer to another, the actual format of the instruction varies also. Regardless of the computer system used, however, an instruction contains at least an operation code and a reference to an operand.

Registers

A register is a device in the computer which is used for storing temporarily a specific amount of information, an example of which is the accumulator (explained in Chapter 12). To illustrate the use of registers, assume the availability of a fixed word-length computer that holds ten BCD positions in each word and consists of 5,000 words. First it will be necessary to have some registers. In addition to an accumulator, another type of register called an "R-register" is used. The accumulator and the R-register each can hold ten digits. The R-register also may be used as an extension register; for example, multiplying

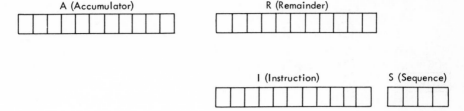

FIG. 13-5. Major registers in a hypothetical computer.

a 10-digit number by a 10-digit number produces a 20-digit result, thus utilizing the accumulator and the R-register. The accumulator holds the ten high-order (right-most) digits of the product; the R-register holds the ten low-order digits.

Assuming the use of the same computer, other registers also are needed. One is the Instruction Register (I-register), which retains each instruction (both operation codes and operand) until it is executed. The size of the I-address register is equal to the length of the word in memory (in this illustration, it is ten BCD digits).

A Sequence Register (S-register) controls the sequence of the instructions; that is, it refers to the location of each instruction as it is used. It requires only a four-digit position, since the memory addresses of the computer are 0000 through 4999 (Figure 13-5).

Each instruction in this hypothetical machine occupies ten positions or a complete word in storage. The first two positions hold the operation code. The last four positions hold the operand (the location, address, or other specific related data). Assume for the moment that the middle four positions are not used. When the necessary instructions are placed (loaded) into the primary storage, the program is ready to process data.

In executing a program the first step involves the console (the unit on the central processor which displays the registers in their BCD form), where the sequence register is set to 0000. When the operator pushes a certain console button, all other registers are cleared to zero to be sure that the accumulator doesn't have any "leftovers" from a previous program (Figure 13-6). When

FIG. **13-6.**

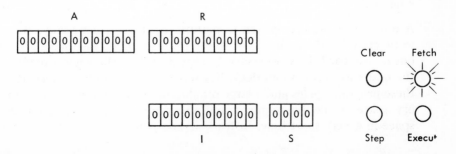

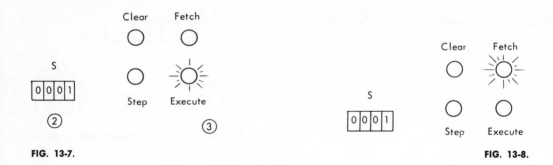

FIG. 13-7.   FIG. 13-8.

this is done, the "Clear" button causes the "Fetch" light to turn on. This means that the computer is in a "fetch" phase for retrieving an instruction specified by the sequence register.

Upon the depression of the "Step" button, the contents of the memory location indicated by the sequence register (which is the first instruction) are picked up by the control unit and placed in the instruction register (I-register). Once this is accomplished, the sequence register is incremented automatically by one (to the next word), thus making sure that instructions are being retrieved, one at a time, in a predetermined sequence. Thereafter, the content of the sequence register will increase by one each time an instruction is executed to show that it is ready for the next instruction (0001 in this case) to be fetched.

At this point, the control unit manipulates the first instruction through an execute phase as indicated by the "Execute" light (Figure 13-7). The execute light tells us that the processor is now ready to execute the instruction loaded in the I-register. Once this is done, the execute light is turned off automatically and the "Fetch" light is turned on instead, ready for retrieving the next instruction in sequence (Figure 13-8). This process continues until the whole program is loaded and its instructions are executed.

Assuming the use of cards for input, information is "read" into memory from the card, some calculations are performed on the data from each card, and a new card is usually punched out or a line is printed (one at a time) in its final form. This is done by a duplication of some of the information from the input side, plus the calculated answer. The process of "read a card into memory, calculate, punch out new card" is an example of a *program cycle*.

Branching

A program is usually written to perform as if there were only one input card to be considered. At the point where the instruction has been given to punch out a new card, it is necessary to repeat exactly the same program steps for the next card in the input deck. If a separate program were needed for each of these program cycles and a large number of cards were to be read, much memory space would be required and programmers would run out of memory space in a very short time. Instead, all computers are provided with a branching, or jump, instruction which takes the program out of its normal sequence (S) and to another instruction instead, resetting the S-register.

Computers must have this branching ability to turn away from a sequential path in the program, not only to enable them to repeat the same program over and over again, but also to deviate from the normal path (the main-line routine) and branch off in another direction. The fact that there are "compare" instructions in a computer indicates the presence of alternative paths provided by the programmer.

To summarize the foregoing description: a computer is able to distinguish between an instruction and the data because (1) the programmer tells the computer where the first instruction is located, and (2) through the use of the fetch and executive controls in connection with the sequence register, instructions are fetched to the instruction register automatically and then executed. If the programmer does not set up the program and data locations properly, it is possible for the computer to treat the data as a series of instructions. Ultimately, however, it would get an invalid operation and code, causing the computer to stop.

Instruction Formats

Computer systems differ from one another in terms of requirements and the manner in which they are programmed. In addition to the requirement for different operation codes, they also must be programmed according to a specific instruction format built into the machine. At present, there are four common variations in instruction formats. The ones with which the industry is most familiar are single-address, two-address, three-address, and one-plus address systems.

In a single-address instruction, each instruction word contains only one memory reference, or operand address (Figure 13-9). To do addition, for example, requires three instructions: (1) an instruction to place a quantity into the accumulator; (2) an instruction to add the second amount to the accumulator; and (3) an instruction to move the result from the accumulator and store it into a selected memory location.

Op.Code	Address

FIG. 13-9. Single-address instruction format.

With a two-address machine, one instruction is used (rather than three) to add the contents of one address to the contents of another. The accumulator is not used by the programmer. Both the address of the first quantity and the address of the second are in the instruction word. The result

Op. Code	Address 1	Address 2

FIG. 13-10. Two-address instruction format.

of the addition replaces the second quantity in memory (Figure 13-10).

A three-address instruction provides for three addresses in the instruction word. For an "ADD" instruction, the contents at the first address are added to the contents of the second address and the sum is stored in the third address (Figure 13-11).

Generally speaking, the word length (number of bits) in multiple-address computers is longer than in single-address machines to accommodate the additional addresses. This is compensated for by the fact that fewer instructions will be needed to do a job. Multiple-address systems also are employed in character-oriented computers. The length of their instructions is not fixed by the length of a word. In the case of one popular machine the instructions may vary from one to eight characters in length.

Op. Code	Address 1	Address 2	Address 3

FIG. 13-11. Three-address instruction format.

The one-plus system is utilized on some drum-memory computer systems to take advantage of the rotation of the drum. If instructions are stored sequentially on a drum, a minimum of one revolution to fetch each instruction would be necessary. An instruction could not possibly be executed before the very next instruction has been passed over, so the one-plus system, in effect, carries its own sequence register in the instruction. Basically, the instruction is a single-address instruction as far as reference to an operand is concerned. However, it carries along with it the address of the next instruction to be fetched, which is not necessarily the next instruction on the drum itself (Figure 13-12).

Op. Code	Address 1	Address of next instruction

FIG. 13-12. One-plus instruction format.

A programmer might calculate that an "add" can be performed in half the revolution time of the drum. If this were the case, the next instruction to be fetched could be stored half a revolution around the drum. This is called *optimizing* the program, and is not an easy thing to do. If instructions are misplaced, for example, as much as a full revolution can be missed. It takes a skilled person to time out each of the instruction executions so that the next command is properly spaced.

GLOSSARY OF TERMS

ACCUMULATOR: A register in which the result of an arithmetic or logic operation is formed.

ADDER: A device whose output is a representation of the sum of the quantities represented by its inputs.

BRANCHING: The selection of one or more alternative actions in a program based on a specific condition.

LOGIC: 1. The science dealing with the criteria or formal principles of reasoning and thought. 2. The systematic scheme which defines the interactions of signals in the design of an automatic data-processing system. 3. The basic principles and application of truth tables and interconnection between logical elements required for arithmetic computation in an automatic data-processing system.

OPERAND: That which is operated upon. An operand is usually identified by an address part of an instruction.

OPERATION CODE: The part of an instruction which tells the computer which operation is to be performed.

PROGRAM: 1. A plan for solving a problem. 2. Loosely, a routine. 3. To devise a plan for solving a problem. 4. Loosely, to write a routine.

REGISTER: 1. A device capable of storing a specified amount of data, such as one word.

TOGGLE: 1. Same as flip-flop. 2. Pertaining to any device having two stable states.

QUESTIONS AND PROBLEMS FOR REVIEW

1. Explain the difference between a parallel and a serial adder. Illustrate.

2. Add the following values in binary. Check by converting to decimal:

(a) 100 (b) 011 (c) 101 (d) 101 (e) 101
    011   101   011   110   100

(f) 111 (g) 10111 (h) 11011 (i) 10111 (j) 11111
    111   11011   11110   01011   11111

3. Subtract the following problems in binary. Check by converting to decimal.

(a) 10 (b) 11 (c) 11 (d) 01 (e) 101 (f) 010
    01   10   01   10   100   101

(g) 1011 (h) 0100 (i) 1111
    0100   1101   1000

4. Multiply the following problems in binary. Check also by converting to decimal:

(a) 100 (b) 101 (c) 111 (d) 111 (e) 1011
    11   11   11   111   1101

5. Multiply each of the problems in Problem 4, using the shift method.

6. Divide the following:

(a) 100/10 (b) 110/10 (c) 111/10 (d) 1001/11
(e) 10010/11 (f) 11110/110 (g) 11101/101

7. How does a computer compare two values? Explain.

8. Describe the control unit of the central processor.

9. What are the two parts of an instruction? Describe each part briefly.

10. What is a register? A sequence register? An I-register? A data register?

11. What is meant by a "program cycle"?

12. Describe briefly the four common variations in instruction formats. Illustrate.

chapter

14

Input-Output—
Cards,
Paper Tape, and Printers

The "magic" of computers is attributed to the capabilities and characteristics of the central processing unit. But, as mentioned in previous chapters, the central processor cannot function alone. A company owning a computer is more concerned with the over-all operation of a system than with the central processor only. This requires auxiliary media and devices to transfer the data from secondary storage to the computer (input) or to receive processed data from the computer and store it externally until needed (output).

Input units, regardless of the type of medium they use, perform the function of transferring human or machine language to the central processing unit, where they are retained either temporarily or permanently. In the case of human language, the input unit must be capable of translating it into a computer language. Output units, on the other hand, are designed to take the processed results from the computer and make them available to the user or to another machine for further processing. Like an input device, output units must be capable of translating output from computer language to human language before the data can be used effectively.

This points out that input and output devices are, in effect, communication links that make it possible for the computer to process the necessary facts and contribute favorably to the solution of the problems encountered. In the search for more comprehensive, and better, ways of handling computer input and output data, the industry has developed a large number of solutions, some general in purpose and others serving specific needs only. At present, there are five basic input techniques available to an electronic data-processing system:

1. Document translation, specifically in cases involving keypunching.
2. Punched paper tape, or punched cards created as a by-product of another document-creation process.
3. Automatic character recognition, where the source document itself is used as input.
4. On-line input, where certain information is transmitted directly from the source, an example of which is a system for handling airline reservations.
5. Magnetic tape.

Selection of input equipment is based largely on the language, translation, and speed at which output is required. Generally, slower methods of input are more economical, and may be more than adequate in situations where the desired results are not required immediately. However, as the time requirement for answers to specific problems becomes more stringent, improved input techniques must be devised to meet this need. This clearly has been the trend in the development of input devices to date.

The units described here have the characteristics of:

1. Using media of various types. This takes the form of holes punched in cards or paper tape, printed patterns on paper forms, or magnetized spots on tape (magnetic tape). Both punched cards and magnetic tape are used as input and/or output media; however, print patterns on paper, or printout, is realized only as output.
2. Being used for either input, or output, or both. Some devices are used as input machines only (for example, punched paper-tape readers), others for output only (for example, printers), or for both input and output (for example, magnetic-tape units).
3. Error-checking capability. Input or output units may have a "built-in" checking device to detect any errors that might have originated either in the source data or during the reading of the data. This feature is of vital importance.

Punched Cards

For several years, the punched card was man's primary means of communication with the computer. Compared to presently available media, it has serious limitations. Normally, it is prepared by someone who selects coded information from the original document and punches it manually into the card. This process allows a chance for errors, in addition to being relatively slow.

Punched cards most commonly are used in small-to-medium-scale computer systems. Large-scale computer systems use magnetic tape because of the tape's speed, which facilitates more efficient use of the central processing unit. Details on the characteristics of the punched card and its uses have been explained in Chapter 7.

The Punched-Card Reader

The card reader is one of the most popular devices in use today. It is designed to recognize holes punched in a card, and transmit their meaning to the central processor. Once punched-card data enter the computer, they are stored internally in a computer language. The language which is used depends on the make and type of computer. It should be noted at this time that only valid characters are transferred to and stored in the computer. A card reader usually has a built-in device to discontinue reading when an invalid character is sensed. In this case, the operator must check the type of error and correct it before any further reading can be done.

Depending on the technique used, card reading employs one of two methods: serial or parallel. The *serial* method is a *column-by-column* reading (columns 1–80); the *parallel* method reads either rows 12 through 9 (when the card enters 12-edge first), or rows 9 through 12 (when it enters 9-edge first).

With the parallel method, the entire card must be read before any meaning can be realized from any of the columns. That is, there are no distinguishing punches until all the rows have been read and reassembled into columns. A hole is judged to be a particular character, based on its distance from the leading edge of the card and the amount of time it would take the reading brushes to reach that hole. Assuming a constant card-reading speed, the holes in the 0-row, for instance, are read at zero time (zero being a prescribed amount of time away from the leading edge of the card).

More recently, serial reading has become popular. Even though the parallel method has been used for a long time, it is felt to be more practical to read one column at a time, since the information punched in each column is a

FIG. 14-1. Reading a punched card—the brush type.

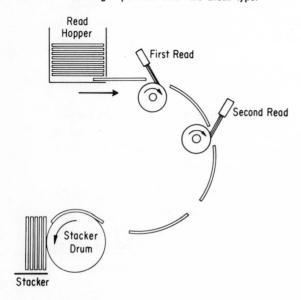

complete character. This method eliminates the need for putting together fragmented data, sensed in each of the 12 rows, as in the case of parallel reading. The only major limitation of the serial method is the extra time it takes to read 80 columns, compared to 12 rows read under the parallel method. In modern serial readers, the time problem has been overcome and they are now capable of reading a card at the same speed as a parallel reader. Further, validity checking in a serial reader is much more feasible, since each column can be checked individually as reading goes on.

Physically, the reading process is done in one of two ways: (1) via the brush-type reader or (2) via the brushless-type reader. The brush-type method of reading punched data is the same as that used in most punched-card data-processing equipment; that is, a reading brush on the top of a card makes contact with a roller beneath the card every time a hole is detected. This contact activates a circuit which manipulates the data based on the instructions stored in the unit (Figure 14-1).

The brushless type is simply a light-sensing device, shining light on the face of the card passing under it. Holes in the card allow the light to shine through them, thus establishing contact with photoelectric cells (Figure 14-2).

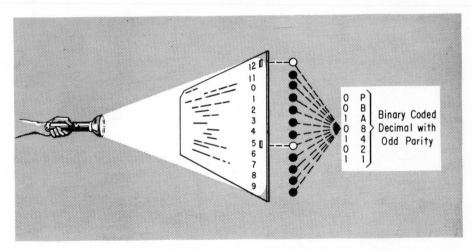

FIG. 14-2. Serial photoelectric reading.

Light sensing is less likely to cause a "mis-read" since there are no brushes to get caught, cause jamming, or cause possible subsequent intermittent reading failures.

Card readers used in computer systems are designed to read various sizes and thicknesses of punched cards. Gas companies, phone companies, or other utilities use punched cards which contain 51, 60, 66, 80, or 90 columns. Any size having less than 80 or 90 columns is considered a *stub card*. Readers also must be capable of handling them effectively. Today's typical reading speeds

FIG. 14-3. High speed card reader—(courtesy National Cash Register Co.).

vary from 100 to 1,000 cards per minute, with some devices reading at 2,000 cards per minute.

Output Card Punch

Punching is done by means of a set of punches which produce holes in certain locations in a card, based on the information they receive (Figure 14-4). Other methods such as burning, etc., have been tried, but none has proved as effective as the punch.

Punching, like reading, can be either serial or parallel. The internal codes of the computer are translated into standard punched-card codes before the information is transferred to the punch. Since the equipment is mechanical in design, punches operate at a limited speed, a feature which limits the effectiveness of punching a card as output compared to the use of other devices.

In a typical computer system, the card punch moves blank cards (one card at a time) from the hopper to the punches, which punch according to pulses received from the computer memory. Next, the punched columns are read at a reading station (brush-type) to check on the accuracy of the punched data. If no errors are detected, the punched card is ejected into its designated pocket (Figure 14-4). Depending on the make and type of equipment used, some card-punch devices are integrated as a part of the card reader.

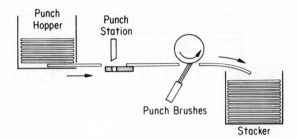

FIG. 14-4. Card punch mechanism.

Punched Paper Tape

Paper tape is another input and/or output medium, used most often in systems where information is received over wire communication circuits and in scientific applications involving limited input and output. In the past, it has not been widely used as an input/output medium due to the lack of tape-preparation devices. Most of the tapes had to be prepared manually or, in some cases, punched by units which provided limited flexibility. Presently, this difficulty has been overcome with relative success through the introduction of better punching devices. Although still comparatively less popular than other input/output media, paper tape currently is being used more effectively than in the past.

Recording on paper tape is performed by some machines that punch data in it by a direct connection to a typewriter or a keypunch. Other machines are used to transmit data punched into paper tape over telephone or telegraph lines in order to produce a duplicate tape at the other end of the line, where the newly punched paper tape can be used for further processing.

Data stored on paper tape are recorded in patterns of round punched holes, located in parallel tracks (channels) along the length of the tape. A character is represented by a combination of punches across the width of the tape. Paper tapes vary according to the number of channels they contain. Most of them are either five or eight channels wide. Consequently, the methods of coding data also vary.

In Figure 14-5, numeric, alphabetic, and special characters are represented by various combinations of punches in seven channels of an eight-channel tape. The eighth channel (the *EL* on the top channel) is used to signal the end of a record on tape. Note that the coding of punches on the tape follows a pattern similar to the one developed for representing characters in computer memory. The four lower channels are *1-2-4-8* (BCD code). Two other channels (*X* and *0*) are used in combination with the numeric channels to represent alphabetic or special characters. The seventh channel is used for checking the validity of characters (parity check), the same technique used in the computer's internal-memory parity check. Running horizontally along the length of the tape are

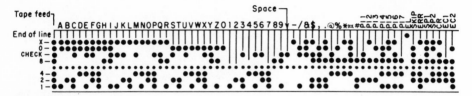

FIG. 14-5. Paper tape—the eight-channel code.

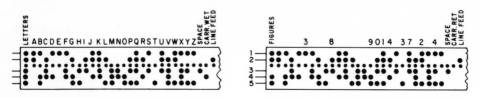

FIG. 14-6. Paper tape—the five-channel code.

small sprocket holes, used to feed the tape into the paper-tape reader mechanically. In any other location on the tape, however, the presence of a round hole indicates that a *bit* of information is recorded.

The five-channel paper tape (Figure 14-6) is used in communication equipment. It employs the telegraphic code, providing the convenience of being transmittable over common telegraph wires. Alphabetic, numeric, and special characters are coded in five punching positions. There is no "parity-check" punch, and therefore, no parity checking. With only five punch positions available, there are up to 31 possible combinations, not enough to represent all the numeric and alphabetic characters. To solve this difficulty, a shift system is used to double the number of possible combinations. A special symbol is punched to indicate that all following codes are alphabetic characters; another symbol is punched preceding sections where numeric or special characters are punched.

There are two basic ways of reading tape: mechanically and photoelectrically. In mechanical reading, pins sense the round holes. Mechanical reading speed is frequently about 20 characters (frames) per second. In photoelectric reading, a light shines through the holes, generating a pulse from a light-sensitive cell behind the tape, and typical photoelectric reading speed is 1,000 frames per second.

Data from the computer may be punched directly onto tape by automatic paper-tape punches (Figures 14-7 and 14-8). Paper-tape punching is comparatively slower than reading, because of the mechanical makeup of the punching device. Punching speed is commonly about 60 characters per second.

Advantages and Limitations of Punched Paper Tape

Punched paper tape has the advantage of allowing easy and relatively compact storage. It takes less space for storage than does the punched card. Being light

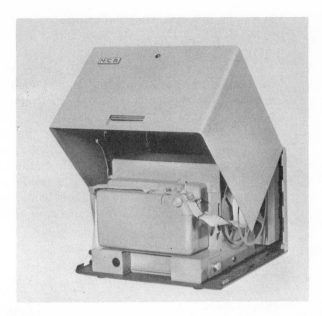

FIG. 14-7. Paper tape punch—NCR model 461.

FIG. 14-8. Paper tape reader and punch—(courtesy *General Electric* Co.).

in weight, it is easier to handle and cheaper to mail. It also is more ·economical to use than punched cards owing to the low cost of the tape and the transport units.

Compared with more advanced media, however, punched paper tape has been found to be as impractical as the punched card. Coded information being punched into it manually allows considerable possibility of error. Like the punched card, it is relatively slow. Being made of paper, it is more likely to break during processing (giving rise to the expression, a "torn-tape system"). Other disadvantages include the fact that paper tape cannot be split apart for sorting, collating, and other related operations like punched cards. Visual reading of punched paper tape also is a problem for someone who is untrained, although there are certain machines which are capable of interpreting and printing the characters on the paper tape in the same fashion that cards may be interpreted.

Printers

One of the most important output devices on a typical data-processing system is the printer. By comparison, all other devices can be considered "data-collection" devices. They are used to collect, sort, and update information which is kept in the computer. Although the printer has none of these capabilities, it is considered a most important device because of its role in communicating results (through printing) from the computer to the user on continuous paper forms.

The two main purposes of a business data-processing installation are to provide customer service and to keep management informed on the status of the business. In order to do either of these things, a way must be found to communicate pertinent reports to management and customers in the fastest and clearest possible form. Therefore, the printer is the most valuable output device for human communication.

A printer translates the computer's internal character representations into alphabetic or numeric information understandable to the human eye. There are three basic kinds of printers:

1. Character-at-a-time printers, which print each character serially, a position at a time, similar to the way a typewriter prints.
2. Line-at-a-time printers, which print all characters on a given line simultaneously.
3. Other machines employing various, less common printing techniques.

Character-at-a-time Printers

Stick printer. An early printer, which consisted of a single type bar with characters embossed on its face. To print a line, the stick would move from left to right, one position at a time, stopping only to move up or down so that the

```
0 ● ● ● 0        0 ● ● ● 0
0 0 0 ● 0        ● 0 0 0 ●
0 0 0 ● 0        ● 0 0 0 ●
0 0 0 ● 0        ● ● ● ● ●
0 0 0 ● 0        ● 0 0 0 ●
0 0 0 ● 0        ● 0 0 0 ●
● ● ● ● ●        ● 0 0 0 ●
```

FIG. 14-9. The matrix printer (schematic)—digit 1 and letter A.

A	B	C	D	E	F	G
H	I	J	K	L	M	N
O	P	Q	R	S	T	U
V	W	X	Y	Z		0
1	2	3	4	5	6	7
8	9		#	.	,	/
@	*	ℋ	&	-	%	$

FIG. 14-10. Teletype printer (schematic).

proper character was properly positioned for printing. This method was relatively slow and was not used in later computer systems.

Matrix printer. A matrix printer consists of pins placed in a 5×7 array. Characters are formed by causing the appropriate pins to strike against the paper. This is a relatively fast technique, providing there is a matrix for each print position. Speeds of 900 lines per minute are not unusual. The characters shown in Figure 14-9 represent *1* and *A*.

Teletype printer. The Teletype printer is similar to the stick printer, since it operates by printing one character at a time. The primary difference between the two is that the Teletype presents type in a square block (Figure 14-10), whereas the stick printer has a single long bar. This type square moves from left to right, positioning the proper character at each print position. As it stops at each position, a hammer behind the character in the matrix strikes it from behind, depressing it against an inked ribbon, which in turn imprints the character on the paper form. Maximum speed for this type of printing is approximately 10 characters per second.

Console printer. Several computer systems are provided with an auxiliary output printer called a console, message, or supervisory printer. It normally is a typewriter device used by the computer for relaying messages to the operator. For instance, a program may be written to check for specific codes on card input. When an error card is sensed, the console printer will print a message describing the nature of the error.

Line-at-a-time Printers

The bar printer. One of the first and best-known types of printer is the one using type bars. It still is in use today in connection with most types of general accounting machines, and consists of a series of type bars, positioned side by side, with one type bar for each print position across the line. The number of print positions varies from one model to another, usually from 55–88.

A printer using type bars is a relatively slow one, because of the mechanical positioning of the bars. A rated speed of 150 lines per minute is about average for straight numeric printing. Alphabetic information is restricted to a section of the type bars, further reducing the printing speed to 100 lines per minute.

The wheel printer. The wheel printer is an improvement over the bar

FIG. 14-11. The drum printer—schematic diagram.

printer. It is similar to it in design, except that the bars are replaced by a disk (wheel) around which all characters are embossed. Generally 120 print positions are available with alphabetic, numeric, and special characters being printed. It has a rated speed of 150 lines per minute, which makes it a faster printer than the type-bar printer despite the fact that the number of characters on each wheel far exceeds that of a type bar, because there is less mechanical effort in activating a circular wheel than in activating a vertical moving type bar.

Drum printer. A drum printer employs a solid cylindrical drum, around which characters are embossed (Figure 14-11). The drum rotates at a constant speed. As the A-row passes the line to be printed, hammers behind the paper strike the paper against the drum, causing one or more A's to be printed. As the B-row moves into place, any print position requiring the letter B is printed in the same manner. One complete revolution of the drum is required to print each line. Drum printer speeds range from 700 to 1,600 lines per minute.

Chain printer. A chain printer consists of a series of "links," arranged side by side (Figure 14-12). In a five-part chain, for instance, a complete set of

FIG. 14-12. The chain printer (courtesy International Business Machines Corp.).

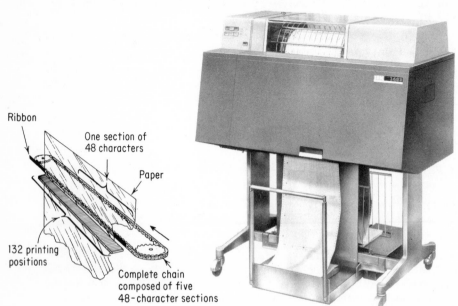

Ribbon

One section of 48 characters

Paper

132 printing positions

Complete chain composed of five 48-character sections

alphabetic, numeric, and special characters is included on each part. The chain is mounted horizontally, so that it revolves from left to right at constant speed. As the chain rotates, hammers behind the paper are timed to select the desired characters and strike the back of the paper to force it against the designated character. The inked ribbon between the character and the form leaves an imprint of the selected character. Speeds range from 600 to approximately 1300 lines per minute.

Comb printer. As the name suggests, this printing mechanism resembles a comb. A complete set of characters is mounted on a solid bar, and the bar is placed horizontally in front of the paper form so that it slides from left to right. As the bar passes in front of the paper, hammers strike the desired character(s) onto the form. When the bar has passed over the width of the paper, it returns to a home position to print another line. The comb printer was developed as an inexpensive device, since the entire comb contains 47 pieces of type, compared to the same number for each print position required by a wheel printer. Speed averages 150 lines per minute for mixed alphabetic and numeric data.

Other Printing Techniques

Electrostatic printing. The electrostatic method is considered the fastest method of printing since it is limited only by the speed at which paper can be moved. The printing process involves placing "spots" of electricity on a special paper, backed with a coating which allows the paper to hold a charge. These spots are assembled in matrix form. Next, the paper moves through a powdered ink bath, which clings to the paper wherever a character has been placed, before moving to a high-temperature area, where the ink is permanently melted on it. Speeds of 2,000–5,000 lines per minute are typical. The major disadvantages are the expense of the special paper and the fact that only one copy can be produced.

Other printing devices have been developed, including Addressograph plates, which are used to print an entire four-line address at one time. Other information can be combined with it from punched cards. Photographic reproductions through cathode-tube or Xerox processes are also in use.

GLOSSARY OF TERMS

BAR PRINTER: A printing device that uses several type bars positioned side by side across the line. Printing data on a line involves activating specific bars to move vertically until the characters they contain are properly aligned. Then, the data are printed simultaneously.

CHAIN PRINTER: A device which uses a chain of several links, each of which contains alphabetic and numeric characters. The chain rotates horizontally at constant speed. Hammers from the back of the paper are timed to fire against selected characters on the chain, causing the printing of a line.

CHARACTER-AT-A-TIME PRINTER: A device that prints one character at a time, similar to the way a typewriter prints.

COMB PRINTER: A device which consists of a set of characters mounted on a bar facing a paper form. As the bar passes over the paper (left to right), hammers strike the selected characters onto the form. When the bar reaches the right edge of the form, it returns to a home position to print another line.

CONSOLE PRINTER: An auxiliary output printer used in several computer systems for relaying messages to the computer operator.

DRUM PRINTER: A printing device which uses a drum embossed with alphabetic and numeric characters. As the drum rotates, a hammer strikes the paper (from behind) at a time when the desired character(s) on the drum passes the line to be printed. To complete printing a given line, further rotation of the drum containing the remaining characters is necessary.

ELECTROSTATIC PRINTER: A device that prints an optical image on special paper. Spots of electricity are placed in matrix form on paper. When the paper is dusted with powdered ink material, the particles cling to the electrically charged characters. Later, they are moved to a high-temperature zone where the ink is melted and is permanently fixed to the paper.

LINE-AT-A-TIME PRINTER: A device capable of printing one line of characters across a page; i.e., 100 or more characters simultaneously as continuous paper advances line-by-line in one direction past type bars or a type cylinder that contains all characters in all positions.

MATRIX PRINTER: Synonymous with *wire printer*. A high speed printer that prints character-like configurations of dots through the proper selection of wire-ends from a matrix of wire-ends, rather than conventional characters through the selection of type faces.

ON-LINE INPUT: A system in which the input device transmits certain data directly to (and under control of) the central processing unit.

PARALLEL READING: "Row-by-row" reading of a data card.

SERIAL READING: "Column-by-column" reading of a data card.

STICK PRINTER: An early printer which consists of a stick which prints one character at a time as the stick moves from left to right.

STUB CARD: A card that measures less than the standard 80- or 90-column cards used in industry.

TELETYPE PRINTER: A device that presents type in a square block. The type square moves from left to right and positions one character at a time. When this happens, a hammer strikes the character from behind, depressing it against the inked ribbon that faces the paper form.

WHEEL PRINTER: Similar in method of operation to the bar printer except that the type bars are replaced by wheels around which all the necessary characters are embossed.

QUESTIONS FOR REVIEW

1. What is the primary function of an input unit?
2. What basic input techniques are available to computer systems? Explain.
3. Describe the operation of a punched-card reader.
4. What is the difference between the serial and the parallel method of card reading? Include in your answer any advantages or limitations of each method.
5. Contrast the brush-type and the brushless-type readers.
6. What is the primary function of the output card punch? Explain.
7. Discuss the functions, uses, types, and methods of reading and recording data on punched paper tape.
8. What are the advantages and limitations of paper tape?
9. Describe the following types of printers:
   (a) Stick printer
   (b) Matrix printer
   (c) Teletype printer
   (d) Console printer
   (e) Bar printer
   (f) Wheel printer
   (g) Electrostatic printer
   (h) Drum printer
   (i) Chain printer
   (j) Comb printer.

Input-Output—
Magnetic Tape
and Direct-Access Devices

Magnetic Tape Input-Output

A major departure from punched-card input and output has been provided by the recording of data on *magnetic-tape*. In medium- to large-scale computer systems, magnetic tape is the most widely used source of secondary storage and high-speed read-in and write-out. In addition to the speed with which it transfers data to and from internal storage, magnetic tape's main advantage lies in the relatively reduced data-storage space requirements. The fact that tape may be erased and re-used repetitively further qualifies it as one of the most economical and versatile forms of storage.

Magnetic tape used in home tape recorders was developed many years prior to its application for computer data storage. The principle of the two applications is quite similar. In recording a human voice, a tape-recorder head forms magnetic patterns on a tape. During playback, the same patterns are amplified to duplicate the original sound. A computer tape unit does much the same thing, recording bits of information sent from the central processing unit in patterns on the tape. Once stored, the information can be "read" back to the computer at a later time. Like sound recording, magnetic-computer tape recording may be "read" again and again without destroying the information it contains. It can be erased and re-used indefinitely for rewriting new information.

Physical Characteristics of Magnetic Tape

While some of the early magnetic tapes were made of metal, all popular tapes now are made of a plastic material, coated on one side with a metallic oxide about the same color as the tape used in home tape recorders. The metallic oxide can be easily magnetized and is capable of retaining its magnetism indefinitely. Bits of information in the form of magnetic fields, referred to as *magnetic spots,* are recorded on the oxide side of the tape by the read-write heads of the tape unit. The spots, which are invisible to the eye, are placed across the width of the tape on parallel tracks running along its entire length. Each track is assigned a read-write head for later recording.

In the more expensive tape, a very thin coat of polyester on top of the oxide inhibits wear on it. Despite this added feature on "sandwich" tape, it is likely to have a certain amount of wear over a long period of time; the oxide usually wears off little by little. However, this is not considered a serious problem, and does not hinder the use of the tape.

Magnetic tape is manufactured to meet rigid specifications. It is wound on spools, called reels, which are kept in dust-resistant plastic cases while in storage. Although tape length on the individual reels varies from system to system, it usually comes either in 2,400 or 3,600 foot reels. The width of the tape varies also; however, one-half inch, three-quarter inch, and one inch widths are the most common sizes.

Data Representation

Although the number of tracks on magnetic tape varies with its width, a seven-channel tape is very common today with a tape width of one-half inch. The pattern of the magnetized spots across the width and along the length of the tape is a *coded representation* of the data stored on it. These spots are magnetized in one of two directions of polarity, indicating either a zero- or a one-bit to correspond with the pulses received from the computer.

Looking across the width of the tape, the seven tracks provide one column of data (*frame*), or simply one character (Figure 15-1). The presence of a

FIG. 15-1. Magnetic tape—the seven-channel code.

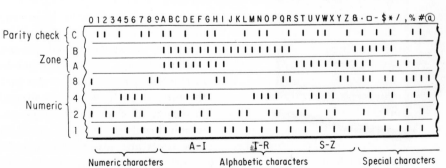

dash or a short line stands for one bit of information which, combined with zero-bits (the absence of a dash) in a seven-channel code, can represent a letter, a digit, or a special character. The zone (A and B) and numeric (1, 2, 4, 8) channels on the tape correspond to the same channels on a paper tape, and also are a coded representation of the zone and numeric rows on the 80-column punched card.

Characters are recorded on tape serially; that is, one or more characters at a time, as the tape passes by the read-write heads. In the tape system illustrated (Figure 15-1) one complete character is read at a time since there are seven read-write heads across the seven channels on the tape. On other tapes, more than a single character may be read at a time depending on the number of tape channels and the coding format.

Reading from and writing on tape is performed by a tape unit (Figure 15-2) at a constant rate of speed. The transfer rate of information to and from tape depends largely on two factors: (1) the actual movement of the tape across the read-write heads, and (2) the number of characters that can be stored on an inch of tape, referred to as its *packing density*. For example, assume a tape movement speed of 100 inches per second and a density of 200 characters to the inch. At those rates, the character transfer rate would be 20,000 characters per second. In typical systems on the market today, tape speed is about 90 inches per second, with a common packing density of 556 characters per inch, giving a transfer rate of approximately 50,000 characters per second. In the early tape systems, transfer rates commonly were in the 6,000 to 15,000 character-per-second range. Each year brought improved methods of tape handling and packing, however, so that today tape systems are marketed with transfer rates of more than 200,000 characters per second.

FIG. 15-2. Tape unit (courtesy International Business Machines Corp.).

Several methods have been employed to move the tape across the read-write heads in a fast, yet synchronized, manner to prevent breakage. The sudden burst of speed in starting a tape and the abrupt jolt when the tape stops have been "softened" by the provision of slack in the tape at areas in which breakage is likely to occur. Most tape units are designed to include vacuum columns to house a loop of tape on both sides of the read-write head which take up and give the required slack before and after recording is done.

The loop in each vacuum column acts as a buffer to prevent high-speed starts and stops from breaking the tape. Vacuum-activated switches in the columns allow the file reel and take-up reel to act independently. The file reel *feeds* tape when the loop in the left chamber reaches a minimum point, and the take-up reel *winds* tape when the loop in the right chamber reaches a minimum point. During the rewinding or backspacing of tape, the two reels simply reverse their roles. The vacuum action is the same, although rewinding speeds generally are faster than reading or writing speeds.

Other methods provide slack in the tape before it moves across the read-write head. In any case, a file reel and a take-up reel are mounted on the tape unit, followed by the threading of the tape through the tape transport mechanism. Recently, automatic tape threading has been developed, by which tape cartridges are mounted in the tape drive mechanism and self-threading by the machine takes place. Some tape units use pinch rollers to move the tape; others make use of suction only, with rotating capstans to pull the tape past the read-write heads. Some machines read the tape in one direction only; others are capable of reading in the reverse direction as well. During operation, tape is fed from the file tape, down through the vacuum chamber, across the read-write heads, down through the right vacuum chamber, and up to the take-up reel (Figure 15-3).

Major safety features are built into magnetic-tape units to prevent accidental erasure of data while reading is taking place. A common one consists of a plastic ring (Figure 15-4). When installed in its groove, reading or writing may take place. When writing is to be suppressed to safeguard the recorded data from being overwritten inadvertently, the plastic ring is removed. This aspect is well-known among tape operators, whose jargon is "no ring, no write."

FIG. 15-3. Magnetic tape mechanism—schematic diagram.

FIG. 15-4. IBM file protection device.

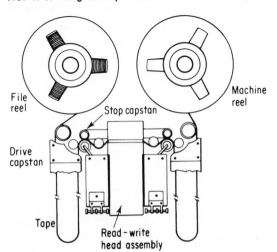

Accuracy Control

Data characters stored on magnetic tape must be checked constantly for accuracy and for any possibility of accidental erasure of magnetized bits that constitute a part of a given character or characters. In order to maintain accuracy, manufacturers have built into the tape unit one or more of three basic safeguards: parity checking, dual recording, and the dual-gap read-write heads.

Parity Checking

Parity checking is a technique whereby the machine counts the total number of one-bits representing each character on tape. Figure 15-5 shows the tape channel which is reserved for parity checking, with emphasis on even parity. Even parity involves the maintenance of an even number of one-bits representing each character on tape. If a given character is represented by an odd number of one-bits, an extra one-bit is added to the parity-check track to make the total even. For instance, the digit "seven" ordinarily is represented by three one-bits in frames 4, 2, and 1. Under an even-parity code, a fourth one-bit is added to make the total one-bit count even (Figure 15-5). When this is accomplished, the accidental loss of one of the four bits would signal an error in future processing, since the remaining bit count would be odd. If you look at the characters in Figure 15-5, you will find that each and every character is represented by an even number of one-bits.

Odd parity is the reverse of even parity. When used, a character is represented by an odd number of one-bits. A parity check bit (1-bit) is added to each character which originally is coded with an even number of one-bits.

The foregoing discussion is related to lateral or vertical parity check. That is, the number of one-bits is counted across the width of the tape, representing an individual frame. The tape unit is further designed to take a horizontal, or longitudinal, parity check at the end of a segment of tape, usually at the end of a record. Horizontal parity checks assure the number of one-bits in

FIG. 15-5. Even-parity checking.

Vertical Parity Check
Even Parity

	1	3	4	5	9	2	7
C							
B	0	0	0	0	0	0	0
A	0	0	0	0	0	0	0
8	0	0	0	0	1	0	0
4	0	0	1	1	0	0	1
2	0	1	0	0	0	1	1
1	1	1	0	1	1	0	1

Before

	1	3	4	5	9	2	7
C	1	0	1	0	0	1	1
B	0	0	0	0	0	0	0
A	0	0	0	0	0	0	0
8	0	0	0	0	1	0	0
4	0	0	1	1	0	0	1
2	0	1	0	0	0	1	1
1	1	1	0	1	1	0	1

After

each of the channels used to represent alphabetic, numeric, or special characters. If the check is for even parity, an extra bit is added to each channel that contains an odd number of one-bits (to make it even); it is vice versa in the case of odd parity check.

Horizontal parity checking is performed to double-check the accuracy of recorded data, since it is possible that two bits could be reversed in a single frame and remain undetected under a system using only vertical parity checking.

Dual Recording and Dual-Gap Read-Write Heads

In *dual recording systems,* a character is written twice in each frame across the width of the tape. It is compared for equality when it is being written and again when it is being read. This method is used only on tape systems with enough channels to record two characters side by side.

To insure the accuracy of data recorded on tape, *dual-gap read-write heads* are also used. A character written on tape is immediately "read" by a read head to verify its validity and readability. If the character is not readable, an error signal is given. Under the direct control of the computer, the tape can be backspaced and instructed to rewrite the proper data. Even then, the dual-gap feature will check the accuracy of the rewrite before any further recording continues.

The main causes of tape errors stem from physical and environmental factors. Flaws in the tape itself due to faulty manufacturing processes probably are the most common causes of error. Also, tape normally wears out after a certain amount of repetitive use, and this, plus a drastic change in temperature and/or humidity, may cause chipping of the oxide on which the magnetized spots are made. When reading from tape, dust particles or a weakness in the magnetic field of the recorded bits often contribute to poor results and frustrations in the processing cycle.

The correction of errors during the reading phase usually requires backspacing a portion of the tape to be read again. If the cause of the reading difficulty is dust or a weak magnetic signal, corrected reading often resumes after the second or third try. Manufacturers have developed schemes for internally correcting "uncorrectable" errors on tape; the usual alternative is to rerun the program that created the tape containing the errors. In most cases, however, tapes have proven very reliable and this alternative is seldom necessary.

Tape Records

Related data usually are written on tape as a group or as a complete unit of information, called a *record.* In an accounts-receivable application, for example, each customer's account, including such data as previous balance, current receipts, and outstanding balance, may be considered as a record. Information received from the central processor continues to be written on tape until a special character or mechanism built into the computer signals the transmission of information to stop. Some tape systems use a fixed block of characters in each record; however, the more common practice is to write variable-length records, limited primarily by practical considerations of available space and the storage capacity of the central processing unit.

Each record is separated from the succeeding one by an "interrecord gap." Gaps vary from about half an inch to an inch (Figure 15-6). Once the size of the interrecord gap is determined for a particular tape system, it is not likely to change. Interrecord gaps are created automatically at the time data are written on tape, and no information is recorded within them. Their presence also allows the tape unit to accelerate and decelerate when starting or stopping, without failing to read or record the desired information. Encountering an interrecord gap causes the unit to stop reading; that is, it denotes the end of a physical record. Decelerating to a stop takes place within the interrecord gap, taking approximately half the length of the gap. The remaining half is used upon acceleration before the next sequential record is read. A new "read" command from the central processor initiates the tape to move again, and by the time it reaches the next tape record, it is at the proper speed to read and transfer the stored data to the computer.

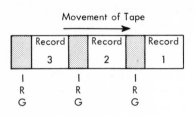

FIG. 15-6. The interrecord gap.

Many records in data-processing activity are not of great length. Considering records of 50 characters and a recording density of 556 characters per inch of tape, for instance, they are written on a fraction of one inch of tape, while allowing a constant three-fourths of an inch for the interrecord gap (the size of the gap depends on the manufacturer). This clearly is a waste of tape and a problem which has been solved by "blocking" such short records. Blocking consists of grouping more than one logical record into a physical record separated from the next block by an interrecord gap. Figure 15-7 shows two blocks of three records each. The interrecord gap used between records in Figure 15-6 is eliminated, thus realizing a saving of tape.

There is an even more important saving of computer time since the central processor isn't waiting constantly while the tape stops and starts between records. Reading a blocked record proceeds from one gap to another, making it possible to read into computer memory several individual records with a single "read" instruction. Once read, records within each block are separated by the program in the primary storage of the computer. Related blocks make up a

FIG. 15-7. Blocked records.

I R G	Record 6	Record 5	Record 4	I R G	Record 3	Record 2	Record 1

block 2   block 1

complete application, which may be a fraction of, or in excess of, one reel of tape.

Direct-Access Mass-Storage Files

Much has been done to supplement primary storage. Secondary-storage devices have been used to hold related data until they are needed by the computer. When they are needed, they are transferred to the computer's primary storage for processing. It is helpful to remember that data stored in primary storage are considered temporary, and generally remain there only during the operation of the program; if certain information must be stored for a longer period of time, it is transferred to a secondary-storage medium for that purpose. Magnetic tape and punched cards are examples of secondary-storage media.

A *mass-storage file* pertains to a unique type of temporary secondary storage designed to supply the computer with the required facts for an immediate up-to-date report on a given account. To do so, a direct, rather permanent hookup (on-line) to the computer system is required. Insurance companies utilize this system, usually through a direct-access device, to satisfy customers' inquiries regarding policy billing information. This service can be provided manually, but because of the thousands of policyholders and hundreds of daily inquiries, it would be both costly and inefficient.

A mass-storage file is similar to a library card catalog. When someone wishes to know about a particular book, he searches in the card file, which normally is arranged alphabetically either by subject or by author. New book information may be added to the file with little difficulty. The cards for lost books may be removed from the file with relative ease. Such flexibility and convenience also is desired of a computer mass-storage device. It must be large enough to accommodate new data, as well as being capable of dropping or altering old data.

Data File

The first devices made for mass storage were called *data files,* produced by the Burroughs Corporation for its 205 computer system and still being used today. The data file is a large coffinlike box which contains 50 individual pieces of nonremovable magnetic tape, each of which is 250 feet in length, draped over a center bar which runs the length of the file. Lengthwise, the tapes are divided into two lanes, each of which contains 1,000 "blocks." A block is large enough to accommodate 20 words of 10 digits each, plus the sign. In one complete unit (called a bin), there are 100 lanes containing 100,000 blocks, two million words, or a total of 20 million digits of information. On the Burroughs 205 computer system, there can be a maximum of 10 bins, thus providing a total secondary storage of 200 million digits.

To transfer data from the bin to primary storage, read-write heads move along the bar and stop on a designated lane. The tape is positioned either forward or backward to the desired block on that lane. The data stored in the block are then transferred to the computer for processing.

RAMAC Disks

Another equally flexible mass-storage device used in a large number of computer installations is the IBM RAMAC (Random Access Method of Accounting and Control). RAMAC is a different storage concept. It consists of a series of rotating disks, much like phonograph records, stacked one on top of the other to make up a file. The disk is divided into a series of concentric circles called *tracks,* which in turn are divided into segments called *records* (Figure 15-8). Each segment is individually addressable; that is, it can be located individually.

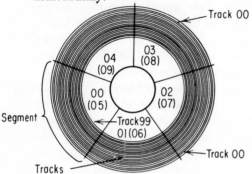

FIG. 15-8. A RAMAC disk (*courtesy International Business Machines Corp.*).

The first RAMAC system was designed with one arm to read and write information. The arm positions itself up and down a vertical shaft to the proper disk, and then moves horizontally to the designated track. Next, it drops on the track and reads the desired record. The basic RAMAC system contains five million character positions of storage, divided into 100-character records. Average access time (the average time it takes the arm to locate a specific record in storage) is about 600 milliseconds or 0.6 seconds. In improved models, more arms have been added to reduce the average access time.

Other disk-file systems have been marketed since the RAMAC by companies such as IBM, Burroughs, Bryant, and Analex. Newer disk files have average access times as short as 20 milliseconds and virtually unlimited storage capacity (Figures 15-9 and 15-10).

Magnetic Drum

Another type of random-access device is the *magnetic drum.* It is similar in nature to the drums used as primary storage, except that it is strictly an auxiliary device. The Univac File Computer drum, for instance, has a storage capacity of 18,000 characters. Ten drums can be hooked together for a total storage capacity of 180,000 characters. Access time to any word on the drum is 17 milliseconds or 0.017 seconds, but storage capacity is not very great. More recently, Univac has developed a magnetic-drum file called Fastrand, which

FIG. 15-9. Interior of the Burroughs disk file.

FIG. 15-10. General Electric disk storage unit.

FIG. 15-11. Interior of the Burroughs B-5500 drum storage unit.

can be obtained in increments of two drums per unit, and has a minimum capacity of 64,880,640 characters and a maximum capacity of 6,228,541,440. Average access time is about 92 milliseconds. The Burroughs B-5500 computers have an attached drum for auxiliary storage which accommodates approximately 512,000 48-bit words with an average access time of 8.4 milliseconds (Figure 15-11).

Card Random-Access Memory (CRAM)

Another related mass-storage device is the NCR CRAM unit (Figure 15-12). The CRAM package consists of a removable cartridge containing 256 magnetic cards of material similar to magnetic tape. These cards store magnetic bits of information totaling 5.6 million characters per cartridge. Cards drop from the cartridge onto a cylinder drum, at which time reading or writing takes place (Figure 15-13). Sixteen cartridges, or 89 million characters, can be on-line at one time.

In summary, we note that direct-access devices are useful in terms of their ability to hold large amounts of data at reasonable cost, in forms prescribed for processing. A business firm integrating direct-access devices into its system

FIG. 15-12. CRAM unit—NCR.

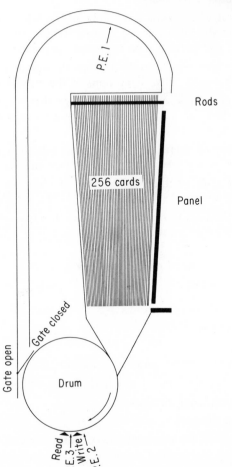

P.E. 1

Rods

256 cards

Panel

Gate closed

Gate open

Drum

Read

P.E. 3

Write

P.E. 2

FIG. 15-13. CRAM unit—NCR (schematic).

must maintain an efficient balance between storage volume and unit cost of storage. Compared to magnetic tape, however, these devices have certain disadvantages in the way of control and comparatively higher cost. As cost is reduced, direct-access devices are likely to become the most popular form of secondary storage.

GLOSSARY OF TERMS

BLOCK: A set of things, such as words, characters, or digits, handled as a unit.

CRAM: *C*ard *R*andom-*A*ccess *M*emory, a mass-storage device that consists of a number of removable magnetic cards, each of which is capable of storing magnetic bits of data.

DUAL-GAP READ-WRITE HEAD: Used in magnetic-tape data processing to insure the accuracy of recorded data on tape. A character written on tape is read immediately by a read head to verify its validity.

INTERRECORD GAP: An interval of space or time, deliberately left between recording portions of data or records. Such spacing is used to prevent errors through loss of data or overwriting, and permits tape stop-start operations.

MAGNETIC DRUM: A right circular cylinder with a magnetic surface on which data can be stored by selective magnetization of portions of the curved surface.

MASS-STORAGE FILE: A type of temporary secondary storage that supplies the computer with the necessary data for an immediate up-to-date report on a given account.

PACKING DENSITY: The number of useful storage elements per unit of dimension, e.g., the number of bits per inch stored on a magnetic tape or drum track.

PARITY CHECK: A check that tests whether the number of ones (or zeros) in an array of binary digits is odd or even. Synonymous with odd-even check.

RAMAC: *R*andom-*A*ccess *M*ethod of *A*ccounting and *C*ontrol, a mass-storage device that consists of a number of rotating disks stacked one on top of another to make up a data file.

RECORD: A collection of related items of data, treated as a unit.

QUESTIONS FOR REVIEW

1. How is sound recording similar to computer tape recording?
2. What is a magnetic tape? Present some of its physical characteristics.
3. How are data represented on tape? Illustrate.
4. What is meant by packing density?
5. Describe briefly the methods by which reading from and writing on tape are performed.

6. What is a parity check? Even parity? Odd parity?

7. What are some of the main causes of tape errors? Explain.

8. Define the following terms:
   - (a) Logical record
   - (b) Interrecord gap
   - (c) Single read block
   - (d) Multiple record block.

9. Explain a mass-storage file. Give an example.

10. What is a RAMAC system? Explain.

11. What is a magnetic drum? A card random-access memory?

chapter

16

Input-Output—
Miscellaneous Devices

Chapters 14 and 15 emphasize the more popular types of input and output media and devices. In addition to these, there are other devices on the market today which are quite useful and hold great promise for the future.

Data Collection and Transmission

Historical

Data transmission is considered an important, though a relatively new, area. Since the time when man developed the alphabet, he has shown interest in establishing contacts with other peoples. The earliest known organized postal service is recorded during the time of King Cyrus of Persia about 500 years before Christ. Since communications through "foot carrying" was a slow method, techniques such as the use of smoke signals and drums were developed.

During the early development of the United States, the pony express was established. It operated in 1860 for only one year, and might have lasted longer had it not been for the arrival of a complete coast-to-coast telegraph link in 1861.

In 1910, the first Teletype equipment was installed for the Postal Telegraph System. Two years later, it was used by the railroad, thus marking the beginning of the first business data-communications system in 1912.

FIG. 16-1. Cathode ray tube data display device (*courtesy Control Data Corp.*).

Fifteen years prior to the Postal Telegraph System, Guglielmo Marconi experimented with a "land-to-ship" wireless transmission. So, in the early 1900's, both the wire and the wireless systems were available as basic communication devices, and still are widely used.

Other methods also are used today in transmitting or receiving information. *Closed circuit television,* for example, is used in airline terminals to communicate flight information, in manufacturing plants to monitor production processes, and in hospitals for student lectures about surgery techniques. Through the cathode ray tube (television screen) information from computer storage may be displayed directly to an individual in the computer room or miles away (Figure 16-1). *Facsimile transmission* involves the process of sending a copy of a printed page by sensing the "black" and "white" areas. *Telemetering* is used to remotely control the physical movement of fluids and gases. Missiles are guided from the ground with measurements recorded by devices inside the missile and relayed to the ground station for evaluation and control.

Information Flow

In its simplest form, the transmission of coded information is accomplished in a *flow* involving five stages. The first stage includes the input and the reading devices. Data are read and then sent by the transmitter through a data set, where they are translated from the source language into pulses and transmitted over teletype-grade channels, voice telephone channels, or broad-band

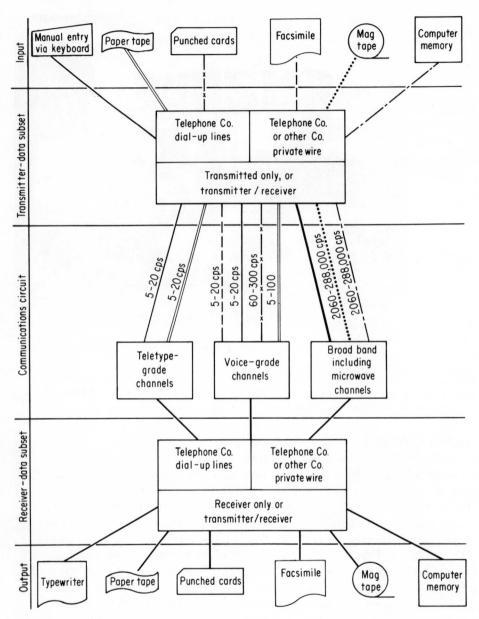

FIG. 16-2. Data transmission—schematic.

channels. These pulses, which travel at high speeds, are then sensed by a receiver or data set and retranslated into an output form. In other words, information goes from (1) an input device to (2) a transmitter, then through (3) a communications circuit to (4) a receiver and finally to (5) an output device (Figure 16-2).

Input. The data are sent by recording them in punched cards, punched paper tape, magnetic tape, or computer memory. Any of these media can be used as the data originator, and in addition, manual keyboards such as the teletypewriter may be used. The speed of each output device varies considerably, a factor which requires the use of a host of different transmitting devices to match the type of input equipment being used. Differences in the rate of speed of input devices also have a bearing on the rate at which data are transmitted.

Transmitter. Transmitting sets also vary in capabilities and in speed. The best-known transmitting system is the Dataphone data set, manufactured by the Bell Telephone System. Basically, it consists of a telephone which can be used either for voice or data transmission. One need only dial the number at the station to which information is being sent, and when the Dataphone set is answered at the other end, the transmitting party indicates the beginning of an information transmission. At that moment, both parties depress buttons marked "Data," which suppress the voice capability and begin sending data instead. Dataphone sets may be either transmitters or receivers, or may have the combined capability of transmitting and receiving (Figure 16-3).

There are three basic kinds of data sets: serial, parallel, and analog. The serial set sends information one bit at a time at a rate ranging from 75 to 2,400 bits per second (BPS). The parallel set transmits one complete character at a time. Low speed parallel sets send 20 and 75 characters per second

FIG. 16-3. Data phone (*courtesy American Telephone & Telegraph*).

(CPS). Analog sets are used especially to transmit handwriting or facsimiles. A printed page would be sent over an analog set to a receiver capable of duplicating the original document from the information it receives.

In addition to the Dataphone, the Bell Telephone Company makes a device which transmits and receives five-, six-, seven-, or eight-channel paper tape at a speed of 1,050 words per minute.

Dial-up. Another choice available to the user is the type of line to be selected for the transmission. The Dataphone set requires the use of the Bell System line; however, other manufacturers producing similar equipment provide other lines for transmission.

The Bell System sets up a long-distance call through wire lines, through coaxial cable, or by microwave. The most common technique is to use normal wire lines, despite the fact that many areas use coaxial cables (a type of wire capable of carrying several calls at the same time). The most recent development, however, is the microwave transmitter. Microwaves are similar to radio waves, except that a microwave cannot be sent from one point to another unless there is a clear line of sight between them. The presence of a mountain or other obstruction causes difficulty which has to be overcome by relay stations along the way.

A normal phone call might be placed on any of these three systems. A long-distance call travels over at least two of them, and sometimes all three by means of switching devices which allow this selection automatically. Wherever there is a clear path through a particular medium, that system switches in. A call from Chicago to New York City could go through switches as far south as Atlanta, for instance, with no human intervention. When data is transmitted on normal dial-up lines, it is routed just like a regular long-distance call. The advantage of this system is that cost is based only on the time used, rather than on a flat rate. Data sets are leased full time at any end of the network, but the circuitry in between is paid for only as it is used.

Private wire. A firm that has a large amount of data transmission to do can use a private wire. A private wire system provides the sender with a direct line to the receiving office, thus making the line available at all times. Since the hookup is a preset path, the line can be conditioned in such a way as to permit the transmission of data at relatively greater speeds.

The receiving station may have several devices for receiving information. These devices are not necessarily the same type which did the sending; for instance, punched-card data can be sent directly to a printer on the other end. Before the information is received, however, it must be reconverted, or "conditioned," from telephone signals to those which can be properly interpreted by the receiving device.

Before a business firm makes a commitment regarding the adoption of a specific piece of data-communication equipment, it should especially consider:

1. Compatibility of equipment at the various sending and receiving points. The equipment must maintain a balance between the speed at which data is sent and that at which it is received. It would be inefficient, for instance, to send data from magnetic tape at a speed of 50,000 characters per second and to receive it on a printer at the receiving end at 10 characters per second.

2. The length and number of messages to be sent.

3. The economics, with regard to accuracy, speed, cost, and urgency. A firm investigating data-communication equipment should take a look at the amount of data, the availability of data, and all other related factors to see whether the need for this type of equipment actually exists. If so, the cost will have to be weighed against the need for speed. A rule of thumb is that the greater the volume of data, the greater the need for speed; if the volume is low, speed will not be such a factor. As a result, the cost has to be based on the speed of the equipment needed.

4. The type range of distribution involved; that is, whether communication is only between two points, from one point to several other points, or between several points.

5. Scheduling problems of the work involved, and other possible alternative methods. Scheduling involves planning and organizing data transmission at a favorable time, avoiding peak loads as much as possible.

To illustrate the use of data-transmission equipment, assume a grocery chain has five main warehouses located throughout the country. Each warehouse is tied to several local stores which order nonperishable goods. Each warehouse also has a computer which contains a mass-storage device for maintaining its inventory. For communicating orders to its warehouse, each store has a teletypewriter installed for this function (Figure 16-4).

FIG. 16-4.

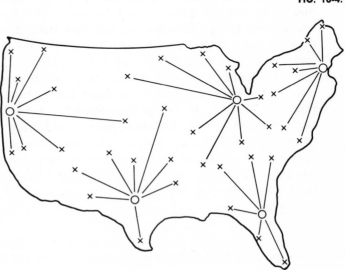

Each day, the stores make a quick list of items which need reordering. The information is sent by Teletype to the main warehouse while a copy of the order is being printed automatically. When the warehouse receives the data, it punches them in cards, each of which includes such information as the item number, quantity, and the number of the store requesting the item. As the cards are punched, they are gathered into batches for processing by the computer. The warehouse computer looks up each item in its random-access unit and, if it is available, prints a "pick list" to be sent into the warehouse, where the items will be gathered and shipped to the requesting store. If an item is not available, the system punches a card which is transmitted back to the store, informing it that the item is out of stock. The store then matches the out-of-stock items to the original request and thus determines which items are on the way. The unavailable items can be solicited from other stores by communicating with them later; meanwhile, the warehouse uses the punched cards representing its out-of-stock items to issue a purchase order that will replenish its own supplies.

Future Data Communications

Much intensive research is being conducted toward advancing the technique and speed of data transmission. New ideas are constantly being tried out and new equipment designed and tested. Voice communication has been sent by means of radio waves fed through underground copper pipes, for example. The radio waves are capable of carrying up to 200,000 simultaneous conversations without the likelihood of one conversation interfering with another.

The principles of light also are being researched for voice transmission. Bell Laboratories has been able to isolate a beam of light of a single frequency by using a device called the *laser*. The future for the use of lasers appears relatively unlimited. Its use has been applied to medicine, where delicate brain or heart operations are performed. The laser has the unique feature of piercing a designated organ without breaking the skin. Future scientific applications include its use in sending data from earth to other planets. For commercial uses, the laser will be beamed through underground pipes, with mirrors to change the path whenever a bend in the pipe is necessary. It is anticipated that these lasers could carry an estimated one million conversations at the same time. The perfection of this principle is an important one. Relieving the maintenance problem of wires and microwave equipment to the point where only a single beam of light is necessary will save telephone and data-transmitting customers untold amounts of money each year.

Magnetic-Ink Character Recognition

The widespread use of *magnetic-ink character recognition* (MICR) by the banking industry deserves special mention as a major breakthrough in standardizing documents for automated input. In 1955, the American Bankers Association realized a great need for some way to automate the processing of bank paperwork. The check, which is the basis for most bank transactions, must be used or else some other document would have to be produced for use as input to an automatic computer system.

Even though they are used successfully by the government and other agencies, punched-card checks require standard sizes and thicknesses. The size requirement of a punched-card check was unsatisfactory to the personal checking accounts carried by commercial and other banks, since their printed checks come in various sizes, shapes, and thicknesses. A check written on a particular bank may be processed by as many as four other banks before the bank on which it originally was drawn receives it. If you look at a used personal check, you will notice on the back the names of all the banks through which the check has passed. Consequently, it is necessary that any approach to automation must be acceptable and agreeable to all banks concerned.

FIG. 16-5. The E 13B type font.

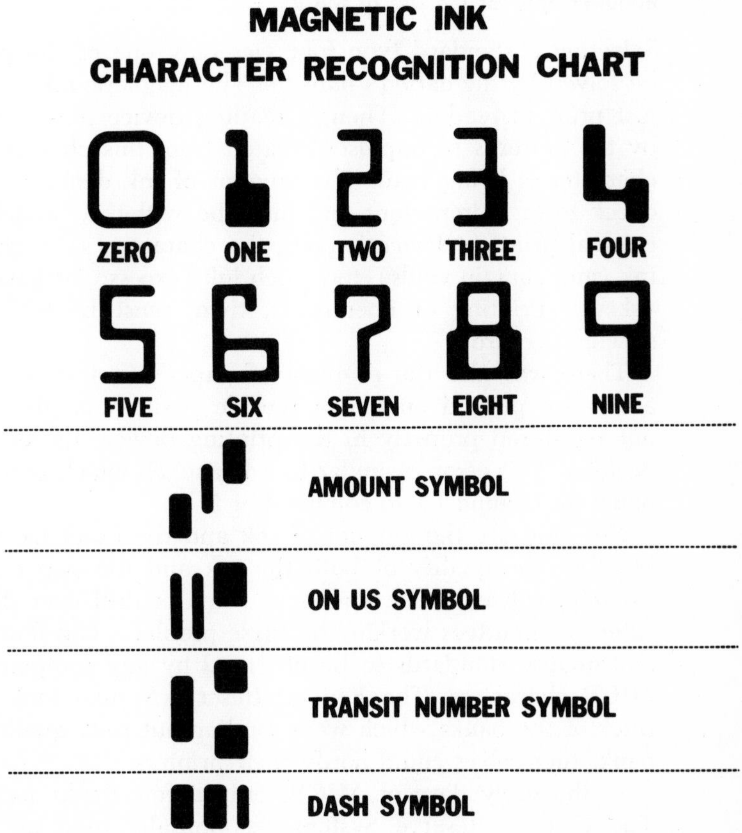

MAGNETIC INK
CHARACTER RECOGNITION CHART

| ZERO | ONE | TWO | THREE | FOUR |
| FIVE | SIX | SEVEN | EIGHT | NINE |

AMOUNT SYMBOL

ON US SYMBOL

TRANSIT NUMBER SYMBOL

DASH SYMBOL

After some research, it was proposed, and later agreed to, that coding the desired information on the check in magnetic ink would be a suitable solution to the problem. Magnetic ink, in this case, solves three major problems: (1) The original document can be used directly as input to the computer so that no substitute document has to be prepared. (2) The necessary information can be coded on checks of any size within a reasonable range. (3) The information is easily readable by persons handling the document.

For several months, committees discussed all possible type font characteristics, and discarded many along the way as being unusable, impractical, or of poor quality. Finally, the E 13B type font was agreed upon and was adopted (Figure 16-5). The E 13B type font was selected because the characters are visually readable, and each of them also can be distinguished through electronic reading devices; that is, a 0 cannot be mistaken for an 8, etc. There are fourteen different characters in E 13B: digits 0 through 9, and the four special characters illustrated in Figure 16-5. Magnetic-ink character recognition (MICR) cannot be used in many data-processing problems since the alphabetic characters were not considered. However, the MICR characters meet the operating needs of most types of financial institution.

Requirements for the Use of MICR

Selecting a standard type font was only one of the problems which had to be solved by the nation's bankers. The magnetic ink on a check is magnetized just prior to reading. Then, a reading device senses the magnetic field, and by the patterns of impulses created from this character, distinguishes which character is being read. The amount of ink denoting each character on the check form is important and must be within a predetermined range. If the original printing device is poor, the character(s) might either have too little ink (and contain voids), too much ink (excess), or have been printed crooked (skew). Printing of documents, then, must be restricted and kept under specified controls.

There was also the problem of paper registration, since the MICR characters are printed only in a specific position on the check. If the check is not registered properly in the printing device, the characters will be out of position. This error is similar to a keypunch which punches information designated for column 1 into column 4 or 5.

Not only are the amount of ink and the exact location of characters critical, but the quality of both the ink and the paper are equally important. To standardize MICR, and have some control over the quality of the characters, committees working on these problems laid down the rules, tolerances, and quality standards to be observed by any company printing checks with MICR characters. The Federal Reserve System took it upon itself to keep track of the banks which were sending out poor quality checks, so that these banks themselves could notify their printers.

In the early days of MICR, only a few banks used this new technique. The Federal Reserve System was initially used as a testing ground and shared most of the headaches in ironing out certain problems. Printers were not the only ones at fault; in fact, the only information which a printer could put on the check was the bank number, and the account number where individual banks had account numbering systems. The first bank to receive the checks (and which had an automatic system) was to imprint the amount of the check with the MICR font in the designated location on it. This was necessary since the printer could not predict the amount for which a check would be written. In order to do the job, it meant that there had to be a device which could imprint characters with magnetic ink. Again, the burden fell on the Federal Reserve Banks, in that they subsidized the purchase or lease of equipment from data-processing equipment manufacturers to imprint magnetic ink characters on checks. At that time, the emphasis was put on building a device which would have good paper registrations, contain the right amount of ink, and be easy to operate. Thus, along with the printers, manufacturers of imprinting equipment likewise shared in the problems.

Since MICR was developed to enable banks to process information automatically through computer systems, manufacturers of these systems were busy developing the equipment to read MICR documents. A popular machine for this purpose is called the *reader-sorter* (Figure 16-6). It is designed to read checks of various length, width, height, and thickness, and transmit the information to the memory of the central processor, which is used later to update the customers' accounts. In addition, the reader-sorter actually is capable of sorting the check to any one of its pockets. Eventually, all checks must be sorted by account number so that they can be returned to the person who wrote them; therefore, the reader-sorter performs the dual function of

FIG. 16-6. Burroughs B100 check sorter-reader.

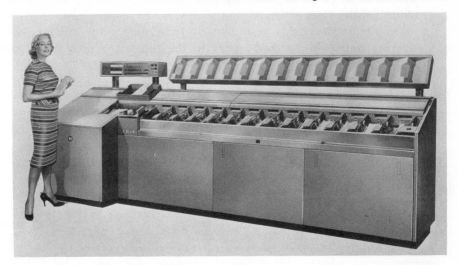

208 Input-Output—Miscellaneous Devices

reading information for automatic processing and physically sorting them. It may either be hooked up to the central processor, whereby information is transferred directly to memory (on-line), or be connected to tape units for data storage on magnetic tape, which can be processed later by the computer. Physical sorting of checks can be performed by the reader-sorter whether or not information is transferred to magnetic tape or to the computer. This is done by detaching the machine from the computer system (off-line processing).

The reader-sorter is the final judge regarding the proper coding of documents. Any unreadable information goes to a separate pocket, called the *reject pocket*. If an unreasonable number of documents are rejecting, it is an indication that the checks have been badly coded.

The check illustrated in Figure 16-7 shows the location in which MICR coding must appear. The coding is divided into three fields: (from left) the *transit field*, which is the bank's serial number; the *on-us field*, reserved for the customer's account number and a translation code to indicate the type of document involved; and the *amount field*, indicating the amount of money involved. There also is an auxiliary on-us field which may be used for the bank's own purposes to contain such things as the check serial number for bank reconciliation or the date of the check. It is not in wide use today. When shown, it would be to the left of the transit field, providing the check is of sufficient length.

The amount symbols always are found in positions 1 and 12 of the item (Figure 16-8). A fixed 10-digit amount field is located between positions 2 and 11, inclusive. The account number and transaction code are found between positions 14 through 31. The account number always is enclosed by the "on-us" symbol, and may contain dash symbols. The transit field always is in positions 33 through 43, with a transit symbol, four digits (ABA number), a dash, four more digits (bank number), and another transit symbol. The transit, on-us (account), and amount symbols are located only in their designated fields.

Despite what might seem like overwhelming odds against MICR, it is thriving today. Much credit goes to the diligent efforts of the committees

FIG. 16-7. A check layout for MICR.

FIG. 16-8. A sample check coded with magnetic ink.

organized by the American Bankers Association (ABA), the Federal Reserve System (which, at present, is utilizing successful automatic systems all over the country), and the equipment manufacturers, whose cooperation with the ABA made the system possible. Consequently, savings and loan institutions as well as banks are using MICR satisfactorily, processing items as quickly as 1,600 checks per minute. In England, the British Bank Association also has accepted the E 13B type font as a standard. It could very well be true that MICR in its present form will become something of an international symbolic banking language in the future.

Optical Scanning

Basically, *optical scanning* is the translation of printed or handwritten characters into machine language. This field has been relatively slow in developing, despite the fact that there has been a need for such devices from the beginning of automatic data processing. Optical scanning holds perhaps the greatest promise for future cost and error reduction in automatic data processing.

Generally speaking, optical scanning is performed by a device which converts a character into a "picture" through the use of an electric eye. The circuitry is designed to break up this image into pulses which identify the specific character. The pulses are used to punch a card, to punch a tape, to store information on magnetic tape, or transfer the information to primary storage.

To illustrate the advantages of optical scanning, let us take an insurance company which stores policyholder information on magnetic tape. In the normal processing routine, the computer system calculates charges during each billing period and prints the results, showing related details by coverage (for example, medical payments). When the bill is received by the policyholder, and later returned with the proper amount of premium, a card is punched to show the amount received and other data, such as the policy number, policyholder's name, amount of bill, and so on. The punched card and others representing premiums received from other policyholders later are used to update the policy files on magnetic tape.

In the foregoing procedure, there always is the possibility of error, since original documents are first translated into punched cards before the information is used. Optical scanning minimizes this possibility because the information from the original document is read directly into the computer system, therefore eliminating the keypunching operation.

Magnetic-ink character recognition (MICR) is a relatively limited form of scanning. It is limited in that the reading device can distinguish only among 14 characters, which are specific as to size, quantity of ink, registration, and so forth. MICR is no doubt a significant improvement over old techniques, but its application is generally limited to the needs of financial institutions.

Although optical scanning devices have their major applications in areas such as tax and social-security reporting, insurance billing, public utilities, and credit-card processing, they are equally effective in certain other areas. In most large post offices today, scanning devices are used to read typewritten addresses on letters, and to sort them geographically by machine. That feature in itself is a feat, since there are hundreds of different typewriter styles. Any nonreadable addresses are sorted out and handled manually. The present use of zip codes should prove to be a tremendous help in this sorting operation.

Another type of special-purpose scanning device is being developed for the blind. It consists of a pencil-like instrument attached to a long cord with a button which fits into the ear. The pencil has several photoelectric cells on the tip. As it is moved along a printed line, the characters cause these cells to make a sound much like static; however, each character makes a different sound. The person using this device can be taught to recognize the various sounds, and thereby learn to "read." The pencil will be able to read books, magazines, and newspapers. Like other optical scanners, this device allows direct reading of the original document, rather than waiting for a time-consuming and error-producing translation.

Most scanners in use today are bound by specific limitations. For the most part, standard type is necessary, as well as standard size paper. They still are considered relatively slow compared to an MICR reader-sorter, which reads up to 1,650 documents per minute and can be used on-line to the computer. Normally, translation from a scanner is done off-line; that is, cards or tape are prepared away from the computer system before the newly produced information is transferred to the computer for processing.

Buffering

A computer system requires that the component units work together in a compatible and harmonious manner so that meaningful results can be expected. No individual unit is capable of functioning effectively unless it becomes a part of the whole system. To do so, cables are used to connect the auxiliary units to the central processing unit which controls their work and the extent to which they are used in getting the job done.

A *buffer* is a device used on some computers to hold temporary information being transmitted between external- and internal-storage units, or between input-output devices and internal storage. An unbuffered system performs a "read-compute-write" cycle in serial fashion; that is, one operation after another: *READ–COMPUTE–WRITE*. A buffered system allows all three operations to proceed simultaneously:

Read	A	B	C	D	E	etc.
Compute		A	B	C	D	etc.
Write			A	B	C	etc.

The need for buffers is readily apparent when the timing of a computer system is considered. Today's electronic computers execute instructions at microsecond speeds, while most input and output equipment (being mechanical) still operate relatively slowly. There is no compatibility, for instance, between a computer executing an instruction in as little as 10 microseconds (ten millionths of a second), and a card reader that reads data to the computer in 75 milliseconds, or 7,500 times as slow. A buffer is designed to compensate for this imbalance. It can be described as an electronic memory device, connected directly to the main computer memory, but not available to the programmer.

In the system illustrated (Figure 16-9), two buffers are added: an input buffer with a holding capacity of 80 characters (one punched card) between the card reader and the computer; and an output buffer, one line of print between the computer and the printer. Being electronic in nature, this device makes it much faster to transfer the 80 characters in the buffer to another electronic device (the computer) than it is to transfer the same positions directly from the card reader to the computer. The computer will be processing one record while the next record is filling the buffer from the card reader.

FIG. 16-9.

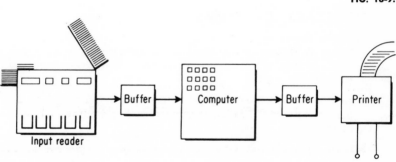

Input reader

To illustrate the role of a buffer when integrated into a computer system, the following is a step-by-step process of a card deck with printed data as output:

1. Input deck is fed into the card reader.
2. Information from the first card goes automatically into the *input buffer*.
3. The stored program calls for a card to be read. Information from the buffer is transferred to memory.
4. Card 2 begins to transfer automatically to the buffer.
5. Card 1 is processed while the buffer contains the data from card 2.
6. Processed information from card 1 is sent to the *output buffer*.
7. The stored program calls for another card to be read. Information from the buffer (card 2) is transferred to memory.
8. Card 3 begins to transfer automatically to the input buffer.
9. Output buffer is automatically sending processed data of card 1 to the printer.
10. Information from card 2 is processed, while the input buffer fills with the next card's contents.

At the end of this processing, card 1 is completely read, processed, and printed. The information from card 2 is ready to be sent to the output buffer, and the data of card 3 are available in the input buffer. The process between steps 6 through 10 continues until the entire deck of cards is processed. You will note that at the input stage, a card is always being prepared ahead of time by moving it into the buffer while the card ahead of it is being processed. Likewise, at the output stage, a card is always in the process of being printed while the card preceding it is being processed. Through the use of such overlapping with buffers a great deal of total processing (throughput) time is saved.

In brief, the use of a buffer aids the mechanically driven input or output units to keep up with the electronic computer, thus maximizing the efficiency of the system. This includes the two primary functions of speed change and time sharing. Other functions involve the buffer's ability to change a code from machine to human language or vice versa, and to change the mode of data transmission; i.e., from serial to parallel or from parallel to serial transmission.

GLOSSARY OF TERMS

BUFFER: A storage device used to compensate for a difference in rate of flow of data, or time of occurrence of events, when transmitting data from one device to another.

FACSIMILE TRANSMISSION: Reproduction of printed matter by a process which picks up the light and dark areas of an object and converts it into a facsimile (copy) of the same.

MICR: *Magnetic-Ink* Character *Recognition*, a process involving the use of a device that senses and encodes into a machine language characters printed with an ink containing magnetized particles.

OFF-LINE: Pertaining to equipment or devices not under direct control of the central processing unit.

ON-LINE: Pertaining to peripheral equipment or devices in direct communication with the central processing unit.

OPTICAL SCANNING: Translation of printed or handwritten characters into machine language.

QUESTIONS FOR REVIEW

1. Present the significant events leading to the beginning of data communication systems.
2. What are the stages through which information flows? Explain each stage briefly.
3. Describe the role of the Dataphone in data communication.
4. What factors are generally considered by a business firm prior to the adoption of a data-communication system? Explain.
5. What is magnetic-ink character recognition? How does it aid banks in processing information? Explain.
6. Describe the E 13B type font.
7. What are the requirements for the use of MICR?
8. Describe the functions of the reader-sorter.
9. What are the primary fields where MICR coding appear on a check? Explain each field briefly.
10. What is optical scanning? Explain its operation, advantages, and use in business data processing. In what other areas is optical scanning applied?
11. What is meant by buffering? Why is it used? What are its advantages?

part 4

Computer Programming and Systems Design

The Programming

Cycle

Stress in this chapter will be upon the methods used to direct a system in processing business data. This involves the specialized field of "programming" and the people (programmers) who perform this function.

Generally, a *program* is defined as a set of instructions. The term "program" is not new, nor is it applicable only to computers. Any activity, whether it is social, economic, or political, has its own program. For example, an athletic field day provides a program for the spectators to use as a guide to the events and the participants. It outlines the steps that will be followed, one after another, during the day. Likewise, computer data processing is conducted according to a program or set of events (instructions).

Preparing the computer program and checking it out are both critical and time-consuming. Every single detail must be carefully considered, every possible contingency provided for, and the whole operation reduced to computer instructions written in computer language. Although the final computer run often is quite short, there usually is a great deal of time-consuming work to be done in analyzing, programming, and coding before the run. *Analyzing* is performed in order to determine the over-all method of solving the problem; *programming* consists of preparing a flow chart to map the means of solving the problem; and *coding* is the final conversion (translation) of the program into the language of the computer. The dividing lines between these functions are not always clear or well-defined in the total solution of the problem.

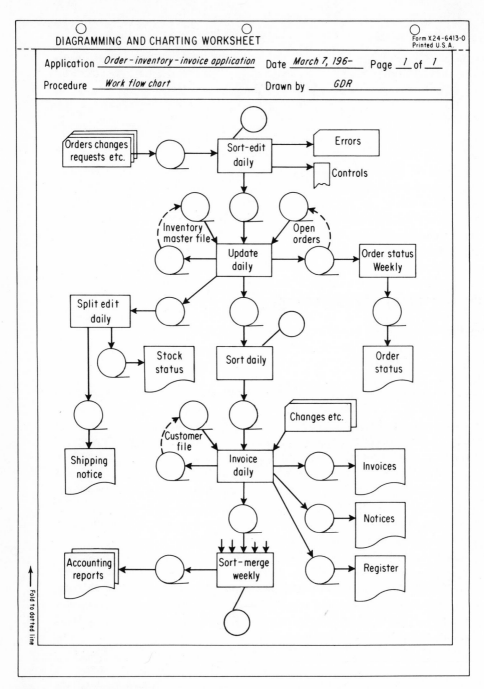

DIAGRAMMING AND CHARTING WORKSHEET

Form X24-6413-0
Printed U.S.A.

Application _Order-inventory-invoice application_   Date _March 7, 196–_   Page _1_ of _1_

Procedure _Work flow chart_   Drawn by _GDR_

Orders changes requests etc.

Sort-edit daily → Errors

Controls

Inventory master file

Open orders

Update daily → Order status Weekly

Split edit daily

Order status

Stock status

Sort daily

Shipping notice

Customer file

Changes etc.

Invoice daily → Invoices

Notices

Accounting reports

Sort-merge weekly

Register

Fold to dotted line

FIG. 17-1. Systems flow chart.

Steps Involved in the Preparation of a Program

A programmer first becomes acquainted with the systems flow chart of the job to be done (Figure 17-1). This chart describes the over-all requirements of the application and indicates how the data are expected to pass from one stage to the next. Of course he must be familiar with the system flow chart symbols used.

At this time the programmer is prompted to ask pertinent questions; for example: How will the input data for this run appear? What medium is to be used (that is, punched cards, magnetic or paper tape, etc.)? How many different files of input data are available? Is the format of these data (its internal arrangement) to be the programmer's decision or is it fixed by a previous operation? In regard to the required output data, what medium is to be used (cards, magnetic or paper tapes, printed reports, etc.)? How many different output files are required? How are the output data to be arranged for reading purposes (in case of reports) or for later computer runs (in the case of machine-readable output)? Regarding the particular processing required in the computer run, the programmer wants to know what must be done to change the files of input data into the required output files: what rules or guidelines of the business is he to implement?

This last factor is very important. The programmer must be aware of the arithmetical and logical choices involved in the situation. To illustrate an *arithmetic* choice, suppose a programmer's job is to prepare bills for the firm's customers. The question arises: Are any customers entitled to a discount? If so, how much? In such a case, the programmer needs to integrate a step into the program to tell the computer that it must multiply the selling price by the discount percentage to arrive at the amount of the discount. The discount then must be subtracted from the selling price to obtain the net billing amount for the customer. This illustration, like many others, involves basic arithmetic.

An example of a *logical* choice related to the same billing situation arises when a discount is allowed for volume purchases (say, more than 100 units). The programmer can include instructions in his program to compare the total order quantity to 100. In this case, the comparison is relatively simple and can be easily stated.

The important thing to note at this stage of programming is that the programmer is attempting to settle, right at the outset, the "rules" of the job. These should be well defined in advance, and fixed by operating management. Even though the arithmetic operations appear lengthy at times, it should be noted that they are broken down into a number of simple sequential steps involving basic addition, subtraction, multiplication, or division.

After the programmer has determined how to process *normal* situations, he checks to see if any *exceptions* are expected and plans in advance the steps to be taken to handle each exception. If several alternative courses of action are possible or desirable, a particular alternative usually is specified for him to implement. Referring to the billing illustration, for instance, a transaction from today's file may indicate a customer for whom no record exists in the master file. The procedure to follow might be one of the following alternatives:

1. If the customer is new, a new record should be inserted in the output master file and a regular bill should be produced. Also an additional message should be written out to draw the attention of the sales department to the situation.

2. The transaction could be withheld from processing as a regular bill, pending investigation. It could be written out as it appears onto a separate output exception file and be given special consideration in another computer run.

It should be remembered that this particular phase of problem definition by the programmer is the most difficult and is highly susceptible to error. The error usually results from a failure to account for all of the possible exceptions, rather than from a poor choice in how to handle one. An exception may not come up at the beginning, but when it does occur later, major time losses can result in an attempt to rectify the situation. The programmer must be alert to the types of exceptions which are likely to occur in the future processing of a given application.

Data Description

Having obtained satisfactory answers to his questions, the programmer is now ready to begin his detailed work. The outward appearance of the "working" programmer can be very deceptive, in that there is limited evidence of physical activity. He does most of his work alone, away from the machines, and often over a relatively long period of time.

To organize his thinking, a programmer first records the manner in which the data are to appear at the various stages of processing. He writes down pertinent information regarding any input files to be used, including the number and type of records they contain. Although a rough draft is prepared first, the final format is written on a special preprinted form similar to the one shown in Figure 17-2. Likewise, when printed reports are desired as output, the printed format is determined in advance and laid out on a special form used for that purpose (Figure 17-3).

After the desired formats have been established, the programmer plans the locations where data records will be stored in the primary-storage area of the computer during actual processing. To do this, he records his plans on a form commonly referred to as a *storage map* or memory map (Figure 17-4). Each particular computer has a fixed amount of internal storage available. The storage map provides the programmer with a pictorial representation of that capacity to help in estimating the proportion of this storage that must be allocated to data.

Having advance knowledge of the processing requirements and the type of

FILE NAME			FILE NO.	
Line item file			F 3404.1	

LOCATION		STORAGE MEDIUM	
Tab room		Card tub file	

ACCESS REQUIREMENTS Data for order must be available within 2 minutes.

SEQUENCED BY Stockroom location within customer number.

CONTENT QUALIFICATIONS Name and address cards and line item cards for picking tickets in process or back – ordered.

HOW CURRENT 1 to 5 hours old when entered. Remain in file until stockroom has attempted to fill picking ticket.

RETENTION CHARACTERISTICS Data normally removed upon receipt of picking ticket. Special purge run once every 2 weeks.

LABELS ___

REMARKS ___

CONTENTS

SEQUENCE NO.	MESSAGE NAME	VOLUME		CHARACTERS PER MESSAGE	CHARACTERS PER FILE	
		AVG.	PEAK		AVG.	PEAK
01	Customer name card (R 3001)	320	400	61	19,520	24,400
02	Customer address cards (R 3004)	640	800	65	41,600	52,000
03	Line item cards (R 3008)	2250	2800	62	139,500	173,600
	TOTALS	3210	4000	188	200,620	250,000

DATE	ANALYST	SOURCE	PAGE

STUDY

FIG. 17-2. File sheet.

facilities available, the programmer weighs alternative choices in the use of the storage. The storage map is changed or revised until he finally arrives at a proper balance among the storage requirements of the data, the expected storage requirements of the program, and the processing objectives of the particular computer run.

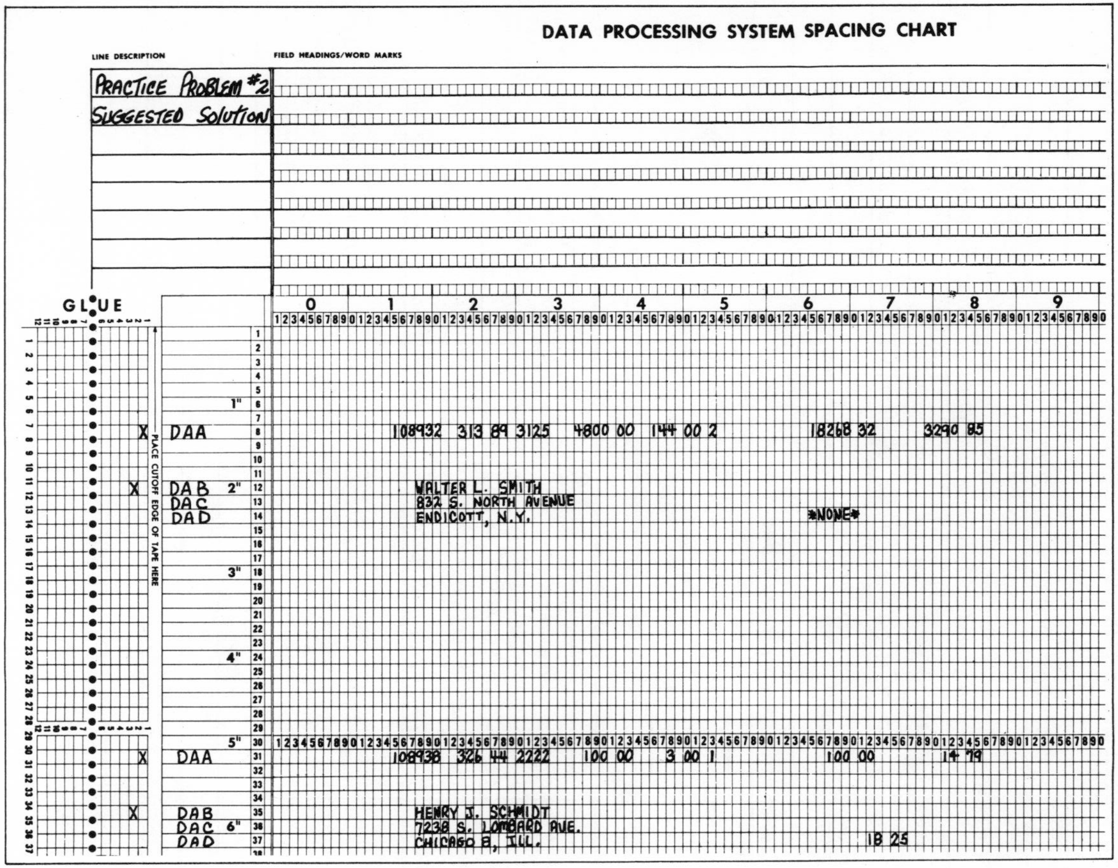

FIG. 17-3. Report format sheet.

STORAGE SCHEMATIC 2000 POSITIONS

APPLICATION _____

DATE _____

	00 01	05	10	15	20	25	30	35	40	45	50	55	60	65	70	75	80	85	90	95	99
100 101											150						180				199
200 201											250										299
300							332 334				350		363								399
400											450										499
500											550										599
600											650										699
700											750										799
800											850										899
900											950										999
1000	1005	1010	1015	1020	1025	1030	1035	1040	1045	1050	1055	1060	1065	1070	1075	1080	1085	1090	1095	1099
1100										1150										1199
1200										1250										1299
1300										1350										1399
1400										1450										1499
1500										1550										1599
1600										1650										1699
1700										1750										1799
1800										1850										1899
1900	1905	1910	1915	1920	1925	1930	1935	1940	1945	1950	1955	1960	1965	1970	1975	1980	1985	1990	1995	1999

FIG. 17-4. Memory map.

223

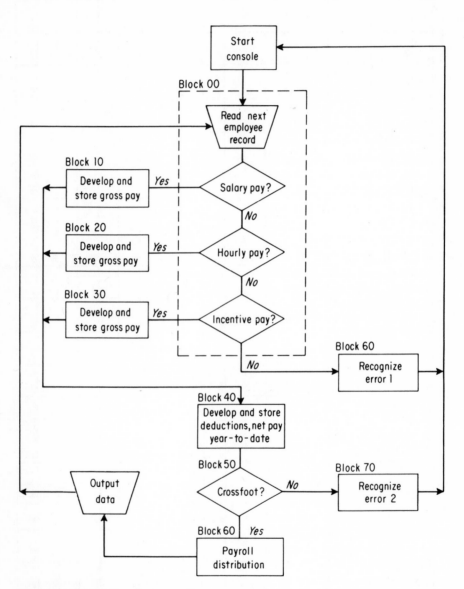

FIG. 17-5. Systems flow chart—payroll.

Logic Description

Before any processing can be performed, the programmer records the processing sequence of the operation by *programming flow charts, decision tables,* or both, in several stages. These are considered the two most common descriptive methods, and since the programmer's task is to write down precise instructions for each machine step, these diagramming stages begin at a very broad level of "general logic" and proceed to a level which breaks down broad functions into individual elements. Figure 17-5 is considered a rather broad presentation of the necessary elements for a payroll application, for instance. By contrast, Figure 17-6 is a detailed chart since it shows the steps performed during the processing of only one block (block *40*) of the previous chart. This shows that the elements included in any given flow chart depend upon the extent and type of details which the programmer feels should be included in the actual processing.

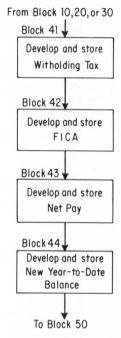

FIG. 17-6. Systems flow chart—block 40.

The Initial Coding Step

After file descriptions, record descriptions, storage maps, and logic diagrams have been prepared, the programmer begins coding. Special forms are used in coding and require that certain data be written in special designated areas on the form (Figure 17-7). Different computers require the use of different languages and this, in turn, requires the use of different coding forms.

COBOL (Common Business-Oriented Language) is a language that can be used on most computer systems, and for this, a special form also is provided (Figure 17-8). FORTRAN (Formula Translator), a procedure-oriented language used mainly in programming scientific applications, also is a "common" language for which special coding sheets are provided (Figure 17-9).

Any programming language will look and sound strange to the layman. However, the programmer is well trained in the particular language he employs in writing computer instructions. A considerable amount of time usually is consumed between the job-definition stage and the completion of initial coding. This ranges from several hours to several months, depending on the complexity of the computer run and on the coding languages used. When the programmer has completed the coding stage, he finally is ready to use the computer.

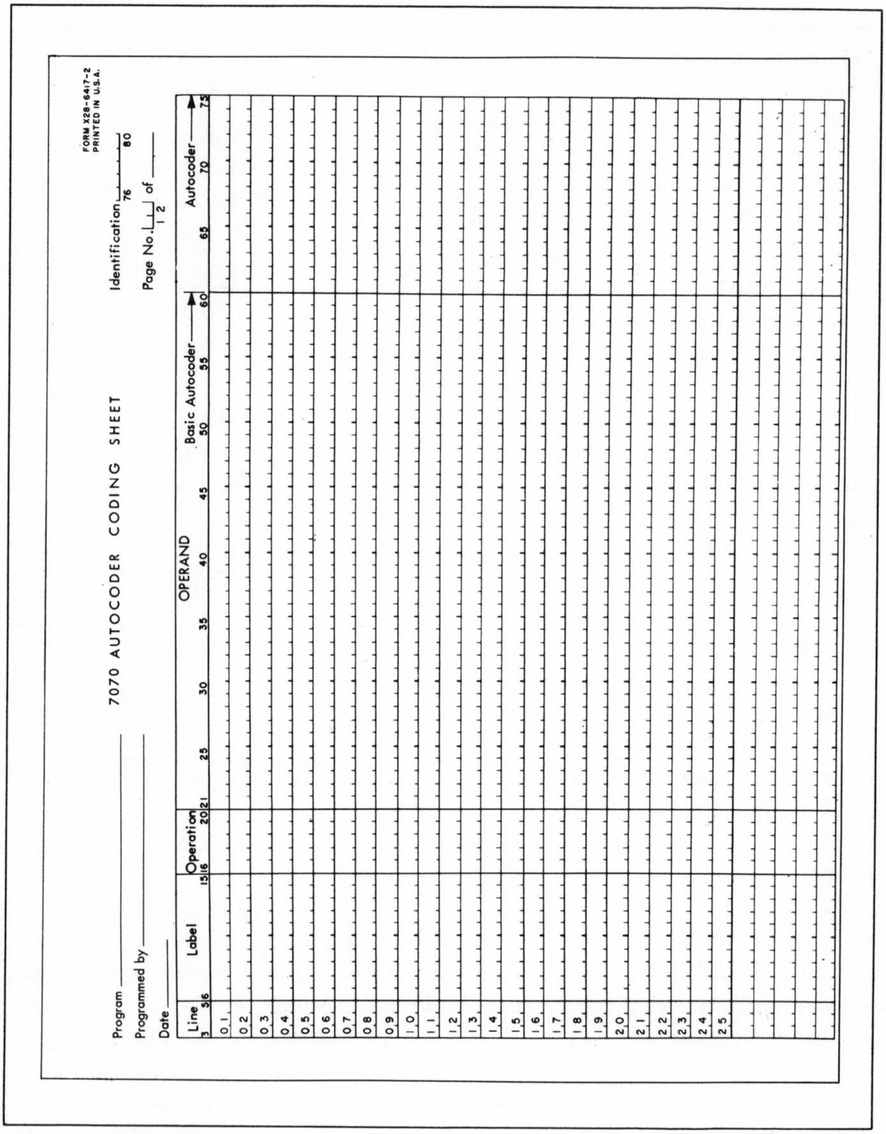
7070 AUTOCODER CODING SHEET

FORM X28-6417-2
PRINTED IN U.S.A.

Program ______
Programmed by ______
Date ______

Identification ______ (76–80)
Page No. ___ (1 2) of ______

Line (3–5)	Label (6–15)	Operation (16–20)	OPERAND — Basic Autocoder (21–60)	Autocoder (61–75)
01				
02				
03				
04				
05				
06				
07				
08				
09				
10				
11				
12				
13				
14				
15				
16				
17				
18				
19				
20				
21				
22				
23				
24				
25				

FIG. 17-7.

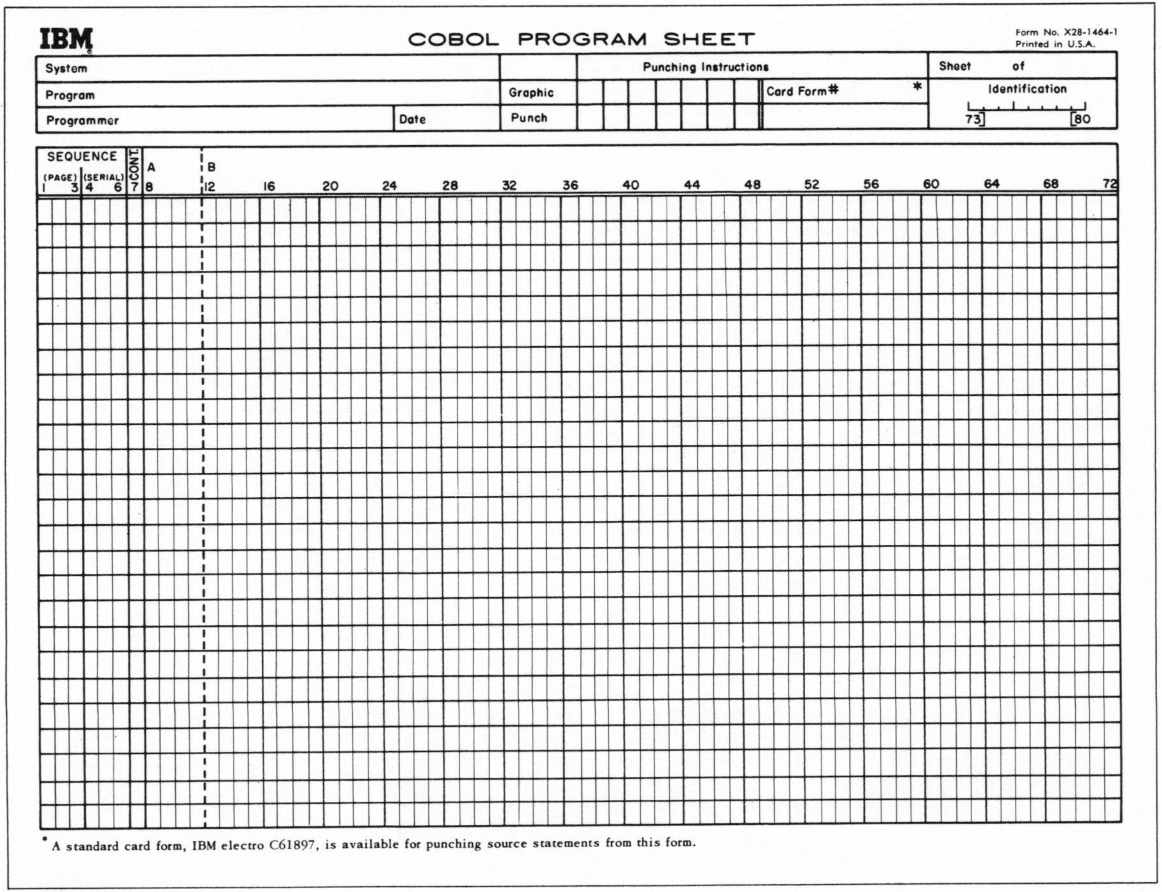
IBM

COBOL PROGRAM SHEET

Form No. X28-1464-1
Printed in U.S.A.

System | Punching Instructions | Sheet of
Program | Graphic | Card Form# * | Identification
Programmer | Date | Punch | 73 80

SEQUENCE (PAGE) 1 3 (SERIAL) 4 6 | CONT. 7 | A 8 | B 12 16 20 24 28 32 36 40 44 48 52 56 60 64 68 72

* A standard card form, IBM electro C61897, is available for punching source statements from this form.

FIG. 17-8. COBOL programming sheet.

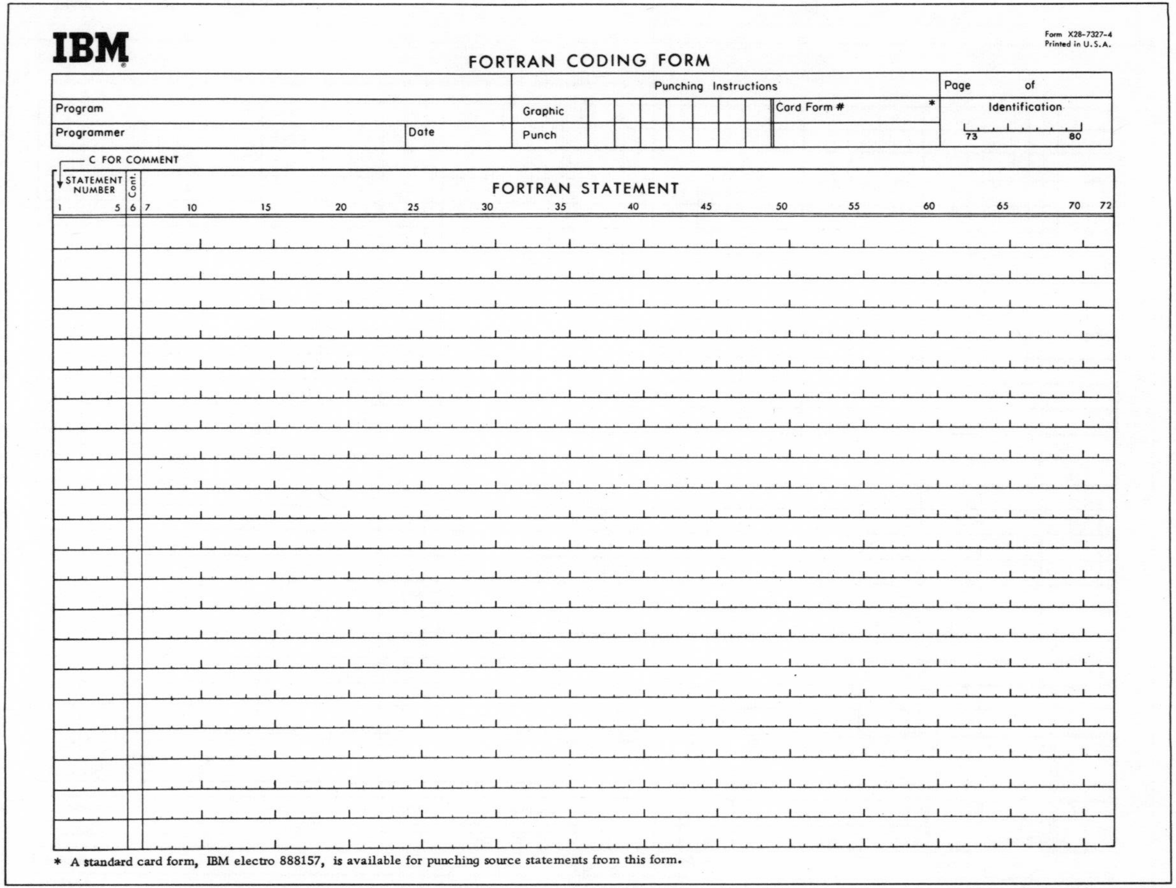
IBM

FORTRAN CODING FORM

Form X28-7327-4
Printed in U.S.A.

	Punching Instructions		Page of
Program	Graphic	Card Form # *	Identification
Programmer / Date	Punch		73 80

C FOR COMMENT

STATEMENT NUMBER | Cont. | FORTRAN STATEMENT

1 5 6 7 10 15 20 25 30 35 40 45 50 55 60 65 70 72

* A standard card form, IBM electro 888157, is available for punching source statements from this form.

FIG. 17-9. FORTRAN programming sheets.

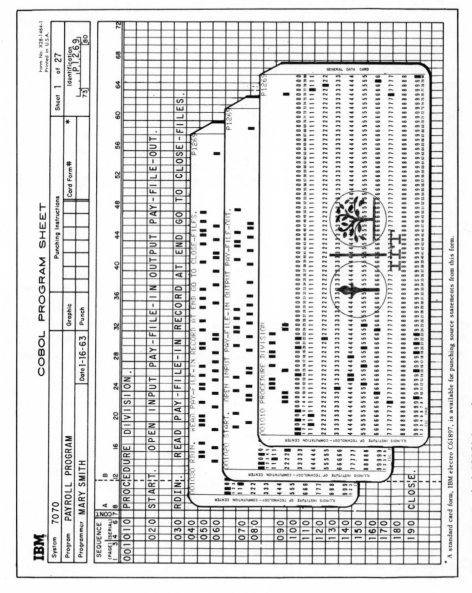

FIG. 17-10. Punched COBOL instructions.

Pre-Compile Preparation

When a program initially is coded in a special language (not directly that of the computer), the computer translates this symbolic language into one it can understand (a machine language). The process is called *compiling*.

In compiling, the various coding sheets are turned over to a keypunch operator, who punches the data from each line onto a separate card, in exactly the same way in which they are written on the coding form. If the coding sheet contains 16 lines (instructions), then 16 cards are punched, constituting the over-all program (Figure 17-10). In keypunching, the operator punches data into the card in specific locations, just as they appear on the coding sheet. For example, page number *001* is shown in the top left corner of the coding sheet. Digits *1* and *3* in that box refer to the column numbers in which the page number must be punched. The keypunch operator then punches *001* in columns *1*, *2*, and *3* as shown in Figure 17-10. This procedure also applies to the remaining characters on that line and to the remaining lines to be punched in their respective cards.

Listing the Punched Program

When the deck of cards representing the program (called the *source* program) has been keypunched, it is run through either an accounting machine or the computer system to produce a *listing* (printing). The listing usually shows what has been punched into the cards, and often other information related to the deck. If a computer system is used for listing, it is common to find additional information included in the printout, such as the total number of cards in the deck, the amount of storage the program will occupy, and even the identification of those areas where there has been an obvious misuse of the language (for example, unintelligible symbols, spaces where there should be none, etc., Figure 17-11).

The programmer thoroughly reviews the listing to make sure that no clerical or mechanical errors have been made in the program. He evaluates the messages supplied in the listing, corrects his original coding sheets in places where language errors have been made, pulls the corresponding cards out of the card deck, and replaces them with new cards punched with the corrected codes. A second listing usually is made of the corrected deck for future reference.

Once all this is accomplished, the programmer refers to his storage map and begins to fill in the amount of storage to be allocated to the program. Even though it is considered a relatively rough estimate, this process nevertheless serves as an aid in determining how reasonable is the approach taken.

Compiling

The prepared deck of source program cards is taken to the computer, and a separate program, called a *compiler*, is first read (loaded) into the machine.

```
AG05            *           DESCRIPTION OF TEMPORARY STORAGE FIELDS
AG06      WORKAREA    DA     1
AG07      GROSSPAY           03,09A5.2
AG08      TAX                13,19A5.2
AG09      FICA               25,29A3.2
AG10      TFICA              35,39A3.2
AG11      NETPAY             43,49A5.2
AG12            *
AG13      ERMESSAGE   DC     -RDW
AG14                         'MASTER IS MISSING FOR MANNUMBER'
AG15      ERRORNO            '          '
AG16            *
AG17            *     PROGRAM
AG18      IOPEN       OPEN   IMASTER,DETAIL,MASTEROUT,CHECKTAPE
AG19      START       GET    DETAIL
AG20      NEXTMASTER  GET    IMASTER
AG21                  COMP   DMANNUMBER,IMANNUMBER,NOMASTER,,NODETAIL
AG22                  ARITH  GROSSPAY=IPAYRATE*DHOURS+DSALES*ICOMISRATE
AG23                  ARITH  TAX=.18*(GROSSPAY-IDEPENDNTS*13.00)
AG24                  ZSIGN  TAX,,,ZEROTAX
AG25      FICATEST    ARITH  FICA=GROSSPAY*.03
AH01                  ARITH  TFICA=IYTDFICA+FICA-144.00
AH02                  ZSIGN  TFICA,FICALC,,FICALC
AH03                  ARITH  FICA=FICA-TFICA
AH04      FICALC      ARITH  IYTDFICA=IYTDFICA+FICA
AH05                  ARITH  IYTDPAY=IYTDPAY+GROSSPAY
AH06                  ARITH  NETPAY=GROSSPAY-TAX-FICA
AH07                  EDMOV  IMANNUMBER TO CMANNUMBER,INAME TO CNAME,NETPAY TO
AH08                         CNETPAY
```

FIG. 17-11. Source program listing—an example.

The compiler program is stored on disks, punched cards or on a reel of tape kept in the installation's library. Once the compiler program is loaded into primary storage, control is transferred to it automatically and the programmer's deck of cards is read in as input data for the compiler program.

The compiler program converts the programmer's punched instructions to machine-language instructions. Output begins to develop from the computer, in the form of punched cards, paper tape, magnetic tape, printed listings, console-typewriter messages, or any combination thereof. Figure 17-12 shows a listing of the program produced in a machine language. The instructions as written by the programmer (*source* program) are on the left and the resulting machine-coded instructions (*object* program) are on the right.

Message Analysis

A listing provides several advantages. First, in addition to a printed copy of the recorded instructions in the input deck, it also shows several columns of numbers. One of these columns represents a sequential numbering of each output line in the listing. Another represents the machine-language coding of the instructions. A third represents the machine addresses of the locations reserved for these instructions.

The listing also includes notes to the programmer regarding the validity and correctness of his coding. He examines each note and takes appropriate action where necessary. For example, a correction usually involves making changes in the coding sheet, repunching the corrected instruction in a new card, and inserting it in the program deck. After corrections are made, the revised input

```
                PROGRAM
CDREF  LABEL      OP   OPERAND                                     CDNO   FD  LOC   INSTRUCTION    REF

AG05   *               DESCRIPTION OF TEMPORARY STORAGE FIELDS                   +0017,41728
AG06   WORKAREA   DA   1
AG07   GROSSPAY        03,09A5.2                                          39   1724                1724
AG08   TAX             13,19A5.2                                          39   1725                1725
AG09   FICA            25,29A3.2                                          59   1726                1726
AG10   TFICA           35,39A3.2                                          59   1727                1727
AG11   NETPAY          43,49A5.2                                          39   1728                1728
AG12   *
AG13   ERMESSAGE  DC   -RDW                                       00232
AG14                   'MASTER IS MISSING FOR MANNUMBER'          00233   09   1729  +0017291738   1729
  X                                                                       09   1730  +0017301738   1730
  X                                                                       09   1731  '7490698200   1731
  X                                                                       09   1732  '7461828269   1732
  X                                                                       09   1733  '7567006676   1733
  X                                                                       09   1734  '7900746175   1734
AG15   ERRORNO                                                    00234   09   1735  '7584746265   1735
                                                                          01   1736  '79           1736
  X                                                                       29   1736  00000000      1736
  X                                                                       09   1737  '000000000    1737
AG16   *                                                                  01   1738  '00           1738
AG17   *
AG18   IOPEN      PROGRAM  !MASTER,DETAIL,MASTEROUT,CHECKTAPE      00235        1739  +0200040578
  X    IOPEN      OPEN     IOCSIXG,IOC,IOPEN                                    1740  +0100091327
  X               BLX      TAPEFILE!M                                           1741  +0100091345
  X               B        TAPEFILEDI                                          1742  +0100091336
  X               B        TAPEFILEMO
```
```
  X    M.22-3+MACREG,02                                           00257        1748  +0110092107
  X    M.23      ST3   CNETPAY(0,1)                                            1849  +3200891611
  X              ZA3   COMAREA.A(6,7)                                          1850  +3300672121
  X              ST3   CNETPAY(2,3)                                            1851  +3200011612
  X              ZA3   COMAREA.A(8,9)                                          1852  +3300892121
  X              ST3   CNETPAY(4,5)                                            1853  +3200231612
  X              ZA3   ','                                         00258        1854  +3300452127
  X              ST3   CNETPAY(6,7)                                            1855  +3300451612
  X              ZA3   COMAREA.A(10,11)                                        1856  +3300012122
  X              ST3   CNETPAY(8,9)                                            1857  +3200671612
  X              ZA3   COMAREA.A(12,13)                             00259        1858  +3300232122
  X              ST3   CNETPAY(10,11)                                          1859  +3200891612
  X              ZA3   COMAREA.A(14,15)                                        1860  +3300452122
  X              ST3   CNETPAY(12,13)                                          1861  +3200011613
  X              ZA3   ','                                                     1862  +3300012127
  X              ST3   CNETPAY(14,15)                               00260        1863  +3200231613
  X              ZA3   COMAREA.A(16,17)                                        1864  +3300672122
  X              ST3   CNETPAY(16,17)                                          1865  +3200451613
  X              ZA3   COMAREA.A(18,19)                                        1866  +3300892122
  X              ST3   CNETPAY(18,19)                                          1867  +3200671613

AHO8A  *         PREPARE TAPE RECORD FOR PRINTING CHECKS OFFLINE
```

FIG. 17-12. Listing—source and object program.

deck is taken back to the computer and the compiling routine is repeated until the output messages during this compiling stage indicate that there are no more obvious errors in the program. After compilation, the output listing represents the compiled (object) program in machine-language form and is presented either on a reel of magnetic tape, on paper tape, or as a deck of punched cards.

Testing and "Debugging"

The machine-language deck (the *object* program) is tested for accuracy by using it in the processing of sample data. This process is called "debugging" the program. It is here that "bugs" in the program logic and coding should be discovered by testing the results of all possible types of transactions and alternatives that could occur in using "live" data. Once debugged, the program is tested with "live" data, a process which is necessary to allow the computer, under the control of the object program, to process data previously processed manually, and compare the results of the two methods. This parallel operation is called *cutover.*

Cutover may also include the conversion of input files to the form used by the new computer method. This usually involves keypunching and special computer runs.

The programmer observes the testing operation, making corrections, and with his management, reviews the results. It is at this time in particular that the importance of identifying all exceptions during the job-definition stage is brought into focus. If the job definition was well done, no "surprises" are likely to occur. However, if an exception is detected for which no provision has been made, *patching* or updating of the program must be done.

Production

Before a computer run is initiated, instructions are given to the machine operators to tell them how the computer components should be set up for the job, what to do when any particular message is typed out, and where output is to be forwarded and filed. When this is done, the installation is ready to use the object program over and over again whenever the application for which it was written is repeated. The job of carrying out the daily production is turned over to the operating personnel, and the programmer is now ready to begin a new project.

The foregoing cycle (problem definition to production) points out that no end result could be accomplished without the creative and ingenious efforts of human beings. Although a powerful tool, the computer could not, for example, change time-card information into an employee's paycheck, create customer bills, or do any other routine without the advance preparation and loading of a program which can "tell" it what to do. Man is still the "master" and the computer is the "slave."

GLOSSARY OF TERMS

COBOL: *C*ommon *B*usiness-*O*riented *L*anguage. A computer language used in business data processing to prepare a program.

CODING: The translation of flow diagrams into the language of the computer.

COMPILE: To prepare a machine language program from a computer program written in another programming language by making use of the over-all logic structure of the program, generating more than one machine instruction for each symbolic statement, or both, as well as performing the function of an assembler.

DEBUG: To detect, locate, and remove mistakes from a routine or malfunctions from a computer. Synonymous with *troubleshoot*.

FLOW CHART: A graphical representation for the definition, analysis, or solution of a problem in which symbols are used to represent operations, data, flow, and equipment.

FORTRAN: *Fo*rmula *tran*slator. Any of several specific procedure-oriented programming languages.

OBJECT PROGRAM: The program which is the output of an automatic coding system. Often the object program is a machine language program ready for execution, but it may well be an intermediate language.

SOURCE PROGRAM: A program written in a source language. A language that is an input to a given translation process.

STORAGE MAP: A pictorial aid used by the programmer for estimating the proportion of storage capacity to be allocated to data.

QUESTIONS FOR REVIEW

1. What is a program? Give an example.
2. What are the steps involved in the preparation of a program? Explain fully.
3. What is a storage map? Why is it used?
4. List and describe the advantages of listing program instructions prior to their use in a computer run.
5. What factors are involved in the testing and debugging stage?

chapter

18

Control
and the Stored Program

Control is defined as mastery over starting or stopping the computer system, either manually or automatically. Manual control often is used when it is necessary to load input data or machine instructions. Certain buttons are depressed which cause an input device to read-in or "load" the data into primary storage; then the computer is started manually. From this point on, the instructions stored in the computer control its operations automatically. This is referred to as *automatic control*. The instructions placed in primary storage are called *the stored program.*

The control unit consists of computer elements which aid in executing the stored instructions in a logical sequence. They interpret each instruction in the order given by the programmer and execute the command, depending on the type of interpretation made. Without this, no instruction could be executed automatically; neither could any interpretation be applied toward the achievement of the required output.

The Stored Program

To understand the stored-program concept, assume that the object program already is loaded into the computer and is undergoing the processing of data records systematically. This status is referred to as the *object time,* or the time span during which a stored program is in active control of a given application.

As described in a previous chapter, the computer system is made up of a central processing unit containing primary storage, the arithmetic unit, a control unit, and input/output units of various types. Referring to the **pro-**

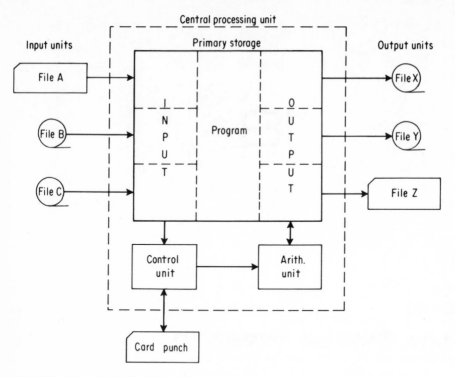

FIG. 18-1. Generalized description of computer system.

grammer's storage map, we would find that certain areas of primary storage are reserved for the temporary retention of the current-data records until they are processed. At that time, new data are read in, stored in the reserved area, and processed by the program in control. The transfer of new input data occurs when a signal is directed to the proper input unit, commanding it to read the next record into the same primary-storage area, thus completely replacing the previous contents. Likewise, the same situation exists in the output areas. As each output record is formed in the storage area, a signal is directed to the proper output unit, causing the record to be written out. The next output record is then formed in the same area, completely replacing the previous one. In this case, the printer advances the form one line in order to print the new data, thus avoiding double printing on the same line.

The remaining areas of primary storage are set aside to store the object program (Figure 18-1). Looking at the memory map shown in Figure 18-2, we see that primary storage might contain the following data:

LOCATION	CONTENTS
062	+ 16093
063	+ 21462
064	− 11104
065	+ 37178

In this example, it is assumed that the storage area is divided into many

STORAGE SCHEMATIC – 400 WORDS

APPLICATION _____   DATE _____

000	1	2	3	4	5	6	7	8	9	010	1	2	3	4	5	6	7	8	9
020										030									
040										050									
060			+ 16093	+ 21462	– 11104	+ 37178					070									
080										090									
100										110									
120										130									
140										150									
160										170									
180										190									
200										210									
220										230									
240										250									
260										270									
280										290									
300										310									
320										330									
340										350									
360										370									
380										390									

FIG. 18-2. Memory map for sample problem.

separate locations, each of which is capable of storing five digits, plus an accompanying sign in a coded form. This size has been chosen for purposes of illustration only, since one could select any number of positions in a given location. The contents of each location—that is, the data it contains—are referred to as a *word*. A word may represent either coded data or an instruction. If the word contains data to be processed, it is called a *data word;* if it contains an instruction, it is called an *instruction word.*

A computer word is the basic unit of information in a computer. In some machines, it is of a fixed length; that is, the number of characters it contains is limited to a predetermined size and is handled as a group. This is referred to as *fixed word-length.*

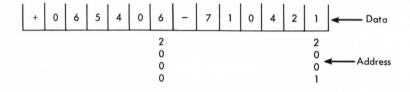

| 6 | 4 | 1 | 7 | 0 | 2 | ◄——— Data |

2	2	2	2	2	2	
0	0	0	0	0	0	◄——— Address
0	0	0	0	0	0	
0	1	2	3	4	5	

(A) An example of a variable word length.

| + | 0 | 6 | 5 | 4 | 0 | 6 | – | 7 | 1 | 0 | 4 | 2 | 1 | ◄——— Data |

		2					2	
		0					0	◄——Address
		0					0	
		0					1	

(B) An example of a fixed word-length.

FIG. 18-3.

Other machines that do not impose a limit on the length of a given word are called *variable word-length,* or "character" machines. Figure 18-3A shows an example of a variable word-length. Each character has its own address (location number); for example, digit 2 is located in *2005* and digit 4 is located in *2001*. Figure 18-3B illustrates a fixed word-length and defines the length of a word to be six characters, plus its sign. These characters are addressed by one address only; for example, the word containing −*710421* is addressed as a group by *2001* and the word containing +*065406* also is addressed as a group by *2000*.

Fixed word-length computers have the following chief characteristics:

1. No storage positions are required to define fields. Since the length of each transmission is determined by the computer itself, the fixed-word concept automatically defines the fields.

2. Since the instructions are of fixed length, parallel access is possible. All fixed-word machines have this capability.

3. Fixed-word machines usually have higher speed because of their parallel access characteristics; in some machines, since arithmetic circuits also can be parallel, the speed can be many times faster than others.

4. Storage may be pure binary or in some other code structure.

By comparison, in variable word-length computers, each position in storage (whether a digit or a character) is individually addressable. Units of transfer are governed only by the practical limits of total storage. Fields or records are usually defined by a special character in the high-order position (left column) of a given record to separate it from an adjacent one. This character is called a flag bit or a word mark.

In order to code data in the BCD or other codes, the computer converts decimal representation at the input stage to the required computer code for processing. At the end of the processing, a converter transforms the coded output back into decimal representation, understandable by the programmer or the user.

Finally, arithmetic circuitry usually is serial, by digit. The variable nature of the fields makes it difficult to design parallel devices. In the previous illustration, it also is assumed that each location is identified by a three-digit address (again, an arbitrary size selected for the purpose of the example). The address itself is not physically labeled in storage; the address simply is a label determined by those who designed and built the machine. In Figure 18-2, each of the three-digit numbers is called an address and each box on the map represents one word of storage; for instance, the word containing +16093 is one word of storage, the address of which is 062.

Instructions

A stored program consists of a set of *instructions* (commands) to put the computer into a cycle for executing each instruction, one after the other, until the job is done. It has been mentioned that both data and instructions are stored in primary storage. Through the stored program the control unit can decide whether a particular word is a data word or an instruction word.

At the beginning of each instruction cycle, an instruction word is channeled to the control unit, where designated electrical equivalents of the digit values cause circuits to be set up to control the next part of the cycle. In the next part of the cycle, another data word generally is brought out to the arithmetic unit, where other circuits are affected and a result is established in a specific register. Then the cycle is repeated, and normally the sequential organization of the program directs that the instruction word following the previously used instruction word will be called into the control unit. Again, the electrical analysis is effected and the rest of the cycle goes on as before, acting upon one instruction at a time automatically.

Although electronic speeds give the impression that many things are happening at the same time, a look into the design of the computer shows the contrary. In most computers each cycle representing an instruction is carried out independently and alone. The word which reaches the control unit at the beginning of the cycle is interpreted as an instruction. The next word in storage will be used as the next instruction unless the effect of the first instruction causes a transfer or change in the normal sequence. It remains for the programmer to take advantage of these facts and organize both instructions and data in storage to do useful work.

An instruction, then, is contained in a word transmitted from primary storage to the control unit at the beginning of a machine cycle. Its function is to set up the necessary circuits so that the rest of the cycle can perform some useful purpose. In order to carry out this function, an instruction affects the control unit by its two parts: the *operation code* and the *operand* or address portion (Figure 18-4).

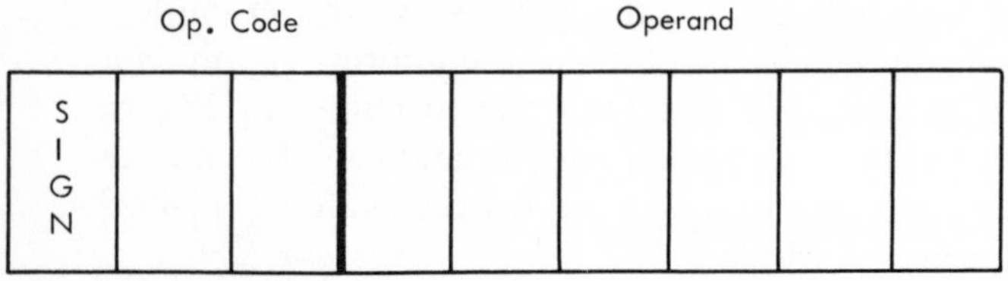

Op. Code Operand

FIG. 18-4. The instruction format.

The effect of the operation code is to set up what is to be done during the rest of the cycle. The operand portion has the effect of specifying the part of the computer system to be used in that operation. When a computer is being designed, the manufacturer has several choices to make concerning instructions, but the real choice is the number of circuits that should be built in to handle the number of desired operations. The final decision is related to (1) the cost of incorporating the necessary circuits, (2) the cost involved in programming it with fewer instructions, and (3) the cost at object time in carrying out the operations. The final choice results in the *instruction set* of the machine. An example of an instruction set is shown in the sample program later in this chapter.

There are other factors which the designer must consider in developing an instruction set for a computer. For example, let us consider the function of addition. To add, a computer must (1) clear a register of any previous contents; (2) move a word from storage to that register; (3) add another word to the first, so that the sum ends up in the register; and (4) store the sum in a specific location in primary storage. It is quite possible to build circuits to perform one, two, three, or all four functions in one cycle. Whatever the designer decides will have a bearing on the cost of the equipment, the amount of programming time that will be required, and the execution time for the completion of a given application.

Once this decision is made, other matters begin to require attention. For example, if an instruction set of more than ten separate operations is decided upon (0–9), then the number of digits in the word needed to represent the operation code will have to be a minimum of two digits (assuming that only numeric codes are used). This allowance makes it possible to have a unique code for 100 different operations (00–99). If 100 operations are too many, however, then a protection device must be built into the control unit to recognize invalid codes. The net result is to come up with a well-defined "instruction set" considering the codes used and any problems created as a result of this choice.

When one is given the designer's decisions, the concept of storing a program, and the definition of an instruction, another fact becomes clear: since instructions and data are stored in the same place and in the same way, and since an instruction can cause an operation on any word in storage, it follows that one instruction can operate on another. This ability represents the real power of the stored program. When one sequence of instructions recognizes certain facts about the data being processed, other sequences of instructions can be altered, at object time, to cause different operations to occur. This capability brings about a remarkable expansion of the power available to the programmer, although it also requires that he be careful and precise in his logic and in the type of instructions he writes for the computer to execute.

Computer Operation and Input/Output Units

The computer *console* is used to perform two main functions: (1) to initiate the execution of the stored program and (2) to provide a communication link between the operator and the system after the stored program is under way (Figure 18-5).

To aid in communicating data between man and machine, the console is equipped with buttons, switches, and related circuits for (1) inserting a missing or needed word into storage manually, (2) accessing a particular word as the first cycle begins, and (3) setting up an impulse for starting the first cycle (see Figure 18-1). To load the program, the operator depresses some keys on the console and places specific instructions in storage. These instructions are called a "load program." The load program now takes over and causes the object program to be read through the proper input unit into a specific area in storage. The last instruction of the load program causes the sequence of instructions to transfer to the word containing the first instruction of the ob-

FIG. 18-5. A computer console (*courtesy Honeywell EDP Division*).

ject program just stored. From then on, the object program is in direct control. This process is called *program loading*.

As the object program begins to function, the flow of data to be processed proceeds from the input units to storage, through the processing sections, and then to the output units. It is continuous and automatic. The role of each of these components is known and clear to the programmer. The input unit(s), for instance, supply the data records, one or more at a time, as requested by the program through the control unit. The storage unit holds the data received from the input unit as well as the program for the use of the control unit as processing progresses. The arithmetic unit combines words in a specified fashion as established by the instructions in the control unit. The output unit(s) accepts the complete data records at times selected by the program through the control unit. Throughout this whole process, the console provides a monitoring station to observe signals sent from the control unit, indicating the current state of the processing routine.

A Sample Program

The following program is presented to illustrate the basic functions of a computer system as operated by a stored program. For the illustration several assumptions are made, as follows:

Input Units: one card reader.

Output Units: one printer.

Control Unit: normal circuits and four indicators called high, low, equal, and end-of-file, each of which has two settings (on or off).

Console: has button for word entry, a CLEAR button to clear all storage to blanks, and a typewriter.

Storage: 1,000 eight-character words, with signs, location addresses running from 000 to 999.

Arithmetic Unit: one eight-digit register, with sign.

Instruction Set: In the following section, the name of the operation is given first, followed by the manner in which this instruction would appear in storage. Letters *AAA* are used to represent any three-digit address. Finally, a description of the function performed is given. All instructions are made up as shown in Figure 18-4; that is, the sign is shown in the sign column, the next two digits represent the operation part (operation code), and the remaining six digits represent the operand part.

READ: +01 000AAA, read one 80-column card from the input unit into a 10-word storage area beginning in location AAA. (Ten words would be necessary for storage of all 80 columns.)

WRITE: +02 000AAA, write one record of 10 words beginning in location AAA on the output unit (80 characters sent to printer).

CLEAR AND ADD: +03 000AAA, clear the contents of the arithmetic register (accumulator), and then add into the register the word located at AAA.

ADD: +04 000 AAA, add the word located at AAA to the word in the arithmetic register. Place the sum in the arithmetic register.

SUBTRACT: +05 000AAA, subtract the word located at AAA from the word in the arithmetic register. Place the difference in the arithmetic register.

MULTIPLY: +06 000AAA, multiply the word in the arithmetic register by the word located at AAA. Place the product in the arithmetic register.

DIVIDE: +07 000AAA, divide the word in the arithmetic register by the word located at AAA. Place the quotient in the arithmetic register.

COMPARE: +08 000AAA, compare the value of the word located at AAA with the word in the arithmetic register. If the number in the arithmetic register is higher, set the "HIGH" indicator in the control unit "ON." If the word in the arithmetic register is lower, set the "LOW" indicator "ON." If the two words are exactly the same, set the "EQUAL" indicator "ON."

BRANCH: +09 000AAA, instead of using the next sequential word as the next instruction, use the word located at AAA as the next instruction.

TEST BRANCH HIGH: +10 000AAA, if the "HIGH" indicator is "ON," turn it "OFF" and take the word at AAA as the next instruction.

TEST BRANCH LOW: +11 000AAA, if the "LOW" indicator is "ON," turn it "OFF" and take the word at AAA as the next instruction.

TEST BRANCH EQUAL: +12 000AAA, if the "EQUAL" indicator is "ON," turn it "OFF" and take the word at AAA as the next instruction.

BRANCH END OF FILE: +13 000AAA, if the "END OF FILE" indicator has been turned "ON" because the last input record has been read, turn it "OFF" and take the word at AAA as the next instruction.

STORE: +14 000AAA, replace the word at AAA by the contents of the arithmetic unit register.

HALT: +15 000AAA, stop the machine and type the digits AAA on the console.

Given the computer specifications and instruction set above, the programmer is asked to add two numbers from each input record and print the sum. When the last sum is printed, the grand total of all the sums is to be printed, preceded by the word "TOTAL." As the records are processed, a check is made to insure that the deck is in ascending sequence. If any card is out of order, the run is to be terminated and the operator is to be informed. In this case, cards would be resequenced and the entire run started over. These steps are shown graphically in Figure 18-6.

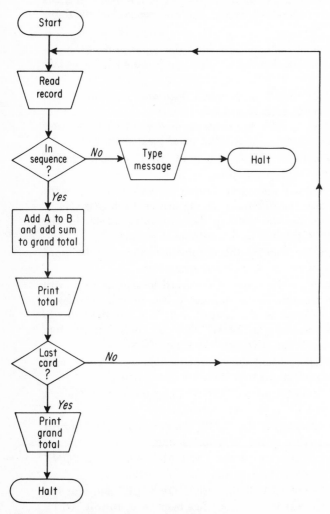

FIG. 18-6. Programming flow chart—sample problem.

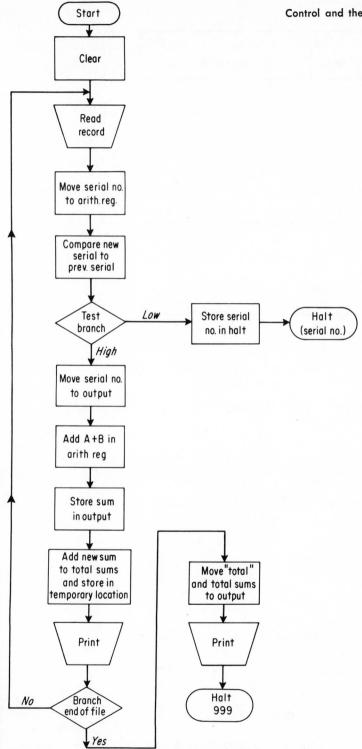

FIG. 18-7. Detailed flow chart—sample problem.

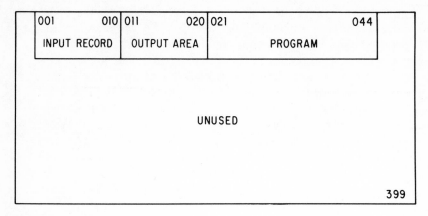

FIG. 18-8. Memory allocation.

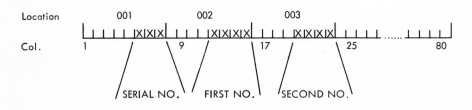

INPUT RECORD LAYOUT

FIG. 18-9.

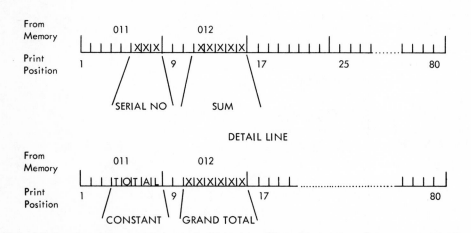

DETAIL LINE

TOTAL LINE

OUTPUT RECORD LAYOUT

FIG. 18-10.

Another step in programming this problem calls for the programmer to prepare a more detailed flow chart showing the exact functions which the computer must perform to process the data (Figure 18-7). The memory allocation is determined next to ascertain the availability of space for input records, output area, and the stored program (Figure 18-8).

The layout of the records as they should appear in the cards and on the printed page are shown in Figures 18-9 and 18-10, respectively.

Once completed, the detail flow chart is coded into the proper set of machine instructions and later punched into cards for loading the program (Figure 18-11). Figure 18-12 shows the detail flow chart for the processing, keyed to the coded program. One address of the instruction that carries out the function is written just above and to the left of the corresponding block. These numbers are inserted after the coding has been completed.

In examining the sequence of coding performed, we find that the first instruction is "read." The programmer then determines the way in which he can check the sequence. Except for the first record, the serial number of the previous record can always be found in the first word of the output area. When the first record is being processed, location 011 should be blank (as a result of a previous clearing of the memory) so that the compare instruction can be addressed to location 011.

The next instruction breaks the sequence if a record is found out of place. When the programmer writes the instruction, he is not really sure how many locations will be necessary for the normal processing. His procedure is to leave the last three digits unfilled and to underline them to remind himself that these must be filled in later (Figure 18-11).

Instructions located in 025, 026, 027, and 028 perform the detail arithmetic required. The next two instructions (in locations 029 and 030) are used for storing the running grand total. When he comes to these instructions, the programmer knows that he can use any word in storage located outside either the record area or the instruction area for this purpose. He leaves the address part of the instruction blank, underlines it, and goes on.

The next instruction (031) causes a detail line to be printed. Instructions 032 and 033 are included to test for the last record. If the last card read is the last record, then instruction 033 is skipped and instruction 034 is executed, resulting in branching to print the TOTAL as output (instruction 044), and then HALT. However, if the last card read is *not* the last record, instruction 033 is executed, which in effect branches the program to the top instruction (021), which is to read the next record in sequence. It should be noted that by using the word "TOTAL," the programmer has the facility to load the word along with the letters "TOTAL" at the same time he is loading the program. This type of word is called a *constant* to differentiate it from the instructions and the data.

Instructions at 036 to 038 complete the preparation of the grand total line and execute its printing. As shown in Figure 18-11, instruction 036 refers to the running total location, which still is not fixed. This causes the programmer to

Address	Contents
021	+01 000 001
022	+03 000 001
023	+08 000 011
024	+11 000 040
025	+14 000 011
026	+03 000 002
027	+04 000 003
028	+14 000 012
029	+04 000 043
030	+14 000 043
031	+02 000 011
032	+13 000 034
033	+09 000 021
034	+03 000 044
035	+14 000 011
036	+03 000 043
037	+14 000 012
038	+02 000 011
039	+15 000 999
040	+04 000 042
041	+14 000 042
042	+15 000 (000)

Constants

| 043 | +00 000 000 |
| 044 | Total |

FIG. 18-11. Machine language flow chart—sample problem.

underline the address for future reference. When the instruction at 039 is reached, the job is completed. The message "999," a common convention among programmers, is typed to inform the operator of the end of the operation. These digits fill out the "HALT" instruction.

At this time, the programmer may write an instruction to check whether a record is out of sequence. Now that he knows the exact instruction address, he goes back on the coding sheet and fills out the instruction 024 with the digits "040." Instruction 041 stores the contents of the next instruction (042) which is a "halt" instruction. The instruction located at 042 is written on the coding sheet as + 15 000 (000). The parentheses serve as a reminder that the address will be modified before it is executed. These parentheses are not key-punched.

The programmer has now completed all the necessary instruction coding except for filling in the address portions of those to be located at 029, 030,

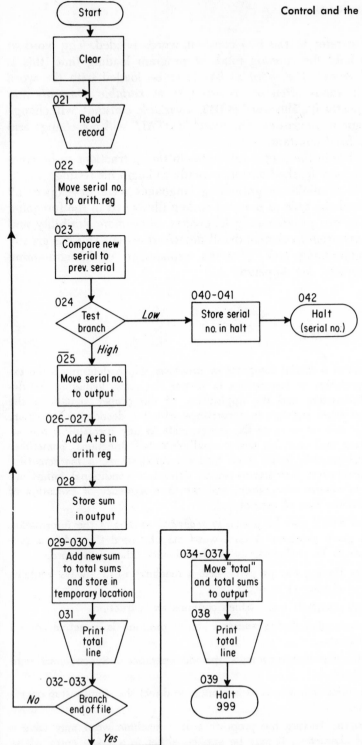

FIG. 18-12. Detailed flow chart for processing—sample problem.

034, and 036. These refer to the two constant words needed. The word at 043 is assigned to hold the running total; at program loading time, this is started out as "all zeros." The word at 044 is to be loaded with the word "TOTAL." These locations often are referred to as *variable constants* and *fixed constants,* respectively. The word at 043, a variable constant, will change in value as the program progresses. The word "TOTAL" will not change and is an example of a fixed constant.

The programmer fills in the proper addresses in the instructions to be completed. His coding is now finished and he is ready to begin his testing.

Until higher level symbolic programming languages were developed, all programming required the type of detailed coding illustrated in the foregoing sample program. Modern programming languages allow more flexibility and do not require the attention to clerical detail described above. This has greatly simplified the programming task. (For an explanation of "Programming Languages and Systems," see Appendix A.)

GLOSSARY OF TERMS

CONTROL: 1. The part of a digital computer or processor which determines the execution and interpretation of instructions in proper sequence, including the decoding of each instruction and the application of the proper signals to the arithmetic unit and other registers in accordance with the decoded information. 2. Frequently, it is one or more of the components in any mechanism responsible for interpreting and carrying out manually-initiated directions. Sometimes it is called manual control. 3. In some business applications, a mathematical check. 4. In programming, instructions which determine conditional jumps are often referred to as control instructions, and the time sequence of execution of instructions is called the flow of control.

DATA WORD: A word which may be primarily regarded as part of the information manipulated by a given program. A data word may be used to modify a program instruction, or to be arithmetically combined with other data words.

FIXED WORD-LENGTH: Having the property that a machine word always contains the same number of characters or digits.

INSTRUCTION WORD: A computer word which contains an instruction.

OBJECT TIME: The time span during which a stored program is in active control of a specific application.

OPERATION CODE: A code that represents specific operations. Synonymous with *instruction code*.

STORED PROGRAM: A series of instructions in storage to direct the step-by-step operation of the machine.

VARIABLE WORD-LENGTH: Having the property that a machine word may have a variable number of characters. It may be applied either to a single entry whose information content may be changed from time to time, or to a group of functionally similar entries whose corresponding components are of different length.

WORD: An ordered set of characters which occupies one storage location and is treated by the computer circuits as a unit and transferred as such. Ordinarily a word is treated by the control unit as an instruction, and by the arithmetic unit as a quantity. Word lengths may be fixed or variable depending on the particular computer.

WORD-LENGTH: The number of bits or other characters in a word.

QUESTIONS FOR REVIEW

1. What is meant by control? By automatic control?
2. Describe the main function(s) of the stored program.
3. What are the two main parts of an instruction? Describe each fully. Give an example.
4. How does the control unit carry out the interpretation of instructions?
5. Discuss the role of the console in the processing of data.
6. What is meant by program loading? How is a program loaded in the computer?

chapter

19

Program Preparation— Flow Charts and Decision Tables

What is Flow Charting?

A flow chart or diagram is defined as a means of expressing a solution to a given problem. Flow charts commonly are used in several fields of endeavor, including physics and architecture. They are used in business as well, and are a basic step in programming procedure.

Before programming an application, it is important to develop the logic to be used for the solution of the various aspects of the problem. This approach is similar to that of "laying out" a long motor trip in advance, or of diagramming a football play on the blackboard before the game is played. Figure 19-1 shows the logic involved by a student in getting ready to go to school in the morning.

In order to flow chart correctly and properly, a programmer must be acquainted with the basic techniques and be familiar with selected symbols, each of which represents a specific action. Once completed, the flow chart can be converted into a machine-language program, ready to process data.

The main symbols in flowcharting are the input/output symbol, the processing symbol, and the logic symbol. Others include the connector and the terminal symbols (Figure 19-2). While different symbols are used by various organizations, there has been a serious effort to standardize them. The symbols used in the following examples have been recommended by the American Standards Association Committee on Computers and Information Processing.

The input/output symbol may be used to show either an input or an output step required in the processing of given data. For example, "read a card" (input) and "punch or print the results" (output) use the same symbol. To help us distinguish between an input and an output step, however, the former usually is located on top (at the beginning) of the flow chart, and the latter is located at the bottom (end).

FIG. 19-1. Sample flow chart—on getting to school in the morning.

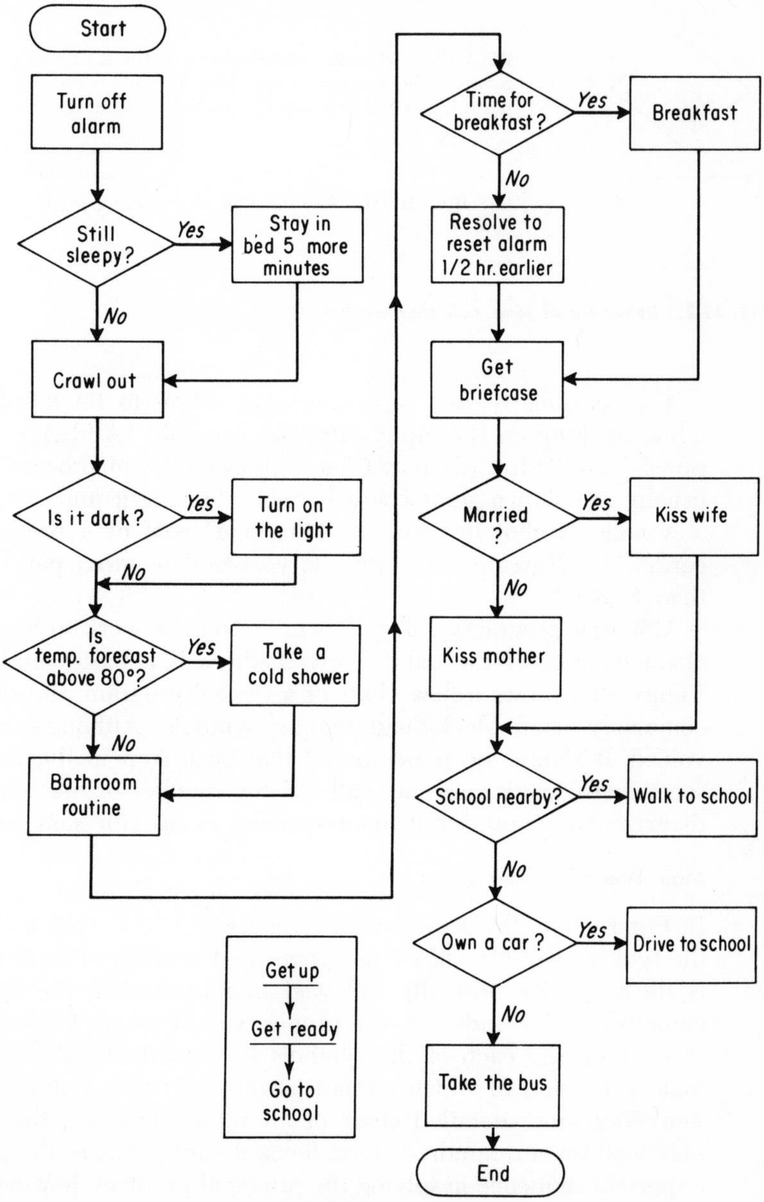

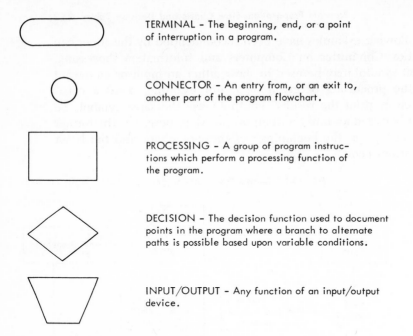

TERMINAL – The beginning, end, or a point of interruption in a program.

CONNECTOR – An entry from, or an exit to, another part of the program flowchart.

PROCESSING – A group of program instructions which perform a processing function of the program.

DECISION – The decision function used to document points in the program where a branch to alternate paths is possible based upon variable conditions.

INPUT/OUTPUT – Any function of an input/output device.

FIG. 19-2. Definitions of some flow chart symbols.

A processing symbol represents any action to be taken by the computer while working on the input data. For example, "Add $A + B$," "Move data to punch," and "Multiply $B \times C$" are all examples of processing instructions and usually are shown somewhere between the input and output symbols.

A logic symbol involves the "thinking" part of a program. "Is it the last card?" "Is A greater than B?" "Is year-to-date gross pay equal to or greater than $4,800?"

Although programs differ, depending on the work to be performed and the characteristics of the data involved, there is a basic similarity among them. Figure 19-3 shows a flow chart of a typical program, illustrating the five most commonly used block-diagramming symbols. Although other ideas are involved, it should be remembered that each step in the logic diagram represents useful work and may call for any number of machine instructions. The diagram can be used to define terms and to describe some common techniques.

Main Line of a Flow Chart

In Figure 19-3, the sequence of steps from A to E (top to bottom) represents the typical idea flow of all programs, and is referred to as the *main line*. This is the sequence normally followed in representing the major job to be accomplished, and indicates the proper way in which to read a flow chart. The steps following each of the symbols B, C, and D indicate the presence of a logical decision in which circumstances can cause a deviation from the main line. In a more detailed chart of an actual program, these "decision points" may total several hundred steps. Since the main line of the program is the most important sequence in solving the principal problem, however, the programmer pays special attention to the way in which he implements it. The goal is to minimize the time required to execute the main line, thus producing a workable and efficient program.

Housekeeping

In every program, a certain amount of "housekeeping" is necessary. This requirement involves setting up basic steps in the computer's internal registers or storage areas, such as steps to clear certain areas to blank or to zero, reading in the input record, resetting accumulators, etc. A programmer usually is aware of the importance of the housekeeping (initialization) stage, since it

FIG. 19-3. Sample flow chart—main line and subroutine.

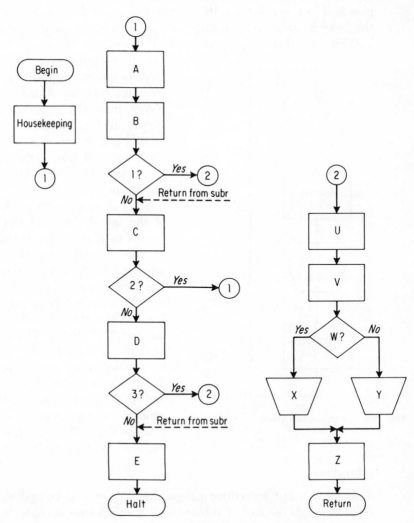

might be required more than once during processing, especially in the event it is necessary to restart the program. When this happens, the tedious routine of reloading the entire program becomes unnecessary.

Looping

Certain calculations involve the repetition of a number of instructions over and over again. The programmer can avoid wasted storage space and effort by writing out one set of instructions in which the last instruction directs the control unit to "branch" back (or repeat) the process, rather than writing a complete set of instructions for each record read. This repetitive operation is termed *looping*.

Figure 19-4 shows a flow chart which simply calls for an input card to be read, its contents to be moved to the punch area, and then the data to be punched in a blank card. In a 1,000-card input deck, this flow chart (through the branch instruction at the bottom) would be used repetitively until the 1,000th card has been processed. Without the "looping" feature, the programmer would have to write out a 3,000-step program, duplicating the first three steps for each input card in the same deck. Every time the program flow-charted in Figure 19-4 is looped back to process another card, it executes a *pass*. In this example, it will take 1,000 passes to process the entire deck of 1,000 cards fed in for processing.

The necessary elements for a loop consist of the initial data and the instructions required to perform the operation, some sort of counter, and a storage location in which intermediate results are temporarily stored. The loop begins when a counter is fed with a predetermined beginning value, usually 1 or 0. Then, the operation is performed and the result is stored. The counter is tested against a predetermined value, and if the comparison does not indicate the end of the operation, a fixed amount is added to the counter, typically +1, while the whole process is repeated. When the counter reaches the end value, the loop is broken and the program continues.

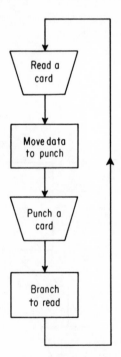

FIG. 19-4. A simple flow chart—an example.

Subroutines

A major attempt to reduce programming cost and compiling time has been made through the use of *subroutines*. A subroutine occupies a secondary or a subordinate function within the over-all program, and one of its main features is that it can be written separately from the main program and be kept in a "library" until it is needed, at which time it is integrated into the main program for proper use.

A subroutine is a set of instructions which varies in size, ranging from a few to several hundred instructions. When it is in operation, a subroutine derives its information (input) from the main program, performs the required steps

FIG. 19-5. Sample program flow chart—no subroutine.

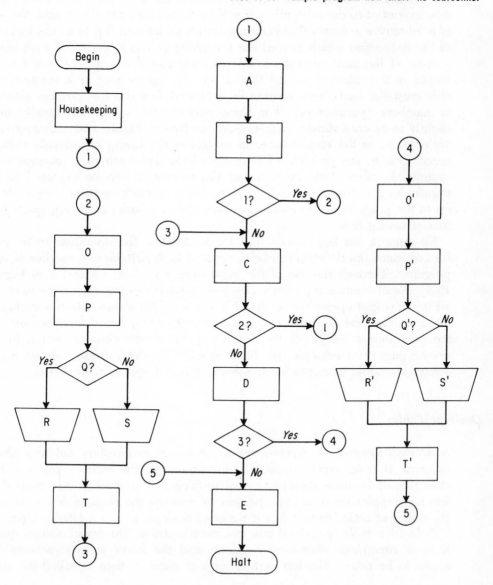

within its capacity, and then furnishes its results (output) back to the main program. These inputs to and outputs from a subroutine often are referred to as *entrance parameters* and *exit parameters*.

To illustrate, Figure 19-3 shows a subroutine in the set of symbols beginning with block U and ending in block Z. Looking at Figure 19-5, we see that there is a slight difference between its O-to-T sequence and the U-to-Z sequence in Figure 19-3. Blocks U to Z use more core storage. Since the subroutine can be initiated from several places in the program, provision must be made to be sure control is returned to the proper instruction. If entry is made from decision point 1, for instance, control will return to block C, but if decision point 3 returns control to the subroutine, it will be to block E. For this reason, the use of a subroutine requires that certain information be supplied to it: the location of the instruction which caused the *branching* (change of control sequence).

Some of the most common subroutines are completely generalized; for example, in the subroutine used to evaluate the square root of a number, not only must the instruction location be indicated, but also the variable number or numbers (parameters). For these reasons, the subroutine usually uses slightly more core storage than the one written in Figure 19-5; however, the multiple use of the same subroutine results in the saving of valuable storage space. Due to the problem of branching back and forth to a common subroutine, the object-time execution of the subroutine can be expected to be slightly longer than that needed to execute a specially written routine. It is up to the programmer to choose between the economics of saving space and that of saving time.

No attempt has been made thus far to describe the operation to be performed, since the diagram can be thought of as describing any number of real programs. Through the use of the input/output symbols (X and Y in Figure 19-3), the illustration represents a very common use of the subroutine to cause all input/output operations. Only 18 blocks have been shown in this example, and from this, one can assume that it represents a very broad level of logic. As the programmer works out the flow chart, the reader could expect it to fill several pages; for example, the block labeled X, which might indicate input operations, could be expanded to several hundred operations in detail.

Decision Tables

A *decision table* is an effective substitute for or an auxiliary aid to a block diagram. It is an excellent notation for expressing the logic required in the definition of business data-processing problems. It is used in situations that involve complex decision logic because it presents the original condition and the course of action to be taken if the conditions are met in a tabular form.

A decision table is divided into two main sections. The upper section questions or *conditions* what must be done, and the lower section presents the *action* to be taken. The left part of each of these sections is called the stub (that is, *condition stub, action stub*). The right part is called the entry (*condition entry, action entry*)—Figure 19-6.

Further elements of a decision table include a line (row) for each condition or action. Several columns are added to show certain rules or instructions, each of which pertains to a specific condition and the manner in which the condition is acted upon (Figure 19-7).

In Figure 19-7, the *table header* shows the table number and/or table name (for example, table number 1). *Rule reference* indicates the rule number (for example, rule 1, rule 2, etc.) The *condition stub* describes all or part of a condition statement. That is, a logical question, or relational or state condition that is answerable by a yes or no. The *condition entry* provides completion of the condition statement (extended entry) or Y(yes), N(no), or *blank* (limited entry). The *action stub* describes all or part of an action statement, or

FIG. 19-6. A decision table—basic elements.

IF...
(CONDITION STATEMENT)

THEN...
(ACTION STATEMENT)

CONDITION STUB	CONDITION ENTRY
ACTION STUB	ACTION ENTRY

FIG. 19-7. Further elements of a decision table.

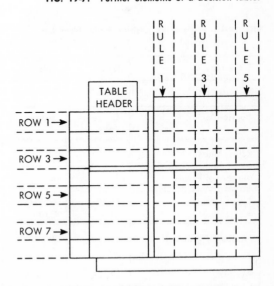

an explicit statement of where to go next for each rule, if not specified in the table header. Finally, the *action entry* shows completion of the action statement (extended entry), or X, or blank (limited entry).

An Example—Design Engineering

With this general background on decision tables, let's see how they can be profitably applied to *design engineering*. Initially, a decision table skeleton is prepared. Customer specifications are shown in the condition area of the table and the product characteristics are shown in the stub. Names of the specifications and names of the characteristics are shown in the stub, while various values for those names are displayed in the entry area (Figure 19-8).

In the filled-out engineering decision table shown in Figure 19-9, various customer specifications (for example, service, application, etc.) are listed on the left. The resulting action (or product characteristics) are presented below the horizontal double line and to the left of the vertical double line. To the

FIG. 19-8. Skeleton structure of an engineering decision table.

STUB   ENTRY

Customer Specification Names	Specification Values and Ranges
Product Characteristic Names	Characteristic Values and Ranges

FIG. 19-9. Engineering decision table—filled out.

Table No. 1	Rule 1	Rule 2	Rule 3	Rule 4
Service	DC	DC	AC	AC
Application	Temperature	Speed		
Rating Units	MV	MV	MV	MA
Number of Phases	1	1	1	1
Type of Armature	Moving Coil	Moving Coil	Electro-dynamic	Inductive
Number of Windings	1	2	2	1 + Number of Phases
Part No.	012526	012526A	012530	012535
Assembly Drawing No.	A26	A26A	B30	B30A
Next table	2	2	2	10

right of the vertical double line are the values for the customer specifications and product characteristics. A decision rule is a unique combination of specifications and characteristics.

Reading a part or parts of a decision table is relatively easy. For example, in Figure 19-9, rule 1 reads: "IF the service is DC, and the application is temperature, and the rating units are MV and the number of phases is 1, THEN the armature is a moving coil type and the number of windings is 1 and the part number is 012526 and the assembly drawing number is A 26 and the next table is 2."

Programming Hints

Many attempts have been made to list desirable programming habits as guidelines for those involved in this work. One of the best of these lists has been written by Daniel D. McCracken in "Source Program Efficiency." * Three of these rules are particularly important:

1. Don't Do Anything Twice if You Can Avoid Doing So

The programmer can realize major savings in both storage space and computer time, particularly when it is necessary to use the result of a calculation within a loop. For example, where it is necessary to calculate the space occupied by a set of crates, all of which have the same width and height, but various lengths, assume that the volume of one crate is expressed as "$V = 1\ wh$." The total volume is the sum of the individual crate volumes. Figure 19-10 shows the different ways in which this basic calculation can be performed. Although Figure 19-10b gives the appearance of being simpler, it is the one which breaks the first rule listed above. If the number of crates is very large, the method shown in Figure 19-10a will result in significant timesaving.

Suppose the example shown in Figure 19-10a saves only 100 milliseconds (0.1 second) each time the loop is executed. If there are 1,000 crates, this means only one minute and 40 seconds will be saved in all. However, it is the good habit of making such savings that can make a real difference in the long run. The crate problem actually is an application of the distributive law of algebra: $ABC + ABD + \ldots = AB(C + D + \ldots)$.

2. Arrange Branch Testing So That the Most Probable Choice Is Tested First

An example of this rule is shown in Figure 19-11a. The problem to be solved involves processing only certain situations in the current month. Items over 100 pounds are handled differently. Figure 19-11b illustrates a very poor habit among programmers, and is tricky in its use of Switch *A*, but even a casual observer can detect the inefficiency caused. Trickiness for the sake of being tricky is not only unwise, but may prove to be expensive.

* *Datamation Magazine,* February 1963, pages 31–33.

FIG. 19-10. Programming hints—rule 1.

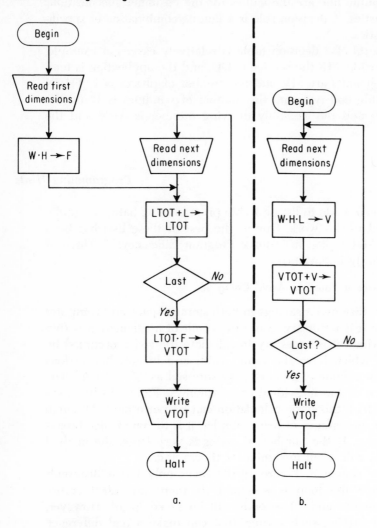

a.

b.

3. Edit Input Data for Reasonableness

This rule deals with identifying things which obviously are absurd. If the program is working with dates, for instance, a month coded 21 is unlikely (probably an error at the keypunch when the operator meant to indicate December). Sometimes, the error is a combination of factors. The programmer should check inconsistent data before going any further. The point is that if the input record is inconsistent with the known facts, it is wasteful to proceed. In addition, erroneous information may get into the permanent file, where it might go unnoticed until a much later date. Then, it becomes necessary to go back and try to reconstruct the data, which is both difficult and expensive.

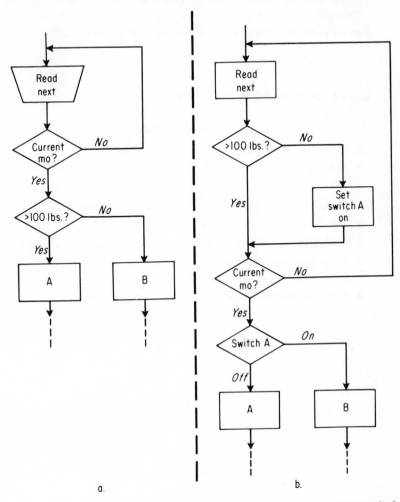

a.

b.

FIG. 19-11. Programming hints—rule 2.

GLOSSARY OF TERMS

BRANCH: A set of instructions that is executed between two successive decision instructions.

HOUSEKEEPING: For a computer program, housekeeping involves the setting up of constants and variables to be used in the program.

LIBRARY SUBROUTINE: A set of tested subroutines available on file for use when needed.

LOOP: A sequence of instructions that is repeated until a terminal condition prevails.

PARAMETER: A variable that is given a constant value for a specific purpose or process.

SUBROUTINE: A routine that can be part of another routine.

QUESTIONS FOR REVIEW

1. Explain a flow chart. Give an example.
2. What are the main flowcharting symbols?
3. What part of a flow chart is called the main line? Illustrate.
4. What is involved in a housekeeping routine? Where in the program is it located?
5. What is meant by looping a program? Illustrate.
6. What is a subroutine? A library subroutine? Explain.
7. Define the terms "parameter," "branching," and "decision table."
8. Why is a decision table used? Explain in detail its parts and their functions. Give an example to illustrate.
9. List and explain three chief programming guidelines.

Systems Analysis
and Procedure

For a long time, large companies have employed experts to study the efficiency of the methods and procedures used in their daily activities. You probably have heard of the efficiency expert, characteristically pictured with a stop watch in his hand. His primary duty is to measure the time required to perform given tasks, examine the flow of work from one employee to another, and analyze or evaluate the required number of finished items per day. His analysis and observations help him to devise a plan showing the number of employees required, their responsibilities, and the equipment they must have to meet the planned output.

Modern business employs another type of efficiency expert: the systems or methods analyst. The term "systems" implies the logical over-all approach or method that is used to carry out a program to its ultimate conclusion. In a more complex system, it often becomes necessary to break the system into segments for ease of handling and to check each step so that all possible exceptions may be recognized.

The systems analyst (or systems engineer) is the focal point in the over-all system concept. He is the one in charge of directing the "task force" designated to develop the necessary means for attaining a given end result. He insures that his company's systems are kept at maximum efficiency through the employment of the latest management techniques and data-processing equipment. Management techniques such as PERT (a specialized way of keeping management informed of the progress of large-scale projects) give information for making better decisions and allowing executives to offer better services at lower cost. The systems analyst constantly must examine new techniques to see if, through their utilization, he can design a better system for his firm.

A systems analyst fills the gap between input and output and should be ready to optimize the system once the program is established and operates satisfactorily. Although complete knowledge of all the hardware is not necessary, he must be able to distinguish between the various types of requirements and know the capabilities of the equipment involved. He also must be prepared to evaluate cost differential and to assume responsibility for incorporating the system as an integral unit into the business. It is his business to make sure that the record keeping and paperwork of a business meet the desired specifications smoothly and efficiently.

The systems analyst's continued job of attaining systems efficiency is important. The dynamic nature of a business firm requires periodic adjustment in the system. As a company grows, its needs and structure change, often making current procedures inefficient and costly to operate. Suppose, for instance, Department *A* of a given firm forwards to Department *B* a complex weekly report which has taken 40 hours to prepare. In the event the company later decides to shift certain functions from Department *B* to the main office, Department *A*'s report may provide more details than necessary. If this has gone unnoticed, inefficiency results. The systems analyst occupies a helpful role by instituting new procedures at the time of the change.

In the past, the systems analyst dealt with machine operators and their key-driven devices. He thought of reports and procedures passing from person-to-person and department-to-department. This thinking pattern has gradually changed to the present concept of evaluating the increasingly larger segments of the total business. In his attempt to integrate man's superior ability to reason with a machine's superior speed and accuracy, the analyst must justify the need for current reports, integrate individual steps into fewer ones, and relieve as many people as possible of routine duties so they can devote more time to creative work.

Steps Involved in Solving a Business Problem

The advent of data-processing equipment shifted much of the routine work from the hands of people to the data-processing machines. Beyond the basic decision-making stage lies the field of operations research and scientific management. Computers today have taken over much of the work considered critical by executives. This work includes establishing safe stock levels, product mix for maximum profitability, and optimum shipping and distribution patterns. Computers also have proved an aid in displaying true operating conditions to management, improve the present business system in general, and guide that business in a way approved by top management.

This evolution made it necessary to design new business systems with the idea of unifying all the factors involved for attaining the desired business goals set by management and for making use of the capabilities of the available data-processing equipment. In order to do this, a systems planner should take into account the three chief phases of *systems study and design, implementation,* and *operation.*

Study and design of a new system involves primarily a clear and thorough understanding of the present business system. In other words, information on what is being done can be used as a guide to a more realistic and accurate understanding of the business firm under study.

Once knowledge has been acquired regarding the present system, the next logical matter to be considered is determining the requirements of the system under study. This step actually is a transition between understanding the present system and designing a new one. Present facts about the existing system are used in conjunction with a projection of future needs of the business through a new system. The systems analyst defines the problem of future goals, makes necessary modifications on present functions, analyzes, and determines measures of effectiveness for each element involved.

The last stage of systems study and design involves a critical review of the alternative designs and equipment selection made earlier in the study, leading to the development of the design which would best serve the purpose. Once systems study and design is completed, the remaining phases (implementation and operation) follow. As soon as the new system has been determined and designed, implementation and operation of the new system are conducted to check and test the effectiveness of the new system. This involves implementation costs and economic analysis of the new system as compared with the present one. Other factors such as programming, physical planning, conversion and systems testing, and personnel responsibilities and relationships as a result of the new system are also considered.

The Manual System

A business organization employing systems analysts would have a set of rules or a series of steps for preparing the flow of business applications. There must be a way of stating the procedure by which each department receives, processes, and distributes its paperwork.

In a *manual system,* a basic list of instructions will suffice. An insurance company might keep policyholder information in file drawers, arranged alphabetically by the policyholder's last name. Periodically, the folders are pulled from the files, perhaps to make a change or to process a claim. Whatever the case, a specific department may request a certain folder by sending a slip of paper containing the policyholder's name to the filing division. When a number of these requests has been received, a file clerk pulls the folders and sends them to the departments concerned. This is a relatively simple

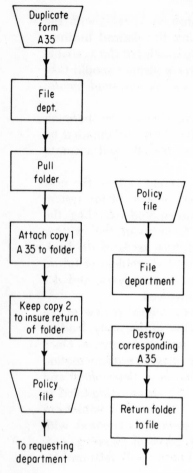

FIG. 20-1. System description—request for policyholder file.

FIG. 20-2. System description — return of policyholder file.

problem. A systems analyst might make out a list of instructions for the file clerk, so that when a new person is hired or temporary help is needed, the duties and procedures of the job will be readily apparent. The list might include:

1. All requests to be made on a special form containing policyholder's name and name of the requesting party. The form then is sent to the filing division to be placed on the clerk's desk.

2. The file clerk accumulates a minimum number of requests (for example, five).

3. When five or more requests have been accumulated, the clerk sorts them manually into alphabetical sequence.

4. The file clerk pulls the desired folders from the file.

5. The form requesting each policyholder folder is attached to the proper folder; the name of the requesting department is encircled; and the folder is placed in the "out" box for delivery. The clerk at this time maintains a record of each folder that leaves the file.

6. Folders in the "out" box should be picked up by a mail clerk once every hour. The clerk also brings back (to the box) any folders which have been used.

7. When at least five folders have been accumulated in the box, the file clerk places them in the file and removes the note indicating that the folder had been removed.

Instead of preparing a list of instructions, the analyst might produce a rather general chart, called a "systems-description" chart. For the operation just described, the chart would be similar to the one shown in Figures 20-1 and 20-2. When the chart is being prepared, the systems analyst considers the waste in time if the file clerk has to seek a folder each time a request comes in, and decides it would be more efficient to have the job done whenever five or more requests have been accumulated. He knows that it will speed up the process by placing the requests in alphabetical sequence before the folders are pulled from the file. Knowledge about the frequency of intercompany mail pickup and delivery further helps to systematize this routine. These and other related points had to be thought out before an efficient and effective system could be devised.

The Punched-Card Method

In a *punched-card system,* the instructions normally are more complicated than in a manual method. The analyst lays out the process by developing a systems flow chart. Systems flow charts are maps that show the processing procedure. Special symbols represent machines and processes involved in a punched-card installation (Figure 20-3).

Assume that the insurance company mentioned earlier has its policyholder information on punched cards, rather than in folders. A systems flow chart

FIG. 20-3. Punched-card flow chart symbols.

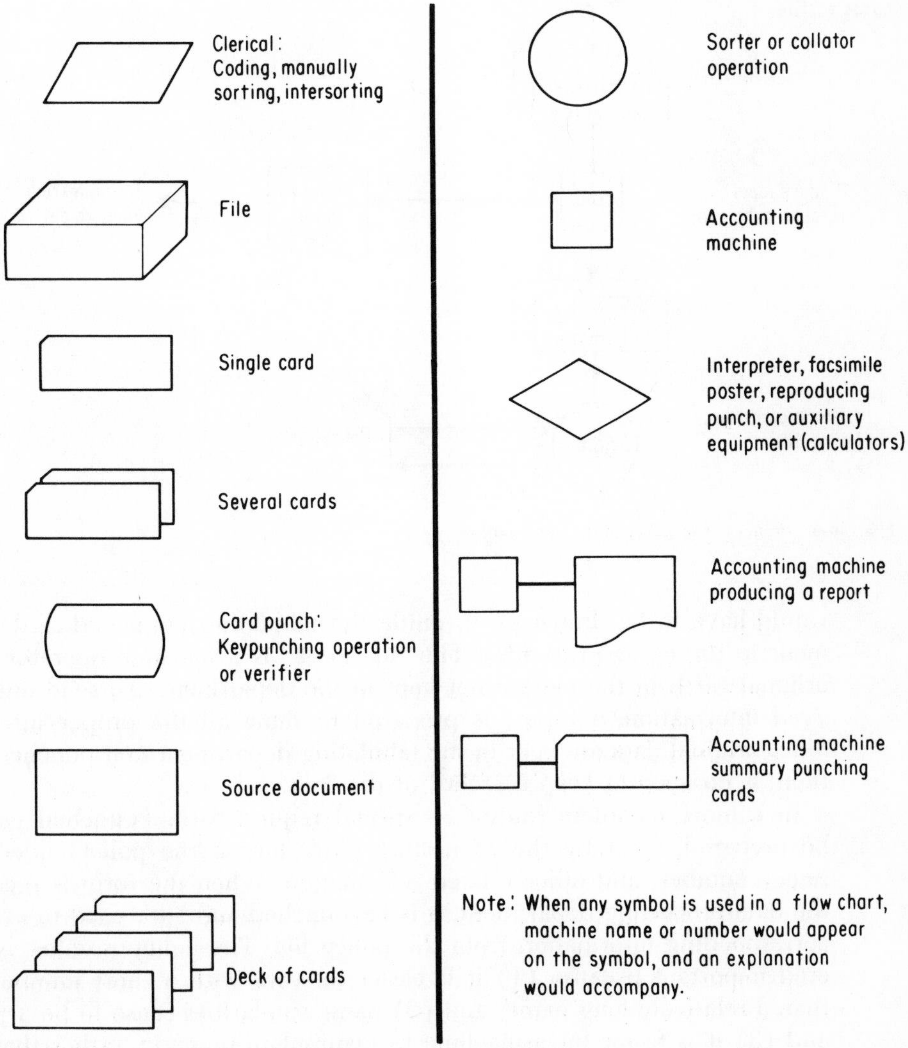

Clerical:
Coding, manually sorting, intersorting

File

Single card

Several cards

Card punch:
Keypunching operation or verifier

Source document

Deck of cards

Sorter or collator operation

Accounting machine

Interpreter, facsimile poster, reproducing punch, or auxiliary equipment (calculators)

Accounting machine producing a report

Accounting machine summary punching cards

Note: When any symbol is used in a flow chart, machine name or number would appear on the symbol, and an explanation would accompany.

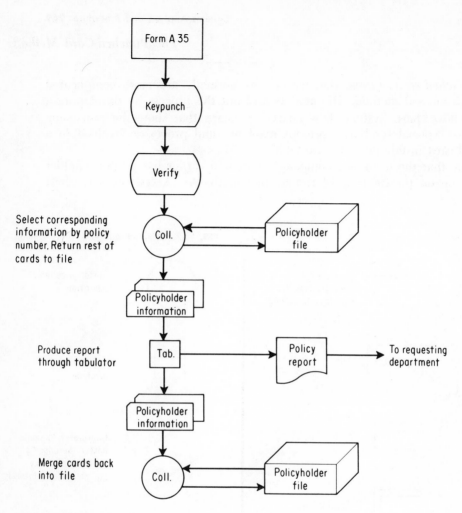

FIG. 20-4. Request for policyholder information.

would have to be drawn up to guide the tabulating (punched-card) department to the cards in its files. The "file clerk" is a machine operator and the original cards in the file are not kept in the department. To send out the desired information, a report is prepared to show all the proper information. Since original data are kept in the tabulating department (on punched cards), there is no need to keep a record of the "out" folders.

In a more complete routine, a special request form (punched card) can be prepared, whereby the requesting party fills in the policyholder's name, policy number, and other related information. When the form is received by the data-processing department, it is keypunched and later used to extract the corresponding information from the policy file. The policy number is considered important because (1) it is easier to work with a short number, rather than a relatively long name; and (2) name similarities cease to be a problem; and (3) it is faster for a machine to manipulate numeric, rather than alpha-

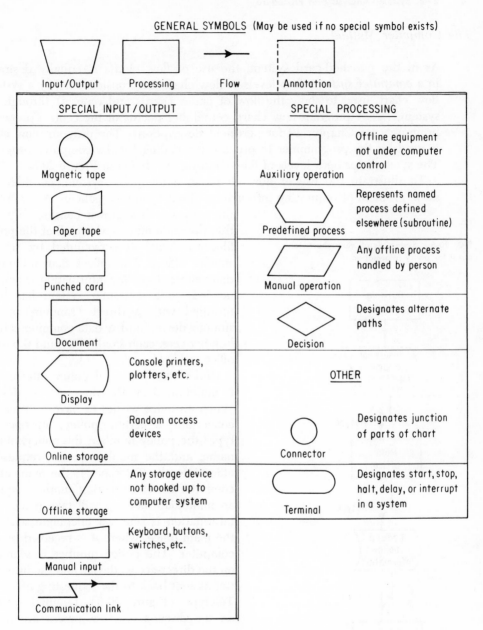

GENERAL SYMBOLS (May be used if no special symbol exists)

Input/Output   Processing   Flow   Annotation

SPECIAL INPUT/OUTPUT		SPECIAL PROCESSING	
Magnetic tape		Auxiliary operation	Offline equipment not under computer control
Paper tape		Predefined process	Represents named process defined elsewhere (subroutine)
Punched card		Manual operation	Any offline process handled by person
Document		Decision	Designates alternate paths
Display	Console printers, plotters, etc.	OTHER	
Online storage	Random access devices	Connector	Designates junction of parts of chart
Offline storage	Any storage device not hooked up to computer system	Terminal	Designates start, stop, halt, delay, or interrupt in a system
Manual input	Keyboard, buttons, switches, etc.		
Communication link			

FIG. 20-5. Standard flow chart symbols.

betic, information. Under the manual system, if Department *A* had requested a particular policy also needed by Department *B*, *B* would have to wait until *A* was finished and had returned the folder to the filing department. With the punched-card system, Department *B* would wait only until the original punched cards are returned to the file, at which time a report is prepared and promptly sent out (Figure 20-4).

The Computer Method

As in the punched-card system, the use of flow charts is equally desirable in a *computer system*. Two levels of flow charts are considered: (1) a systems flow chart, used to show the flow of paper (cards and reports) through the system. (2) A program flow chart, containing details of the central processor program (see Chapter 19 for pertinent description). The program flow chart is used by the programmer to prepare the coding for the computer program. The symbols for both levels of flow-charting are shown in Figure 20-5.

To illustrate the use of flow charts in a computer system, consider the same problem of requesting information about insurance policies. Assume that the company has grown considerably and that the main office (where all of the policy files are kept) is surrounded by several smaller offices. The offices demand immediate access to policy information whenever needed, so a computer system has been installed with a direct (random) access storage device and a data-communications link between each small office and the main office.

Under this setup, all policy information is maintained on the direct-access device. When an office wishes to have information concerning a certain policy, an operator types the policy number, the policyholder's name, and the number of the requesting office into the Teletype. If the main office computer is not answering another request, an immediate hookup will take place. The information is sent via telephone wires to the main office, where it is received by the computer. The policy number is searched on the direct-access device and the information is sent back to the requesting office via Teletype (Figure 20-6). Original records on the direct-access equipment are never removed, not even for a short period. Requests do not have to be accumulated to attain maximum efficiency; to the contrary, such an accumulation of requests would slow down the operation. Requests are answered within minutes or a fraction thereof.

FIG. 20-6. System detail flow chart—request for policy information.

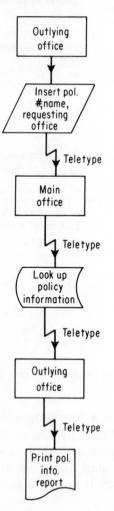

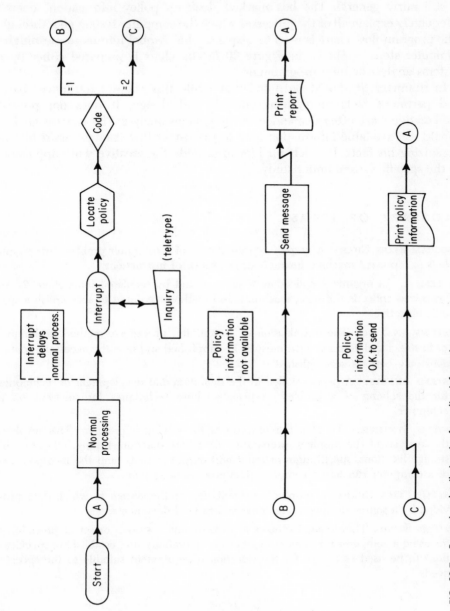

FIG. 20-7. Processing detail—inquiry for policy information.

The foregoing method of direct access to original data is considered the most productive method. Its main disadvantage is cost, but such systems are becoming more economical. The systems detail chart presented in Figure 20-6 is still fairly general. The box marked "look up policy information" doesn't adequately explain all of the processes which the computer system goes through. The program flow chart is used to "expand" this symbol into more meaningful computer steps as shown in Figure 20-7. The chart is prepared either by a systems analyst or by a programmer.

In summary, it should be noted that while this chapter introduces basic and pertinent facts on systems analysis and design, it does not present the creative work often demanded of the systems analyst. The systems analyst should use available information only to the extent that it might assist him in organizing his facts. It is left for him to provide the creative work applicable to the specific system under study.

GLOSSARY OF TERMS

PROGRAM FLOW CHART: A graphic representation of a computer problem using symbols to represent machine instructions or groups of instructions.

SYSTEM: 1. An organized collection of parts united by regulated interaction. 2. An organized collection of men, machines, and methods required to accomplish a specific objective.

SYSTEMS ANALYSIS: The examination of an activity, procedure, method, technique, or business to determine what must be accomplished and how the necessary operations may best be accomplished.

SYSTEMS ANALYST: A person skilled in the definition and development of techniques for the solving of a problem; especially those techniques for solutions on a computer.

SYSTEMS SYNTHESIS: To plan the procedures for solving a problem. This involves the analysis of the problem, preparation of a flow diagram, testing, allocation of storage locations, specification of input and output formats, and the incorporation of a computer run into a complete data-processing system.

SYSTEMS FLOW CHART: A graphic representation of the system in which data provided by a source document are converted to final documents.

SYSTEMS STUDY: The detailed process of determining a system or set of procedures for using a computer for definite functions or operations and establishing specifications to be used as a base for the selection of equipment suitable to the specific needs.

QUESTIONS FOR REVIEW

1. What are some of the functions and duties of a systems analyst? Explain.
2. List and discuss the primary phases considered important in designing new business systems.

3. Explain the primary stages of systems study for:
   (a) The manual method
   (b) The punched-card method
   (c) The computer method

chapter

21

Basic Processing Methods— Sequential (Batch) Processing with Magnetic Tape

Business activity grows with the steady increase of population and its demand for more and better products and services. Accelerated growth induces small firms to expand or to merge with other firms so that the skills of the craftsmen, the salesmen, the rank-and-file workers, and the financial administrators can be organized to best serve the needs of the consumer—the user of the finished product.

To operate a large and complex organization involves obtaining executive and managerial talent and securing the necessary capital to finance its projects. Direction requires the coordination of the various elements of the organization and the supply of vital information. This requires an information system which has the ability to collect and maintain up-to-date files of descriptive and quantitative data, reorganize them, and present them in a readable summary manner that can be used for decision-making.

The method chosen for file maintenance is dependent on the requirements of the system, cost of equipment, and related side benefits. The terms used to describe the two most popular methods of approaching a file maintenance application are *sequential (batch) processing* and *on-line (random) processing*.

Sequential (Batch) Processing

Historically, the processing of business data originated as an "on-line" operation. That is, transactions were handled in their entirety as they occurred. In the direct-barter system, data processing began and ended when the bartered material changed hands. Before there was a credit system, currency was immediately exchanged for goods, creating an immediate data-processing cycle. As more formal business-accounting systems developed, transactions were recorded by posting them in a ledger each time a transaction occurred. If a bootmaker sold a pair of shoes, for example, he immediately reduced the inventory account and increased his cash account or his receivable account. Thus, he posted two accounts. If his next transaction happened to be the receipt of a cash payment for a previous sale, he would post the amount to his cash and receivable accounts.

Although this system of accounting was relatively slow and subject to many clerical errors, it had the distinct advantage of being constantly in balance. Since it offered immediate access to ledger accounts, transactions could be recorded as they occurred in random order.

With the steady increase in the number of transactions and ledgers that businesses have had to maintain, this manual approach made it impossible to handle the volume and keep the records up to date. Even when additional clerks were hired, it was difficult to post the ledgers soon after the transactions occurred. An apparent solution was to batch transactions by type, so that selected clerks could handle each type with greater efficiency. Even this system had its limitations, however. Ledger posting often was delayed, with the result that accounts were not current.

The mechanization of business data processing appeared to offer a solution. The concept of batching—that is, accumulating transactions which require the same data-processing steps—became an inherent characteristic of mechanization.

The development of punched-card (unit-record) data processing is an excellent example of employing the same batching principles that are so successful in the mass production of manufactured goods. Following the tradition of mass production technology an array of single-purpose machines was built to perform a series of simple repetitive operations as batches of cards passed through each of them in turn.

Naturally, the time necessary to accumulate an economically efficient batch before processing creates delays, but that time has been generally accepted as a small loss in view of the large amount of over-all time and money saved through mechanization.

Magnetic Tape Processing

Commonly then, the techniques of automatic processing of business data are (1) to collect data in "batches"; (2) sort it into the sequence of the master file, which is on tape or cards; and (3) "update" this master file at a specific time. In magnetic-tape systems, input data are usually punched into cards, the cards converted to tape, sorted, and then run against the master tape to create a new master. This necessarily means delay, especially since it is uneconomical to run a few input cards (say on a daily basis) against a comparatively large master file. In a discussion of magnetic-tape data-processing techniques, stress is placed on the proper ways of handling magnetic tape and the sorting of the information it contains into desired sequences.

There are several ways of setting up tape files. In each particular installation, some standards should be followed. Since reels of tape contain invisible characters, there is nothing to distinguish one reel from another. The plastic case (and in most cases, the tape reel) carries a label identifying the information it contains as to application, date last used, etc. However, this does not guarantee that the operator will select the right tape for use in running a program.

Tape Labels

When a new application is set up and the initial records for that application are copied onto the magnetic tape (for example, from punched cards), a special record, called a *tape label,* is written as the first block of the tape. Like other data on the tape, the label is readable only to the read-write head of the unit. The tape label usually has a standard size (length) and contains such data as the name of the application, date of tape creation, record length of data within the file, reel number, etc.

Once all records have been placed in the file, an ending tape label is necessary. Like the beginning tape label, the ending tape label is of a specific length. It indicates whether it is the last label (last reel of tape in the file) or whether there are other reels to be used. Further, it contains the number of records stored on the tape. This particular information is useful when the reel is used for updating purposes, since the number of records always is counted by the program and checked against the number stored in the ending tape label. There is a beginning and an ending tape label on each reel, even if the records extend to more than one reel.

A programmer not only is responsible for writing the tape labels as new files are created, but he also is in charge of checking them in any program he writes. A program involving magnetic-tape input reads the beginning tape label and checks to make sure it is the proper reel to be processed. If the operator fails to place the right reel on the tape unit, the program detects the error, notifies the operator by printing out an indication of what is wrong, and then halts the system.

Tape File Handling

There are certain operations which are common to most magnetic-tape file-processing applications. The most important of these are:

1. At some time during or after the transfer of the input transactions onto magnetic tape (usually from punched cards), the data must be edited. Input editing consists of reviewing data in an effort to insure accuracy. This might be a programmed operation involving the checking of data between limits, checking batches of data to control totals, checking data for improbable combinations of factors, double punches and blank columns.

2. Before updating on tape, input transactions must be sorted into the same sequence as that of the tape file.

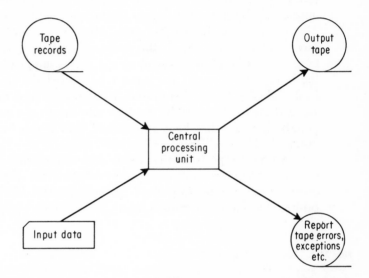

FIG. 21-1. Updating tape—basic routine.

3. During the updating routine, the following steps (called the "copy technique") take place: (a) The tape label from the input tape is read and the tape itself is checked to make sure it is the right one. Thus, the tape label is copied onto the blank tape to create a new label showing the correct date. (b) An input transaction is read, followed by the reading of a tape record and adding "one" to the record count. When the two types of data become available, the identification of the input transaction is matched against the tape-record identification number * to see if they are the same. If they are not the same, the tape record is written on the output tape and another tape record is read and compared. These two steps are repeated until a match is detected, in which case the tape record is updated in memory and finally is

---

* Data records are identified by individual identification numbers (ID), which may be numeric or alphanumeric. The (ID) numbers in a customer file might be the account numbers, the customer numbers, or even the customer names and/or addresses. Each data record is stored in a definite position within the storage unit and each such place has a numeric address.

written on the output tape (Figure 21-1). (c) The program reverts to reading another input transaction, going through the same procedure until the last one has been processed. (d) The last step involves writing onto an output tape any tape records remaining in the input file. When the ending tape label from this input file is read, the record count accumulated during the processing is checked against the ending label count. If the two counts are the same, the new ending label is written onto the output tape.

4. When a new file has been created through an updating procedure, it becomes input for the next processing run. The former (older) tape is stored for safety's sake until the next processing occurs, at which time the tape from the output run becomes the "safety" tape and another becomes the most current. This routine is called *cycling tape*. After two updating runs have been made, there will be three tapes: the new updated tape, called the "son" tape; the tape used as input to this most recent processing, called the "father" tape; and the tape used to create the input tape, called the "grandfather" tape (Figure 21-2). This technique establishes backup reference in case any failure occurs along the way. Usually, by the time the third tape is built, the validity of the grandfather tape has been established, and it can be put back into the computer system as a "free" or "scratch" tape.

5. A report tape is created which lists information pertinent to management reports, exceptions, errors, or documents. This tape must be run through other programs later to pull off the appropriate information and list it on the printer. During these runs output editing takes place, which includes the in-

FIG. 21-2. Tape updating cycle.

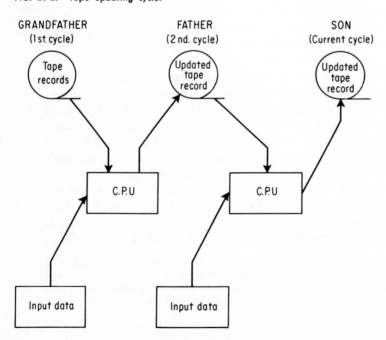

GRANDFATHER
(1 st. cycle)

FATHER
(2 nd. cycle)

SON
(Current cycle)

Tape records

Updated tape record

Updated tape record

C.P.U

C.P.U

Input data

Input data

sertion of punctuation and special characters, the elimination of lead zeros from numeric fields, etc. Special instructions are available in most computer languages to provide this type of editing automatically.

Some people wonder why a complete file is always copied, even though only a few records may require updating. To update records without recopying the tape would involve backspacing the tape, to reposition it after reading so that the same record may be rewritten in the same area.

There are several obstacles inherent in such an updating system:

1. It is impractical, considering the possibility of failure in the event the tape is backspaced too far, thus causing it to write over the wrong record.

2. There is the possibility that the tape mechanism will not write exactly at the beginning of a given record, but in such a place as to absorb the interrecord gap.

3. If the input transactions are incorrect and the record is updated incorrectly, there is no convenient way of tracing the original record. Auditing the information from files being updated in this manner can be a painstaking and futile task. Discovery of the error might come too late and the entire record would need to be removed and re-created from the beginning.

Tape Sorting

Sorting is basic to batch processing, whether by card or tape. However, the fact that a reel of tape represents a great many records, all strung together, with no way to break them apart physically creates a vastly different sorting problem than dealing with a deck of cards. A card deck can always be broken apart and resorted into any desired sequence. In an inventory application, for example, each card could represent an item taken from stock, and could be arranged in part-number sequence. For use in billing the customer, they could be resorted into customer-number sequence (customer number was added to the card when the item was removed from stock). But what about magnetic tape? Must the tape be converted to punched cards before resorting? No, magnetic tape can be sorted, but the sorting is done on the computer.

Generally speaking, to sort a tape, the records are read into the memory of the computer, rearranged into a different sequence, and written onto an output tape. The program (or sort routine) which performs this function is a fairly complicated one. Regardless of the specific sort routine used, the job is basically the same: to sort an input file into a different sequence and write out a new tape file. Depending on the size of the system (the memory size, the number of tape units on the system, the speed of the instructions, etc.), tape sorting varies in method and in total sorting time.

Tape Timing

Tape timing (the time it takes to read and write information) is based on two factors: (1) the start-stop time, and (2) the transfer rate of the data. Start time is the time it takes the tape unit to overcome its inertia and bring the tape to the speed at which reading or writing is done. This wastes tape, which is a portion of the interrecord gap. Stop time is the time it takes the unit to come to a stop after the record has been written. In a sort run, the computer "loafs" during acceleration or deceleration of tape. Not until actual data have been transferred to memory does it really operate efficiently.

Stringing

A stringing phase refers to a stage in which the input file is read completely (the first pass). The number of records (the length of the string) is determined by the amount of memory available in the system.

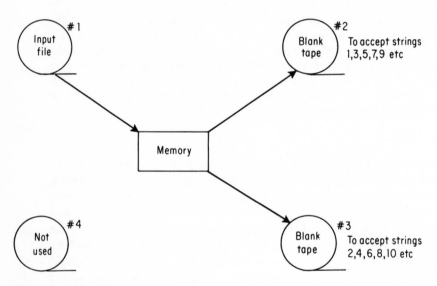

FIG. 21-3. Tape sorting—first pass.

Initially, a specific number of records from the input file is read into memory. The string in memory is rearranged into the desired sequence. When the string has been sorted, it is written onto the first reel of output tape (Figure 21-3).

Next, another string is read in, sorted, and this time, written onto the second reel of tape. This "ping-pong" effect continues—one string to the first output tape, the next to the second tape—until the input file is finished. At that time, the input tape is dismounted to be replaced by a free tape.

Merging

The next pass consists of taking the two output tapes and merging one string from the first unit with one string from the second unit. This is much like the work done by a punched-card collator, in which cards from the secondary hopper are merged with those from the primary hopper. The two strings are

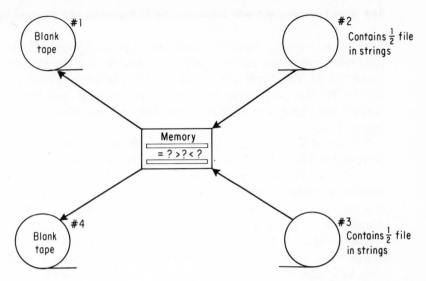

FIG. 21-4.   First merge.

combined into a longer string (twice the length of the initial string size) and in the proper sequence (Figure 21-4).

The merge routine involves comparing the first record from the first string with the first record from the second string. The lower record of the two will be written onto the third tape unit (formerly the input unit, but now containing a free tape) and another record is compared. The two strings are intermixed until the merge is finished. When this takes place, two more strings are read into memory—one from each of the two units now being treated as the input file. This string goes to the fourth tape unit (Figure 21-5). Merging continues

FIG. 21-5.   Merging continues.

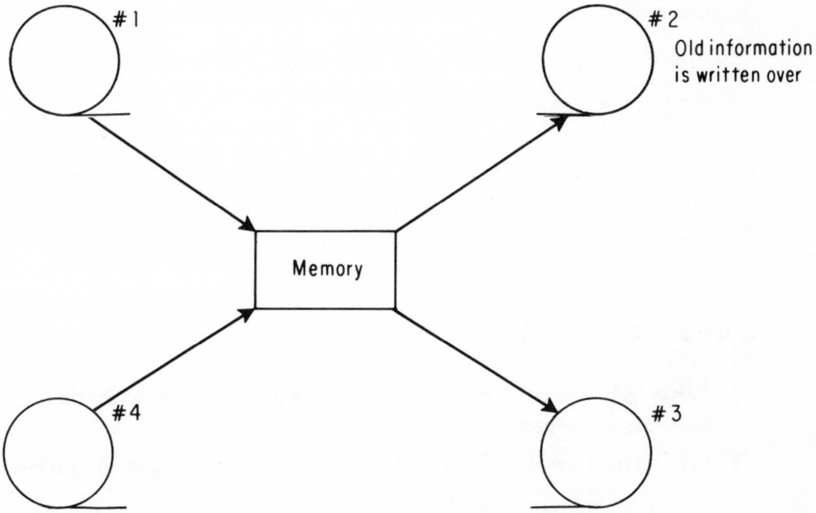

until all the strings from the two units are completed. Each time a merge pass takes place, the size of the strings double and the number of the strings is cut in half. The result is two reels of tape (in strings) representing the entire file. In the last pass, these two strings are merged, and the final string (the entire sorted file) is written onto one output tape. We now have a completely resorted tape.

Timing of a tape sort is based primarily on how many times the file must be reshuffled from tape to tape, consisting of the reading and writing of the first pass, plus all the subsequent merges. The number of merges depends upon the number of strings created on the first pass (the fewer the strings, the fewer the merges). The number of strings, on the other hand, depends upon the number of records in a string, which in turn depends upon how much memory space is available to build the string in the first place.

File time is the time it takes to transfer the required characters, plus start-stop time. Assuming a transfer rate of 50,000 characters per second and 10 million characters in the file (50,000 records of 200 characters each), read time is 200 seconds and write time is 200 seconds—a total of 6.7 minutes per read and write of the file. After allowing five milliseconds per record for start time and five milliseconds for stop time (a total of 8.4 minutes), it would take 15.1 minutes to completely read and write a file. With 12 merges, and one initial stringing phase, the total sort time would be 12 × 15.1 minutes or 3.02 hours.

To show the clear advantage of using magnetic tape, let us contrast it with a punched-card installation, specifically a 1,000-card-per-minute sorter. Assuming the processing of 50,000 records (200 characters each), we would need three cards to store one record—150,000 cards in all. At a speed of 1,000 cards per minute, it would take 150 minutes to sort each column. For 50,000 records, there usually is at least a five-column identification field, which would increase the sorting time by a factor of five. Thus, it would take 12.5 hours of machine sorting, plus approximately 1.3 hours of handling time and full-time human supervision, or 13.8 hours, to handle this assignment.

GLOSSARY OF TERMS

BATCH PROCESSING: A technique by which items to be processed must be coded and collected into groups prior to processing.

CYCLING TAPE: Creating a new tape file through an updating procedure.

QUESTIONS FOR REVIEW

1. What advantage does the batching process have over the manual method of business data processing?
2. What steps are involved in the automatic processing of business data?

3. Why is a tape label used? Where on tape is it located? Who is responsible for preparing it? Explain.

4. List and explain some of the main operations common to most magnetic tape file processing applications.

5. In an updating routine, a computer file is copied even though only a few records may require updating. What are some of the obstacles inherent in such a routine? Explain.

6. Explain how a tape is sorted, the factors which determine the methods used, and the over-all sorting time.

7. What two factors determine tape timing? Explain each factor briefly.

8. What is meant by stringing? Give an example.

9. Explain the routine used in merging records on tape. Illustrate.

10. What is file time?

chapter

22

Basic Processing Methods—
On-Line Processing

On-Line Processing Versus Batching

The use of punched-card and magnetic-tape systems implies that transactions would have to be batched for economical handling. That is, it would not be practical to process transactions as they occur, since so much time would be consumed in looking up items randomly. Also, for tape systems, there is the cost of recopying the file on a new tape as a usual part of the updating procedure. However, there also are applications which, because of a time factor, require files to be updated as transactions occur.

On-line processing means that data may be processed as they become available regardless of the order in which they arrive. It means that input data are not subjected to editing or sorting prior to entering the system, whether the input is for various transactions of a single application or for intermixed transactions of many applications (Figure 22-1). This presents problems of accuracy control which are not encountered in batch-processing systems.

The ability to process transactions on-line, as they are received, has been of keen interest to computer manufacturers and users. Until the recent development of faster and less expensive direct-access devices it has rarely been practical for large- or medium-scale users. Today, devices are available which are able to store large amounts of data in directly addressable units and to obtain information quickly from each unit with equal ease and at reasonable cost. These devices were introduced in Chapter 15.

Further, the demand for on-line processing has increased because some jobs do not lend themselves well to batch processing. The batching time is often longer than the actual process time. In many cases, a number of other batching problems have been apparent:

1. Certain data are out of date even before they are processed.

2. Reports are available infrequently and often too late to be used as a basis for management decision and action.

3. Requests for information, such as item status or account balance, are sometimes extremely difficult to answer. It often is impossible to locate data records during the processing cycle, and an inquiry may have to go unanswered until the cycle is complete.

4. Since batch processing requires that input data and all files be maintained sequentially, much money and time is spent in sorting data.

FIG. 22-1.   Example of batch and random processing.

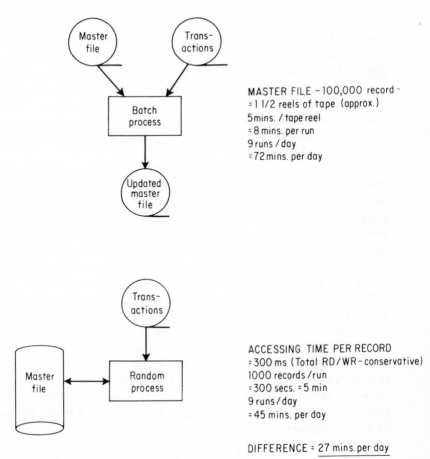

MASTER FILE – 100,000 record –
= 1 1/2 reels of tape (approx.)
5 mins. / tape reel
= 8 mins. per run
9 runs / day
= 72 mins. per day

ACCESSING TIME PER RECORD
= 300 ms (Total RD/WR - conservative)
1000 records /run
= 300 secs. = 5 min
9 runs /day
= 45 mins. per day

DIFFERENCE = 27 mins. per day

For applications that require information in large volumes and on short notice, the disadvantages of the batch approach are even more obvious.

The on-line approach is becoming more vital every day. Some of the reasons are:

1. The computer can directly refer all the necessary data for processing a transaction. Data can be efficiently processed in any sequence as it becomes available.

2. While removing the absolute requirement that file records and input transactions always be available in a fixed sequential order, new disk-storage units can make efficient use of sequential order to do high-speed batch processing for those applications which require it.

3. Jobs are more highly integrated, and manual intervention is less a factor in the processing of an application.

Direct-Access Storage Inquiry

Data-processing installations always have found it necessary to obtain specific information from files during an operation. Prior to the development of direct-access mass storage, the ability to request information directly from temporary or permanent storage devices was relatively limited. Procedures were developed, but at best they resulted in time-consuming interruptions, and often the information was not completely up to date when received. The special ability of disk and other mass-storage systems to process input data of various types on-line and to update all affected records immediately makes it possible to request information directly from storage and receive an immediate reply. This is significant because information requests no longer disrupt normal processing, and there no longer is a need for delay between a request for information and a reply.

To illustrate, a major national airline operated a number of reservations offices throughout the country and attempted to maintain a record of all flights and passenger reservations on ledger-type cards in a central location. The records were updated and inquiries were made by telephone. Replies often were inaccurate and delayed. When a disk-storage system was installed, flight-passenger records were maintained there and communications were linked from the reservations desks to a computer, thus permitting all inquiries to be answered quickly, accurately, and automatically.

The need for immediate retrieval of business information is prevalent in industry. In demand-deposit accounting, for instance, one might ask: "What is the balance of account number 133420?" In inventory control: "How many units of part number 55632 are on order?" In manufacturing: "How many subassemblies of part number 16414 are on hand?" In payroll: "What are the year-to-date earnings of employee number 13862?" It is true that each of these questions could be answered eventually through other data-processing means. However, unreasonable delay might make the resulting information out-of-date or insignificant.

The ability to request information directly from a computer and to receive an immediate response with a minimum of operational procedures is strong justification for the use of direct-access mass-storage devices for a growing number of applications. As costs for such devices are reduced they can be expected to play a leading role in data-processing systems of the future.

Disk Storage and Low-Activity Data Processing

Many applications call for the processing of a limited number of input transactions against very large master files. Although few master file records are altered or referenced by the input data during a particular run on magnetic tape, the entire master tape must be searched. Assume, for example, that a billing system maintains 100,000 customer master records, of which only 9,000 are referenced daily. One approach would be to collect and sort the 9,000 records into customer number sequence and then process them against the master file in a single daily run. If the billing operation requires that bills be completed throughout the day, however, the data would have to be batch-processed nine times a day, resulting in 1,000 input transactions being processed against the 100,000 master records on each run. Since there is no practical way to skip through a file, every record would have to be examined by the system in each of the nine runs.

An answer to the problem lies in the use of direct (random) access devices, which permit the retrieval of records without the examination of intervening records. Figure 22-2 illustrates the difference in the batch and random processes.

High-Activity Data Processing

Direct-access storage also is used in "high-activity" applications where a comparatively small number of records is updated or referenced frequently. For example, assume a company has 10,000 employees and each works on 10 or more different jobs per day with a specific rate and guarantee for each job. In the processing of a piecework payroll such as this, each calculation would be based on the employee's unique work history. In this case, there is a need for continuous reference to a comparatively small number of rate tables.

Using the batch approach, job completion tickets would be batched *by employee* as they are received and a master file of employee rate tables would be searched in order to process each employee's job tickets. As an alternative, a separate edit run could be made to determine which rate tables would be required, but in either case, job-ticket data would be tagged with a rate table code; data would be sorted into rate-table sequence; and all reference to a particular rate table would be completed in sequence order. When all rate data are extracted, another run would be required to complete the calculations. Figure 22-2a shows how such an approach would be implemented.

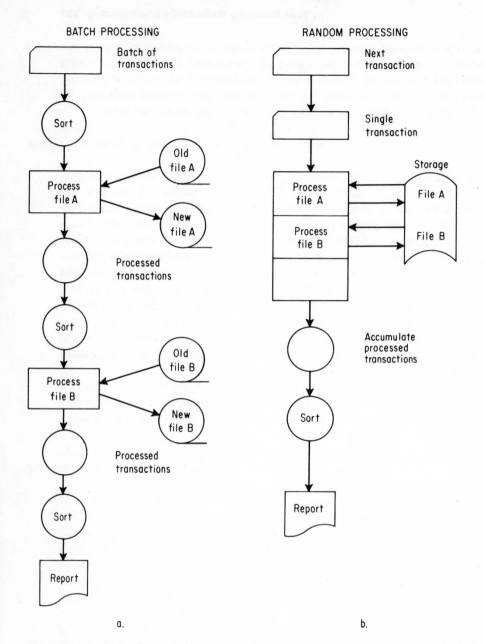

BATCH PROCESSING

Batch of transactions

Sort

Process file A

Old file A

New file A

Processed transactions

Sort

Process file B

Old file B

New file B

Processed transactions

Sort

Report

RANDOM PROCESSING

Next transaction

Single transaction

Process file A

Process file B

Storage

File A

File B

Accumulate processed transactions

Sort

Report

a.

b.

FIG. 22-2. Flow charts—batch and random processing.

By contrast, in a random-access approach all rate tables would be accessible as they are required, without having to batch or search through the file for each one or to go through an involved procedure of repeated sorting and processing to complete the job. Figure 22-2b shows how this approach would work.

Random and Sequential Data Processing

It is important to distinguish between the organization of a master file and the order of the input detail records processed against it. When used with the term "processing," the terms "random" and "sequential" refer to the order of the input transaction records and to the order of reference to records in the master file, respectively. *Random processing* is the processing of detail transactions against a master file, regardless of the order in which they occur. In *sequential processing*, the input transactions are grouped and sorted into master-file control-number sequence, after which the resulting batch is processed against the master file. When the master files are stored on tape or cards, sequential processing is the most efficient procedure.

Direct-access storage units are considered very efficient sequential processors as well as random processors. They make it possible to choose the best processing method to suit the application. Thus, some applications can be processed sequentially, while those in which sorting or batching is undesirable can be processed randomly. Either approach can be used, whether the master file is in random or in sequential order, illustrating the additional flexibility obtained by storing a master file on direct-access storage units.

Real savings in over-all job time often can be made by combining runs in which each input affects several master files. The details can be processed sequentially against a primary file and randomly against the secondary files, all in a single run. This is the basis of on-line processing.

Disk-File Addressing Techniques

When using mass-storage devices, a business firm will make efficient use of every character position possible. Only the amount of usable storage is ordered at a particular point in time since more storage can be added at a later date. Consequently, the firm must consider the matter of "packing" information onto the file, wasting a minimum amount of space, and keeping in mind the problem of cost.

In order to explain disk-file addressing techniques, assume you have a typical disk file in which each disk is divided into segments of 200 alphanumeric character positions of storage.

Addressing: Direct and Indirect

The two techniques used for locating information on a random-access file are *direct addressing* and *indirect addressing*. Generally, direct addressing is used whenever the input data record carries the absolute disk-file address for those data. Indirect addressing, on the other hand, is used when the absolute address on the disk file is first found on a list that carries both the actual identification number and the location of the desired information.

In a direct-access application, an identification code in the input data must be used to locate the corresponding information in the file. This does not imply that the identification number of the input data must be identical to the addressing system of the direct-access device; it simply means that the identification must be used in one way or another to determine the location of the information on the file.

Direct and indirect addressing have their advantages and limitations. At times, a combination of the two techniques is the most efficient. The application under consideration is a major factor in determining which method is to be used.

Direct Addressing Techniques

When a new application is being transferred to an automatic system, it may be assigned the same numbers as the addresses on the disk file. For instance, in a disk file containing addresses which run from 000000 to 999999, a particular application may be assigned by any of these addresses, provided all of its records are contained within this range. The advantage of this system is the speed at which information may be accessed; the absolute address is available immediately for access to the file. Its chief limitation is that once records become obsolete and are dropped from the file, they leave gaps which cannot be used to store other information. If the numbering system does not use all or at least most of the available numbers, much of the file will be left blank.

Recorded Identification Number (Pseudo Direct)

When an application is ready to be recorded on disk storage, an "open list" will be made available to the personnel working on the problem. This list carries all the addresses on the file which are not in use. All existing identification numbers for the particular application are typed up in a sequential list, and an open address from the disk file is placed next to each number. The address just assigned is then crossed off the open list. From that time on, all documents used as input to the computer system must carry both the actual identification of the input data and the assigned disk-file address. If a card is keypunched for a particular item, the operator must look up the disk address from the prepared list so that it also can appear on the card.

The advantage of this system is that as numbers "die out," the disk addresses may be placed back on the open list. This way, the locations do not have to remain filled (as they do in a straight direct address) unless there is no possibility of the number recurring in the system. However, the chief disadvantage is that the maintenance of the dictionary list is very time-consuming, and it is possible that personnel might pick up an incorrect disk address. The latter possibility usually is discovered, however, since the information on the disk file also carries the actual identification number, which is compared to the input document by the program before any updating takes place.

Various Uses of Identification Number

Certain problems might occur in an installation where several applications lend themselves to the direct-addressing scheme. In a billing application, for instance, the account numbers of customers might have the same format as the employee numbers established for the firm's payroll. It would seem at first glance that a customer number and an employee number (both being the same), would have to have the same area assigned to them on the file. Naturally, this is not possible.

To see how a system with more than one file for each identification number works, consider an example in which both the employee numbers and the customer numbers run from 0000000 to 0009999. If we were to assign disk locations 0000000 through 0009999 to employee payroll information, the employee program would have to refer only to the actual employee number to find the proper data. In assigning locations for the billing application, a distinction can be made by assigning them to locations 0010000 to 0099999 (Figure 22-3). These two areas on the file do not cause any conflict.

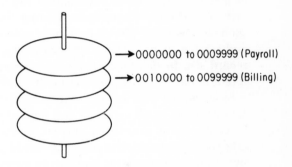

→ 0000000 to 0009999 (Payroll)

→ 0010000 to 0099999 (Billing)

FIG. 22-3.

But how would anyone be able to find the proper billing location for account number 12685, for instance? First the transactions to be processed carry a specific code to distinguish the information they contain from that used in other applications. Payroll cards might carry a "1" code; billing cards might carry a "2" code. Whenever the payroll program is running, the program "knows" that the employee numbers represent the actual disk address. When the billing program runs, the program "knows" that the customer information is addressed by the customer number plus 10,000. The program then adds the account number (12685) to a program constant of 10,000 (which is carried in the program), and comes up with a disk-file address of 0022685. The only apparent danger in this technique is the possibility that improper input data might be used (for example, payroll cards might be used as input to the billing run). However, the program can be instructed to check the application code carried on the input document to avoid any confusion.

Consecutive Multiple Segments for a Record

There are cases where the identification number can be used as a direct reference to a disk-file address, but the information required to be kept on the file exceeds the disk's segment size; that is, the data exceed the assumed segment storage of 200 characters. If, for instance, the record size for a particular application requires two segments (or 400 characters) the 0000000 identification number would occupy locations 0000000 and 0000001, causing identification number 0000001 to "lose a home." To rectify this, the identification number is multiplied by a factor of two, since two segments are used per identification number. To locate the address for a particular identification, the program would be set up to perform the multiplication of the ID by the desired factor. If the application needed three segments for a record (600 characters), the factor would be three; a four-segment requirement, four.

Trailer Record for File Density

A trailer record is used in cases involving identification numbers which match the disk-file addresses and might or might not have more than 200 characters as a requirement for storage on the file. In a commercial bank that keeps records for Demand Deposit Accounting, for instance, certain basic information such as customer name, customer account number, home address, balance, and service charge is retained for every account held. Determining a standard-record size in this type of work is difficult, since each customer writes a different number of checks each month. With the trailer method, each account has a basic record (the home record), containing a standard amount of information common to all accounts and kept at the address corresponding to the ID.

As the file is developed and an "open list" is kept, accounts expanding in information beyond one segment would cause the program to look at a computer table (open list), find a free segment, and assign it as the trailer record. The address of this trailer record then would be inserted into the main record (the last seven positions of the main segment) for reference. When that account comes up for processing, the main record is brought into memory and the last seven positions are examined. If they have a trailer address in them, that segment is sought and also read into memory, making all 400 positions available to the program when updating the account. If more than two segments are necessary, the first trailer will carry the address of the next trailer, and so on.

The advantage of this system is that it sets aside for storage only segments which actually are needed. This keeps the file densely packed. In the previous system (consecutive multiple segments for a record), an account that did not use all of the multiple segments which were set aside simply wasted them.

Indirect Addressing Techniques (Indexing)

Indexing is synonymous with the terms "Dictionary" and "Table Look-Up." It is similar to recorded ID Number (Pseudo Direct), described earlier, except that the computer program, rather than a person, looks up the actual address.

The most popular technique for practicing Table Look-Up on a computer is called a "binary search." A list of numbers is set up in ascending sequence (for example, 64 numbers). Instead of writing a program to look at the first number, the program is set up to look at the middle number 32 and compare it to the one which is being searched. The number in the table will be too high, too low, or equal to the one being matched. If it is equal, the answer has been found. If it is too high, the program examines the 16th number and makes the same comparison. This process continues, taking half of what is left after the comparison, until the actual number is found. For a table of 64 numbers, the maximum number of comparisons would be five.

In indexing, where the range of ID numbers might run to as many as 10,000, it would be impossible to keep the entire dictionary in the memory of the computer. The entire table would require 70,000 positions for the account numbers and 70,000 more for the disk addresses—a total of 140,000 character positions, divided into two types: rough tables and fine tables. The *rough table* is kept in memory constantly and is set up in a practical size for the particular computer being used. *Fine tables,* on the other hand, are kept in an auxiliary storage device (for example, a disk file) in an area not used for normal accounting information, where they will be available to the program at any time they are needed.

Below is an example of a rough table for account numbers 029 through 899:

Account Number	Disk-File Address
029	0000010
059	0000020
089	0000030
119	0000040
149	0000050
179	0000060
209	0000070
239	0000080
269	0000090
299	0000100
329	0000110
359	0000120
389	0000130
419	0000140
449	0000150
479	0000160
509	0000170
539	0000180
569	0000190
599	0000200
629	0000210
659	0000220
689	0000230
719	0000240
749	0000250
779	0000260
809	0000270
839	0000280
869	0000290
899	0000300

The first column of figures shows the account numbers in increments of 30, carrying only the highest number in each 30-number range. The second column represents the address on the disk file where the *fine table* is located (not the account information).

When a transaction is to be processed and an account number is received, it is compared to the first column of figures using the binary search principle. This determines the general range into which it falls. The number 345, for example, falls somewhere between the 11th and 12th entries in the table; in other words, it is greater than 329, but less than 359. The entry at the 12th position tells us that the fine table for the account numbers from 329 through 358 is found on the disk file at location 0000120.

The rough table is composed of the range of numbers, plus a disk-file address. It takes only 300 memory positions (30 numbers at three digits per number plus 30 addresses at seven digits per address).

As soon as the address for the next table is located (0000120), that table is read into memory. It is the fine table for the rough range 329 through 358, and might look like the following:

Fine Account No.	Disk-File Address
329	0000400
330	0000401
331	0000402
332	0000403
333	0000404
334	0000405
335	0000406
336	0000407
337	0000408
338	0000409
339	0000410
340	0000411
341	0000412
342	0000413
343	0000414
344	0000415
345	0000416
346	0000417
347	0000418
348	0000419
349	0000420
350	0000421
351	0000422
352	0000423
353	0000424
354	0000425
355	0000426
356	0000427
357	0000428
358	0000429

Again, the account number would be brought into the table. This time the range has been established however, and the actual number will be found. Account number 345 will be found on the disk file at address 0000416.

The table also requires 300 positions of memory—a total of 600 positions for Table Look-Up. There would be 300 for the rough table (kept in memory at all times) and 300 for a fine table (brought into memory at any time). As different fine tables are used, they simply are written over the ones previously used.

Without this method, 9,000 positions of memory would be required to do the same job done here by 600. Indexing is fairly fast. Two references to the file usually are necessary: one to bring in the fine table, and another to read the actual information desired. The Table Look-Up process would not be possible where random alphabetic characters are part of the ID, as they often are with part numbers in an inventory application.

Randomizing

A firm may retain its present numbering system through randomizing. In this technique, the original ID has a specific type of formula applied to it for producing a generated number or numeric address and is within the range of the addressing system on the disk file. For example, the disk-file address of the number 123456789 is obtained as follows:

(a) Add every other number (1, 3, 5, 7, 9 equal 25).
(b) Add the remaining numbers (2, 4, 6, 8 equal 20).
(c) Multiply the two low-order digits (8 $\times$ 9 equal 72).
(d) Providing a disk-file address of 0252072.

To set up a randomized file, the following steps should be observed:

1. Use a mathematical formula on the ID and create a legitimate segment address.
2. Examine the contents of the segment address just created. If it is not filled, put the ID number and the information belonging to it in that address.
3. Continue seeking successive information until a disk-file address is generated. It should be noted that as this process goes on, the program keeps track of addresses that are being filled, thus allowing the preparation of an "open list."
4. No matter how complicated the formula, duplicates are bound to occur. When a duplicate occurs, the data for that particular ID is punched out in cards, or set aside in some way for later handling.
5. When the rest of the file is finished, certain parts of it (duplicates) are found not copied onto the disk memory. They are processed again, and this time, when the duplicate number is calculated, that segment is read into memory; an address is selected from the open list; and the address is stored, representing the last seven digits of the duplicate segment. Finally, the segment is rewritten on the file.
6. The duplicate information is stored at the selected open-list address, writing the information for that record as well as the original identification. The duplicate-address segment still contains the original information.

Let us see what happens when some information is to be processed for an ID which was a duplicate. The ID is used and the formula used to create the file is applied to it. This disk address reads in the appropriate segment, and the ID from the input transaction is compared to the ID from that segment. If they are not the same, the segment address in the last seven positions of the segment in memory is used to read in the next link of the chain, and the input ID is compared against the ID of that segment. This process continues until the record has been found. In addressing, no set rules can be laid down. Each mass storage installation has different problems, resulting in the need for a careful review of numbering systems so that the disk file can be used as efficiently as possible. Randomizing appears to be the most complicated, and therefore the least desirable. However, it is widely accepted because of its great flexibility.

GLOSSARY OF TERMS

DIRECT-ACCESS STORAGE: (1) pertaining to the process of obtaining information from or placing information into storage where the time required for such access is independent of the location of the information most recently obtained or placed in storage; (2) pertaining to a device in which random access can be achieved without effective penalty in time.

DIRECT ADDRESS: An address that specifies the location of an operand. Synonymous with *one level address*.

INDEXED ADDRESS: An address that is to be modified, or has been modified, by an index register or similar device.

INDIRECT ADDRESS: An address that specifies a storage location that contains either a direct address or another indirect address. Synonymous with *multilevel address*.

ON-LINE PROCESSING: Descriptive of a system and of the peripheral equipment or devices in a system in which the operation of such equipment is under control of the central processing unit, and in which information reflecting current activity is introduced into the data processing system as soon as it occurs. Thus, directly in-line with the main flow of transaction processing.

SEQUENTIAL DATA PROCESSING: A technique by which items to be processed must be coded and collected into groups prior to processing.

TABLE LOOK-UP: A procedure for obtaining the function value corresponding to an argument from a table of function values.

QUESTIONS FOR REVIEW

1. What is meant by on-line processing?
2. For what reasons has the on-line approach become vital? Explain.
3. Explain and illustrate the role of direct access storage systems in data acquisition.

4. What is the difference between low activity data processing and high activity data processing?
5. Distinguish the difference between random and sequential data processing. Give an example.
6. What is an "open list"? Discuss its advantages and limitations.
7. Describe the various uses of identification numbers. Give an example.
8. What is a trailer record? Explain its uses for file density.
9. What is meant by "binary search"? How is it used for practicing table look-up on a computer? Give an example.
10. Distinguish and explain the difference between a fine table and a rough table.
11. What is randomizing? What steps are usually taken to set up a randomized file?

chapter

23

File Organization Techniques

File Organization

File organization is the process of relating the ID number of a file record to the address of that record in the storage unit. The ID numbers used by the outside world must be related to the addressing scheme designed into the equipment. The primary objective of file organization is to retain data in storage systematically so as to retrieve them in the fastest way possible when needed. The method used for a particular file varies, and its final form is dependent on the requirements of the given application.

In setting up a file for a direct-access device, there are many questions to be considered. What addressing technique will be used? How frequently will the file be referred to? Are disk files only to be used, or will there be a combination of other gear, such as magnetic tapes? What are the inquiry requirements? What will be the predominant reporting sequence? In updating records, are all records and information for an application consolidated, or are they kept individually? Will there be random processing, batched sequential processing, or both? What are the file maintenance requirements?

Guidelines for answering the first question are outlined in Chapter 22. The frequency of reference to the file (question 2) can be determined by the past experience of the firm. In considering the use of a combination of magnetic tape and direct-access devices, some believe that at least one tape unit, and probably two, are necessary with a direct-access device. In mass-storage usage, certain errors are bound to crop up, or a malfunction of the hardware may occur. Because of this, the contents of the file often are copied (or "dumped") onto tape periodically.

Another good reason for having a combination of tape and direct-access storage is the cost factor. Mass storage is fairly expensive. A tape unit is expensive also, but the amount of information which can be kept on additional reels of tape is far greater than that of the mass-storage device. Sometimes, it may be feasible to keep only the information needed for inquiries on the disk file and to use magnetic tape to store data which are not referenced as often.

In file organization, reporting sequence is a considerable factor. In a large manufacturing firm where inventory is a major application, for example, it makes a lot more sense to have the disk file in part-number sequence than to have it in vendor sequence. All of this implies that a serious systems study should be made prior to setting up a file for a direct-access device.

In manual or even in tabulating operations, each application usually is handled separately. There might be a group of people who take care of accounts receivable, one for payables, one for payroll, another for stock or inventory control. A mass-storage file may be set up in the same way, part of the file allocated to information on accounts receivable, another section for payables, and so on.

Another, more concise method to set up a file for direct-access is to consolidate all pertinent processing. To illustrate, consider what happens when an order is received from a customer. First, the stock is checked to see if the full order can be filled or if a purchase order must be issued to get the desired parts. Once the order has been filled, the customer must be billed. Each of these steps involves a separate application. The receipt of the order precipitates the calculation of sales commission (payroll application) as well as a stockroom search for parts (inventory application). If parts have to be ordered, a vendor must be notified (order-processing application) and he will send the firm a bill (accounts payable). When the customer's order is sent, he must be billed (accounts receivable). Rather than start documents going to many separate departments, it would be better to handle the entire job at one time (consolidate).

In a manual, semiautomatic, or automatic system not utilizing mass storage, the total system is impractical. With mass storage, however, the file can be set up so that the order starts a search within the device for individual parts records, which also can carry the percentage of commission to be used for the salesman's payroll records. The same records can carry the name of the vendor from whom parts must be ordered if the record shows an out-of-stock condition. An immediate purchase order can be issued by the system, to the proper vendor, after checking the stock records in the disk file. At the same time, the customer's bill can be made up and printed out, and the customer's records can be updated. Certainly, setting up the total system is more time-consuming, but it pays off in the elimination of duplication and saves time in taking care of the customer's and the firm's needs during day-to-day operations.

In setting up mass-storage files, systems people must make decisions on how they should be organized, basing their opinions on factors such as the account-numbering system, speed of access to a file, and so on. The file maintenance requirements also must be estimated. It is relatively easy to dump an entire file and reload it when an emergency occurs, but sometimes a firm might wish to copy the file onto magnetic tape for other reasons. In that case, perhaps the dump will take place according to the application; that is, all of the billing information copied onto one reel, the payroll information onto another, and so on. With a file that has these applications intermixed throughout, the dumping is a problem. If the applications are kept separate, such a dump is relatively simple.

File Composition—Random & Sequential

A file of records can be arranged within a storage unit in two major ways: *randomly* and *sequentially*.

In a random file, each record is at an address computed by a *randomizing routine*—a program that calculates the address from the item's control number. The order of the records within the storage unit generally is not sequential. To find a record in such a file, its address is simply computed from the ID by the same formula used to put it there. The main reason for using the random approach is to eliminate index tables.

In a sequential file, records are sorted and stored in the disk-storage unit in control-number sequence so that records with successively higher ID numbers will have successively higher addresses. It is not necessary (or even usual) for the ID to be the same number as the file address; the only requirement is that the ID's be in sequence.

Each of these two methods involves techniques to minimize the number of accesses to the file.

Random-order Techniques

Activity sequence. When identification numbers are randomized, duplicates or "synonyms" are created. In setting up a file based on activity sequence, it is desirable to put the most active information at the home location and the least active at the farthest location in the chain. In other words, the sequence of the file as it is first loaded onto the disks would not be in ID sequence, but in decreasing activity sequence. A great saving in time can be realized by placing the most active records in such a way that there will be only one access to the file. To maintain the file in the correct activity sequence, it is necessary during the accounting period to tally the number of references to each record. Periodically, based on this tally, the file is reorganized.

Correspondence method. When applications are related to one another, it is simple to set up the first application to occupy just a part of the file. This can be done by altering the randomizing formula to generate addresses which are restricted to a single section. Then, when the next application is put on the file, the corresponding record will be stored in the next section of the file, and will be put at the location relative to the initial record. If the first address were 0000008, for example, and the section to which this application is restricted fills addresses 0000000 through 0000100, the first record of the next application would be stored at 0000108, an increment of 100 addresses away. When the time comes for updating the disk file, the first address would be generated through randomizing, and all other records which might be affected could be accessed easily by adding a factor to the address of the original record.

To see how this technique can save time, consider a record which is fourth in a chain. It would take four accesses to the file to reach that record. For any record which has a correspondence to it, other accesses would have to be made (recalculating or generating each of their individual addresses). With the correspondence method, the addresses for corresponding records are known immediately, even if the records are chained.

Associative method. For somewhat the same purpose as in the foregoing illustration, the original record filed by the associative method would carry the addresses of all associated records. To get an additional record, instead of *incrementing* as one does in the correspondence method, the addresses are kept in the main record.

Tree method. In setting up chained records, the number of accesses to reach the records at the end of the chain can be reduced considerably by using the tree method. The first ID to create an address is stored in the same manner as the first pass of the example illustrating randomizing records. When a duplicate address appears, however, the original ID is tested to see whether it is even or odd. If it is even, an address from the open list will be

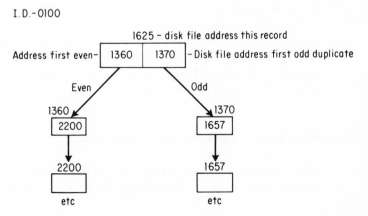

FIG. 23-1. The tree method.

selected and stored in the seven characters of the record just in front of the last seven. If the original ID is odd, the address from the open list is stored in the last seven characters of the original record. As more duplicates occur, the even or odd path is followed (Figure 23-1).

Actually, there are two chains—one for all duplicate records with even ID's and one for all those with odd ID's. Notice that the address of these records can be any address, since it is only the ID which matters. This system cuts down the number of accesses required.

Sequential Order Techniques

Assigned file address. Using the direct-address and indexing techniques, the input file to be stored on the disks is sorted and read into memory, followed by the building of the fine tables. This implies that fine tables do not need to carry all possible ID's—only the ones that actually are going to be used. For a range of 100 numbers in the rough table, for instance, there may be only 30 in the fine table. As soon as a range has been read and the numbers listed, this list is stored on the disk as the fine table and the procedure continues until all addresses have been assigned.

Unassigned file address. This method treats the disk file as if it were continuous reels of magnetic tape with all records in sequence. First, input transactions are presented in batched sequence. Next, as many segments as possible are read into the memory of the computer. One input transaction at a time is read and matched to a memory segment for updating purposes. When the appropriate segment is updated, that segment is rewritten on the disk file. To update an entire file, all segments must be read into memory, but only those segments which have input transactions matching them will be rewritten on the file.

Linkage. In previous automatic-accounting systems, application information was collected on what is called a "minor" level. In a sales organization, for instance, sales information might be collected by product throughout the country. When it was time to prepare reports, the information would be totaled by sorting the product information by salesman and taking salesman totals. Then it would be sorted in branch sequence and totaled by branch, and then perhaps it would be totaled to produce a national figure.

Using the linkage technique, the product record is updated on the disk when product information is received. At the same time, the salesman record is sought and updated, as well as the branch and countrywide records. When reports are needed, all accumulations are readily available, with neither sorting time nor accumulation necessary.

Sequential Versus Random-File Organization

Choosing between sequential and random organizational techniques can be simple in some cases, difficult in others. Basically, it involves choosing either tables or direct computation as a means of finding an address. The following are some comparisons that can be made between the two techniques:

1. The sequential (table) method allows denser packing and permits a higher per cent of disk storage space for use.
2. The random method is faster for random processing.
3. The sequential method is more efficient for generating reports that depend on a search of the file in control-number sequence. To accomplish the same thing with random organization, a finder file (a list of control numbers of all the records in the file) is needed.
4. The random method more readily handles addition to and deletions from the file. With a sequential file, a large number of additions and deletions forces frequent reorganization.
5. With sequential organization, sequential processing is preferable. However, when it is batched, if the input is sorted into randomized formula sequence instead of control-number sequence, the two organizations are equally efficient.

Based upon the foregoing comparisons, the following generalizations can be made:

1. If storage capacity is very limited and files must be tightly packed, the sequential method would be preferable.
2. If random throughput and job time are the main criteria, the random organization may give better performance.
3. If there are numerous additions to and deletions from the file, the random method may be a wiser choice.
4. If there are many reports to be run and the control numbers are long, the sequential method may be the better choice.

Both sequential and random-file organization are valid techniques for doing a job and both should be explored thoroughly. Approaches to file organization may be combinations of the two techniques. After a thorough study, it may be found that some files in an application should be in random order, while others should be sequential.

Record Composition

When getting an over-all view of a direct-access device, the composition of the record is as important as the makeup of the file. There are several ways in which information may be arranged within the record to save time or to make updating easier.

Abstracting

Whenever a firm decides that mass storage is justified on the basis of inquiry purposes, but cannot be justified in terms of size, an abstracting technique may be used to reduce the size and thus reduce the cost of the system. In abstracting, only essential record information is carried on the direct-access file. The rest of the information can be stored on reels of magnetic tape, which are processed together with the direct-access file at regular accounting periods.

Trailer Record

If reference time to the most pertinent data is of more consideration than size and cost, the same technique can apply, but this time the remaining information might appear elsewhere on the file.

Consolidated Files

Often, many firms wish to have different application information consolidated into one record. This is typical of an insurance company that carries Auto, Life, Homeowners, Accident and Health, and other lines of insurance. Rather than having separate files for each of these types, the company might prefer to keep the information by policyholder. Under this set-up, a customer who carries Homeowners, Auto, and Life insurance with the same company will not have his name, address, and other basic information duplicated three times in the file.

Consolidation does save storage space. A more important consideration to the insurance company, however, is customer service. All billing, customer inquiry, etc., can be handled by examining one record, rather than many records.

Multiple Records per Segment

When the size of the segment is larger than the information to be stored (such as records which occupy only 100 out of the 200 available character positions of the segment), it would be desirable to pack more records into it. In a direct-addressing scheme where the ID's of two related application areas coincide, the first part of the record could be used for one application and the last part for the other. For example, payroll information for employee number 2345 would occupy the first 100 characters in the address position. The billing data for customer number 2345 would occupy the last 100 character positions of that same record. The computer payroll program would be instructed to be aware of the sequence of the applications.

Random-Access and On-Line Systems

"On-line" refers to the operation of input/output devices under direct control of the central processing unit. When this can be accomplished, it eliminates the need for human intervention between input origination and output destination within computer processing. "On-line" can be applied to the units near to and under direct control of the central processing unit (for example, an on-line printer), or for units which are not located near the central processing unit, but which require a communication link.

In an airline flight reservation application, the need for data inquiry is considered. The remoteness of the many reservations offices makes communication links necessary. Communication equipment and random-access storage are mutually supplemental. The maintenance of and access to flight records on a computer system would be extremely difficult without disk storage. Without communications on-line equipment, changing records or making inquiries regarding information on those records would also be difficult. The lack of either hardware would make a computerized reservations system impractical.

In batch-type installations, many operations are reserved for "off-line" handling. Typical of these are operations dealing with the transfer of data from cards to tape, tape to printer, etc. Since the card readers and line printers are relatively slow devices, it is less expensive to have them operate separately and not hold up the central processing unit. To do this, the information is written "on-line" on magnetic tape. This tape then is moved to a smaller system when the reports are run.

Mass (Direct Access) Storage and Responsive Systems

The ability to process input data on-line, regardless of the diversity of applications, and the ability to store both master records and programs make mass storage systems uniquely responsive. They can process data randomly, give an immediate response, or even more appropriately, give responses on a priority basis.

When a system is called upon to process many applications, and the input data are received randomly, it often becomes necessary to schedule the processing and establish a priority for processing. The use of mass storage gives unlimited flexibility to this work without creating an overpowering burden upon the operators of the system. For example, a general-file maintenance run can be interrupted to process an inquiry, then the machine can return to its file maintenance run. A payroll job-ticket calculation run can be interrupted to assemble a new program or even to test a new one.

In other words, a mass-storage system responds to changing priorities and requirements. Rather than processing data on a first-come, first-served basis, a mass-storage system can respond effectively on a controlled "first-things-first" priority. Thus, the capability of altering priority according to the immediate requirements of daily activity becomes a practical reality. Significant reduction is found in the tasks of program modification or the incorporation of new programs into an existing system, and both can be accomplished in a minimum time with a minimum of perplexity.

Selective Updating

Where records take up more than one consecutive segment, the most likely information to be updated (the "dynamic" information) is kept in one segment, and the least likely data to be updated (the "static" data) are kept in another segment. Thus, when the segments are read into memory, only one segment needs to be rewritten.

GLOSSARY OF TERMS

TRAILER RECORD: A record which follows a group of records and contains pertinent data related to the group of records.

QUESTIONS FOR REVIEW

1. Define file organization. What is the primary objective of its use?
2. What methods are used to set up a file for direct access? Illustrate.
3. Describe each of the following random-order techniques:
   a. correspondence method
   b. associative method
   c. tree method.
4. Discuss and compare the factors involved in choosing between random and sequential file organization.
5. What is abstracting? Explain briefly.
6. How do insurance companies apply consolidated files to improve customer service?
7. Explain how airlines make use of on-line systems for handling reservations.

chapter

24

Payroll—
A Computer Approach

Background Information

To illustrate a payroll application using a computer system, assume there is an office staff of 300 to be paid on Monday of each week for the hours worked during the previous week. When a person is hired, he completes a form with information to be used in the master personnel record. In Figure 24-1, the employee number, department, pay rate, and starting date are filled in by the personnel manager according to the form completed by the applicant. The last name is given first to facilitate alphabetic filing. Address and phone number are kept in case of an emergency. Sex and marital status are requested for general information. The Social Security number is important in that all Social Security withholdings must be reported periodically to the Social Security office by Social Security number.

There are other ways for an employee to save part of his salary: (1) He might elect to have part of his pay go toward a retirement program. (2) He might have part of his pay go toward the purchase of U.S. Savings Bonds. (3) He might wish to save a portion of his pay in the company's credit union —an organization which invests employee savings and returns a certain amount of interest to the employee each year.

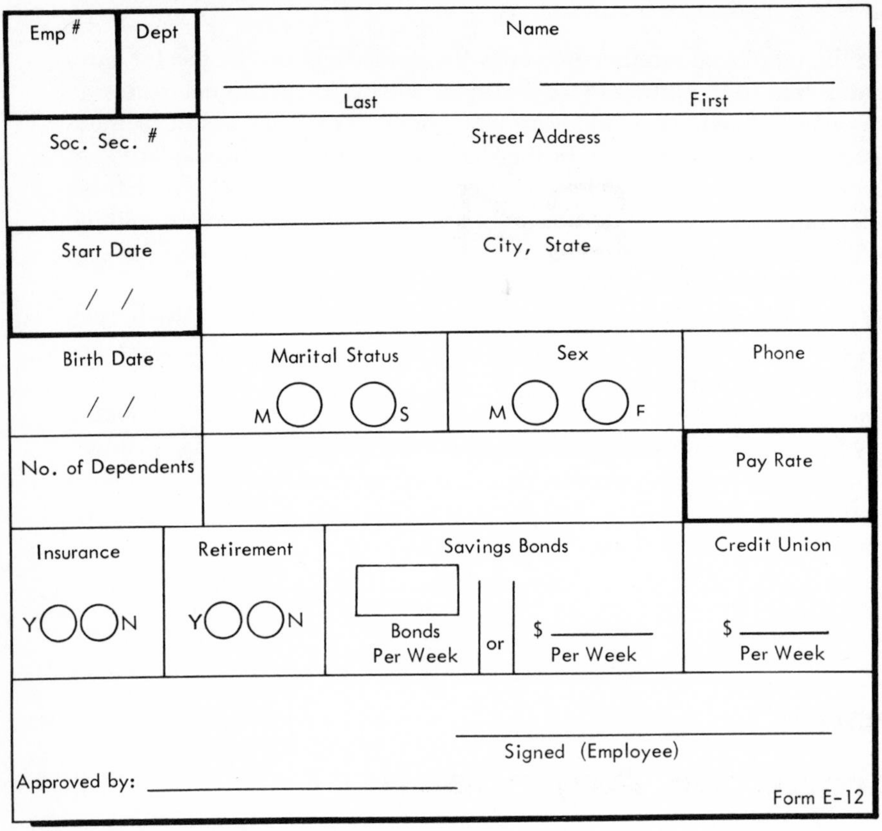
Emp #
Dept
Name
Last
First
Soc. Sec. #
Street Address
Start Date
/ /
City, State
Birth Date
/ /
Marital Status
M S
Sex
M F
Phone
No. of Dependents
Pay Rate
Insurance
Y N
Retirement
Y N
Savings Bonds
Bonds Per Week
or
$ Per Week
Credit Union
$ Per Week
Signed (Employee)
Approved by:
Form E-12

FIG. 24-1. Personnel form.

Preparation of Input Data

The Master Payroll Card

When this personnel form has been properly signed by the personnel manager, it is sent to the data-processing center, where the information is key-punched into a card, referred to as a *master payroll card.* The data fields on the form have been set up in advance by a systems man, thus making the keypunching routine as convenient as possible. In Figure 24-2, note that the areas on the personnel form correspond to the sequence in which they appear on the punched card to simplify the keypunching.

Column *1* on the master card is reserved for a "card code":

1. To distinguish it from another card and to make it easier to extract it from a mixed deck of cards. A master deck may be extracted from a mixed deck by sorting the merged deck on column *1.*

2. It is possible that the person running the payroll application might pick up the wrong deck of cards for processing. With a specific code punched into the card, the computer could be programmed to test for that code and halt processing if the wrong cards turn up. According to the code in Figure 24-2, there always should be a "3" punched in column *1* of each master payroll card.

Note that the employee number precedes the name field on the master card. It is assumed that the personnel department keeps its personnel forms in sequence by name; however, computers lend themselves more easily to number sequences, so the master cards in the data-processing department are kept in employee-number sequence. The employee number field is assigned three columns (columns 2–4), since there are about 300 employees to be accounted for. If the firm increases its personnel to more than 999, the card will have to be redesigned to allow another column (column 5) for proper coding.

Columns 5 and 6 are reserved for the department number to which each employee is assigned. All master cards are kept in employee-number sequence within their respective departments.

The name field has been allocated 20 columns (columns 7–26). Over a period of years, data-processing installations have learned that 20 columns usually are sufficient for this purpose. The last name usually can be punched in this amount of space, and the first initial can be used if there is too little room left for the entire first name.

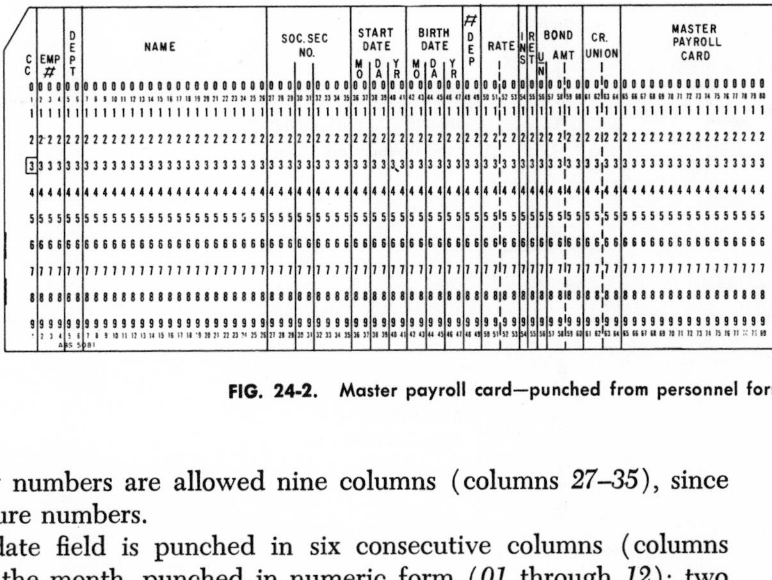

FIG. 24-2. Master payroll card—punched from personnel form.

Social Security numbers are allowed nine columns (columns 27–35), since they are nine figure numbers.

The starting date field is punched in six consecutive columns (columns 36–41): two for the month, punched in numeric form (01 through 12); two for the day; and two for the year (the prefix "19" is not necessary). Following the starting-date field is the birthdate field (columns 42–47). Note that all information to this point is of a fixed nature, except for the possibility of a name change due to marriage.

The field reflecting the number of dependents is given two columns (48–49). Rate of pay requires four columns (50–53). Note that the decimal point is not punched into the card; the dotted line in the face of the card denotes the location of the decimal point. A rate of 3.50, for example, would be punched as 0350; a rate of 4.00, as 0400. The pennies always are indicated in columns 52 and 53, which is called "right justifying" a field.

Column *54* is reserved for insurance. If the insurance box in the personnel card is checked "yes," a "1" is punched in column *54;* otherwise, a zero is punched. The next column (column *55*) is used for a retirement deduction and the same coding applies. Column *56* indicates the number of bonds to be purchased by the employee each week; if none, a "0" is punched. Columns *57–60* are reserved for the amount to be deducted from the employee's pay toward the purchase of bonds; if none, the field is punched with 0000. The last data field, Credit Union (columns *61–64*) is punched with the amount to be deducted each week, if any, for investment purposes.

FIG. 24-3. Setting up the master payroll cards.

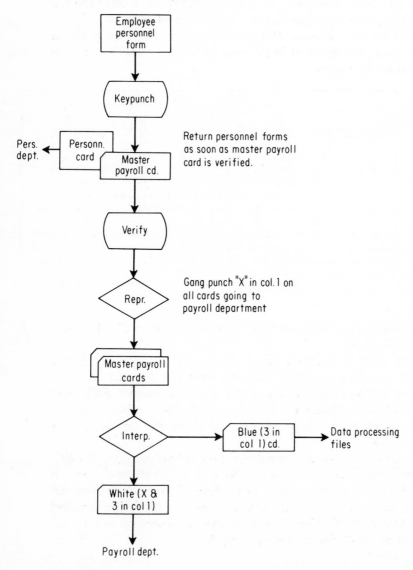

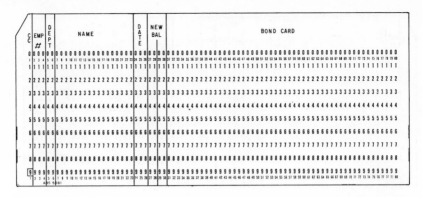

FIG. 24-4. The bond card.

FIG. 24-5. Preparation of the bond card—flow chart.

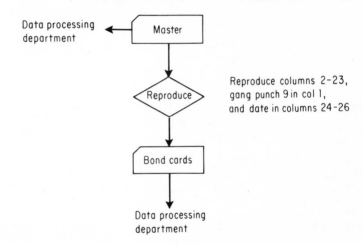

Reproduce columns 2-23, gang punch 9 in col 1, and date in columns 24-26

After the original document (personnel form) has been key-punched, the master payroll card is verified. Then the source document is returned to the personnel department for reference. Pertinent data from the master card are reproduced and sent to the payroll department. The two data cards are distinguished by using different colors (for example, blue for data processing and white for the payroll department). An X-punch also is made in column *1* of the payroll department's card. This step, as well as others mentioned to date, are shown in Figure 24-3.

The Bond Card

Before the master card is filed, it is used for creating another card, called the *bond card* (Figure 24-4). This card is punched by reproducing columns *2–23* from the master, and gang punching a "9" in column *1* and a date in columns *24–26*. Columns *27–30* are left blank. The flow chart for the preparation of a bond card is shown in Figure 24-5.

In the bond card, the date consists of a week number (1–52) and the last digit of the year. Other details are presented later in this chapter.

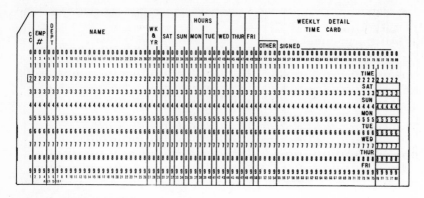

FIG. 24-6. Weekly detail time cards.

FIG. 24-7. Preparation of the weekly detail time card—flow chart.

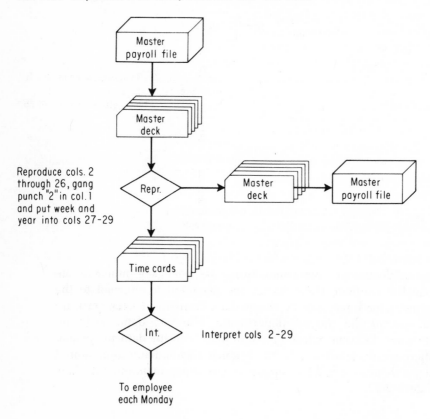

The Time Card

Toward the end of each week, the data-processing department must prepare individual time cards to be given to each employee for recording the hours he has worked. Employees, especially those who work over the weekend, must have the cards no later than Friday. Prepunched into the card are a card code (assume a "2"), department number, employee number, name, week, and year (Figure 24-6). Any prepunched data are interpreted for readability before they are sent out to the employees. The system flow chart for this routine is shown in Figure 24-7.

As the week progresses, each employee fills in the hours worked in the appropriate space on his card. On Friday, all cards are signed, collected by the department, and sent to the data-processing center. There, the information concerning hours is punched, verified, and then sorted into employee sequence and department sequence, respectively. If the keypunch operator makes a mistake, one of two things can happen. Either a new card is prepared and the incorrect card kept aside until all payroll processing is complete (this is called preparing a substitute document), or a small piece of tape can be placed over the incorrect hole, thus preventing any equipment from reading the incorrect punch, and the correct punch can be made.

Since the master card contains certain information required in the processing of a paycheck, (for example: deductions, exemptions, pay rate, etc.) it is merged on a collator with the detail card. It should be noted that the master file is sorted in the same sequence as the detail cards.

The Year-to-Date Card

Included in the processing of employee payroll is the preparation of required reports to be submitted periodically to the government. One of these reports is a quarterly statement showing the amount withheld for FICA (Social Security). A special file is provided for keeping a running total of year-to-date figures for each employee. The *year-to-date card* contains such identifying information as card code (7), department number, employee number, and name (Figure 24-8). Other information also is included and is updated each week whenever a new card is produced.

Other than the date, all fields will contain year-to-date information (progressive totals) regarding gross pay (total money earned), FICA (Social Security withheld) to date and for the quarter, withholding tax (income tax withheld),

FIG. 24-8. Year-to-date card.

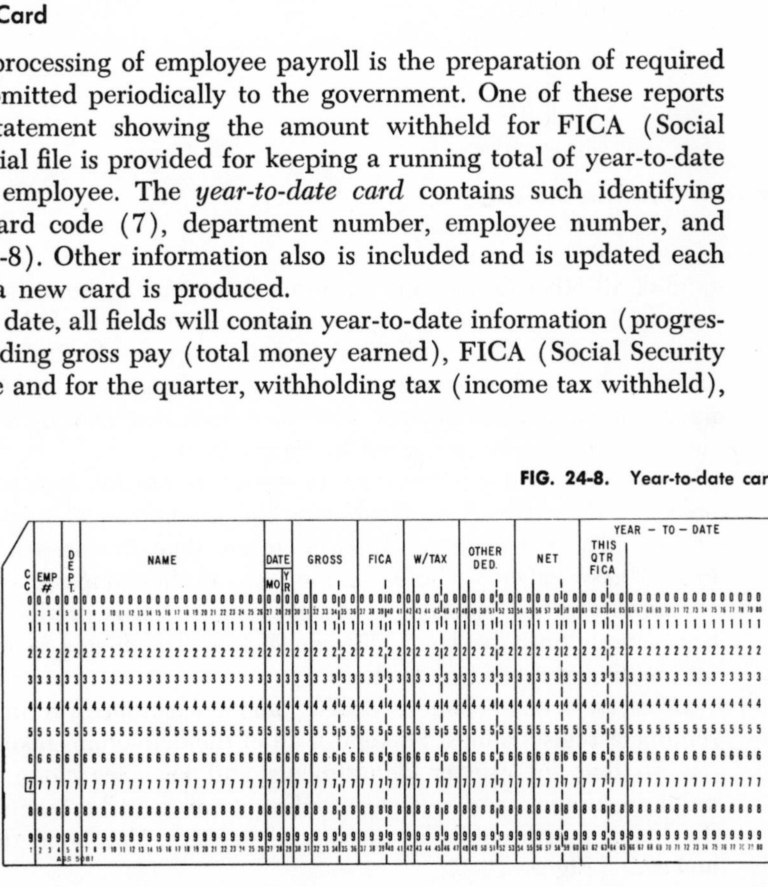

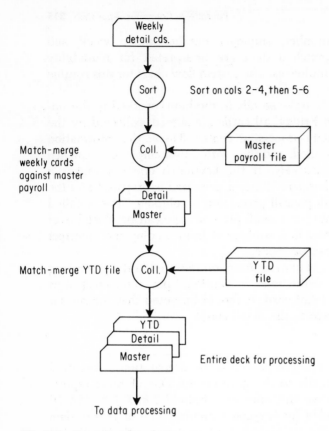

Weekly
detail cds.

Sort   Sort on cols 2-4, then 5-6

Match-merge
weekly cards
against master
payroll

Coll.   Master
payroll file

Detail
Master

Match-merge YTD file   Coll.   YTD
file

YTD
Detail
Master   Entire deck for processing

To data processing

FIG. 24-9. Operations flow chart.

total of all other deductions (insurance, retirement, bonds, credit union), and
net pay (amount of check: gross, minus all taxes and deduction). At the end
of the 13th, 26th, 39th, and 52nd weeks, the quarterly FICA figure is dropped,
since it does not represent a year-to-date figure, but only an accumulated
figure for the current quarter. The flow chart prepared by the systems analyst
for this operation is presented in Figure 24-9.

It can be concluded from the foregoing discussion that although the prime
objective of a payroll application is the production of a paycheck, the "side
effects" take more time and consideration than the preparation of the check
itself. These "offshoots" affect many areas of the company, some of which are:

Payroll register (journal). As each paycheck is produced, a listing of all
transactions must be kept (Figure 24-10). The listing is prepared from the
information recorded on a check.

Other registers (bonds, credit union, insurance, retirement). Separate
reports or registers must be kept of all of the deductions taken from employees'
pay so that the proper departments and agencies can give credit. Credit
union, insurance, and retirement information may be taken from the second,
third, and fourth copies of the payroll register. The bond register is separate,
however (Figure 24-11).

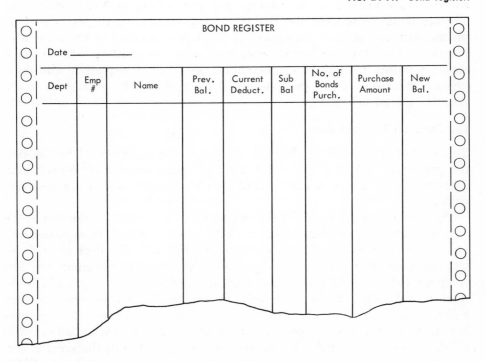

PAYROLL REGISTER

Date

Dept #	Emp #	Name	Reg. Hrs	O.T. Hrs	Reg. Pay	O.T. Pay	Tot. Gross	FICA	W/tax	Misc. Ded. Other	Ins.	Ret.	Bonds	Cr. Union	Check No.	Net Pay
(2)	(3)	(20)	(3)	(3)	(5)	(5)	(5)	(3)	(4)	(4)	(3)	(3)	(4)	(4)	(3)	(5)

FIG. 24-10. Payroll register.

FIG. 24-11. Bond register.

BOND REGISTER

Date _____

Dept	Emp #	Name	Prev. Bal.	Current Deduct.	Sub Bal	No. of Bonds Purch.	Purchase Amount	New Bal.

Government reports (FICA and withholding tax). Information must be collected in order to prepare quarterly reports to the government (Figures 24-12 and 24-13).

Gross pay by department. In making business decisions, cost or overhead often is considered, especially in matters relating to budget appropriations on a departmental basis. The payroll register is set up to show totals in all fields by department. In manufacturing, management needs more data than department totals. Manufacturing employees often fill out a time card showing the amount of time worked to complete a specific job. Job-cost data are valuable to management in determining the cost to be charged to the customer. At the end of the week, the data-processing department sorts out all time cards by job number and produces a report showing the payroll involved in each of the jobs in the factory. This is called a labor distribution report.

Miscellaneous reports. The personnel department might wish to make morale surveys and needs information regarding absenteeism. A weekly report could be run by department, showing hours not worked and overtime hours worked (hours over 40 per week per employee). This report would give the personnel department an idea of how many people were late to work and how many had to work beyond the 40-hour limit to get the job done. It also might tell them if there are particular times of the year when absenteeism is at its height.

Other special management reports also might be presented upon request, covering such matters as the average pay per person, over-all average pay increase or decrease over the last year, projected pay next year based on present increases in pay, percentage of employees enrolled in the retirement program versus the number of employees who are quitting, etc. When a manager wishes to have this information, he sends a request to the data-processing manager and a programmer is assigned to write a program to obtain this special information.

The Computer Paycheck Run

To complete the payroll application, the processing is performed by the central processing unit. It is assumed that the computer system includes a central processing unit, a card reader, a card punch, a printer, and a console typewriter.

The most important aspect of the payroll job is the actual production of the paycheck, which is prepared before any other work is done. The steps involved in a paycheck processing run are shown in Figure 24-14. The deck of cards for all employees (three cards per employee) is the input to the computer. The computer calculates the pay of each employee and prints the paychecks at the same time it punches out two cards: an employee's new year-to-date card and a journal card. As each employee's record is processed, any discrepancies are noted on the console printer. For instance, if the year-to-date card is missing, a note is printed. The record is not processed until the error is corrected. To complete the application, another computer run is made which

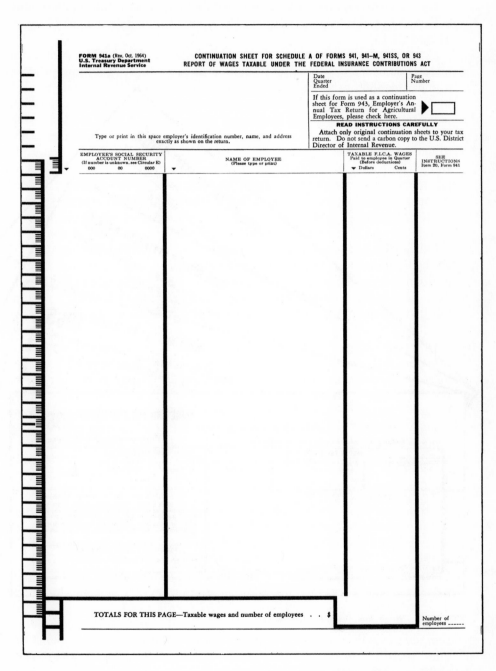

FORM 941a (Rev. Oct. 1964)
U.S. Treasury Department
Internal Revenue Service

CONTINUATION SHEET FOR SCHEDULE A OF FORMS 941, 941—M, 941SS, OR 943
REPORT OF WAGES TAXABLE UNDER THE FEDERAL INSURANCE CONTRIBUTIONS ACT

Date
Quarter
Ended

Page
Number

If this form is used as a continuation sheet for Form 943, Employer's Annual Tax Return for Agricultural Employees, please check here.

READ INSTRUCTIONS CAREFULLY

Type or print in this space employer's identification number, name, and address exactly as shown on the return.

Attach only original continuation sheets to your tax return. Do not send a carbon copy to the U.S. District Director of Internal Revenue.

EMPLOYEE'S SOCIAL SECURITY ACCOUNT NUMBER (If number is unknown, see Circular E) 000 00 0000	NAME OF EMPLOYEE (Please type or print)	TAXABLE F.I.C.A. WAGES Paid to employee in Quarter (Before deductions) Dollars Cents	SEE INSTRUCTIONS Item 20, Form 941

TOTALS FOR THIS PAGE—Taxable wages and number of employees . . $

Number of employees _____

FIG. 24-12. Report of taxable wages.

WAGE AND TAX STATEMENT 1965

Copy D—For employer

SOCIAL SECURITY INFORMATION

Total F.I.C.A. wages paid in 1965

WAGE AND TAX STATEMENT 1965

Copy C—For employee's records

SOCIAL SECURITY INFORMATION

employee | Total F.I.C.A. wages paid in 1965

WAGE AND TAX STATEMENT 1965

Copy B—To be filed with employee's tax return

SOCIAL SECURITY INFORMATION

employee | Total F.I.C.A. wages paid in 1965

1

WAGE AND TAX STATEMENT 1965

Copy A—For District Director

Type or print EMPLOYER'S identification number, name, and address above.

INCOME TAX INFORMATION			SOCIAL SECURITY INFORMATION	
Federal income tax with-held	Wages [1] paid subject to with-holding in 1965	Other compensation [2] paid in 1965	F.I.C.A. employee tax withheld	Total F.I.C.A. wages paid in 1965

Type or print EMPLOYEE'S social security number →

[1] Before payroll deductions or "sick pay" exclusions.
[2] The block marked "Other compensation" is for use in reporting salary or other compensation which was not subject to withholding and which was heretofore reported on Form 1099. In 1965 this type of income may be shown on either the W–2 or the 1099 (but not on both).

FOR USE OF INTERNAL REVENUE SERVICE

Employee's copy and employer's copy compared . . . .

Type or print EMPLOYEE's name and address above.

FORM W-2—U.S. Treasury Department, Internal Revenue Service   EMPLOYER: See instructions on back of copy D.   10—78420–1

FIG. 24-13. Wage and tax statement—sample.

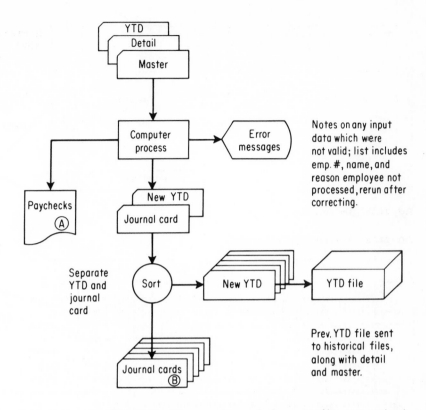

FIG. 24-14. The computer paycheck run (weekly)—systems detail.

includes all the employees who were not included on the original run (Figure 24-14).

A paycheck is divided into two parts: the check and the stub. The former is the negotiable section and represents the employee's net pay. The blank checks come through the printer in a continuous sequence (Figure 24-15). These "continuous forms" are fed into the printer by a sprocket wheel which engages the holes on the edges of the paper. The wheel turns as printing occurs, one line at a time, in a predetermined manner.

The stub of the check is detachable by the employee and is prepared for the employee's own record. It contains all the information regarding payroll deductions. Total hours worked are recorded from the weekly detail card, and any hours over eight hours per day are considered overtime. During the computer run, a constant of eight is subtracted from each day's hours, and the total number of overtime hours is accumulated. Separating regular hours from overtime hours is necessary because regular hours are multiplied by the normal pay rate; overtime hours are paid at time and a half. Total gross pay is the sum of regular and overtime pay. Social Security (FICA) is a tax based upon a percentage of the gross pay. A maximum limit is set by the Social Security

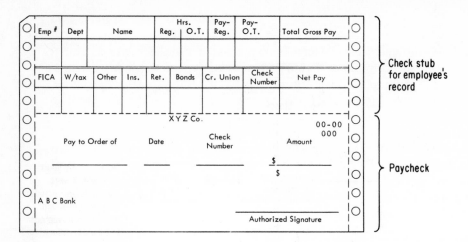

FIG. 24-15. The paycheck.

FIG. 24-16. A journal card.

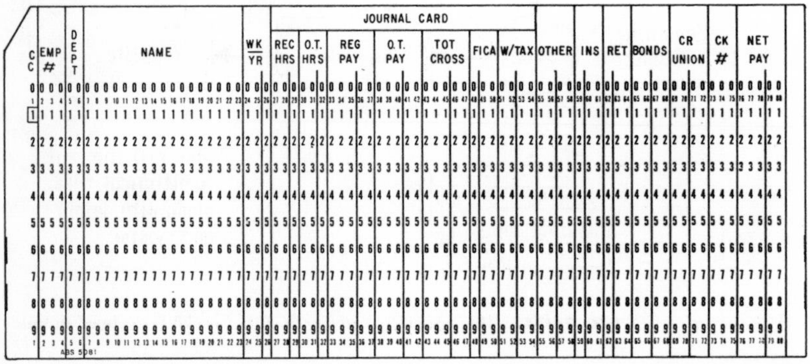

office regarding the amount of tax which can be deducted during the year. The FICA year-to-date figures are kept on the year-to-date card.

"W/tax" is the federal income tax. It is based on a percentage of gross pay, depending on the number of dependents claimed.

The next five fields are miscellaneous deductions. The field entitled "Other" represents such things as a salary advance made to the employee or a correction to his pay, perhaps from a mistake made the previous week.

Insurance is a fixed rate per week per employee and is maintained as a program constant by the computer. If the rate changes, a corrective instruction is made in the program.

Retirement is calculated as a percentage of gross pay. Bonds and credit union deductions are made based on instructions shown on the master card.

The check number is added by the computer. At the beginning of the run, the operator furnishes a starting number to the computer, after which it is incremented by one every time a check is printed.

Finally, net pay represents gross pay minus the sum of all taxes and miscellaneous deductions.

After all the employees' checks have been processed, the checks are separated from the continuous form into individual copies and are run through a machine which prints the authorized signature. This machine also imprints a special ink through the amount (light enough that it does not cover up the amount), so that no changes can be made.

The last step in the payroll run involves separating the journal cards and year-to-date cards by sorting them on column *1*. The new year-to-date card is sent to a file to await other uses. The old file can be sent to the historical files. Just as in magnetic-tape processing, old files are retained until all processing has proved to be correct. Journal cards also will be used for other processes (Figure 24-16).

Preparation of the Payroll Register

As soon as the paychecks have been processed and distributed, other details must be completed. The journal card is used to produce the *payroll register* (Figure 24-17). Since all necessary calculations have been made, the use of a com-
puter is not necessary for this run. Figure
24-10 shows a continuous-form payroll
register for this application. The date
printed on each page is controlled through
the control panel of the accounting machine. Certain wires are changed each
week so that a new date will be printed.

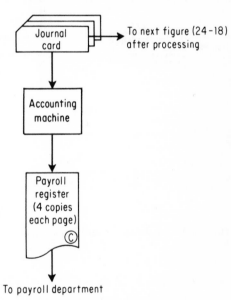

FIG. 24-17. Preparation of the weekly payroll register.

The payroll register includes headings
and columns representing all the information used during payroll processing. The
numbers in parentheses show the number
of print positions set aside for each field.
The continuous-form register can be run
in several copies (with carbons between
sheets). Many of the fields on the register
are accumulated by department as they
are printed on the tabulator. These data
are valuable to the payroll department in
determining the cost of the payroll for
each department of the firm.

Preparation of the Bond Register

The *bond register* is prepared on a computer, since it is a little more complicated. Figure 24-18 shows a systems flow chart of this routine. Before the
beginning of the computer run, the bond cards (with a zero new balance field
for new employees) are match-merged against the journal cards. Not all employees are enrolled in the bond program; therefore, some journal cards fall in
the unmatched pocket of the collator and are sent to the historical file. The

merged deck (bond cards and journal cards) can then be processed. The journal card shows the amount of the current week's bond deduction, previously calculated during the paycheck run. The result of the bond run produces a register and new bond cards; the input deck (old bond cards and matched journal cards) is sent to the historical files; and the new bond cards will be used to run the succeeding week's register (Figure 24-19).

The main problem in processing the foregoing routine is that the total amount collected seldom equals the purchase price of a bond. Each week, the total dollars available for bond purchase are examined. If a total equals or exceeds the bond price (for example, $18.75), a bond is purchased. Any remaining amount is examined again to see if perhaps another bond may be

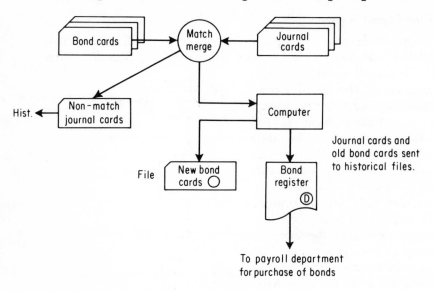

FIG. 24-18. Preparation of weekly bond register—
flow chart.

purchased. If so, another $18.75 is subtracted from the accumulated funds. This process continues until no more bonds may be purchased for the week. The money left over is punched into the new bond card to carry over for the following week. The bond register (Figure 24-11) shows this complete transaction, including the balance from the previous week's card (previous balance); the deduction made this week according to the journal card (current deduction); the sum of the two (sub-balance); the number of bonds purchased and the value they represent; and finally, the new balance, which goes on the register as well as on the new bond card.

Preparation of the Quarterly Earnings Report

As we mentioned before, a report goes to the government each quarter (every 13 weeks) showing employee earnings. A copy of this report is shown in

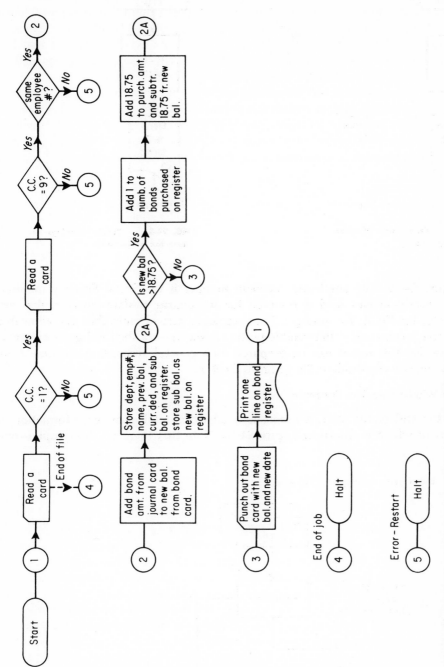

FIG. 24-19. Processing detail chart—weekly bond register preparation.

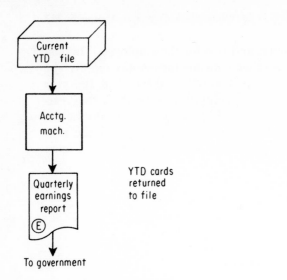

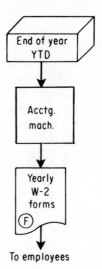

FIG. 24-20. Preparation of quarterly earnings report.

FIG. 24-21. Yearly earnings—income tax preparation.

Figure 24-12. The employee's account number is the Social Security number. The taxable-wages field is reserved for the quarter-to-date earnings that are taxable for FICA; for example, if an employee earned more than the allowable taxable income, only that taxable portion is shown—not the total gross earnings. Note that this report can be prepared on a general accounting machine from the current year-to-date file (Figure 24-20).

The Withholding Tax Statement

At the end of the year, a report is needed for total earnings information, a copy of which is shown in Figure 24-13. Note that there are four copies—one

FIG. 24-22. End of year—creating new YTD cards.

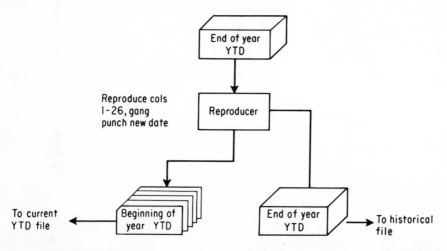

for the government, one for the employer, and two for the employee. The employee keeps one copy and submits the other with his income-tax report. The report may be prepared from the year-to-date cards at the end of the year (Figure 24-21). As soon as all end-of-the-year reporting is finished, the year-to-date cards are run through a reproducer and all accumulated information is dropped. The old cards become part of the historical files, and the new blank cards are used to begin payroll processing for the new year (Figure 24-22).

GLOSSARY OF TERMS

GROSS PAY: An employee's total pay with no deductions.

PAYROLL REGISTER: A record of employees to be paid with the amount due to each.

TIME CARD: A card used for showing the number of hours an employee has worked.

QUESTIONS FOR REVIEW

1. Describe the steps involved in the preparation of payroll input data.
2. What is the difference between a bond card and a time card?
3. What is the main function of a year-to-date card? What information does it contain?
4. What types of reports and records are prepared as a part of a payroll application? Explain each briefly.
5. Explain the actual payroll routine performed by the central processing unit.
6. What type of information does a paycheck include?
7. Summarize briefly the computer routine involved in the preparation of the following reports:
   (a) Payroll register
   (b) Bond register
   (c) Quarterly earning report.

Career Opportunities
and Management's Role

The topics discussed in the text thus far stressed the need, the operations, and manipulating aspects of data-processing hardware with a brief coverage of computer-programming techniques and methods. Behind all the equipment and the various components making up a computer installation are men and women whose jobs vary from keypunching the data in cards and preparing source data for input to the task of programming, debugging, operating, and managing a computer system. In this chapter, emphasis will be placed upon career opportunities which have grown out of the increasing need for better electronic data-processing systems.

Every year, more computers (in number and complexity) are introduced on the market requiring more specialized and highly trained data-processing personnel at all levels. The more an organization depends on a computer, the more it realizes the need for qualified people to plan, organize, direct, and control the many data-processing tasks.

Not all computer systems have been successful. A major reason behind either a successful or unsuccessful computer system is the caliber of the people involved with and responsible for its operation. A successful installation is one which is run by competent data-processing personnel and supported by key managers. The need for highly skilled data processors has created a new profession for thousands of men and women.

Career Positions in Automatic Data Processing

Working efficiency in the EDP system has been shown to be based to a large degree on a new profession of specialists. The computer is a helpless tangle of wires until a "program" has been prepared to direct its action—and programs are prepared by human beings. A computer program may be the result of weeks or months of analysis to determine exactly how output information may be obtained from the input data available. This calls for the combined talents of (1) data-processing managers, (2) systems analysts, and (3) programmers. Behind them a whole echelon of operations personnel must control the day-to-day "care and feeding" of the equipment itself.

Data-Processing Management

The Data-Processing Manager

A data-processing department is organized along the same patterns as that of a formal organization. At the top is a *data-processing manager* aided by one or more assistants who act in his behalf to carry out assigned duties. Below the top position are several subordinate employees responsible for producing predetermined results.

The data-processing manager is responsible for the planning, coordinating, and directing of data-processing activities for the entire organization. He must supervise the work of others and should possess high managerial as well as technical skills. Many of those now occupying this position have moved up the ladder from within the department after acquiring the necessary background and experience. Persons seeking a career in computer management should, however, attempt to earn a college degree since "outsiders" considered for a top position usually are expected to present a more attractive background than those from within the firm. In many cases a master's degree will be desired. The college course required will vary according to the type of installation. For example, a degree in business administration with some emphasis on data processing would be more suitable for work in a business-oriented computer installation than a scientific-oriented one. The latter one would require, in most cases, a degree in mathematics, physics, statistics, or other related fields with a background in management and some practical experience in computer science.

It should be emphasized at this point that a data-processing manager must, in addition to his technical and practical background, possess a "know-how" to lead and get things done through people, since it is people who operate and produce the over-all detailed activities of the department. A good manager will be instrumental in optimizing the output of the computer department.

A data-processing manager's salary varies with different companies, geographic locations, and size of data-processing installations. A recent survey,* presenting salaries by metropolitan areas, shows a national average of $280 per week. The salaries ranged widely, from a low of $121 to a high of $600 per week.

Manager of Computer Operations

The next management position in a data-processing department is the direction of computer operations. The *manager of computer operations* directs the computer installation, plans the scheduling of computer time, allocates personnel, maintains the program library, and controls operations within the computer center.

The educational requirements for this position vary considerably, depending on the size and functions of the computer. Although many persons presently holding the position of computer-operations manager do not have college degrees, the tendency is toward hiring and promoting operations managers who have completed degrees, or at least a significant amount of college work. The college course should include business subjects as well as mathematics, statistics, and computer science.

Like the data-processing manager's salary, the manager of computer-operation's salary also differs depending on the size, type of firm, and the geographic location of the installation. The same survey mentioned earlier shows a national weekly salary average of $184.

Systems Analysis and Programming

The Systems Analyst

As explained in a separate chapter, the *systems analyst* is responsible for creating an ordered system for data collection, processing, and the production of useful information. His objective is to improve control and decision making and at the same time to make the most efficient use of available data-processing equipment. The highly abstract nature of his work, like that of the computer programmer, requires strong logical and creative abilities.

On the basis of present practices for hiring systems analysts, a college graduate appears to be the best prospect for receiving the job and advancing in this area. Again, the desired major field of college study depends on the type of installation and the specific projects to be worked on. Generally speaking, however, a balanced background in mathematics, computer science, and business management would be desirable.

Senior systems analysts are paid about $200 per week on the average; the

---

* *Business Automation,* Business Publications International, 288 Park Avenue West, Elmhurst, Ill., June 1965.

manager of systems analysis is generally paid between $200 and $300 per week.

The Computer Programmer

The job of *programmer* is one of the newest in the country. Before 1950, this job classification did not exist, since it wasn't until early 1951 that commercial computers were first installed. In 1951, only one computer (Univac) was installed. In 1952, 7 (4 Univacs, 3 NCR) computers; in 1955, 309 computers; in 1958, 3,638 computers; in 1960, 4,519 computers; in 1963, 17,840 computers; and today (latest figures available), about 28,600 computers.*

With the steadily increasing demand for computers comes an equal demand for programmers (at all levels) to "put the computer to work." It is estimated that as many as 200,000 programmers will be needed by 1970. In large computing systems, several programmers at different levels of responsibility work as a team on a given project, often a complex one. The highly experienced, or *senior* programmer usually directs the work of junior and other programmers throughout the duration of the whole project. Each programmer is assigned a part of the system to program.

Except for sophisticated, highly specialized, or scientific engineering applications, programming does not necessarily require a college background. Still, college work is desirable since many employers use the degree as a screening device for applicants. Also, a background of general education helps programmers understand the basis for the company procedures and problems. Programming requires a logical mind, an attention to detail, and an ability to determine what steps are necessary to complete a task or solve a problem. Some of the best programmers in industry today have a college background in music, philosophy, and the liberal arts since data processing courses were not available. But new programs are being designed especially to train programmers in high schools and colleges. This should result in better prepared programmers for industry in the future.

Persons seeking an opportunity in a scientific oriented computer installation (scientific programming) would find it helpful to have taken as many college courses in mathematics and computer science as possible. On the other hand, those interested in working in a business-oriented installation (business programming) would find a background that includes business subjects and some mathematics most valuable. For a top position in programming sophisticated projects, a bachelor's or master's degree in mathematics, computer science, or business administration is an important asset in the long run.

How does one know whether he has the aptitude for programming? A number of computer users, manufacturers, and employment services offer various programming aptitude tests which measure the applicant's logical ability and to a degree, his ability to manipulate and work with figures. Those

* *Business Automation*, August 1965. Ned Chapin, *An Introduction to Automatic Computers*, 2nd ed. D. Van Nostrand Co., Inc., Princeton, N.J. Page 199.

interested might wish to inquire about these tests through their school guidance counselor, the State or Federal Employment Service, or by getting in touch with the educational center of a computer manufacturer.

Financial remuneration and working conditions for programmers are generally good. A beginning programmer should start at $5,000 to $6,000 per year depending on his school and work experience, and gradually move up to a senior programmer's level at about $10,000. Many senior programmers, however, with a college or a graduate degree in a specialized science area, earn well over $13,000 a year and some with management responsibility and extensive experience earn as high as $20,000.

Data-Processing Operations

The Computer Operator

A *computer operator* is in direct command of the computer during a program run. He must load and unload programs, prepare input data for entry, and be on hand to monitor error messages and keep the machines operating smoothly. He should be intelligent, alert, and mindful of the expensive equipment he is operating.

At the present time most computer operators are high school graduates who were previously operators of unit record (tabulating or EAM) equipment. However, the more sophisticated computer systems being marketed today promise to place additional educational demands on operators.

Training for computer-operating jobs is provided through private business and technical schools, junior colleges, and some high schools. Most operators have learned on the job and through schools conducted by the computer manufacturers for their customers' personnel. Most of those who train for computer-operating jobs either have a high school diploma or are presently in high school and are preparing to enter the computer-operation field after graduation. Persons planning to attend a private data-processing training institution are advised to check first the reputation of the private school. The state departments of education and the local Better Business Bureaus may be of assistance in locating the best schools. Salaries for computer operators range on the average from $88 per week for beginners to $128 for senior operators.

The Tabulator Operator

The *tabulator operator* works with unit-record equipment, transferring the cards being processed from machine to machine and controlling the operation of various accounting machines. Required educational background is similar to that of a computer operator but with less emphasis on the technical knowledge of electronic computers. Salaries for tabular operators average from $80 per week for trainees to $150 for supervisors and group leaders. Some supervisors earn as much as $280 per week. Geographic location and the size and type of installations are among the chief determinants of the tabulator operator's income.

Keypunch Operator

Keypunch operators transcribe input data from the original documents to punched cards using keypunch equipment. Keypunch supervisors schedule activities in the keypunch section and instruct operators on procedures for keypunch applications. The educational background necessary is similar to that of tabulator operators: a high school diploma is desirable but not necessarily required. Salaries for keypunch operators average between $66 per week for trainees to $123 for supervisors. Some keypunch supervisors earn over $200 per week.

Entry-level jobs in computer, tabulator, or keypunch operations generally do not require the breadth of educational background or abstract logical ability necessary for systems and computer programming work. They do require a high level of manual dexterity, alertness, and practical thinking.

Management and Automatic Data Processing

There has been a great deal of misleading publicity about computers, but the less publicized fact is that before any machine can function, a human being first has to think through the problem, reduce it to its most basic logic, and then prepare a machine program to follow that logic. Buried under the millions of published words about computers is the truly significant fact that we have at last begun to analyze our problems in a disciplined and logical manner, reducing them to basics and assigning quantitative measures where only subjective analysis and emotion existed in the past. The desire to use this relatively new tool in solving our problems has forced us to become more scientific in our thinking about them.

This is not a lesson that has been learned easily, as evidenced by the disappointments many companies have experienced in their early attempts to use computers for problem-solving. The fault is not with the machines—the hardware technology is far ahead of the applications and is accelerating more rapidly. The problem is directly attributable to the scarcity of competent, experienced people and the traditional caution of many people in management positions. It is just as important for management to know the capabilities and limitations of the computer as it is for the shop foreman to know the capabilities of the machines in his shop.

The Management Tool

How does one learn about computers to be able to use them intelligently in a business situation? The problem is primarily one of attitude—of placing the use of the machine in its proper perspective. The manager must overcome the fear that the machine poses a threat to his ability to exercise full control over operations, and realize that a computer, properly used, can increase his ability to exercise control by making more information available to him when he needs it. It is important for him to know comparatively little about the machine itself as long as he realizes that:

1. The computer is only a tool, one component in a man-machine-information system.

2. Information coming out of the machine can be only a combination or permutation of the data which went into it. The machine cannot create information, nor can it extract information which is not inherent in the raw data going in.

3. Information coming out of the machine is useful only when it is interpreted in terms of the combined limits of error of the input data and the program which processed it.

In order to apply this knowledge, the manager must have considerable depth of understanding about each subsystem in which the computer is used. But in assessing and evaluating what comes out of the machine, he now must analyze what he knows about his operations more exactly than ever before. He must take the time to state his information requirements precisely, so that the people who are directing the machine will develop answers within the limits he sets forth.

In the rapidly changing environment of today's business, high-speed data processing machines offer a means through which the manager of a business can respond dynamically to the challenge of making fast decisions correctly. That, for the manager, is the most significant "why" of automatic data processing.

part 5

Appendices

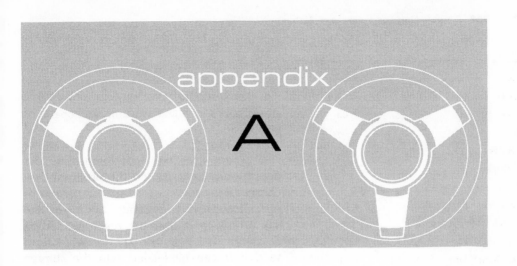

Programming Languages
and Systems

Machine-Language Coding

As we look back at the programmer's work described in Chapter 18, we note many complications:

1. The programmer deals almost exclusively in numbers. When he wants to add a quantity to the arithmetic unit register, for example, he must search in the operation code list to get the right digits (Figure A-1). This is a relatively minor problem with the type of computer used for the example which has only 15 instructions. Most computers, however, have many more instructions in their sets; in some, there are well over 200 different types of possible operations.

2. Constant underlining of blank spaces to be filled in later can be an annoying phase of the program and may cause errors. The example problem in Chapter 18 was accommodated by a 22-instruction program. By contrast, it is common for major business programs today to require thousands of machine instructions. For example, a modest program designed to write customers' bills for a department store, using sales-slip input data and customer master-file information, and designed to check the input data for accuracy and validity, required 1,216 instructions.

3. In addition to keeping track of branch locations and constant words, a programmer must be prepared to handle any exceptions that may arise in the most efficient way possible. These errors usually occur as a result of the many lists and

Name	Code
Read	+ 01
Write	+ 02
Clear and Add	+ 03
Add	+ 04
Subtract	+ 05
Multiply	+ 06
Divide	+ 07
Compare	+ 08
Branch	+ 09
Test Branch High	+ 10
Test Branch Low	+ 11
Test Branch Equal	+ 12
Branch End of File	+ 13
Store	+ 14
Halt	+ 15

FIG. A-1. Operation code list.

other details that must be checked, such as updating the storage map. Some of the common lists include those of instruction locations, constant locations, data locations, storage locations used and available, and operation codes.

A programmer also has to translate the descriptions he writes on the program flow charts into the numerical language of operation codes and storage addresses. He has to see to it that the resulting coding is transcribed into machine-readable form so that it can be loaded into the storage when needed.

Since the early 1940's, programmers have been thinking about better ways of transcribing source programs into machine readable form and reducing coding errors. This has led to the development of programming aids. The functions mentioned above can be performed by using a computer; what is needed is simply a program to do them. Such a program is called a *processor program*.

The Processor Program

As input, the processor program uses the recorded coding of the programmer, presented in a language similar to the English language. This language is commonly called "symbolic" language. Loaded along with the processor program are fixed and variable constants to be used for translation purposes and for recording the assignment of addresses in the object program (the program when coded in a machine language). The processor program can produce the object program in the necessary machine-readable form, as well as in a printed form. It also is capable of supplying the storage map and certain messages concerning any clerical errors which may have occurred in transcribing the source coding (Figure A-2).

It should be noted that the processor program performs very little arithmetic. Its major work consists of reading the lines of coding (which have been punched into cards), treating them as input records, comparing the operation code with a table to find the right machine code, comparing the address portion with symbolic addresses to find the proper machine address, assembling the instructions for output, and then writing the necessary output. As a precautionary measure, many exceptions are provided for, an approach considered desirable in all programs.

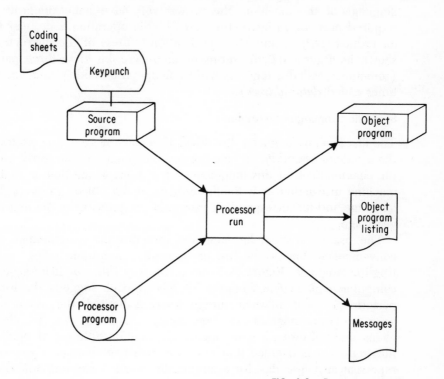

FIG. A-2.   Processor program run.

This points out the programming economy realized for the use of processor programs. Computer manufacturers employ a large staff of programmers for this purpose. When a new computer is announced today, it is expected that the total computer system will include not only the equipment hardware, but also the accompanying processor programs ("software").

Languages—Formats and Types

The programmer who uses a processor program is expected to specify the layout of his input and output records. Most importantly, he must specify what kind of characters will be recognized and in what order they should be read and/or handled. This specification results in what is called the *language* of the processor system.

FIG. A-3.   Coding sheet for processor language.

Label	Op Code	Operand
(Basically, the address of the instruction)	(The symbol describing what is to be done)	(The description of the things to be operated upon)

Since the language of the processor program is to be translated into the language of the machine, the format will have some similarity. The three required parts of an instruction are (1) the operation code, (2) the operand or address portion, and (3) the location address of the instruction itself. As shown in Figure A-3, the terms used to describe these three parts are *label* (sometimes called a tag), *op-code* (or operation code), and *operand* (sometimes called *data address*).

Symbolic Language—Assembler

The first level of language described for a class of processor programs is called the *symbolic assembly,* or "one-for-one" language. As the third term indicates, the characteristic of this language is that there is one line of coding for each machine instruction as it finally appears in the object program. This type of language and its corresponding processor programs were the first type defined years ago.

The use of a symbolic language provides the programmer with several conveniences. One is the use of op-codes (operation codes) similar to the English language. Figure A-4 shows the way this would be specified for the computer explained in Chapter 18. The op-code suggests the function to be performed. Since internal storage space is limited, the writer of the processor program must decide how many characters can be allotted to op-codes and still provide some mnemonic function (the use of symbols). In this illustration, it is decided that no more than five characters are to be used to represent any op-codes; for example, the words *Clear and Add* are condensed

FIG. A-4. Mnemonic op-codes.

Name	Op Code	Machine Code
Read	Read	+ 01
Write	Write	+ 02
Clear and Add	Cladd	+ 03
Add	Add	+ 04
Subtract	Subt	+ 05
Multiply	Mult	+ 06
Divide	Div	+ 07
Compare	Comp	+ 08
Branch	Br	+ 09
Test Branch High	Brhi	+ 10
Test Branch Low	Brlo	+ 11
Test Branch Equal	Breq	+ 12
Branch End of File	Breof	+ 13
Store	Store	+ 14
Halt	Halt	+ 15

into *CLADD* to conform to the five-character requirement. This type of contraction is very common and leads a newcomer to comprehend the meaning rather easily. As in any other language, when a person uses symbolic language for some time, he becomes very familiar with the symbols.

A second accommodation symbolic language affords the programmer is that of facilitating references to other instructions by using symbolic names rather than numbers. Once again, the author of the processor program must decide how large these symbols should be and where they must appear in input records. As shown in Figure A-3, the usual order is *Label, Op-Code, Operand*. Labels commonly are restricted to five, six, or seven characters, depending on the specifications stored in the processor program.

Another consideration is the kind of characters to be used. To protect the programmer from confusion and the processor program from unnecessary difficulty, one restriction might be to prohibit the use of the op-code symbols as labels. Another restriction might be that the first character of the label-symbol should be a letter of the alphabet. In this way, the author of the processor program would reserve anything beginning with a digit for other purposes, usually constants or actual machine-word locations.

It is obvious that the author of the processor program has many decisions to make regarding the instruction format and, in particular, the format of input records to be processed by the program. After these decisions are made, however, the rules must be communicated to user programmers for proper application. Learning these language rules is one of the first requirements faced by those who want to program a particular computer system.

Providing a way to write symbolic labels and op-codes leaves only the need to do the same thing for data and constants. This is performed through a device commonly called the *declarative operation,* which is a coding sequence made up of a symbolic label, a declarative operation code, and an operand. Figure A-5 shows the use of a declarative operation code symbolized as *DA*. This type of operation code differs from the ones previously described in that it represents a signal to the processor program that the items associated with it are to be entered into one of the address lists for later reference. Such an operation is not to be performed at object time as are operations like ADD, STORE, etc.

The sample coding shown in Figure A-5 is interpreted by the processor program as follows: the first line indicates that an area 10 words long is to be reserved. This whole area then can be addressed by using the symbol *INPUT*. The areas of storage for the object program are assigned according to the order in which the various coding sequences are "read-in" during the

FIG. A-5. Declarative operations.

Label	Op Code	Operand
Input	DA	10
Serial		1
Fact 1		2
Fact 2		3
		4, 10
Output	DA	10
Outser		1
Sum		2
		3, 10

Coding			Object Program	
Label	Op Code	Operand	Loc	Word Contents
Input	DA	10	000	
Serial		1	000	
Fact 1		2	001	
Fact 2		3	002	
		4, 10		
Output	DA	10	010	
Outser		1	010	
Sum		2	011	
		3, 10		
Runsum	DC	+ 00 000 000	020	+ 00 000 000
Word	DC	Total	021	Total
Begin	Read	Input	022	+ 01 000 000
	Cladd	Serial	023	+ 03 000 000
	Comp	Outser	024	+ 08 000 010
	Brlo	Seqchk	025	+ 11 000 041
	Store	Outser	026	+ 14 000 010
	Cladd	Fact 1	027	+ 03 000 001
	Add	Fact 2	028	+ 04 000 002
	Store	Sum	029	+ 14 000 011
	Add	Runsum	030	+ 04 000 020
	Store	Runsum	031	+ 14 000 020
	Write	Output	032	+ 02 000 010
	Breof	Exit	033	+ 13 000 035
	Br	Begin	034	+ 09 000 022
Exit	Cladd	Word	035	+ 03 000 021
	Store	Outser	036	+ 14 000 010
	Cladd	Runsum	037	+ 03 000 020
	Store	Sum	038	+ 14 000 011
	Write	Output	039	+ 02 000 010
	Halt	999	040	+ 15 000 999
Seqchk	Add	Hltseq	041	+ 04 000 043
	Store	Hltseq	042	+ 14 000 043
Hltseq	Halt	000	043	+ 15 000 (000)

FIG. A-6. Fully coded program.

processor run (Figure A-2). For instance, if line 1 is the first one read, the area 000 to 009 will be reserved and "INPUT" will be entered in a list indicating that it represents 000. Later, if a READ INPUT instruction is encountered, the machine instruction will be +01000000.

Next, line 2 is interpreted. Since there is no operation code, it is interpreted as one of the data items within the area *INPUT*, and is the first word (operand = 1) tagged by the symbol *SERIAL*. Machine location 000 will be associated with this symbol. Line 3 associates the symbol *FACT 1* with machine location 001, and line 4 assigns 002 to *FACT 2*. Line 5 simply means that the remaining seven words of the area are not used, but should be saved because of the special type of read instruction designed into the equipment. The sixth line begins the same sequence for the *OUTPUT* area as the one for the *INPUT* area. Figure A-6 presents a fully coded program showing the symbolic language written by the programmer. The three left columns usually are referred to as the "source program," and the machine language equivalent (the two right columns), is called the "object program."

Macro Languages

The next level of languages takes the coding idea one step further. Programmers began to notice that certain sequences of instructions had a tendency to be repetitive. The most common example is the one which moves a word from one place in storage to another (CLADD, STORE). Since this is such a common instruction, two choices were available: (1) To change the design of the equipment so that two address instructions were available, a change that has been made in many modern computers; or (2) to expand the function of the processor program beyond the strict one-for-one situation.

If one could predict what combination of machine instructions would be needed in these common instances, it would be relatively simple to add new

FIG. A-7. Macro instructions—a sample.

Macro Formal	Equivalent Symbolics	
Move A, B	Cladd	A
(Meaning – Move word at A to loc B)	Store	B
Accum A, B, C	Cladd	A
(Meaning – Add word at A to word	Add	B
at B and store sum in loc C)	Store	C
Cmpar A, B, H, L, E	Cladd	A
(Meaning – Compare value of	Comp	B
word at A with word at B, if A is	Brhi	H
high, branch to H, if low to L,	Brlo	L
and if equal to E)	Breq	E

Label	Op Code	Operand
Begin	Read	Input
	Cmpar	Serial, Outser, Next, Seqchk, Next
Next	Store	Outser
	Accum	Fact 1, Fact 2, Sum
	Accum	Sum, Runsum, Runsum
	Write	Output
	Breof	Exit
	Br	Begin
Exit	Move	Word, Outser
	Move	Runsum, Sum
	Write	Output
	Halt	999
Seqchk	Accum	Serial, Hltseq, Hltseq
Hltseq	Halt	000

FIG. A-8. Example program using macro instructions.

operation codes to the processor program vocabulary. Such operation codes are called *macro operation codes,* or simply *"macros."* Macros differ from the symbolic one-for-one, in that more than one object-program machine instruction can be produced for the use of each macro instruction.

The languages that evolved from this thinking were a combination of declarative op-codes, symbolic one-for-one op-codes, and macros. The sample macro instructions shown in Figure A-7 could be easily added to our basic processor language. Once again, the format of the input record (the instruction) must be fixed. The format is shown first to the left; the equivalent symbolic one-for-one instructions, to the right. Given this facility, the processing part of the coding for our example program is shown in Figure A-8.

Comparing figures A-7, A-6, and A-8, one begins to appreciate what this development is really designed to do. Basically, it is designed to conserve the energy of the creative worker—the programmer—so that he can accomplish his work more quickly and with less chance of error.

There are other improvements in this macro-language idea. For example, looking at the second instruction in Figure A-8, we learn that if we are using a language with the format and results shown in Figure A-7, the equivalent symbolic instructions to this statement would be:

BEFORE:	CMPAR	SERIAL, OUTSER, NEXT, SEQCHK, NEXT
		translated as
AFTER:	CLADD	SERIAL
	COMP	OUTSER
	BRHI	NEXT
	BRLO	SEQCHK
	BREQ	NEXT

A reference to Figure A-6 shows that this translation results in two more instructions (the third and fifth above) than we had felt necessary in the one-for-one coding.

A common way to avoid this apparent waste of storage and time in the object program is to change the description of the macro instruction slightly. Then the processor program is changed accordingly so that the proper instructions are produced. In this case, the definition of CMPAR is stated:

> CMPAR   A, B, H, L, E
>
> Meaning: Compare value of the word at A with the word at B. If A is high, branch to location H; if low, branch to location L; if equal, branch to location E. If, however, any particular branch possibility is not anticipated, omit any symbol between commas.

With this definition, we now can write:

> CMPAR   SERIAL, OUTSER, SEQCHK,

It is translated as:

> CLADD   SERIAL
> COMP   OUTSER
> BRLO   SEQCHK

This is what originally was wanted.

Variations on this theme are many. When approaching a new language, it is important to be familiar with its rules. The macro language comes closer to the kind of language we use in every-day life, which makes the macro language easy to learn and use.

Procedure-Oriented Languages

The obvious goal of these programming languages is to come as close as possible to our common language. There have been many approaches to this idea of "procedure-oriented" languages. Those which are best known and are being used most widely today are COBOL, FORTRAN, and ALGOL. COBOL stands for Common Business-Oriented Language and is designed for use in normal commercial, nonscientific situations.* FORTRAN stands for Formula Translator and is particularly suited to the needs of the scientist and engineer for the statement of solutions to arithmetic problems. ALGOL stands for Algorithmic-Oriented Language and has basically the same function as FORTRAN with some additional features.

Figure A-9 shows a page of coding from the processing part of a program

---

* Further information on the specifics of the COBOL language may be obtained from a U.S. government publication, "COBOL–1965."

COBOL PROGRAM SHEET

PAGE 1 3	PROGRAM			FOR	1401	SYSTEM	1401		SHEET	6	OF	7
006	PROGRAMMER	PROBLEM	−13			DATE 11/15/62			IDENT.	73 P,R,O,B, ,1,3 80		

SERIAL	CONT A B																		
4 6	8 12 16 20 24 28 32 36 40 44 48 52 56 60 64 68 72																		
0,1,0	PROCEDURE DIVISION.
0,2,0	HOUSEKEEPING SECTION.
0,3,0	HK.. OPEN INPUT MASTER-FILE TRANSACTION-FILE OUTPUT OUTPUT-FILE
0,4,0	ORDERS-CANCELLED-FILE ERROR-OUT.. MOVE ZERO TO SKIPIT.
0,5,0	BEGIN.. READ MASTER-FILE AT END GO TO CLOSEM.. GO TO SWITCH-OFF.
0,6,0	DEPENDING ON SKIPIT.. READ TRANSACTION-FILE AT END GO TO
0,7,0	CLOSET.
0,8,0	PRE-TEST.. IF CANCEL-ORDER GO TO TEST-AGAIN..
0,9,0	CMP.. IF ADDITIONAL-QTY AND MOD-ORD-NO EQUAL TO TMOD-ORD-NO NEXT
1,0,0	SENTENCE ELSE GO TO TEST.. ADD NEW-QTY TO QUANTITY..
1,1,0	OUT.. WRITE MASTER-OUTPUT FROM MASTER.. GO TO BEGIN.
1,2,0	TEST.. IF QTY-CANCELLED AND MOD-ORD-NO EQUAL TO TMOD-ORD-NO NEXT
1,3,0	SENTENCE ELSE GO TO TEST-AGAIN.. SUBTRACT NEW-QTY FROM
1,4,0	QUANTITY.. IF QUANTITY IS NEGATIVE NEXT SENTENCE ELSE GO TO
1,5,0	OUT.
1,6,0	CANCEL-IT.. WRITE CANCEL-RECORD FROM MASTER GO TO BEGIN.
1,7,0	TEST-AGAIN.. IF CANCEL-ORDER AND MOD-ORD-NO EQUAL TO TMOD-ORD-NO.2
1,8,0	GO TO CANCEL-IT.. IF TMOD-ORD-NO.2 IS GREATER THAN MOD-ORD-
1,9,0	NO MOVE I TO SKIPIT GO TO OUT ELSE WRITE ER-OR FROM MASTER
2,0,0	GO TO BEGIN.

FIG. A-9. Program coding in COBOL.

FIG. A-10. Program coding in FORTRAN.

```
C  DETERMINATION OF CURRENT IN AC CIRCUIT
     7  READ 1,OHM,FREQ,HENRY
   1,0,0  READ 2,FRD1,FRDFIN
   1,0,1  PRINT 1,OHM,FREQ,HENRY
   1,0,2  VOLT = 1.0
     9  PRINT 1, VOLT
   1,0,3  FARAD = FRD1
     5  AMP = VOLT/SQRTF(OHM**2 +(6.2832*FREQ*HENRY
     1        -1./(6.2832*FREQ*FARAD))**2)
   1,0,4  PRINT 2,FARAD,AMP
   1,0,5  IF(FARAD-FRDFIN)3,4,4
     3  FARAD = FARAD +0.000 000 01
   1,0,6  GO TO 5
     4  IF(VOLT-3.0) 6,7,7
     6  VOLT = VOLT+0.5
   1,0,7  GO TO 9
     1  FORMAT (3F14.5)
     2  FORMAT (2E14.5)
```

Comment quadratic equation Y equals 5X squared plus 6X plus 7 for values of X from 1 through 11;

begin

    integer X, Y;

    for X:=1 **step** 1 **until** 11 **do**

        begin

            Y:= ((5X + 6) X + 7);

            print (X, Y)

        end

end

FIG. A-11. Program coding in ALGOL.

stated in COBOL. Figure A-10 shows a similar section of coding for a separate problem written in FORTRAN. Figure A-11 shows a sample ALGOL problem. Processor programs to translate COBOL, FORTRAN, and ALGOL statements into machine-coded object programs, have been prepared for many of today's computer systems.

Although there appears to be a tremendous difference between the work of the programmer using a symbolic language and one using a procedure-oriented language, a search for similarities is very revealing. The most striking similarity is the sequential nature of the thinking involved. This is primarily because of the design of the equipment to be used. Although the language tends to look less and less similar to the machine equivalent, the programmer still thinks about one step at a time. Whether the free form of COBOL or the stylized, rigid format of a one-for-one language is used, the sequential nature of the processing section of coding remains evident.

There is even greater similarity when we look at the coding required to define the data. In fact, this part of the work is the most difficult to separate from machine considerations. Figure A-12 shows a data-division coding sheet for the COBOL language. Compare it with Figure A-6 and note the similarity. The format requirements of FORTRAN and ALGOL problems usually are quite similar. To carry out the significance of COBOL, the example problem presented in this chapter is shown in COBOL language in Figure A-12.

COBOL PROGRAM SHEET

PAGE 1 3 004	PROGRAM PROBLEM - 13		FOR 1401	SYSTEM 1401	SHEET 4 OF 7
	PROGRAMMER			DATE 11/15/62	IDENT. 73PROB 1360

SERIAL 4 6	CONT 8	A 12	B 16	20	24	28	32	36	40	44	48	52	56	60	64	68	72

```
010      DATA DIVISION.
020      FILE SECTION.
030      FD  MASTER-FILE BLOCK CONTAINS 7 RECORDS, LABEL RECORDS ARE STAND-
040          ARD VALUE OF IDENTIFICATION IS 'MASTER-INS', DATA RECORD IS MA-
050          STER.
060      01  MASTER.
070          02  MOD-ORD-NO USAGE COMPUTATIONAL PICTURE IS 9(19).
080          02  QUANTITY USAGE COMPUTATIONAL PICTURE IS 99999.
090          02  FILLER SIZE IS 65 USAGE COMPUTATIONAL OCCURS 5 TIMES.
100      FD  TRANSACTION-FILE BLOCK CONTAINS 10 RECORDS LABEL RECORDS ARE
110          STANDARD VALUE OF IDENTIFICATION IS 'TRANS-INSS', DATA RECORDS
120          ARE TRAN1, TRAN2.
130      01  TRAN1.
140          02  TMOD-ORD-NO USAGE COMPUTATIONAL PICTURE IS 9(10).
150          02  CODE PICTURE IS 9.
160              88  ADDITIONAL-QTY VALUE IS 1.
170              88  QTY-CANCELLED VALUE IS 2.
180          02  NEW-QTY USAGE COMPUTATIONAL PICTURE IS 9999.
190          02  FILLER SIZE IS 26.
200      01  TRAN2.
```

FIG. A-12. Data-division coding sheet—COBOL.

Generalized Programming Aids

Over the past several years, certain programs have been extremely common to most business operations. Consequently, computer manufacturers have organized their own programming staffs to develop these programs in the best possible way and to make these programs available to their customers. This approach makes efficient use of the best talent available. Programmers in "user" installations can take advantage of the generalized routines available from the manufacturer and direct their attention to problems peculiar to their own industry or company.

Assemblers and Compilers

The following section describes the basic characteristics of the most common packages supplied by manufacturers and gives an indication of their current state. To review, processor programs are used to take care of translating programmer's language to machine language. The terms "compiler" and "assembler" have different meanings. A *compiler* permits statements which produce whole subroutines, while an *assembler* works only on one-for-one statements. In fact, a complete compiler program usually is made up of several parts, the last of which is an assembler. The first phases of the compiler break down the source statements and call from an internal library the one-for-one statements which make up the necessary subroutine. These statements are then passed on to the assembler phase, where translation to machine language and assignment of locations are performed.

The procedure-oriented languages described previously are examples of compiler programs. Today, the creation of good assemblers and compilers is taken for granted. Almost every machine system on the market has an associated assembler. In addition, it is expected that there will be at least one business language compiler (most often COBOL), and one scientific language compiler (usually FORTRAN), or one designed for both (PL/1). Some machine systems also are available with another macro-level compiler using a language specifically chosen to take advantage of the design elements of the equipment.

The result of all this work is to provide tools for programmer use which permit programmers to concentrate on the job at hand and describe their solutions to problems in a language close to their own. Through the skill of the programmers who design and implement these processor programs, the application programmer can obtain the proper balance between two economic measures: space and time. The "space" referred to is that available in the various types of storage: magnetic core, magnetic tape, magnetic disk, magnetic drum, or punched cards. The "time" refers to programming time, compiling run time, or object-program run time. The extent to which a compiler or assembler provides a good choice to the programmer is the best measure of its usefulness.

Input/Output Control Systems

A special element of a processing system is the section which accommodates input and output requirements. As explained earlier, getting information into and out of the central processor is relatively more time-consuming than internal calculations. The use of buffers, channels, and multiplexors have helped the situation in terms of time but have made programming more complicated. This requires that their complexities be minimized. Fortunately, things to be done with input/output devices are predictable. Following is a list of the operations to be handled and a very brief description of the type of operation:

1. SEEK-READ-WRITE: These are the obvious elements of introducing data into central storage and of recording the results after processing.
2. BLOCK-DEBLOCK: In several of the input/ouput (I/O) media, it is most efficient to group logical records into blocks of information in order to save time. When such blocks are read into storage, they are separated into logical records for processing and then reblocked before writing.
3. SCHEDULING: Now that it is possible to carry out processing, input and/or output simultaneously overlapping, it is necessary to schedule the demands on the input/output devices to achieve maximum use of all equipment. Although this is

7070 AUTOCODER CODING SHEET FOR 7070 10CS TAPE FILE SPECIFICATIONS

			Punching Instruction										
Program **PAYROLL**			Graphic						Card Form #		*	Page	of
Programmer **MARY SMITH**		Date **AUG.63**	Punch									Identnification	P,2,6,3 76 80

Sequence (Pg) (Lin)	Name (Label)	Operation Code	Operand 21 25 30 35 40 45 50 55 60 65 70 75
0,1,	T,A,P,E,F,I,L,E,A,	D,T,F,	M,A,S,T,E,R,
0,2,	F,C,H,A,N,N,E,L,/,	1	
0,3,	B,A,S,E,T,A,P,E,	1	
0,4,	A,L,T,1,T,A,P,E,	1	
0,5,	A,L,T,2,T,A,P,E,	2	
0,6,	A,C,T,I,V,I,T,Y,		
0,7,	B,L,O,C,K,C,N,T,		
0,8,	F,I,L,E,F,O,R,M,	1	
0,9,	F,I,L,E,T,Y,P,E,	1	
1,0,	R,E,C,L,N,G,T,H,	0,0,1,0,	
1,1,	B,L,O,C,K,I,N,G,	0,0,0,5,	
1,2,	O,P,E,N,P,R,O,C,	2	
1,3,	C,L,S,E,P,R,O,C,	3	
1,4,	T,P,E,R,R,O,P,T,	1,6	
1,5,	I,O,R,D,W,L,S,T,	D,A,T,A,I,N,	
1,6,	I,O,M,E,T,H,O,D,		
1,7,	T,I,O,A,R,E,A,S,	2	
1,8,	P,R,I,O,R,I,T,Y,	1	
1,9,	I,N,D,X,W,R,D,A,	X,W,D,1,	
2,0,	I,N,D,X,W,R,D,B,	X,W,D,2,	
2,1,	T,D,E,N,S,I,T,Y,	2	
2,2,	S,L,R,P,R,O,C,D,		
2,3,	L,L,R,P,R,O,C,D,		
2,4,	S,C,L,P,R,O,C,D,		
2,5,	T,P,E,R,R,F,L,D,		
2,6,	T,P,S,K,P,F,L,D,		
2,7,	E,O,S,P,R,O,C,D,		
2,8,	E,O,R,P,R,O,C,D,		
2,9,	E,O,F,P,R,O,C,D,	D,A,T,A,E,O,F,	
3,0,	R,W,D,P,R,O,C,D,	3	
3,1,	C,H,E,C,K,P,N,T,		
3,2,	L,A,B,E,L,I,N,F,	M,A,S,L,A,B,	
3,3,	S,R,B,F,O,R,M,4,		
3,4,	R,L,I,F,O,R,M,3,		
3,5,	S,P,A,R,E,I,N,F,		
3,6,	S,C,H,E,D,I,N,F,/,		

7070 AUTOCODER CODING SHEET

			Punching Instructions										
Program			Graphic						Card Form #		*	Page **04**	of **04**
Programmer		Date	Punch									Identification	0,0,0,0,1 76 80

Sequence (Pg) (Lin)	Name (Label)	Operation Code	OPERAND 21 25 30 35 40 45	Basic Autocoder → 50 55 60	Autocoder → 65 70 75
	*DEFINE	INPUT/OUTPUT	AREA OF STORAGE		
	DATAFIELD	DA	1,RDW		
	PRINCIPAL		10,14		
	INTRATE		17,19		
	PERIOD		20,29		
	NEWPRINCPL		30,39		

FIG. A-13.

complicated and calls for great precision on the part of the program, it nevertheless is completely feasible and can be generalized.

4. ERROR PROCESSING: Many factors can contribute to errors in the I/O operations. Often it is a human error (mounting a wrong tape reel, error made in keypunching, or using a control card that is out of sequence), but other times, it is equipment trouble (dust deposits on a recording surface, oxide flaking off, etc.). The main requirement of an I/O routine is to correct the error, if possible, within the minimum period of time.

5. END OF REEL–END OF FILE: Special consideration must be made when either an element of a file or the entire file has reached an end. One of the major jobs at "end-of-reel" time is to switch to an alternate device where the next reel should have been mounted by an operator. To eliminate the chance of operator error and to provide auditing controls, it is common to check the sequence number of the next reel, the total of records on the reel just finished, the date when the next reel was written, and so on.

6. CHECKPOINT–RESTART: When a computing run takes a long time, it becomes expensive to start all over again if something happens to interrupt. For this reason, a *checkpoint* record is written periodically, the purpose of which is to record the vital elements of the system at a particular moment. Then if something happens, the only necessary step is to activate the *restart* program (a special program which reads in the last checkpoint record, re-establishes the central storage, repositions the input/output devices at their proper positions, and transfers control to the processing program).

The items in the foregoing list represent at least 40 per cent of the total job in most business-programming activities. These functions can be programmed basically as subroutines and made available to the compiler. The language usually is designed so that the programmer can describe his records and files in a "check-list" manner (Figure A-13). In his file lists, he usually indicates what optional subroutines he would like compiled, keeping in mind the space–time equation. After that, he can forget this part of the work and think of the records as being available to his program one at a time and in proper sequence. This greatly simplifies the total job.

Present-day compilers include very efficient I/O sections. Because of its importance, this preprogramming of I/O subroutines usually is included even in assemblers. The major difference between the two processors is that the programmer using the compiler writes statements such as "GET IN RECORD" or "FILE PAY LINE," while the assembler language requires the programmer to write a few "bridging" instructions to transfer from his main line of coding to the preassembled subroutines.

Utilities

There are many common jobs which recur frequently. These are serviced by a set of programs referred to as *utility programs* or *utilities*. Their function is to aid in the production of programs for the computer system. Some of these include:

1. Card to tape, tape to card, tape to printer. These are programs used to transfer data from one medium to another.

2. Memory print—used to write out complete areas of central storage up to and including the entire storage capacity. The program also is referred to as a "dump."

3. Program loader—introduces a new program into storage.

4. Tape duplication—this program permits the user to reproduce a reel of tape on another reel.

5. File routines—the use of large capacity, random-acess files requires the user to copy the information from these files onto magnetic tapes with some regularity for protection purposes. With so much of a firm's active data in these files, it is necessary to be sure that the files can be reconstructed if a major stoppage occurs. This is similar in concept to the checkpoint previously discussed.

Naturally, there are many other utilities; however, the foregoing list should give the reader an idea as to the kind of work they can do. Almost all of these utilities take a common form: each is supplied as an assembled program, ready to be run. The user puts it to work either through some well-defined console operation or a combination of the console and a control card(s) which contains initializing data. For example, the Memory Print program usually requires the programmer to specify the locations in storage which are the boundaries of the area to be written. These are punched into specific columns of a control card. After the Memory Print program is loaded, the card is read; the program is initialized; and the printing takes place.

There are several computer users' organizations which have common interests. These organizations maintain whole libraries of generalized programs. Thousands of them are available. The best advice one can give to any learning programmer is to make sure that he becomes aware of what others have done and are doing. Much valuable time can be saved by such sharing.

GLOSSARY OF TERMS

ALGOL: Algorithmic-oriented language. An international procedure-oriented language.

ASSEMBLE: To prepare a machine language program from a symbolic language program by substituting absolute operation codes for symbolic operation codes and absolute relocatable addresses for symbolic addresses.

DECLARATIVE OPERATION: A coding sequence which involved writing symbolic labels and operation codes for data and constants. It is made up of a symbolic label, a declarative operation code, and an operand.

HARDWARE: Physical equipment, e.g., mechanical, magnetic, electrical, or electronic devices. Contrasts with software.

LABEL: One or more characters used to identify an item of data. Synonymous with *key*.

MACRO INSTRUCTION: 1. An instruction consisting of a sequence of micro instructions which are inserted into the object routine for performing a specific operation. 2. The more powerful instructions which combine several operations in one instruction.

PROGRAMMING LANGUAGE ONE: A new high level procedure-oriented language designed to satisfy the needs of business and scientific applications as well as processor programming.

PROCESSOR PROGRAM: A programming aid which prepares an object program first by reading symbolic instructions and then compares and converts the instructions into a suitable computer language.

SOFTWARE: 1. The collection of programs and routines associated with a computer, e.g., compilers, library routines. 2. All the documents associated with a computer, e.g., manuals, circuit diagrams. 3. Contrasts with *hardware*.

QUESTIONS FOR REVIEW

1. What are some of the complications involving the job of a programmer? Explain.
2. What is a processor program? How is programming economy realized through the use of a processor program? Explain.
3. List and describe the three parts of a symbolic language instruction.
4. What is meant by "one-for-one" language?
5. What accommodations does a symbolic language provide a programmer?
6. What is a macro language? How do macros differ from the "one-for-one" language?
7. List and explain three main "procedure-oriented" languages.
8. What similarities are there between a symbolic language and a procedure-oriented language?
9. List and explain briefly five operations handled by input/output devices.
10. What is a utility program? Why is it used? Give three examples of utility programs.

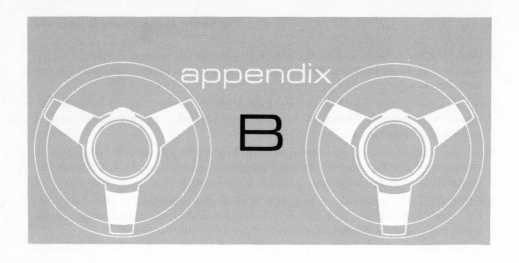

appendix

B

Glossary
of Data-Processing Terms

ABACUS: A manual calculating device that uses beads to represent decimal values.

ACCESS TIME: 1. The time interval between the instant at which data are called for from a storage device and the instant delivery is completed, i.e., the read time. 2. The time interval between the instant at which data are requested to be stored and the instant at which storage is completed, i.e., the write time.

ACCOUNTING MACHINE: 1. A keyboard actuated machine that prepares accounting records. 2. A machine that reads data from external storage media, such as cards or tapes, and automatically produces accounting records or tabulations, usually on continuous forms.

ACCUMULATOR: A register in which the result of an arithmetic or logic operation is formed.

ADDER: A device whose output is a representation of the sum of the quantities represented by its inputs.

ADDRESS: 1. An identification, as represented by a name, label, or number, for a register, location in storage, or any other data source or destination such as the location of a station in a communication network. 2. Loosely, any part of an instruction that specifies the location of an operand for the instruction.

ALGOL: Algorithmic-oriented language. An international procedure-oriented language.

ANALOG COMPUTER: A computer which represents variables by physical analogies. Thus any computer which solves problems by translating physical conditions such as flow, temperature, pressure, angular position, or voltage into related mechanical or electrical quantities and uses mechanical or electrical equivalent circuits as an analog for the physical phenomenon being investigated. In general, it is a computer which uses an analog for each variable and produces analogs as output. Thus an analog computer measures continuously whereas a digital computer counts discretely.

ASSEMBLE: To prepare a machine language program from a symbolic language program by substituting absolute operation codes for symbolic operation codes and absolute relocatable addresses for symbolic addresses.

AUTOMATION: 1. The implementation of processes by automatic means. 2. The theory, art, or technique of making a process more automatic. 3. The investigation, design, development, and application of methods of rendering processes automatic, self-moving, or self-controlling.

AUXILIARY STORAGE: A storage that supplements another storage.

BAR PRINTER: A printing device that uses several type bars positioned side by side across the line. Printing data on a line involves activating specific bars to move vertically until the characters they contain are properly aligned. Then, the data are printed simultaneously.

BATCH PROCESSING: A technique by which items to be processed must be coded and collected into groups prior to processing.

BINARY: 1. Pertaining to a characteristic or property involving a selection, choice, or condition in which there are two possibilities. 2. Pertaining to the number representation system with a radix of two.

BINARY-CODED DECIMAL: Pertaining to a decimal notation in which the individual decimal digits are each represented by a group of binary digits, e.g., in the 8-4-2-1 binary-coded decimal notation, the number twenty-three is represented as 0010 0011 whereas in binary notation, twenty-three is represented as 10111.

BIQUINARY CODE: A two part code in which each decimal digit is represented by the sum of the two parts, one of which has the value of decimal zero or five and the other the values zero through four. The abacus and soroban both use biquinary codes.

BIT: 1. An abbreviation of *bi*nary digi*t*. 2. A single character in a binary number. 3. A single pulse in a group of pulses. 4. A unit of information capacity of a storage device.

BLOCK: A set of things, such as words, characters, or digits, handled as a unit.

BRANCH: A set of instructions that is executed between two successive decision instructions.

BUFFER: A storage device used to compensate for a difference in rate of flow of data, or time of occurrence of events, when transmitting data from one device to another.

BUSINESS DATA PROCESSING: Data processing for business purposes, e.g., recording and summarizing the financial transactions of a business.

BUSINESS ORGANIZATION: A framework by means of which the activities of a business are tied together to provide for integrated performance. Also, a human relationship in group activity.

CALCULATING: Reconstructing or creating new data by compressing certain numeric facts.

CALCULATOR: 1. A device capable of performing arithmetic. 2. A calculator as in (1) that requires frequent manual intervention. 3. Generally and historically, a device for carrying out logic and arithmetic digital operations of any kind.

CARD STACKER: An output device that accumulates punched cards in a deck. Contrast with card hopper.

CASH DISCOUNT: A fixed amount or a percentage deducted by the seller from the price of an item for inducing cash payment by the buyer.

CHAIN PRINTER: A device which uses a chain of several links, each of which contains alphabetic and numeric characters. The chain rotates horizontally at constant speed. Hammers from the back of the paper are timed to fire against selected characters on the chain, causing the printing of a line.

CHARACTER: An elementary mark or event that is used to represent data. A character is often in the form of a graphic spatial arrangement of connected or adjacent strokes.

CHARACTER-AT-A-TIME PRINTER: A device that prints one character at a time, similarly to the way a typewriter prints.

CLASSIFYING: Arranging data in a specific form, usually by sorting, grouping, or extracting.

COBOL: Common Business-Oriented Language. A computer language used in business data processing to prepare a program.

CODING: The translation of flow diagrams into the language of the computer.

COLLATOR: A device to collate or merge sets of cards or other documents into a sequence.

COMB PRINTER: A device which consists of a set of characters mounted on a bar facing a paper form. As the bar passes over the paper (left to right), hammers strike the selected characters onto the form. When the bar reaches the right edge of the form, it returns to a home position to print another line.

COMPILE: To prepare a machine language program from a computer program written in another programming language by making use of the over-all logic structure of the program, generating more than one machine instruction for each symbolic statement, or both, as well as performing the function of an assembler.

COMPOSITE CARD: A multipurpose data card, or a card that contains data needed in the processing of various applications.

COMPUTER WORD: A sequence of bits or characters treated as a unit and capable of being stored in one computer location. Synonymous with machine word.

CONSOLE PRINTER: An auxiliary output printer used in several computer systems for relaying messages to the computer operator.

CONTROL: 1. The part of a digital computer or processor which determines the execution and interpretation of instructions in proper sequence, including the decoding of each instruction and the application of the proper signals to the arithmetic unit and other registers in accordance with the decoded information. 2. Frequently, it is one or more of the components in any mechanism responsible for interpreting and carrying out manually-initiated directions. Sometimes it is called manual control. 3. In some business applications, a mathematical check. 4. In programming, instructions which determine conditional jumps are often referred to as control instructions, and the time sequence of execution of instructions is called the flow of control.

CONTROL PANEL: 1. A part of a computer console that contains manual controls. 2. Same as plugboard.

CONTROL PUNCH: A specific code punched in a card to cause the machine to perform a specific operation.

COUNTER: A device such as a register or storage location used to represent the number of occurrences of an event.

CRAM: *C*ard *R*andom-*A*ccess *M*emory, a mass storage device that consists of a number of removable magnetic cards each of which is capable of storing magnetic bits of data.

CRYOGENICS: The study and use of devices utilizing properties of materials near absolute zero in temperature.

CYCLING TAPE: Creating a new tape file through an updating procedure.

DATA PROCESSING: Any operation or combination of operations on data.

DATA-PROCESSING CYCLE: The sequence of steps involved in manipulating business information.

DATA WORD: A word which may be primarily regarded as part of the information manipulated by a given program. A data word may be used to modify a program instruction, or to be arithmetically combined with other data words.

DEBUG: To detect, locate, and remove mistakes from a routine or malfunctions from a computer. Synonymous with *troubleshoot*.

DECLARATIVE OPERATION: A coding sequence which involves writing symbolic labels and operation codes for data and constants. It is made up of a symbolic label, a declarative operation code, and an operand.

DETAIL PRINTING (*listing*): The printing of one line for each card read by the tabulator.

DIGIT-PUNCHING POSITION: The area on a punched card reserved to represent a decimal digit.

DIGITAL COMPUTER: A computer that operates on discrete data by performing arithmetic and logic processes on these data. Contrast with analog computer.

DIRECT-ACCESS STORAGE: (1) Pertaining to the process of obtaining information from or placing information into storage where the time required for such access is independent of the location of the information most recently obtained or placed in storage; (2) Pertaining to a device in which random access, as defined in definition 1, can be achieved without effective penalty in time.

DIRECT ADDRESS: An address that specifies the location of an operand. Synonymous with *one level address*.

DOCUMENT CARD: A special card form used in preparing a document such as a check, a purchase order, etc.

DRUM PRINTER: A printing device which uses a drum embossed with alphabetic and numeric characters. As the drum rotates, a hammer strikes the paper (from behind) at a time when the desired character(s) on the drum passes the line to be printed. To complete printing a given line, further rotation of the drum containing the remaining characters is necessary.

DUAL-GAP READ-WRITE HEAD: Used in magnetic tape data processing to insure the accuracy of recorded data on tape. A character written on tape is read immediately by a read head to verify its validity.

EDVAC: An electronic automatic computer which represents data in a binary form.

ELECTROSTATIC PRINTER: A device that prints an optical image on special paper. Spots of electricity are placed in matrix form on paper. When the paper is dusted with powdered ink material, the particles cling to the electrically charged characters. Later, they are moved to a high temperature zone where the ink is melted and is permanently fixed to the paper.

ENIAC: A high-speed electronic computer designed and built by Mauchly and Eckert at the University of Pennsylvania.

FACSIMILE TRANSMISSION: Reproduction of printed matter by a device which picks up the light and dark areas of an object and converts it into a facsimile (copy) of the same.

FEEDBACK: The part of a closed loop system which automatically brings back information about the condition under control.

FIELD: A specified area of a record used for a particular category of data, e.g., a group of card columns used to represent a wage rate or a set of bit locations in a computer word used to express the address of the operand.

FIXED WORD-LENGTH: Having the property that a machine word always contains the same number of characters or digits.

FLOW CHART: A graphical representation for the definition, analysis, or solution of a problem in which symbols are used to represent operations, data, flow, and equipment.

FORTRAN: Formula translations. Any of several specific procedure-oriented programming languages.

GANG PUNCH: To punch identical or constant information into all of a group of punch cards.

GENERAL-PURPOSE COMPUTER: A computer that is designed to solve a wide class of problems.

GROSS PAY: An employee's total pay with no deductions.

GROUP PRINTING: A procedure whereby one line is printed for each group of cards having similar characteristics.

GROUPING: Arranging a mass of data into related groups, having common characteristics.

HARDWARE: Physical equipment, e.g., mechanical, magnetic, electrical, or electronic devices. Contrast with software.

HOLLERITH: A widely used system of encoding alphanumeric information onto cards, hence Hollerith cards is synonymous with punch cards.

HOUSEKEEPING: For a computer program, housekeeping involves the setting up of constants and variables to be used in the program.

INDEXED ADDRESS: An address that is to be modified, or has been modified, by an index register or similar device.

INDIRECT ADDRESS: An address that specifies a storage location that contains either a direct address or another indirect address. Synonymous with *multilevel address.*

INPUT: 1. The data to be processed. 2. The state or sequence of states occurring on a specified input channel. 3. The device or collective set of devices used for bringing data into another device. 4. A channel for impressing a state on a device or logic element. 5. The processes of transferring data from an external storage to an internal storage. 6. *See* MANUAL INPUT.

INPUT DEVICE: The mechanical unit designed to bring data to be processed into a computer; e.g., a card reader, a tape reader, or a keyboard.

INSTRUCTION WORD: A computer word which contains an instruction.

INTERPRETER: 1. A program that translates and executes each source language expression before translating and executing the next one. 2. A device that prints on a punched card the data already punched in the card.

INTERRECORD GAP: An interval of space or time deliberately left between recording portions of data or records. Such spacing is used to prevent errors through loss of data or overwriting and permits tape stop-start operations.

KEYBOARD: A group of marked levers operated manually for recording characters.

KEYPUNCH: A keyboard-operated device that punches holes in a card to represent data.

LABEL: One or more characters used to identify an item of data. Synonymous with *key.*

LIBRARY SUBROUTINE: A set of tested subroutines available on file for use when needed.

LINE-AT-A-TIME PRINTER: A device capable of printing one line of characters across a page; i.e., 100 or more characters simultaneously as continuous paper advances line-by-line in one direction past type bars or a type cylinder that contains all characters in all positions.

LOGIC: 1. The science dealing with the criteria or formal principles of reasoning and thought. 2. The systematic scheme which defines the interactions of signals in the design of an automatic data-processing system. 3. The basic principles and application of truth tables and interconnection between logical elements required for arithmetic computation in an automatic data-processing system.

LOOP: A sequence of instructions that is repeated until a terminal condition prevails.

MACRO INSTRUCTION: 1. An instruction consisting of a sequence of micro instructions which are inserted into the object routine for performing a specific operation. 2. The more powerful instructions which combine several operations in one instruction.

MAGNETIC CORE: A configuration of magnetic material that is, or is intended to be, placed in a spatial relationship to current-carrying conductors and whose magnetic properties are essential to its use. It may be used to concentrate an induced magnetic field as in a transformer, induction coil, or armature, to retain a magnetic polarization for the purpose of storing data, or for its nonlinear properties as in a logic element. It may be made of such material as iron, iron oxide, or ferrite, and in such shapes as wires and tapes.

MAGNETIC DRUM: A right circular cylinder with a magnetic surface on which data can be stored by selective magnetization of portions of the curved surface.

MANIPULATION: The actual work performed on source data-processing.

MARK-SENSE CARD: A card designed to allow entering data on it with an electrographic pencil.

MASS-STORAGE FILE: A type of temporary secondary storage that supplies the computer with the necessary data for an immediate up-to-date report on a given account.

MATCHING: A data-processing operation similar to a merge, except that instead of producing a sequence of items made up from the input, sequences are matched against each other on the basis of some key.

MATRIX PRINTER: Synonymous with *wire printer*. A high speed printer that prints character-like configurations of dots through the proper selection of wire-ends from a matrix of wire-ends, rather than conventional characters through the selection of type faces.

MEMORY: 1. Pertaining to a device into which data can be entered, in which it can be held, and from which it can be retrieved at a later time. 2. Loosely, any device that can store data.

MERGE: To combine two or more sets of data into one, usually in a specified sequence.

MICR: *Magnetic-Ink Character Recognition*, a technique involving the use of a device that senses and encodes into a machine language characters printed with an ink containing magnetized particles.

MICROSECOND: One millionth of a second.

MILLISECOND: One thousandth of a second.

NANOSECOND: One billionth of a second.

NAPIER'S BONES: A technique introduced by John Napier to aid multiplication through the use of data tables or rods.

9-EDGE: Denotes the bottom edge of a punched card.

NUMERALIZATION: Representation of alphabetic data through the use of digits; a desired step in automatic data processing.

OBJECT PROGRAM: The program which is the output of an automatic coding system. Often the object program is a machine language program ready for execution, but it may well be in an intermediate language.

OBJECT TIME: The time span during which a stored program is in active control of a specific application.

OCTAL: 1. Pertaining to a characteristic or property involving a selection, choice, or condition in which there are eight possibilities. 2. Pertaining to the number representation system with a radix of eight.

OFF-LINE: Pertaining to equipment or devices not under direct control of the central processing unit.

ON-LINE: Pertaining to peripheral equipment or devices in direct communication with the central processing unit.

ON-LINE INPUT: A system in which the input device transmits certain data directly to (and under control of) the control processing unit.

ON-LINE PROCESSING: Descriptive of a system and of the peripheral equipment or devices in a system in which the operation of such equipment is under control of the central processing unit, and in which information reflecting current activity is introduced into the data processing system as soon as it occurs. Thus, directly in-line with the main flow of transaction processing.

OPERAND: That which is operated upon. An operand is usually identified by an address part of an instruction.

OPERATION CODE: A code that represents specific operations. Synonymous with *instruction code*.

OPTICAL SCANNING: Translation of printed or handwritten characters into machine language.

ORIGINATION: Determining the nature, type, and origin of some documents.

OUTPUT: 1. Data that has been processed. 2. The state or sequence of states occurring on a specified output channel. 3. The device or collective set of devices used for taking data out of a device. 4. A channel for expressing a state of a device or logic element. 5. The process of transferring data from an internal storage to an external storage.

OUTPUT DEVICE: The part of a machine which translates the electrical impulses representing data processed by the machine into permanent results such as printed forms, punched cards, and magnetic writing on tape.

PACKING DENSITY: The number of useful storage elements per unit of dimension, e.g., the number of bits per inch stored on a magnetic tape or drum track.

PARALLEL READING: Row-by-row reading of a data card.

PARAMETER: A variable that is given a constant value for a specific purpose or process.

PARITY CHECK: A check that tests whether the number of ones (or zeros) in an array of binary digits is odd or even. Synonymous with odd-even check.

PAYROLL REGISTER: A record of employees to be paid with the amount due to each.

PLOTTER: A visual display or board in which a dependent variable is graphed by an automatically controlled pen or pencil as a function of one or more variables.

PROCESS: A general term covering such terms as assemble, compile, generate, interpret, and compute.

PROCESSOR PROGRAM: A programming aid which prepares an object program first by reading symbolic instructions and then compares and converts them into a suitable computer language.

PRODUCTION: Conversion of basic raw materials into a product sold by a business firm.

PROFIT AND LOSS STATEMENT: A financial statement showing the company's earning capability during a specific period of time.

PROGRAM: 1. A plan for solving a problem. 2. Loosely, a routine. 3. To devise a plan for solving a problem. 4. Loosely, to write a routine.

PROGRAM CARD: A coded card inserted in the program control unit of the keypunch to control operations such as skipping, duplicating, and shifting, automatically.

PROGRAM FLOW CHART: A graphic representation of a computer problem using symbols to represent machine instructions or groups of instructions.

PROGRAMMING LANGUAGE ONE: A new high level procedure-oriented language designed to satisfy the needs of business and scientific applications as well as processor programming.

PUNCHED CARD: 1. A card punched with a pattern of holes to represent data. 2. A card as in (1) before being punched.

PUNCHING STATION: The area on the keypunch where a card is aligned for the punching process.

PURCHASE ORDER: A requisition made by the purchasing department to a supplier for meeting the needs of a division or a department (for example, production department) of the firm.

RAMAC: *Random-Access Method of Accounting and Control*, a mass storage device that consists of a number of rotating disks stacked one on top of another to make up a data file.

READING STATION: The area on the keypunch where a data card is aligned for reading by a sensing mechanism to duplicate it automatically into another card located in the punching station.

RECORD: A collection of related items of data, treated as a unit.

RECORDING: The process by which an input device facilitates the presentation of source data for processing.

REGISTER: 1. A device capable of storing a specified amount of data, such as one word.

REPRODUCER: A machine that reproduces a punched card by duplicating another similar card.

SELECTING: Extracting certain cards from a deck for a specific purpose without disturbing the sequence in which they were originally filed.

SEQUENCE CHECK: A data-processing operation designed to check the sequence of the items in a file assumed to be already in sequence.

SEQUENTIAL DATA PROCESSING: A technique by which items to be processed must be coded and collected into groups prior to processing.

SERIAL READING: Column-by-column reading of a data card.

SIMULTANEOUS-PUNCHING PRINCIPLE: Introduced by James Powers, whereby information to be punched is initially accumulated and then punched simultaneously in a card.

SOFTWARE: 1. The collection of programs and routines associated with a computer, e.g., compilers, library routines. 2. All the documents associated with a computer, e.g., manuals, circuit diagrams. 3. Contrasts with *hardware*.

SORTER: A machine capable of sorting punched cards either alphabetically or numerically.

SORTING: Arranging numeric or alphabetic data in a given sequence.

SOURCE DOCUMENT: A document from which basic data is extracted.

SOURCE PROGRAM: A program written in a source language. A language that is an input to a given translation process.

SPECIAL-PURPOSE COMPUTER: A computer that is designed to solve a restricted class of problems.

STANDARDIZATION: Establishment of specific procedural requirements for the efficient production of a large volume of goods or for automatic processing of data.

STICK PRINTER: An early printer which consists of a stick which prints one character at a time as the stick moves from left to right.

STORAGE: The retention of data (source or finished) in memory until needed.

STORAGE MAP: A pictorial aid used by the programmer for estimating the proportion of storage capacity to be allocated to data.

STORED PROGRAM: A series of instructions in storage to direct the step-by-step operation of the machine.

STRINGING: The stage in which an input file is read completely.

STUB CARD: A card containing a detachable stub to serve as a receipt for future reference.

SUBROUTINE: A routine that can be part of another routine.

SUMMARIZING: Condensing a mass of data into a concise and meaningful form.

SUMMARY PUNCH: A card punch operating in conjunction with another machine, commonly a tabulator, to punch into cards data which have been summarized or calculated by the other machine.

SYSTEM: 1. An organized collection of parts united by regulated interaction. 2. An organized collection of men, machines, and methods required to accomplish a specific objective.

SYSTEMS ANALYSIS: The examination of an activity, procedure, method, technique, or a business to determine what must be accomplished, and how the necessary operations may best be accomplished.

SYSTEMS ANALYST: A person skilled in the definition and development of techniques for the solving of a problem; especially those techniques for solutions on a computer.

SYSTEMS FLOW CHART: A graphic representation of the system in which data provided by a source document are converted into final documents.

SYSTEMS STUDY: The detailed process of determining a system or set of procedures for using a computer for definite functions or operations, and establishing specifications to be used as a basis for the selection of equipment suitable to the specific needs.

SYSTEMS SYNTHESIS: The planning of the procedures for solving a problem. This may involve among other things the analysis of the problem, preparation of a flow diagram, preparing details, testing, and developing subroutines, allocation of storage locations, specification of input and output formats, and the incorporation of a computer run into a complete data processing system.

TABLE LOOK-UP: A procedure for obtaining the function value corresponding to an argument from a table of function values.

TELETYPE PRINTER: A device that presents type in a square block. The type square moves from left to right and positions one character at a time. When this happens, a hammer strikes the character from behind, depressing it against the inked ribbon that faces the paper form.

TIME CARD: A card used for showing the number of hours an employee has worked.

TOGGLE: 1. Same as flip-flop. 2. Pertaining to any device having two stable states.

TRAILER RECORD: A record which follows a group of records and contains pertinent data related to the group of records.

12-EDGE: A term used to designate the top edge of a punched card.

TWO-OUT-OF-FIVE CODE: A code in which each decimal digit is represented by five binary digits of which two are one kind (e.g., ones) and three are the other kind (e.g., zero).

UNIT RECORD: 1. A separate record that is similar in form and content to other records; e.g., a summary of a particular employee's earnings to date. (2) Sometimes refers to a piece of nontape auxiliary equipment; e.g., card reader, printer, or console typewriter.

UNIVAC: An early automatic computer designed and manufactured by the Sperry Rand Corporation.

VARIABLE WORD-LENGTH: Having the property that a machine word may have a variable number of characters. It may be applied either to a single entry whose information content may be changed from time to time, or to a group of functionally similar entries whose corresponding components are of different length.

VERIFIER: A device on which a record can be compared or tested for identity character-by-character with a retranscription or copy as it is being prepared.

WHEEL PRINTER: Similar in method of operation to the bar printer except that the type bars are replaced by wheels around which all the necessary characters are embossed.

WORD: An ordered set of characters which occupies one storage location and is treated by the computer circuits as a unit and transferred as such. Ordinarily a word is treated by the control unit as an instruction, and by the arithmetic unit as a quantity. Word lengths may be fixed or variable depending on the particular computer.

WORD LENGTH: The number of bits or other characters in a word.

X-PUNCH: A punch in the second row, one row above the zero row, on a Hollerith punched card.

ZONE PUNCH: A punch in the O, X, or Y row on a Hollerith punched card.

appendix

C

Selected References
for Source Material

Basic Books in Automatic Data Processing

Ackoff, Russell L., and Patrick Rivett, *A Manager's Guide to Operations Research.* New York: Wiley, 1963.

Awad, Elias M., *Business Data Processing.* Englewood Cliffs, N.J.: Prentice-Hall, 1965.

Baumann, Richard, Manuel Feliciano, F. L. Bauer, and K. Samelson, *Introduction to ALGOL.* Englewood Cliffs, N.J.: Prentice-Hall, 1964.

Becker, Joseph and Robert M. Hayes, *Information Storage and Retrieval.* New York: Wiley, 1963.

Brandon, Dick H., *Management Standards for Data Processing.* Princeton, N.J.: Van Nostrand, 1963.

Brooks, Frederick P., and Kenneth E. Iverson, *Automatic Data Processing.* New York: Wiley, 1963.

Buchholz, Werner (ed.), *Planning a Computer System.* New York: McGraw-Hill, 1962.

Business Systems, Volume I and II. Cleveland, Ohio: Systems and Procedures Association, 1963.

Calingaert, P., *Principles of Computation.* Reading, Mass.: Addison-Wesley, 1965.

Chapin, Ned, *An Introduction to Automatic Computers.* Princeton, N.J.: Van Nostrand, 1963.

Churchman, C. West, Russell L. Ackoff, and E. Leonard Arnoff, *Introduction to Operations Research.* New York: Wiley, 1957.

Computer Oriented Mathematics. Washington, D.C.: National Council of Teachers of Mathematics, 1963.

Department of Defense, U.S. Government Printing Office, *COBOL–65,* Washington, D.C., 1965.

Desmonde, William H., *Real-Time Data Processing Systems.* Englewood Cliffs, N.J.: Prentice-Hall, 1964.

Fisher, F. P., and G. F. Swindle, *Computer Programming Systems.* New York: Holt, Rinehart and Winston, 1964.

Gallagher, *Management Information Systems and the Computer,* AMA, 1961.

Galler, Bernard, *The Language of Computers.* New York: McGraw-Hill, 1962.

Grabbe, Eugene M., Simon Ramo, and Dean E. Wooldridge, ed., *Handbook of Automation, Computation, and Control,* Volume 2. New York: Wiley, 1959.

Gregory, Robert H., and Richard L. Van Horn, *Automatic Data-Processing Systems.* Belmont, Calif.: Wadsworth, 1963.

Head, R. V., *Real-Time Business Systems.* New York: Holt, Rinehart and Winston, 1964.

Hein, Leonard W., *An Introduction to Electronic Data Processing for Business.* Princeton, N.J.: Van Nostrand, 1961.

IBM, *General Information Manual: Decision Tables, F20-8102,* 1962.

———, *Programming System Concepts, F20-8149,* 1963.

Iverson, Kenneth E., *A Programming Language.* New York: Wiley, 1962.

Johnson, R. A., et al., *Theory and Management of Systems.* New York: McGraw-Hill, 1963.

Kaufman, Felix, *Electronic Data Processing and Auditing.* New York: Ronald, 1961.

Kemeny, John G., Arthur Schleifer, Jr., J. Laurie Snell, and Gerald L. Thompson, *Finite Mathematics with Business Applications.* Englewood Cliffs, N.J.: Prentice-Hall, 1962.

Laden, H. N., and T. R. Gildersleeve, *Systems Design for Computer Applications.* New York: Wiley, 1963.

Lazzaro, Victor (ed.), *Systems and Procedures: A Handbook for Business and Industry.* Englewood Cliffs, N.J.: Prentice-Hall, 1958.

Leeds, H., and G. Weinberg, *Computer Programming Fundamentals.* New York: McGraw-Hill, 1961.

Leeson, D. N., and D. L. Dimitry, *Basic Programming Concepts.* New York: Holt, Rinehart and Winston, 1963.

Martin, E. W., Jr., *Electronic Data Processing.* Revised edition. Homewood, Ill.: Irwin, 1965.

McCracken, Daniel D., *A Guide to ALGOL Programming.* New York: Wiley, 1962.

———, *A Guide to COBOL Programming.* New York: Wiley, 1963.

———, *A Guide to FORTRAN Programming.* New York: Wiley, 1961.

———, and William S. Dorn, *Numerical Methods and FORTRAN Programming.* New York: Wiley, 1964.

————, Harold Weiss, and Trai-Hwa Lee, *Programming Business Computers*. New York: Wiley, 1959.

McGill, Donald A. C., *Punched Cards: Data Processing for Profit Improvement*. New York: McGraw-Hill, 1962.

McMillan, Claude, and R. F. Gonzalez, *Systems Analysis: A Computer Approach to Decision Models*. Homewood, Ill.: Irwin, 1965.

McNerney, John P., *Installing and Using Automatic Data Processing Systems*. Boston: Harvard Press, 1961.

Morrison, Richard J., Robert E. Nolan, and James S. Devlin, *Work Measurement in Machine Accounting*. New York: Ronald, 1963.

Nelson, Oscar S., Richard S. Woods, *Accounting Systems and Data Processing*. Cincinnati, Ohio: South-Western, 1961.

Neuschel, Richard F., *Management by System*. New York: McGraw-Hill, 1960.

Optner, Stanford L., *Systems Analysis for Business Management*. Englewood Cliffs, N.J.: Prentice-Hall, 1960.

Organick, E. I., *A FORTRAN Primer*. Reading, Mass.: Addison-Wesley, 1963.

Saxon, J. A., *COBOL*. Englewood Cliffs, N.J.: Prentice-Hall, 1963.

Schmidt, Richard N., and William E. Meyers, *Electronic Business Data Processing*. New York: Holt, Rinehart and Winston, 1963.

————, *Introduction to Computer Science and Data Processing*. New York: Holt, Rinehart and Winston, 1965.

Schultz, L., *Digital Processing: A Systems Orientation*. Englewood Cliffs, N.J.: Prentice-Hall, 1963.

Simon, H. A., *The New Science of Management Decision*. New York: Harper & Row, 1960.

Sprague, R. E., *Electronic Business Systems*. New York: Ronald, 1963.

Van Ness, Robert G., *Principles of Punched Card Data Processing*. Elmhurst, Ill.: The Business Press, 1964.

Young, Frederick H., *Digital Computers and Related Mathematics*. New York: Ginn, 1961.

Periodicals

Business Automation, 288 Park Avenue, West, Elmhurst, Illinois.

Communications of The ACM, 211 E. 43rd Street, New York 17, New York.

Computers and Automation, 815 Washington Street, Newtonville 60, Mass.

Computers and Data Processing, 217 Broadway, New York, New York.

Computing Reviews, 211 E. 43rd Street, New York 17, New York.

Data Processing for Management, 22nd floor, Book Tower, Detroit 26, Michigan.

Data Processing Digest, 1140 S. Robertson Blvd., Los Angeles 45, California.

Datamation, 1830 W. Olympic Blvd., Los Angeles 6, California.

Journal of Accountancy, 270 Madison Avenue, New York 16, New York.

Journal of the ACM, 211 E. 43rd Street, New York 17, New York.

Journal of Data Management, 505 Busse Highway, Park Ridge, Illinois.

N.A.A. Bulletin, 505 Park Avenue, New York 22, New York.

Operations Research, Mt. Royal & Guilford Avenue, Baltimore, Maryland.

Systems and Procedures Journal, 7890 Brookside Drive, Cleveland 38, Ohio.

Associations and Other Sources

Administrative Management Society, 212 5th Avenue, New York 10, New York.

American Institute of Certified Public Accountants, 666 Fifth Avenue, New York 19, New York.

American Federation of Information Processing Societies, 211 E. 43rd Street, New York 17, New York.

American Institute of Industrial Engineers, 345 E. 47th Street, New York 17, New York.

Association for Computing Machinery, 211 E. 43rd Street, New York 17, New York.

Association for Educational Data Systems, 1201 16th Street, N.W., Washington, D.C.

Association of Data Processing Service Organizations, 947 Old York Road, Abington, Pennsylvania.

Business Equipment Manufacturers Association, 235 E. 42nd Street, New York 17, New York.

Data Processing Management Association, 505 Busse Highway, Park Ridge, Illinois.

Institute of Electrical and Electronic Engineers, 345 East 47th Street, New York, N.Y.

National Association for Accountants, 505 Park Avenue, New York 22, New York.

Operations Research Society of America, Mt. Royal and Guilford Avenue, Baltimore, Maryland.

Project on Information Processing, Box 201, Montclair State College, Upper Montclair, New Jersey.

Systems and Procedures Association, 7890 Brookside Drive, Cleveland, Ohio.

Manufacturers

Burroughs Corporation, 6071 Second Avenue, Detroit, Michigan.

Control Data Corporation, 8100 34th Avenue South, Minneapolis, Minn.

Friden Corporation, 2350 Washington Avenue, San Leandro, California.

General Electric Computer Division, P. O. Box 270, Phoenix, Arizona.

General Precision Corporation, 101 W. Alameda, Burbank, California.

Honeywell EDP Division, 60 Walnut Street, Wellesley Hills, Massachusetts.

International Business Machines, 112 East Post Road, White Plains, New York.

National Cash Register Company, Main and K Streets, Dayton, Ohio.

RCA Computer Division, Cherry Hill, Camden, New Jersey.

Univac Division, Sperry Rand, 1290 Avenue of the Americas, New York 9, New York.

Index